HOUGHTON MIFFLIN

Spelling and Vocabulary

Senior Author
Shane Templeton

Consultant
Rosa Maria Peña

HOUGHTON MIFFLIN

Boston · Atlanta · Dallas · Denver · Geneva, Illinois · Princeton, New Jersey · Palo Alto

Acknowledgments

For each of the selections listed below, grateful acknowledgment is made for permission to excerpt and/or reprint original or copyrighted material as follows:

UPWORDS®, SCRABBLE®, and BOGGLE® are registered trademarks of Hasbro, Inc. Used by permission of Hasbro, Inc. All rights reserved.

Select definitions in the Spelling Dictionary are adapted and reprinted by permission from the following Houghton Mifflin Company publications: copyright © 1994 THE AMERICAN HERITAGE CHILDREN'S DICTIONARY; copyright © 1994 THE AMERICAN HERITAGE STUDENT DICTIONARY.

Excerpt from *Mister Stormalong,* by Anne Malcolmson and Dell McCormick. Copyright 1952 by Mabel McCormick and Anne Burnett Malcolmson. Copyright renewed © 1980 by Anne Burnett Malcolmson Van Storch and Joshua Tolford. Reprinted by permission of Houghton Mifflin Company.

Excerpt from *Nature's Champions,* by Alvin and Virginia Silverstein. Copyright © 1980 by Alvin and Virginia Silverstein. Adapted and reprinted by permission of Random House, Inc.

Excerpt from *Philip Hall Likes Me. I Reckon Maybe.*, by Bette Greene. Text copyright © 1974 by Bette Greene. Adapted and reprinted by permission of the publisher, Dial Books for Young Readers, a division of Penguin Books USA Inc.

"A puppy whose hair was so flowing" by Oliver Herford from *Century* magazine. Published 1912 by The Century Company.

Excerpt from "Winter Static Magic," by Doris Spaulding, as reprinted in *Cricket* magazine, December 1975, vol. 3, Number 4. Every attempt has been made to locate the rightsholder of this work. If the rightsholder should read this, please contact Houghton Mifflin Company, School Permissions, 222 Berkeley Street, Boston, MA 02116-3764.

Excerpt from *A Zillion Stars,* by Yoshiko Uchida. Copyright © 1983 by Yoshiko Uchida. Adapted and reprinted by courtesy of the Bancroft Library, University of California, Berkeley.

2000 Impression

ISBN: 0-395-85524-1

10 11 12 13 14 -VH- 03 02 01 00

Contents

How to Study a Word   **9**

Using Spelling Strategies   **10**

Cycle 1

Unit 1

Short Vowels   **12**

- Spelling-Meaning Connection
- Proofreading and Writing
  Proofread: Spelling and End Marks
- Expanding Vocabulary
  Recognizing Word Families
- Real-World Connection
  Recreation: Summer Camp

Unit 2

Spelling |ā| and |ē| **18**

- Spelling-Meaning Connection
- Dictionary: Guide Words
- Proofreading and Writing
  Proofread for Spelling
- Expanding Vocabulary
  Using a Thesaurus
- Real-World Connection
  Social Studies: Elections

Unit 3

Spelling |ī| and |ō| **24**

- Spelling-Meaning Connection
- Dictionary: Definitions
- Proofreading and Writing
  Proofread for Spelling
- Expanding Vocabulary
  Thesaurus: Words for *walk*
- Real-World Connection
  Physical Education: Baseball

Unit 4

Spelling |o͞o| and |yo͞o| **30**

- Spelling-Meaning Connection
- Proofreading and Writing
  Proofread: Spelling and Commas
- Expanding Vocabulary
  Easily Confused Words: *loose* and *lose*
- Real-World Connection
  Careers: Police Work

Unit 5

Spelling |ou|, |ô|, and |oi| **36**

- Spelling-Meaning Connection
- Dictionary: Spelling Table
- Proofreading and Writing
  Proofread for Spelling
- Expanding Vocabulary
  Words from *mille* and *centum*
- Real-World Connection
  Science: Birds

Unit 6

Review   **42**

- Spelling-Meaning Strategy
  Silent to Sounded Consonants
- Literature and Writing
  Literature
  from *Philip Hall likes me.*
  I reckon maybe. by Bette Greene
  The Writing Process
  Personal Narrative

sh + blown – bl = shown

Contents

Cycle 2

Unit 7

Spelling |ôr|, |âr|, and |är| 48

* Spelling-Meaning Connection
* Dictionary: Pronunciation Key
* Proofreading and Writing
Proofread for Spelling
* Expanding Vocabulary
Idioms
* Real-World Connection
Language Arts: Tales

Unit 8

Spelling |ûr| and |îr| 54

* Spelling-Meaning Connection
* Proofreading and Writing
Proofreading: Spelling and Possessive Nouns
* Expanding Vocabulary
Recognizing Blended Words
* Real-World Connection
Science: Using a Microscope

Unit 9

Compound Words   60

* Spelling-Meaning Connection
* Dictionary: Stress
* Proofreading and Writing
Proofread for Spelling
* Expanding Vocabulary
Building Compound Words
* Real-World Connection
Recreation: Wheelchair Basketball

Unit 10

Homophones   66

* Spelling-Meaning Connection
* Dictionary: Homophones
* Proofreading
and Writing
Proofread for Spelling

* Expanding Vocabulary
The Word Root *sol*
* Real-World Connection
Math: Surveys

Unit 11

Final |ər| 72

* Spelling-Meaning Connection
* Proofreading and Writing
Proofread: Spelling and Comparing
with *good* and *bad*
* Expanding Vocabulary
Multiple-Meaning Words
* Real-World Connection
Performing Arts: Theater

Unit 12

Review   78

* Spelling-Meaning Strategy
Long to Short Vowel Sound
* Literature and Writing
Literature
based on
"Winter Static Magic"
by Doris Spaulding
The Writing Process
Instructions

Cycle 3

Unit 13

More Compound Words   84

* Spelling-Meaning Connection
* Proofreading and Writing
Proofread: Spelling and Capital Letters
* Expanding Vocabulary
Words That Bridge Ideas
* Real-World Connection
Social Studies: Holidays

watermelon

P5NS313A.01M

Contents

Unit 14

Final |l| or |əl| 90

- Spelling-Meaning Connection
- Dictionary: Parts of Speech
- Proofreading and Writing
  Proofread for Spelling
- Expanding Vocabulary
  The Word Root *ped*
- Real-World Connection
  Science: Gems

Unit 15

VCCV Pattern   96

- Spelling-Meaning Connection
- Dictionary: Different Pronunciations
- Proofreading and Writing
  Proofread for Spelling
- Expanding Vocabulary
  The Word Root *ject*
- Real-World Connection
  Social Studies: Traffic Safety

Unit 17

VV Pattern   108

- Spelling-Meaning Connection
- Proofreading and Writing
  Proofread: Spelling and Commas
- Expanding Vocabulary
  Building a Word Family for *create*
- Real-World Connection
  Language Arts: Poetry

Unit 18

Review   114

- Spelling-Meaning Strategy
  Schwa to Short Vowel Sound
- Literature and Writing
  Literature
  from *Mr. Stormalong* by Anne
  Malcolmson and Dell J. McCormick
  The Writing Process
  Story

Unit 16

VCCCV Pattern   102

- Spelling-Meaning Connection
- Proofreading and Writing
  Proofread: Spelling and Commas in a Series
- Expanding Vocabulary
  Words from Names
- Real-World Connection
  Social Studies: Congressional
  Representatives

Cycle 4

Unit 19

VCV Pattern   120

- Spelling-Meaning Connection
- Dictionary: Homographs
- Proofreading and Writing
  Proofread for Spelling
- Expanding Vocabulary
  Word History
- Real-World Connection
  Science: Robots

Contents

drip **p** ed

Unit 20

Words with *-ed* or *-ing*   126

- Spelling-Meaning Connection
- Dictionary: Base Words and Endings
- Proofreading and Writing
  Proofread for Spelling
- Expanding Vocabulary
  Using a Thesaurus to Find Exact Words
- Real-World Connection
  Performing Arts: Movies

Unit 21

More Words with *-ed* or *-ing*   132

- Spelling-Meaning Connection
- Proofreading and Writing
  Proofread: Spelling and Commas
- Expanding Vocabulary
  Multiple-Meaning Words: *spot*
- Real-World Connection
  Home Economics: Cooking

Unit 22

Words with Suffixes   138

- Spelling-Meaning Connection
- Dictionary: Suffixes
- Proofreading and Writing
  Proofread for Spelling
- Expanding Vocabulary
  Regional Differences
- Real-World Connection
  Language Arts: Mysteries

Unit 23

Final |n| or |ən|, |chər|, |zhər| 144

- Spelling-Meaning Connection
- Proofreading and Writing
  Proofread: Spelling and Quotation Marks
- Expanding Vocabulary
  The Word Root *ven* or *vent*
- Real-World Connection
  Social Studies: Exploration

Unit 24

Review   150

- Spelling-Meaning Strategy
  The Sound of *t*
- Literature and Writing
  Literature
  from "A Zillion Stars" by Yoshiko Uchida
  The Writing Process
  Description

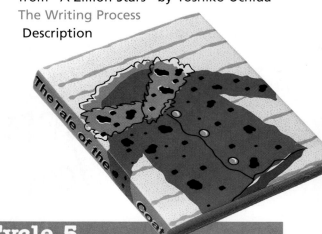

Cycle 5

Unit 25

Final |ĭj|, |ĭv|, and |ĭs| 156

- Spelling-Meaning Connection
- Proofreading and Writing
  Proofread: Spelling and Titles
- Expanding Vocabulary
  Multiple-Meaning Words: *passage*
- Real-World Connection
  Social Studies: Travel

Unit 26

Spelling Unstressed Syllables   162

- Spelling-Meaning Connection
- Proofreading and Writing
  Proofread: Spelling and Titles
- Expanding Vocabulary
  Antonyms
- Real-World Connection
  Social Studies: The Pilgrims

Unit 27

Words with Prefixes   168

- Spelling-Meaning Connection
- Dictionary: Word History
- Proofreading and Writing
  Proofread for Spelling
- Expanding Vocabulary
  Building Words with Prefixes and Suffixes
- Real-World Connection
  Social Studies: The *Titanic*

Unit 28

Changing Final *y* to *i*   174

- Spelling-Meaning Connection
- Proofreading and Writing
  Proofread: Spelling and Business Letters
- Expanding Vocabulary
  Thesaurus: Exact Words for *small*
- Real-World Connection
  Social Studies: The American Revolution

Unit 29

Adding *-ion*   180

- Spelling-Meaning Connection
- Dictionary: Primary and Secondary Stress
- Proofreading and Writing
  Proofread for Spelling
- Expanding Vocabulary
  The Greek Word Part *tele*
- Real-World Connection
  Performing Arts: Television

Unit 30

Review   186

- Spelling-Meaning Strategy
  The Greek Word Part *ast*
- Literature and Writing
  Literature
  based on *Gramp*
  by Joan Tate
  The Writing Process
  Persuasive Letters

Cycle 6

Unit 31

More Words with *-ion*   192

- Spelling-Meaning Connection
- Proofreading and Writing
  Proofread: Spelling and Commas
  in Letter Headings
- Expanding Vocabulary
  Building Words with *impress*
- Real-World Connection
  Health: Pollution

Unit 32

More Words with Prefixes   198

- Spelling-Meaning Connection
- Dictionary: Different Pronunciations
- Proofreading and Writing
  Proofread for Spelling
- Expanding Vocabulary
  Building New Words with Prefixes
- Real-World Connection
  Social Studies: Making Laws

Contents

Unit 33

Suffixes *-ent, -ant; -able, -ible* 204

- Spelling-Meaning Connection
- Proofreading and Writing
  Proofread: Spelling and Using *I* and *me*
- Expanding Vocabulary
  The Word Root *vac*
- Real-World Connection
  Business: Fashion

Unit 34

Three-Syllable Words 210

- Spelling-Meaning Connection
- Dictionary: Prefixes
- Proofreading and Writing
  Proofread for Spelling
- Expanding Vocabulary
  Antonyms and Synonyms
- Real-World Connection
  Social Studies: National Parks

Unit 35

More Three-Syllable Words 216

- Spelling-Meaning Connection
- Proofreading and Writing
  Proofread: Spelling and Contractions
- Expanding Vocabulary
  The Suffix *-ous*
- Real-World Connection
  Recreation: Summer Olympic Games

Unit 36

Review 222

- Spelling-Meaning Strategy
  The Latin Word Root *spect*
- Literature and Writing
  Literature
  from *Nature's Champions* by Alvin and Virginia Silverstein
  The Writing Process
  Research Report

Student's Handbook

Extra Practice and Review 229

Writer's Resources

Capitalization and Punctuation Guide
Abbreviations 247
Titles 248
Quotations 248
Capitalization 249
Punctuation 250

Letter Models
Friendly Letter 252
Business Letter 253

Thesaurus

Using the Thesaurus 254
Thesaurus Index 256
Thesaurus 261

Spelling-Meaning Index

Consonant Changes 270
Vowel Changes 271
Word Parts 274

Spelling Dictionary

Spelling Table 276
How to Use a Dictionary 278
Spelling Dictionary 279

Content Index 336
Credits 340
Handwriting Models 341
Words Often Misspelled 342

How to Study a Word

❶ Look at the word.

- What are the letters in the word?
- What does the word mean?
- Does it have more than one meaning?

❷ Say the word.

- What are the consonant sounds?
- What are the vowel sounds?

❸ Think about the word.

- How is each sound spelled?
- Did you see any familiar spelling patterns?
- Did you note any prefixes, suffixes, or other word parts?

❹ Write the word.

- Think about the sounds and the letters.
- Form the letters correctly.

❺ Check the spelling.

- Did you spell the word the same way it is spelled on your word list?
- Do you need to write the word again?

Using Spelling Strategies

Sometimes you want to write a word that you are not certain how to spell. For example, this student writer wanted to spell the word that named the machine in the picture. She followed these steps to figure out the spelling.

1 Say the word softly. Listen to all the sounds. Then think about the letters and patterns that usually spell each sound. Listen for familiar word parts, such as prefixes, endings, or suffixes.

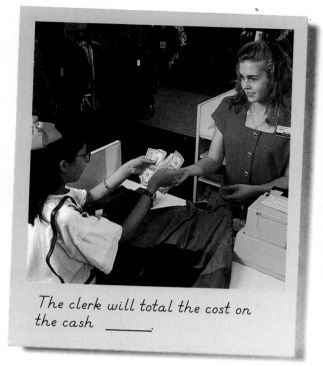

The clerk will total the cost on the cash _____.

The first syllable has the short vowel pattern. The short *e* sound is probably spelled *e*.

The |j| sound could be spelled *j* or *g*. I know that the final schwa + *r* sounds are usually spelled *er, ar,* or *or*.

2 Have a go at the spelling! Write the word a few different ways to see which way looks right. Make a chart like the one shown. In the first column, write one possible spelling. In the second column, write a second possible spelling.

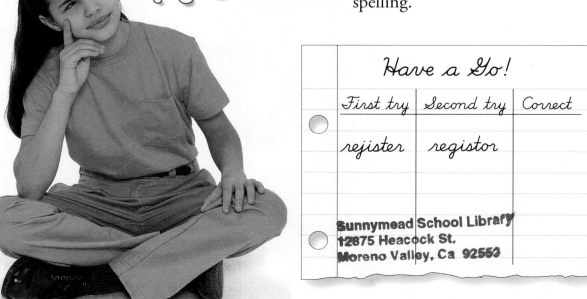

Have a Go!		
First try	Second try	Correct
rejister	registor	

Sunnymead School Library
12875 Heacock St.
Moreno Valley, Ca 92553

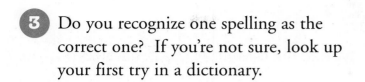

3 Do you recognize one spelling as the correct one? If you're not sure, look up your first try in a dictionary.

> I didn't find it spelled *r-e-j*.

4 It's not there? Look up your second try.

> Oh, here it is. It's spelled *r-e-g-i-s-t-e-r*.

5 Finish your chart by writing the correct spelling. You might want to put a check mark over the letters you spelled correctly and circle the incorrect letters to help you remember.

Have a Go!		
First try	Second try	Correct
register	registor	register

Spelling Strategies

1. Listen for familiar sounds and patterns.
2. Listen for familiar word parts—prefixes, suffixes, and endings.
3. Use the Spelling-Meaning Strategy. Is there a word related in meaning that can help you spell your word?
4. Use a Have-a-Go chart.
5. Use a dictionary.

Short Vowels

|ŭ| |ĕ|
bunk **slept**

Basic

READ the sentences. **SAY** each bold word.

1. bunk — I will sleep on the top **bunk**.
2. staff — The **staff** welcomed the new campers.
3. dock — The boat was left at the **dock**.
4. slept — Have you ever **slept** in a tent?
5. mist — The **mist** changed to rain.
6. bunch — Ann picked a **bunch** of flowers.
7. swift — The **swift** runner won the race.
8. stuck — The car is **stuck** in the mud.
9. breath — I took a **breath** of air.
10. tough — Outdoor clothing must be **tough**.
11. fond — Maria is **fond** of her dog.
12. crush — Do not **crush** the bug with your foot.
13. grasp — Please **grasp** the rope tightly.
14. dwell — Do bears **dwell** in your state?
15. fund — Is there any money in the birthday **fund**?
16. ditch — The car slid into the **ditch**.
17. split — Can we **split** that sandwich in two?
18. swept — He **swept** the floor with a broom.
19. deaf — The **deaf** cat cannot hear the bell.
20. rough — Today the sea is too **rough** for sailing.

Think and Write

Each word has a short vowel sound spelled by a single vowel followed by a consonant sound. This is called the **short vowel pattern**.

|ă| st**a**ff |ĭ| m**i**st |ŭ| b**u**nk
|ĕ| sl**e**pt |ŏ| d**o**ck

• What letter usually spells each short vowel sound? How are the Elephant Words different?

Now write each Basic Word under its vowel sound.

|ă|	|ĕ|	|ĭ|	|ŏ|	|ŭ|

Review
21. trunk
22. skill
23. track
24. fresh
25. odd

Challenge
26. trek
27. knapsack
28. summit
29. rustic
30. mascot

Independent Practice

Spelling Strategy Remember that a short vowel sound is usually spelled by one vowel and followed by a consonant sound. This is the **short vowel pattern**. These vowels usually spell these short vowel sounds:

|ă| *a* |ĕ| *e* |ĭ| *i* |ŏ| *o* |ŭ| *u*

Word Analysis/Phonics Complete the exercises with Basic Words.
1–2. Write the two words that end with double consonants.
3–4. Write the two words that end with the |f| sound spelled *gh*.
5–7. Write the three words that have the |ch| or the |sh| sound.

Vocabulary: Definitions Write the Basic Word that fits each meaning.

8. a wharf
9. to hold on to firmly
10. a double-decker bed
11. unable to hear
12. moving very fast
13. a sum of money

Challenge Words Write the Challenge Word that fits each clue. Use your Spelling Dictionary.

14. a slow, hard journey
15. rural
16. peak
17. holds camping supplies
18. often seen at football games

Spelling-Meaning Connection

Breathe and *breath* have different vowel sounds, but they are related in spelling and meaning. **Think of this:** In cold weather I can see my *breath* when I *breathe*.

19–20. Write *breathe*. Then write the Basic Word that is related in spelling and meaning to *breathe*.

breathe
breath

Review: Spelling Spree

Letter Swap Write a Basic or Review Word by changing the underlined letter to a different letter or to two different letters.

Example: sp_i_ll *skill*

1. _b_rush
2. f_l_esh
3. o_l_d
4. b_e_nch
5. st_i_ff
6. _p_itch
7. dea_d_
8. _d_eath
9. tou_c_h
10. gras_s_
11. f_o_nd
12. b_a_nk
13. s_w_ept
14. swel_l_
15. d_u_ck
16. _t_ough
17. m_u_st

Find a Rhyme Write a Basic or Review Word that rhymes with the underlined word and makes sense in the sentence.

18. When I opened the car _____ , out jumped a <u>skunk</u>.
19. Jeffrey _____ the floors and <u>kept</u> the place clean.
20. A man walked along the _____ , carrying his <u>sack</u>.
21. Anna is _____ of swimming in the <u>pond</u>.
22. How did the <u>truck</u> get _____ in the sand?
23. The _____ current caused the boat to <u>drift</u> toward the shore.
24. If you both want the apple, _____ <u>it</u>.
25. With grace and _____ , Jane skied down the <u>hill</u>.

How Are You Doing?

List the spelling words that are still hard for you. Practice them with a family member.

Proofreading and Writing

Proofread: Spelling and End Marks End every sentence with the correct mark.

DECLARATIVE: At camp we learned the names of birds**.**

INTERROGATIVE: Will we see a red-winged blackbird**?**

IMPERATIVE: Please hand me the binoculars**.**

EXCLAMATORY: How colorful the blue jay is**!**

Find four misspelled Basic or Review Words and two incorrect end marks in these rowing tips. Write the paragraph correctly.

Did you ever row against a
swift river current. It takes skil.
Grasp the oars tightly, or they will
be sweped away by the ruff water?
Take a deep breth, and pull as hard
as you can.

Write a Journal Entry

In your journal write about an outdoor experience that you have had. Try to use five spelling words. You may want to read your journal entry to a classmate.

MY JOURNAL

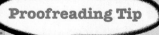

Proofreading Tip

Check that you used the correct end marks. Proofread for one kind of error at a time.

Basic

1. bunk
2. staff
3. dock
4. slept
5. mist
6. bunch
7. swift
8. stuck
9. breath
10. tough
11. fond
12. crush
13. grasp
14. dwell
15. fund
16. ditch
17. split
18. swept
19. deaf
20. rough

Review
21. trunk
22. skill
23. track
24. fresh
25. odd

Challenge
26. trek
27. knapsack
28. summit
29. rustic
30. mascot

Proofreading Marks

¶ Indent
∧ Add
ℱ Delete
≡ Capital letter
/ Small letter

Expanding Vocabulary

Recognizing Word Families The words *slept* and *swept* are the past tense forms of the verbs *sleep* and *sweep*. Other verbs with this spelling pattern spell their past tense forms the same way.

Fill in the past tense forms for *keep, creep,* and *weep* in this chart.

sleep	sweep	keep	creep	weep
slept	*swept*	1. ?	2. ?	3. ?

Work Together Work with a partner to write sentences to describe the pictures. Use the present and the past tense forms of the verbs *sleep* and *creep*. Use your Spelling Dictionary.

4.

5.

Vocabulary Enrichment

Real-World Connection

Recreation: Summer Camp All the words in the box relate to summer camp. Look up these words in your Spelling Dictionary. Then write the words to complete this letter.

Spelling Word Link

rustic

campfire
canoe
mosquitoes
prank
counselor
crafts
archery
poison ivy

22 Willow Avenue
Nashua, NH 03060
July 22, 1998

Dear Carrie,

This summer we went to Camp Huron. Pam, the camp __(1)__, was in charge of our cabin. She taught us how to paddle a __(2)__, hit the target in __(3)__, build a roaring __(4)__, and make different __(5)__. She also taught us how to avoid getting bitten by hungry __(6)__ and to recognize __(7)__ leaves, which can cause an itchy skin rash. At night we laughed a lot because Pam would often play a __(8)__ on us.

Love,
Ana

Try This CHALLENGE

Riddle Time! Write a word from the box to answer each riddle.

9. What does the job of both a stove and a furnace?
10. What is a sport you can play standing in one place?
11. What is green but can make you turn red?
12. What insects get slapped when they have dinner?

★★★ Fact File

Backpacking combines hiking and camping. Backpackers hike into the wilderness carrying food, clothing, shelter, bedding, and cooking equipment on their backs.

Spelling |ā| and |ē|

Read and Say

|ā| |ē|
stray   leaf

Basic

READ the sentences. **SAY** each bold word.

1. *speech* — Did you hear the **speech** about litter?
2. *greet* — I **greet** my guests at the door.
3. *claim* — The boys **claim** that they did not cheat.
4. *stray* — We found a **stray** cat.
5. *brain* — Use your **brain** to solve the problem.
6. *deal* — Sam got a **deal** on a used bike.
7. *male* — The **male** dog is named Max.
8. *raise* — Please **raise** the window higher.
9. *leaf* — This **leaf** fell from that oak tree.
10. *thief* — The police caught the **thief**.
11. *lease* — We have a one-year **lease** on this house.
12. *laid* — He **laid** the paper on the desk.
13. *waist* — The pants are too big around the **waist**.
14. *praise* — Be sure to **praise** Mary's good work.
15. *beast* — The **beast** looked like a bear.
16. *stain* — The ink **stain** would not wash out.
17. *seal* — Did you **seal** the letter tightly?
18. *sway* — The trees **sway** in the wind.
19. *fleet* — The **fleet** of ten boats will sail today.
20. *niece* — My sister's daughter is my **niece**.

Think and Write

The long *a* sound can be spelled *a*-consonant-*e* or with two letters.
The long *e* sound is often spelled with two vowels. The *ai* and *ea*
patterns are often followed by a consonant sound.

|ā| m**a**l**e**, br**ai**n, str**ay** |ē| l**ea**f, gr**ee**t

• What three patterns spell |ā|? What two patterns spell |ē|?
How is |ē| spelled in the Elephant Words?

Now write each Basic Word under its vowel sound.

|ā| Sound	|ē| Sound

Review	23. least	**Challenge**	28. campaign
21. free	24. safe	26. candidate	29. nominate
22. gray	25. gain	27. succeed	30. cease

Independent Practice

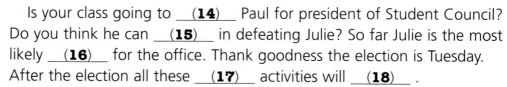

Spelling Strategy When you hear the |ā| sound, think of the patterns *a*-consonant-*e, ai,* and *ay.* When you hear the |ē| sound, think of the patterns *ea* and *ee.*

Word Analysis/Phonics Complete the exercises with Basic Words.

1–2. Write the two words that rhyme with *chain.*

3–8. Write the word that begins with each consonant cluster.

3. pr	**5.** str	**7.** gr
4. sw	**6.** fl	**8.** sp

Vocabulary: Definitions Write the Basic Word that fits each meaning.

9. a person who steals

10. a right to something

11. to lift

12. to rent

13. the daughter of one's brother or sister

Challenge Words Write the Challenge Words to complete this paragraph. Use your Spelling Dictionary.

Is your class going to __(14)__ Paul for president of Student Council? Do you think he can __(15)__ in defeating Julie? So far Julie is the most likely __(16)__ for the office. Thank goodness the election is Tuesday. After the election all these __(17)__ activities will __(18)__ .

Spelling-Meaning Connection

Deal and *dealt* are related in meaning and spelling even though they have different vowel sounds. **Think of this:** When it was Tom's turn to *deal,* he *dealt* the cards quickly.

19–20. Write *deal* and *dealt.* Underline two letters in each word that are the same but that spell different vowel sounds.

Dictionary

Guide Words In a dictionary each main word, or **entry word,** is listed in alphabetical order. Two **guide words** appear at the top of each dictionary page. They show the first and last entry words on that page.

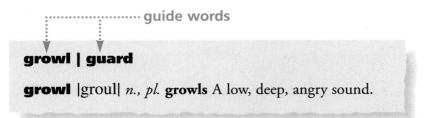

guide words

growl | guard

growl |groul| *n., pl.* **growls** A low, deep, angry sound.

Practice 1–8. Write the words that you would find on the page with the guide words **leader | leather.**

leash	lease	leaf	league	leap
lead	learn	leak	leave	least

Review: Spelling Spree

Word Clues Write a Basic or Review Word to fit each clue.

9. walks on four legs
10. placed or put
11. to achieve
12. part of a plant
13. a homeless cat
14. a boy or a man
15. a color
16. to say hello
17. no cost

18. to swing back and forth
19. many ships
20. robber
21. sister's daughter
22. agreement with a landlord
23. discolored spot
24. opposite of *greatest*
25. between the ribs and the hips

Proofreading and Writing

Proofread for Spelling Find eight misspelled Basic or Review Words in this script for a talk. Write each one correctly.

I am giving this speech today to gain your support. I clame to be the best person for class treasurer. First, I have a good brane for math. Second, I know how to deel with money and keep it saif. My chief concern is to get money for our after-school activities. I have lots of ideas about how we can raze money on our own. I hope I have earned your prais. Give me your seel of approval when you vote.

Write a Speech

Write a speech about something that is important to you. Include strong reasons for your ideas. Try to use five spelling words. You may want to present your speech to some classmates.

Proofreading Tip

Put a strip of paper or cardboard under each line as you read it. This will help you focus on each word.

Proofreading Marks

¶	Indent
∧	Add
⌐	Delete
≡	Capital letter
/	Small letter

Expanding Vocabulary

Using a Thesaurus Where can you find an exact word to replace a general or overused word? Where can you find **synonyms**, words with the same or similar meanings? Use a **thesaurus**. Look at this entry from your Thesaurus.

part of speech ···· ···· definition ····sample sentence

main entry word ········➤ **speech** *n.* a public talk. *The writer gave a **speech** at the high school.*

subentry ····
➤ **address** a formal speech. *We listened to the President's **address**.*
➤ **lecture** a speech providing information on a subject, given before a class. *The class heard a **lecture** about the planets.*

Read pages 254–255 to learn how to use your Thesaurus. Then write the two subentries given in your Thesaurus for each of these words.

1–2. boast   **3–4.** protect   **5–6.** different

Show You Know! Write a caption for each picture, using the subentry for *different* that fits each one.

7.

8.

Vocabulary Enrichment

Real-World Connection

Social Studies: Elections All the words in the box relate to elections. Look up these words in your Spelling Dictionary. Then write the words to complete this chart.

Steps for Electing a President of the United States

When	Step
Summer before the election	Each major political __(1)__ holds a meeting called a __(2)__. The __(3)__ decide who the Democratic candidate will be, and the __(4)__ choose their candidate. Each party also writes its __(5)__, a statement of the party's beliefs and goals.
Anytime before a certain date prior to the election	All citizens eighteen and over who want to vote must __(6)__ if they have not already done it.
Election Day	Each __(7)__ can cast one __(8)__ for one candidate.

Spelling Word Link

campaign

ballot
convention
party
Democrats
Republicans
platform
register
voter

Yes or No? Write *yes* if the underlined word is used correctly. Write *no* if it is not.

9. Mrs. Lewis marked her <u>ballot</u>.
10. On Election Day the people voted at a <u>convention</u>.
11. <u>Party</u> members worked to support their candidate.
12. The party's <u>platform</u> was fifty pages long.

> ⭐⭐⭐ **Fact File**
>
> The right to vote is called suffrage. The United States has not always had suffrage for women. Susan B. Anthony worked to win this right, and suffrage for women became law in 1920.

Spelling |ī| and |ō|

sign   slope

Read and Say

Basic	**READ** the sentences. **SAY** each bold word.
1. strike	Do not **strike** anything with that stick.
2. thrown	The pitcher has **thrown** a fastball.
3. stole	Someone **stole** the book.
4. boast	Do not **boast** about your score.
5. sign	Did you see the name on the **sign**?
6. stroll	Let's **stroll** through the park.
7. thigh	The ball hit my **thigh**.
8. height	You and I are the same **height**.
9. dough	My mother makes bread **dough**.
10. owe	You **owe** me one dollar.
11. loaf	Please buy a **loaf** of bread.
12. stroke	I like to **stroke** my cat's soft fur.
13. growth	The city's **growth** has been quick.
14. stride	That man walks with a long **stride**.
15. code	The note was in a secret **code**.
16. slope	The seats **slope** down to the field.
17. hose	Use the **hose** to water the lawn.
18. mild	The weather is clear and **mild**.
19. flow	Which way does the river **flow**?
20. slight	The difference between the twins is **slight**.

Think and Write

The long *i* and the long *o* sounds can be spelled with the vowel-consonant-*e* pattern or with patterns of one or more letters. The *oa* pattern is usually followed by a consonant sound.

|ī| str**ike**, th**igh**, s**ign** |ō| h**ose**, b**oa**st, thr**ow**n, str**o**ll

• What are three patterns for |ī|? What are four patterns for |ō|? How are |ī| and |ō| spelled in the Elephant Words?

Now write each Basic Word under its vowel sound.

|ī| Sound	|ō| Sound

Review	23. broke	**Challenge**	28. site
21. twice	24. shown	26. opponent	29. plight
22. goal	25. sigh	27. sacrifice	30. reproach

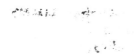

Independent Practice

Spelling Strategy When you hear the |ī| sound, think of the patterns *i*-consonant-*e, igh,* and *i.* When you hear the |ō| sound, think of the patterns *o*-consonant-*e, oa, ow,* and *o.*

Word Analysis/Phonics Complete the exercises with Basic Words.

1–4. Write the four words that begin with the same cluster of three consonants.

5–7. Write the three words that end with the |ō| sound. Then circle the word in which the |ō| sound is the only sound.

Vocabulary: Word Clues Write the Basic Word that fits each clue.

8. the upper part of the leg
9. how tall a person is
10. another word for *gentle*
11. another word for *brag*
12. small in amount
13. can be used to wash a car or water a garden

Challenge Words Write the Challenge Word that fits each meaning. Use your Spelling Dictionary.

14. to blame
15. a rival
16. location
17. to give up something valuable
18. a serious condition

Spelling-Meaning Connection

How can you remember that *sign* has a silent *g*? Think of the related word *signal,* in which the *g* is pronounced.

sign
signal

19–20. Write *sign* and *signal.* Underline the letter that is silent in one word and pronounced in the other.

Dictionary

Definitions A dictionary **entry** may include several numbered definitions. A **sample sentence** or **phrase** is often given to help you understand a specific meaning.

> **height** |hīt| *n., pl.* **heights** **1.** The distance from bottom to top: *The height of the flagpole is twenty feet.* **2.** The distance from foot to head: *My height increased two inches this year.* **3.** The highest point; peak: *the height of the storm.*

Practice Write *1, 2,* or *3* to show which definition of *height* is used in each sentence.

1. The twins were exactly the same height.
2. The height of the building is ninety feet.
3. She won the Nobel Prize at the height of her career.
4. People were amazed by the height of the mountain.
5. What is the height of the tallest person who ever lived?

Review: Spelling Spree

Letter Math Add and subtract letters from the words below to make Basic or Review Words. Write the new words.

Example: sh + blown – bl = *shown*

6. th + sigh – s =
7. fl + show – sh =
8. sl + hope – h =
9. tw + rice – r =
10. d + though – th =
11. m + wild – w =
12. s + fight – f – t =
13. grow + th =

14. str + bike – b =
15. c + rode – r =
16. str + joke – j =
17. load – d + f =
18. throw + n =
19. str + bride – br =
20. h + rose – r =

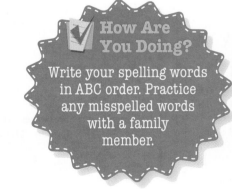

☑ How Are You Doing?

Write your spelling words in ABC order. Practice any misspelled words with a family member.

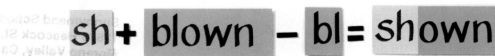

sh + blown – bl = shown

Proofreading and Writing

Proofread for Spelling Find ten misspelled Basic or Review Words in this sports article. Write each one correctly.

HOORAY for HAYS!

Carlton Hays brok a world record in today's ball game. He stol more bases than any other baseball player. That has been his gole since he joined the team.

After the game the fans watched Hays strole across the field to speak. With a slite nod to the crowd, Carlton said, "I want to bost about my teammates. I ow my success to them. They never loaf on the job and have shone what good teamwork can do." Some fans held up a sine that said *Hooray for Hays!* Hays is at the hight of his fame.

Basic

1. strike
2. thrown
3. stole
4. boast
5. sign
6. stroll
7. thigh
8. height
9. dough
10. owe
11. loaf
12. stroke
13. growth
14. stride
15. code
16. slope
17. hose
18. mild
19. flow
20. slight

Review

21. twice
22. goal
23. broke
24. shown
25. sigh

Challenge

26. opponent
27. sacrifice
28. site
29. plight
30. reproach

Write a Description

Write a paragraph about a sports event. What do you see, hear, smell, or feel? Paint a word picture! Try to use five spelling words.

Proofreading Tip

Circle any words that might be misspelled. Then look up their spellings in a dictionary.

Proofreading Marks

¶	Indent
∧	Add
⌐	Delete
≡	Capital letter
/	Small letter

Vocabulary Enrichment

Expanding Vocabulary

Thesaurus: Words for *walk* Which sentence is clearer?

Tim **walks** to first base.   Tim **strides** to first base.

Walks tells you what Tim does, but *strides* is more exact. It tells you that Tim walks with energy, taking long steps.

Look up the main entry *walk* in your Thesaurus. Then draw this word web, and fill in the subentries given for *walk*.

1. ?
2. ?
3. ?
4. ?
5. ?
6. ?

walk

Show You Know! What is the best word in the word web to replace *walk* each time it is used in this personal story? Write the story, using exact words in place of *walk*.

Last Sunday our family went to Briggs Park. My little sister had fun trying to **walk** toward the squirrels without scaring them. We had to watch her closely so that she did not **walk** all over the park without us.

After lunch we watched the members of the high school band **walk** up and down the field, practicing their drills. Then I played softball, but a ball hit me in the leg. I saw my father **walk** across the field to help me. I had to **walk** back to the car at the end of the day.

Vocabulary Enrichment

Real-World Connection

Physical Education: Baseball All the words in the box relate to baseball. Look up these words in your Spelling Dictionary. Then write the words to complete this description.

Spelling Word Link

strike

mound
inning
outfield
league
triple
shortstop
umpire
pitcher

CLEAR CREEK'S ALL STARS
Marlene Zavala

Marlene Zavala, the star __(1)__ in our school's baseball __(2)__ , throws a great fastball. When she takes the __(3)__ , the crowd cheers. The __(4)__ has trouble calling balls and strikes. Marlene plays through the ninth __(5)__ . She strikes out most players, and no one has hit a __(6)__ . Her teammates who play in the __(7)__ rarely see much action. Anyone who plays __(8)__ , the position between second and third base, is bored.

Try This CHALLENGE

Yes or No? Write *yes* if the underlined word is used correctly. Write *no* if it is not.

9. The <u>pitcher</u> threw a curve ball to the batter.
10. In yesterday's game the <u>umpire</u> hit a home run.
11. The batter hit a fly ball into the left <u>inning</u>.
12. The Cardinals are in our baseball <u>league</u>.

Fact File

Jackie Robinson was the first black player on a major league baseball team. A great all-around player, he is honored in the National Baseball Hall of Fame.

Spelling |oo̅| and |yoo̅|

Read and Say

proof
clue

Basic

READ the sentences. **SAY** each bold word.

1. clue   We need a **clue** to guess the secret word.
2. proof   Do you have **proof** that this dog is yours?
3. cruise   Let's **cruise** around the block.
4. choose   I will **choose** two books from this list.
5. rule   This class has a **rule** against shouting.
6. troop   There are ten students in our **troop**.
7. dew   The grass is wet with **dew**.
8. route   What **route** do you take to school?
9. view   There is a pretty **view** from the hill.
10. lose   Did you **lose** my pencil?
11. duke   A **duke** is not as powerful as a king.
12. mood   I am in a happy **mood** today.
13. scoop   Use the shovel to **scoop** up the sand.
14. mule   A **mule** pulled the wagon.
15. youth   My mother looked like me in her **youth**.
16. bruise   I got a **bruise** when I bumped the table.
17. loose   Tighten the lid so that it is not **loose**.
18. rude   It is **rude** to talk back to someone.
19. loop   The path makes a **loop** through the park.
20. flute   Jane plays the **flute** in the band.

Think and Write

The |oo̅| and the |yoo̅| sounds can be spelled *u*-consonant-*e* or with two letters. A consonant sound usually follows the patterns *oo, ui,* and *ou.*

|oo̅| or |yoo̅| r**u**le, cl**ue**, d**ew**, pr**oo**f, cr**ui**se, r**ou**te

• What six patterns spell |oo̅| or |yoo̅|? How are |oo̅| and |yoo̅| spelled in the Elephant Words?

Now write each Basic Word under its spelling of |oo̅| or |yoo̅|.

u-consonant-e	oo	ui or ou	ue or ew	Other

Review
21. shoot
22. true
23. group
24. fruit
25. blew

Challenge
26. subdue
27. pursuit
28. presume
29. accuse
30. intrude

Independent Practice

Spelling Strategy When you hear the |ōō| and the |yōō| sounds, think of the patterns *u-consonant-e, ue, ew, oo, ui,* and *ou.*

Word Analysis/Phonics Complete the exercises with Basic Words.

1–4. Write the four words that have the final |z| sound.

5–7. Write three words by adding letters to the consonant clusters.

    5. cl_____   **6.** tr_____   **7.** pr_____

Vocabulary: Classifying Write the Basic Word that belongs in each group.

  8. spoon, shovel, _____
  9. queen, prince, _____
10. fog, mist, _____
11. violin, tuba, _____
12. road, highway, _____
13. donkey, horse, _____

Challenge Words Write the Challenge Word that completes each sentence. Use your Spelling Dictionary.

14. The police officer tried to _____ the noisy crowd.

15. The police are in _____ of the bank robber.

16. Will the witness _____ the suspect of stealing?

17. We have laws so that others do not _____ on our privacy.

18. Do not _____ that a person who looks suspicious is guilty.

Spelling-Meaning Connection

Can you see *view* in these words: *preview, review?* These words are all related in spelling and meaning. **Think of this:** The critic had a good *view* when she watched the movie *preview.*

19–20. Write *preview.* Then write the Basic Word that you see in *preview.*

Review: Spelling Spree

Puzzle Play   Write a Basic or Review Word to fit each clue. Circle the letter that would appear in the box.

Example: not polite   _ _ □ _   *rude*

1. pick   □ _ _ _ _ _
2. young person   _ _ _ _ □
3. good dessert   _ _ _ □ _
4. stubborn animal   _ _ _ □
5. evidence   _ _ _ _ □
6. a feeling   _ □ _ _
7. an instrument   □ _ _ _ _

8. bunch   _ _ _ _ □
9. misplace   _ □ _ _
10. to govern   _ _ □ _
11. hurt spot   _ _ _ □ _ _
12. to dish out   _ □ _ _ _
13. path   _ _ _ _ □

Now write the circled letters in order. They will spell three mystery words that name a job.

Mystery Words: _ _ ? _ _   _ ? _   _ _ _ _ ? _ _ _

Crack the Code   Some Basic and Review Words have been written in the code below. Use the code to figure out each word. Then write the words correctly.

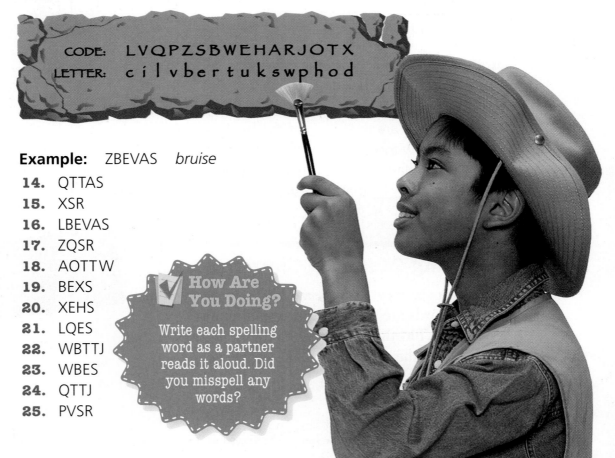

CODE: L V Q P Z S B W E H A R J O T X
LETTER: c i l v b e r t u k s w p h o d

Example: ZBEVAS   *bruise*

14. QTTAS
15. XSR
16. LBEVAS
17. ZQSR
18. AOTTW
19. BEXS
20. XEHS
21. LQES
22. WBTTJ
23. WBES
24. QTTJ
25. PVSR

How Are You Doing?

Write each spelling word as a partner reads it aloud. Did you misspell any words?

Proofreading and Writing

Proofread: Spelling and Commas In a compound sentence, two sentences are joined by the conjunction *and, but,* or *or.* Use a comma before the conjunction.

You must stop at a red light, or you will get a ticket.

Find four misspelled Basic or Review Words and two missing commas in this beginning of a detective story. Write the story beginning correctly.

Who took the floot? Officer Mackey talked to the groupe in the music store. They said the rude yuth was innocent and Mackey knew the story was true. Mackey needed a clew but she did not know where to look.

Write Interview Questions

Write some questions that a reporter might ask a detective about a crime. Try to use five spelling words and at least one compound sentence. You may want to role-play your interview with a partner.

Proofreading Tip

Check that you used a comma to separate the parts of any compound sentences.

Basic

1. clue
2. proof
3. cruise
4. choose
5. rule
6. troop
7. dew
8. route
9. view
10. lose
11. duke
12. mood
13. scoop
14. mule
15. youth
16. bruise
17. loose
18. rude
19. loop
20. flute

Review
21. shoot
22. true
23. group
24. fruit
25. blew

Challenge
26. subdue
27. pursuit
28. presume
29. accuse
30. intrude

Proofreading Marks

¶   Indent
∧   Add
⌐   Delete
≡   Capital letter
/   Small letter

Vocabulary Enrichment

Expanding Vocabulary

Easily Confused Words: *loose* and *lose* *Loose* and *lose* are often misspelled. *Loose* is usually an adjective that can mean "not fitting tightly" or "not tied up." *Lose* is a verb that can mean "to fail to find" or "to fail to win."

The button is **loose**.

Where did she **lose** the button?

You can see *loose* and *lose* in the other words in their word families.

loose	lose
not fitting tightly; not tied up	to fail to find; to fail to win
loosen **loose**ly **loose**st **loose**r	**lose**r **los**ing **los**t

Complete this part of a letter by writing *loose*, *lose*, or another word from their word families. Use your Spelling Dictionary.

Tomorrow I'll be racing in this year's Soap Box Derby. I hope that I don't __(1)__ this year. It's not that I really mind __(2)__, but it's more fun to be a winner than a __(3)__ !

This year I will be sure to check for __(4)__ wheel nuts before the race. I'm also going to try to relax during the race, __(5)__ my grip on the steering wheel a bit, and just have fun. I will tie your good-luck scarf __(6)__ around my neck. See you at the finish line!

Real-World Connection

Careers: Police Work All the words in the box relate to police work. Look up these words in your Spelling Dictionary. Then write the words to complete this announcement.

Davis Receives Promotion

The Police Department announces the promotion of Russell Davis to captain. A party to honor Davis will be held at police __(1)__ on June 22. Abigail Melton, Sheriff Kane's __(2)__, will present Davis with his new __(3)__ before the other members of his __(4)__.

Davis had ten years of experience and was no __(5)__ when he joined the department last year. He had been a police __(6)__ with the Bedford Police Department. On his first day, Davis nabbed a suspected __(7)__ by quickly obtaining a search __(8)__ for the suspect's car.

Try This CHALLENGE

Right or Wrong? Write *T* if the sentence is true. Write *F* if it is not.

9. A squad works like a team.
10. A deputy is in charge of a sheriff.
11. A rookie has a lot of experience.
12. A warrant allows an officer to make an arrest.

⭐⭐⭐ **Fact File**

The most famous police department may be Scotland Yard, in London, England. It has led the world in solving crimes. It was the first to use fingerprinting.

Spelling |ou|, |ô|, and |oi|

Read and Say

|oi| |ou|
royal tower

Basic

READ the sentences. **SAY** each bold word.

1. hawk — The **hawk** flew over the farm.
2. claw — An eagle's **claw** is very sharp.
3. bald — The man's **bald** head felt smooth.
4. tower — The **tower** is one hundred feet high.
5. stalk — Tigers **stalk** other animals for food.
6. prowl — Cats **prowl** at night.
7. loyal — Kate is **loyal** to her friends.
8. pause — Can we **pause** for a short break?
9. moist — The dirt is **moist** from the rain.
10. ounce — This letter weighs one **ounce**.
11. launch — When will they **launch** the new ship?
12. royal — The princess is part of the **royal** family.
13. scowl — My dad will **scowl** when he is angry.
14. haunt — The movie will **haunt** us for days.
15. joint — The elbow is a body **joint**.
16. coward — Only a **coward** would run away.
17. fawn — The deer was followed by its newborn **fawn**.
18. thousand — Ten times one hundred is one **thousand**.
19. drown — How can we **drown** out that loud noise?
20. fault — This broken glass is not my **fault**.

Think and Write

The |ou|, the |ô|, and the |oi| sounds are usually spelled with two letters. The patterns *ou, au,* and *oi* are usually followed by a consonant sound.

|ou| **ou**nce, t**ow**er |oi| m**oi**st, l**oy**al
|ô| cl**aw**, p**au**se, b**a**ld

• What are two patterns for |ou|? What are three patterns for |ô|? What consonant follows the *a* spelling of |ô|? What are two patterns for |oi|?
Now write each Basic Word under its vowel sound.

|ou| Sound	|ô| Sound	|oi| Sound

Review	23. false	**Challenge**	28. loiter
21. south	24. cause	26. grouse	29. somersault
22. dawn	25. howl	27. poise	30. awkward

Independent Practice

Spelling Strategy   When you hear the |ou|, the |ô|, and the |oi| sounds, think of these patterns:

|ou| *ou, ow* |ô| *aw, au, a* before *l* |oi| *oi, oy*

Word Analysis/Phonics Complete the exercises with Basic Words.

1–5. Write the five words that begin with a consonant cluster. (*Th* is not a consonant cluster. It spells one sound.)

6–7. Write the two rhyming words that have the |oi| sound.

Vocabulary: Analogies An **analogy** compares word pairs that are related in the same way. Write a Basic Word to complete each analogy.

Example: *Hot* is to *cold* as *lost* is to *found.*

  8. *Heart* is to *muscle* as *elbow* is to _____ .
  9. *Foot* is to *inch* as *pound* is to _____ .
 10. *Bear* is to *cub* as *deer* is to _____ .
 11. *Mammal* is to *rabbit* as *bird* is to _____ .
 12. *Airplane* is to *takeoff* as *ship* is to _____ .
 13. *One* is to *ten* as *hundred* is to _____ .

Challenge Words Write the Challenge Word that fits each clue. Use your Spelling Dictionary.

 14. to linger
 15. a game bird
 16. to balance
 17. clumsy
 18. to roll the body in a complete circle

Spelling-Meaning Connection

How can you remember that *moisten* has a silent *t*? Think of the related word *moist,* in which the *t* is pronounced.

19–20. Write *moist* and *moisten.* Underline the letter that is pronounced in one word and silent in the other.

Dictionary

Spelling Table How can you find a word in a dictionary when you do not know how to spell it? Use the **Spelling Table**. It lists different spellings for the vowel and consonant sounds. If you wanted to find |houl|, you would check each spelling for the |ou| sound until you found *howl*.

SOUND	SPELLINGS	SAMPLE WORDS
|ou|	ou, ough, ow	l**ou**d, b**ough**, n**ow**

Practice For each pronunciation below, write the spellings given in the Spelling Table on pages 276–277 for the vowel sound. Then find the word in your Spelling Dictionary. Write it correctly.

1–2. |drout| **3–4.** |yēld| **5–6.** |klĕnz| **7–8.** |vôlt|

Review: Spelling Spree

The Third Word Write the Basic or Review Word that belongs in each group.

9. connection, hinge, _____
10. stop, wait, _____
11. scratch, dig, _____
12. mistake, blame, _____
13. morning, sunrise, _____
14. fake, untrue, _____
15. ship, voyage, _____
16. frown, pout, _____
17. wail, hoot, _____
18. wet, damp, _____
19. faithful, true, _____
20. hundred, million, _____
21. spook, ghost, _____
22. ton, pound, _____
23. east, north, _____
24. calf, foal, _____

Bon Voyage!

How Are You Doing?
Write each spelling word in a sentence. Practice any misspelled spelling words with a family member.

Proofreading and Writing

Proofread for Spelling Use proofreading marks to correct nine misspelled Basic or Review Words in this nature article.

The Forest Is Awake

At dawn the forest is awake. Like a king in his royle tawer, the bawld eagle watches the sunrise. The hauk is no caward. It searches the forest floor, ready to stauk mice. A river and a thousand bird songs almost droun out a wolf's howl. A mother deer and her fawn run down to the shining stream. Though the wolf is on the proul, it is too distant to couse them much fear. ●

Basic

1. hawk
2. claw
3. bald
4. tower
5. stalk
6. prowl
7. loyal
8. pause
9. moist
10. ounce
11. launch
12. royal
13. scowl
14. haunt
15. joint
16. coward
17. fawn
18. thousand
19. drown
20. fault

Review

21. south
22. dawn
23. false
24. cause
25. howl

Challenge

26. grouse
27. poise
28. loiter
29. somersault
30. awkward

Write Riddles

Write five riddles that can be answered with a pair of rhyming words. Include at least one spelling word in each answer. Trade riddles with a classmate.
Example: What is a best friend who is a prince? *a loyal royal*

Proofreading Tip **Check that you formed your *u*'s and *n*'s correctly so that they are clear.**

Proofreading Marks

¶ Indent
∧ Add
⌐ Delete
≡ Capital letter
/ Small letter

39

Vocabulary Enrichment

Expanding Vocabulary

Spelling Word Link

thousand

centennial
centenarian
million
millennium

Words from *mille* and *centum* Many words we use come from Latin, a language spoken in ancient Rome. The Latin words *mille* and *centum* are the sources of the words in the box. Look up each word in your Spelling Dictionary.

1. What number did you find in the definitions for words that begin with *mill*?

2. What number did you find in the definitions for words that begin with *cent*?

Work Together Work with a partner to write a sentence to answer each question. Use a word in the box in each sentence.

3. If a man lived for one thousand years, how long would he have lived?

4. Do you know any people who are one hundred years old or older?

5. What kind of celebration did the United States have on its hundredth birthday in 1876?

6. If groups of one thousand people were watching a television show in one thousand different places, how many people would be watching in all?

Fact File

You can see *centum* in the names of money from different countries. In the United States, one hundred **cents** equals one dollar. In Mexico, one hundred **centavos** equals one peso. In France, one hundred **centimes** equals one franc.

Real-World Connection

Science: Birds All the words in the box are names of birds. Look up these words in your Spelling Dictionary. Then write the words to complete this part of a zoo guide.

Spelling Word Link

hawk

falcon
ostrich
penguin
cardinal
flamingo
mallard
condor
quail

ZOO

Birds, Birds, Birds!

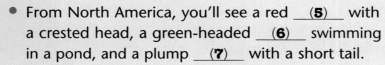

- A huge vulture, the __(1)__ , came from South America.

- Two long-necked birds, the pink __(2)__ and the fluffy __(3)__ , came from Africa.

- A funny black-and-white __(4)__ came from the South Pole.

- From North America, you'll see a red __(5)__ with a crested head, a green-headed __(6)__ swimming in a pond, and a plump __(7)__ with a short tail.

- Notice that the hawklike __(8)__ has the look of a hunter.

mallard

Try This CHALLENGE

Write Shape Poems Write a four-line shape poem about one of the birds listed in the word box. Use the form below. Then draw the shape of the bird around the poem.

adjective noun—
adjective, adjective, adjective—
verb
adverb, adverb, adverb

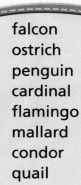

Powerful falcon—
Rare, keen-eyed, courageous—
Diving
Fast, fast, fast.

6 Review: Units 1–5

staff	bunch	slept	breath	tough
ditch	fond	grasp	rough	deaf

|ŭ| |ĕ|
bunk **slept**

Spelling Strategy
Remember that a short vowel sound is usually spelled by a single vowel and followed by a consonant sound.

|ă| → **a** |ĕ| → **e** |ĭ| → **i** |ŏ| → **o** |ŭ| → **u**

Write the word that fits each clue. Circle the words that have the |ĕ| sound.

1. a group
2. unable to hear
3. strong
4. loving
5. a walking stick
6. rhymes with *death*

Write the word that belongs in each group.

7. hold, grab, _____
8. hole, pit, _____
9. napped, dozed, _____
10. bumpy, uneven, _____

brain	male	speech	stray	thief
sway	beast	stain	fleet	niece

|ā| |ē|
stray **leaf**

Spelling Strategy

|ā| → **a-consonant-e, ai, ay** |ē| → **ea, ee**

Write the word that rhymes with each word below.

11. sleet
12. chief
13. least
14. pale
15. piece

Write the word that completes each sentence.

16. In humans the _____ is the memory center.
17. This grease _____ will never wash out of my pants.
18. After winning the election, Li gave an acceptance _____ .
19. The branches of the trees _____ in the wind.
20. Mrs. Johnson always feeds the lost or _____ animals.

Unit 3   Spelling |ī| and |ō| pages 24–29

thigh	stroll	height	dough	owe
growth	stride	mild	loaf	stroke

sign slope

Spelling Strategy

|ī| → **i-consonant-e, igh, i** |ō| → **o-consonant-e, oa, ow, o**

Write the word that completes each sentence.

21. Will you join us for a _____ around the neighborhood?
22. The black horse won the race without breaking _____ .
23. Bread, pastry, and other baked goods are made from _____ .
24. The bells rang at the _____ of midnight.
25. The part of the leg above the knee is the _____ .

Write the word that means the opposite of each word below.

26. work
27. decline
28. pay
29. stormy
30. depth

Unit 4   Spelling |o͞o| and |yo͞o| pages 30–35

dew	clue	cruise	view	lose
mule	mood	duke	youth	loose

**proof
clue**

Spelling Strategy

|o͞o| and |yo͞o| → **u-consonant-e, ue, ew, oo, ui, ou**

Write the word that fits each meaning.

31. to look at
32. a nobleman
33. a sea trip
34. early life
35. not bound together
36. state of mind

Write the word that completes each sentence.

37. The grass sparkled with morning _____ .
38. A missing book was a _____ to the mystery.
39. Many trees _____ their leaves in the fall.
40. I tied the gear onto the gray _____ .

|oi| |ou|
royal tower

Unit 5   Spelling |ou|, |ô|, and |oi| pages 36–41

pause	moist	ounce	loyal	stalk
fawn	scowl	joint	launch	thousand

Spelling Strategy

|ou| → **ou, ow** |ô| → **aw, au, a** before **l**
|oi| → **oi, oy**

Write the word that completes each analogy.

41. *Hot* is to *warm* as *wet* is to _____ .
42. *Smile* is to *grin* as *frown* is to _____ .
43. *Bad* is to *good* as *unfaithful* is to _____ .
44. *Tree* is to *trunk* as *plant* is to _____ .

Write the word that fits each clue.

45. knee
46. less than a pound
47. brief stop

48. a number
49. motorboat
50. young deer

Challenge Words   Units 1–5   pages 12–41

opponent	somersault	summit	accuse	succeed
candidate	sacrifice	subdue	loiter	knapsack

Write the word that means the opposite of each of these words.

51. provoke
52. teammate

53. base
54. hurry

Write the word that completes each analogy.

55. *Sharp* is to *dull* as *defend* is to _____ .
56. *Swimmer* is to *dive* as *gymnast* is to _____ .
57. *Lose* is to *win* as *fail* is to _____ .
58. *Cycling* is to *saddlebag* as *hiking* is to _____ .
59. *Gift* is to *present* as *offering* is to _____ .
60. *Job* is to *applicant* as *public office* is to _____ .

Spelling-Meaning Strategy

Consonant Changes: Silent to Sounded

You know that words, like people, can be related to each other. Read this paragraph.

When you are riding your bicycle, you should always stop at a stop **sign**. Use a hand **signal** when you want to make a turn.

sign
signal

Think

- How are *sign* and *signal* related in meaning?
- Which letter is silent in one word and pronounced in the other?

Here are more related words in which a consonant is silent in one word and pronounced in the other.

colum**n**	**h**eir	mus**c**le
colum**n**ist	in**h**erit	mus**c**ular

Apply and Extend

Complete these activities on a separate sheet of paper.

1. Look up the meaning of each word in the box above. Then write a short paragraph, using one pair of words from the box. Can you make the meaning of each word clear?

2. With a partner list as many words as you can that are related to *sign, column, heir,* and *muscle.* Then look at the section titled "Consonant Changes: Silent to Sounded" on page 270 of your Spelling-Meaning Index. Add any other words that you find in these families to your list.

Summing Up

How can you remember how to spell a word with a silent consonant? Sometimes there is a word that is related in meaning in which the letter is pronounced.

UNIT
6

Personal
Narrative

from
Philip Hall likes me.
I reckon maybe.
by Bette Greene

Usually Beth likes to talk to Philip, but today she has something else on her mind. Why is Beth eager to get home?

As I took a flying leap across the frozen drainage ditch that separated the road from the field, I heard Philip calling me.

"Hey, Beth!" He was still standing on the blacktop just where the bus left him. "You shouldn't be going through the field. You might step into an ice puddle."

Of all days to have to stop and start explaining things to Philip Hall. But at any other time I'd be thinking that he wouldn't be fretting about my feet if he didn't really like me. Now would he? "Frosty feet are nothing," I told him, "when you have a spanking new puppy waiting to meet you."

"What if Mr. Grant wouldn't swap a collie dog for one of your pa's turkeys?" asked Philip, grinning as though he hoped it was so.

"That's all you know! When I left the house this morning, my pa was picking out six of our fattest turkeys for swapping." I turned and began running across the field.

Think and Discuss

1. What information does the author present through the dialogue to explain why Beth wants to get home?

2. Where does this part of the story take place? What details help you picture the scene?

3. From whose point of view is this story told? How do you know?

The Writing Process
Personal Narrative

Write about an interesting experience you have had. Keep the guidelines in mind. Follow the Writing Process.

1 Prewriting
- Write about only one experience.
- Try different beginnings—a surprising statement, action, or dialogue.

2 Draft
- Try tape-recording your story. Replay the tape as you write.

3 Revise
- Add details and dialogue.
- Use your Thesaurus to find exact words.
- Have a writing conference.

4 Proofread
- Did you spell each word correctly?
- Did you use correct end marks?

5 Publish
- Add a good title.
- Illustrate a neat, final copy of your story, and share it.

···· Guidelines for Writing a Personal Narrative

✓ Tell the story from your point of view.
✓ Use dialogue and details to help your readers see, hear, and feel your experience.
✓ Catch your readers' attention with a good beginning.

Composition Words

tough
boast
lose
loyal
stroll
bruise
scowl
slept

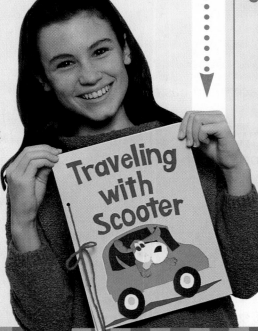

Traveling with Scooter

Spelling |ôr|, |âr|, and |är|

Read and Say

|ôr|	|âr|
sore	hare

Basic

READ the sentences. **SAY** each bold word.

1. hare — Is that a **hare** or a rabbit?
2. scar — I have a **scar** where I cut myself.
3. torch — Light the flame on the **torch**.
4. soar — We watched the hawk **soar** in the sky.
5. harsh — The noise of the drill was **harsh**.
6. sore — My feet were **sore** after the long walk.
7. lord — A duke is one kind of **lord**.
8. flair — Lynn has a **flair** for writing.
9. warn — The siren will **warn** us of danger.
10. floor — I dropped food on the **floor**.
11. tore — Dana **tore** a hole in her skirt.
12. lair — This cave is the **lair** of a fox.
13. snare — The rabbit was caught in a **snare**.
14. carve — This man can **carve** animals out of wood.
15. bore — Does this silly show **bore** you?
16. fare — The bus **fare** is fifty cents.
17. cork — Stick the **cork** in the bottle.
18. barge — The **barge** carries wheat down the river.
19. flare — The fresh log made the fire **flare**.
20. rare — Good friends such as you are **rare**.

Think and Write

Each word has a vowel sound + *r*.

|ôr| t**or**ch, s**oar**, s**ore** |âr| h**are**, fl**air** |är| sc**ar**

• What are three patterns for the |ôr| sounds? How are the |ôr| sounds spelled in the Elephant Words? What are two patterns for |âr|? What is one pattern for |är|?

Now write each Basic Word under its vowel + *r* sounds.

|ôr| Sounds	|âr| Sounds	|är| Sounds

Review		**Challenge**	
21. horse	23. square	26. folklore	28. ordeal
22. sharp	24. stairs	27. unicorn	29. marvelous
	25. board		30. hoard

Independent Practice

> **Spelling Strategy** When you hear the |ôr| sounds, think of the patterns *or, oar,* and *ore.* When you hear the |âr| sounds, think of the patterns *are* and *air.* When you hear the |är| sounds, think of the pattern *ar.*

Word Analysis/Phonics Complete the exercises with Basic Words.

1–4. Write the word that sounds the same as each word below.

    1. boar   **2.** fair   **3.** worn   **4.** hair

5–8. Write two pairs of words that sound alike but are spelled differently.

Vocabulary: Definitions Write the Basic Word that fits each meaning.

  9. a wild animal's den
  10. unpleasant or severe
  11. bottom surface of a room
  12. a bottle stopper
  13. to make by cutting

Challenge Words Write the Challenge Word that fits each meaning. Use your Spelling Dictionary.

  14. a difficult experience
  15. a secret supply
  16. causing wonder
  17. legends, fables, myths
  18. an imaginary animal similar to a horse

Spelling-Meaning Connection

When you form the past tense of *scar,* double the *r* before adding *-ed.* Otherwise, you will have the word *scared,* which is the past tense of *scare.*

scar
scarred

19–20. Write *scar.* Then write the past tense of *scar,* and underline the double consonant.

Dictionary

Pronunciation Key How can you find out how to pronounce *warn*? The dictionary gives its pronunciation. The **pronunciation key** helps you understand the symbols used in the pronunciation. It gives one or more sample words for each symbol. Part of a pronunciation key is shown below.

PRONUNCIATION	PRONUNCIATION KEY
warn |wôrn|	ŏ p**o**t ō g**o** ô p**aw**, f**or**

Practice Write the correct spelling for each dictionary pronunciation. Use the Pronunciation Key on page 279.

1. \|lo͞op\| lope, loop
2. \|skär\| scar, scare
3. \|**prâr**′ ē\| prayer, prairie
4. \|flôr\| floor, flour
5. \|sŏr′ ē\| sore, sorry

Review: Spelling Spree

Crack the Code Use the following code to find a Basic or Review Word in each item below. Write each word correctly.

CODE	1	2	3	4	5	6	7	8	9	10	11	12	13	14	15	16	17	18
LETTER	a	b	c	d	e	f	g	h	i	k	l	o	q	r	s	t	u	v

Example: 8-1-14-15-8   *harsh*

6. 3-1-14-18-5
7. 16-12-14-5
8. 2-12-14-5
9. 2-1-14-7-5
10. 11-1-9-14
11. 6-11-1-14-5
12. 15-12-1-14
13. 11-12-14-4
14. 2-12-1-14-4
15. 15-3-1-14
16. 8-1-14-5

17. 16-12-14-3-8
18. 15-12-14-5
19. 15-13-17-1-14-5
20. 6-1-14-5
21. 3-12-14-10
22. 15-16-1-9-14-15

How Are You Doing?

List the spelling words that are still hard for you. Practice them with a family member.

Proofreading and Writing

Proofread for Spelling Find eight misspelled Basic or Review Words in this tale. Write each one correctly.

Once upon a time the hare had tiny ears. A bird with a hars voice and shap claws saw a snair on the forest flor. This rar bird tried to worn the hare about the trap, but the hare did not listen. A hors with a flar for saving animals pulled the sore hare out by its ears. That is how the hare got its big ears.

Basic

1. hare
2. scar
3. torch
4. soar
5. harsh
6. sore
7. lord
8. flair
9. warn
10. floor
11. tore
12. lair
13. snare
14. carve
15. bore
16. fare
17. cork
18. barge
19. flare
20. rare

Review

21. horse
22. sharp
23. square
24. stairs
25. board

Challenge

26. folklore
27. unicorn
28. ordeal
29. marvelous
30. hoard

Write a Tale

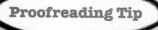

Imagine that at one time zebras did not have black and white stripes. Write a tale that explains how zebras got their stripes. Try to use five spelling words. Read your tale to some classmates.

Proofreading Tip **Say each word aloud to yourself to help you check your spelling.**

Proofreading Marks

- ¶ Indent
- ∧ Add
- ℘ Delete
- ≡ Capital letter
- / Small letter

Vocabulary Enrichment

Expanding Vocabulary

Idioms

Ben **tore his hair out** over the tough decision.

Do you think that Ben really tore his hair out? That wouldn't be wise. The phrase *tore his hair out* is an **idiom**. It means that Ben was very worried. An idiom has a meaning that is different from the meaning of each separate word.

Write the letter of the meaning that matches each underlined idiom.

Meanings

a. very happy **b.** to be part of something from the beginning

c. is easily seen **d.** very nervous **e.** to rise to give a formal speech

1. The spelling mistake <u>sticks out like a sore thumb</u>.

2. Everyone stared at Tom when he <u>took the floor</u>.

3. Abby <u>got in on the ground floor</u> of the new project.

4. Julio was <u>walking on air</u> after he won the blue ribbon.

5. Mary was <u>on pins and needles</u> while waiting for her test score.

Show You Know! Choose three idioms, and use each one in a sentence. Then rewrite each sentence, replacing the idiom with words that show its meaning.

Real-World Connection

Language Arts: Tales All the words in the box relate to tales. Look up these words in your Spelling Dictionary. Then write the words to complete this tale.

Pecos Bill

Pecos Bill will __(1)__ you with his extraordinary, or __(2)__, strength. Once he dug a ditch through __(3)__ Texas country to the Gulf of Mexico and was not even __(4)__ by this incredible __(5)__! Although his girlfriend Slue-Foot Sue was a good rider, Bill told her to __(6)__ of Widow Maker, his wild horse. Sue, being a __(7)__ person, refused to listen. She used her __(8)__ to find a way to ride the horse and was never seen again.

Spelling Word Link

folklore

superhuman
stubborn
astound
exhausted
rugged
beware
feat
cunning

Try This
CHALLENGE

Yes or No? Write *yes* if the underlined word is used correctly. Write *no* if it is not.

9. The <u>rugged</u> mountains were difficult to climb.
10. Did Pecos Bill have big <u>feat</u>?
11. She was <u>stubborn</u> and easy to get along with.
12. This amazing adventure will <u>astound</u> you.

★★★ **Fact File**

The tale of John Henry may be based on a true event. To prove that no machine could replace him, Henry raced his hammer against a steam-powered drill and won.

32 USA

JOHN HENRY

Spelling |ûr| and |îr|

Basic

READ the sentences. **SAY** each bold word.

1. smear	Try not to **smear** the wet paint.
2. germ	A **germ** can cause sickness.
3. blur	The racers sped by in a **blur**.
4. peer	**Peer** into the bottle to see the bug.
5. stir	Please **stir** the yellow paint well.
6. squirm	Did you see the worm **squirm**?
7. nerve	Jed had a pinched **nerve** in his back.
8. early	I get up **early** each morning.
9. worth	The silver dollar is **worth** $20.
10. pier	The boat is docked at the **pier**.
11. thirst	Donna has a **thirst** for juice.
12. burnt	Kim had **burnt** her hand on the hot pot.
13. rear	The emergency exit is at the **rear** of the bus.
14. term	Last **term** at school, we studied hard.
15. steer	I learned how to **steer** a ship.
16. pearl	My ring has one large black **pearl**.
17. squirt	Why did you **squirt** water at me?
18. stern	The **stern** is the back part of the boat.
19. hurl	Can you **hurl** the ball over the fence?
20. worse	My cold got **worse** last night.

Think and Write

Here are more words with a vowel sound + *r*.

|ûr| g**er**m, st**ir**, bl**ur**, **ear**ly, w**or**th
|îr| p**eer**, sm**ear**

• What are five patterns for the |ûr| sounds? What are two patterns for the |îr| sounds? How are the |îr| sounds spelled in the Elephant Word?

Now write each Basic Word under its vowel + *r* **sounds.**

|ûr| Sounds	|îr| Sounds

Review	23. world	**Challenge**	28. emerge
21. learn	24. firm	26. interpret	29. dreary
22. curve	25. year	27. yearn	30. career

Independent Practice

Spelling Strategy When you hear the |ûr|
sounds, think of the patterns *er, ir, ur, ear,* and *or.*
When you hear the |îr| sounds, think of the patterns
eer and *ear.*

Word Analysis/Phonics Complete the exercises with Basic Words.
1–4. Write the four words that begin or end with *st.*
5–6. Write the two words that have the |kw| sounds.
7–8. Write the two words that sound alike.

Vocabulary: Analogies Write the Basic Word that completes
each analogy.

9. *Good* is to *better*
as *bad* is to _____.
10. *Jump* is to *leap*
as *throw* is to _____.
11. *Frozen* is to *thawed*
as *raw* is to _____.
12. *Sunrise* is to *sunset*
as *late* is to _____.
13. *Flower* is to *daisy*
as *gem* is to _____.

Challenge Words Write the Challenge Word that fits each clue.
Use your Spelling Dictionary.

14. opposite of *cheerful*
15. opposite of *disappear*
16. to have a deep longing
17. a chosen profession
18. to explain the meaning
or importance of

Spelling-Meaning Connection

Can you see *worth* in these words: *worthy,
worthless, worthwhile*? These words are all
related in spelling and meaning. **Think of
this:** A *worthy* friend is *worth* your time.
19–20. Write *worthy.* Then write the
Basic Word that you see in *worthy.*

worth
worthy
worthless
worthwhile

Review: Spelling Spree

Puzzle Play Write a Basic or Review Word to fit each clue.
Circle the letter that would appear in the box.

Example: to look hard ☐ _ _ _ (p̃eer

1. a bending line ☐ _ _ _ _
2. throw with force ☐ _ _ _
3. find out _ ☐ _ _ _
4. a blotch _ ☐ _ _ _
5. solid _ ☐ _ _
6. wiggle ☐ _ _ _ _ _
7. value _ _ _ ☐ _
8. to guide _ _ _ _ ☐

9. twelve months ☐ _ _ _
10. scorched ☐ _ _ _ _
11. place for ships _ ☐ _ _
12. less well _ ☐ _ _ _
13. white gem _ _ _ _ ☐
14. Earth _ ☐ _ _ _
15. causes disease ☐ _ _ _
16. not late _ _ _ _ ☐

**Now write the circled letters in order. They will spell two
mystery words that name science subjects.**

Mystery Words: __ __ __ __ __? __ __ __ __ __ , __ __ __ __ __ ?__ __

Find a Rhyme For each sentence write a Basic Word that rhymes
with the underlined word and makes sense in the sentence.

17. Is there a scientific _____ for germ?
18. Put that fern in the _____ of the boat.
19. This photo of Rover is not clear. It is just a _____ of fur!
20. We stopped to _____ at the deer in the forest.
21. What should you do first to satisfy your _____ ?
22. Sir, the chef must _____ the sauce.
23. The tennis player lost his _____ and missed the serve!
24. Do not _____ that water on my clean shirt!
25. Why do you fear sitting in the _____ of the bus?

How Are
You Doing?

List the spelling words
that are still hard for you.
Practice them with a
family member.

Proofreading and Writing

Basic

Proofreading: Spelling and Possessive Nouns A **possessive noun** shows ownership. To form a possessive noun, add 's to a singular noun or a plural noun that does not end with s. When a plural noun ends with s, add only the apostrophe.

Penny**'s** notebook   mice**'s** tails   students**'** jars

Find four misspelled Basic or Review Words and two incorrect possessive nouns in this science journal entry. Write the journal entry correctly.

September 27

This yer we are using a microscope. It brings a new world into view. Everything is a blir when I per through the lens, so I adjust the knob. I have seen a sponges skeleton, a jurm, and several insects wings!

Basic

1. smear
2. germ
3. blur
4. peer
5. stir
6. squirm
7. nerve
8. early
9. worth
10. pier
11. thirst
12. burnt
13. rear
14. term
15. steer
16. pearl
17. squirt
18. stern
19. hurl
20. worse

Review
21. learn
22. curve
23. world
24. firm
25. year

Challenge
26. interpret
27. yearn
28. emerge
29. dreary
30. career

Write a Funny Story

MY DAY AS A GERM

Imagine you are a germ, and today you will be examined under a microscope. Write a story about your day. Try to use five spelling words and at least one possessive noun.

Proofreading Tip

Check that you wrote any possessive nouns correctly.

Proofreading Marks

¶ Indent
∧ Add
⌔ Delete
≡ Capital letter
/ Small letter

Expanding Vocabulary

Recognizing Blended Words When one word can do a better job than two, a new word may be created. When two words are combined, some letters may be dropped out. The new word is a **blended word**. The meanings of the two words are blended too.

squirm + w**iggle** = squiggle

to twist + to turn with winding motions =
to twist with winding motions

Write the blended words by combining the underlined parts in each pair of words.

1. t<u>wi</u>st + wh<u>irl</u> =
2. <u>fla</u>me + g<u>lare</u> =
3. <u>motor</u> + caval<u>cade</u> =
4. <u>helicopter</u> + air<u>port</u> =
5. <u>tele</u>vision + mara<u>thon</u> =
6. <u>sports</u> + broad<u>cast</u> =

Work Together With a classmate write a sentence for each picture. Use a different blended word you made in each sentence. Use your Spelling Dictionary if necessary.

Real-World Connection

Science: Using a Microscope All of the words in the box relate to using a microscope. Look up these words in your Spelling Dictionary. Then write the words to complete this science experiment.

Spelling Word Link

germ

- microscope
- slide
- magnify
- bacteria
- focus
- cell
- experiment
- laboratory

Skin Cells

Perform this __(1)__ in the science __(2)__ .

1. Scrape the inside of your cheek with a tongue depressor.

2. Smear some of the scraping onto a glass __(3)__ .

3. Examine it under a __(4)__ . The instrument will __(5)__ the sample a hundred times. If the image is blurry, turn the knob to bring it into __(6)__ .

4. A skin __(7)__ from your cheek is almost transparent and has a round, flat shape. Do you see any germs or __(8)__ ?

Try This CHALLENGE

True or False? For each sentence write *T* if the statement is true. Write *F* if it is not.

9. You can look at the stars with a microscope.
10. Some bacteria cause disease.
11. If you magnify things, you make them look smaller.
12. When the image is not clear, you should adjust the focus.

Guess what this is!

Fact File

Most microscopes use light to magnify, but an electron microscope uses a beam of electrons. An electron microscope can make an object appear 500,000 times bigger than its actual size.

human scalp and hair

Compound Words

wheel + chair =

wheelchair

Read and Say

Basic

READ the sentences.
SAY each bold word.

1. basketball — Practice dribbling the **basketball**.
2. wheelchair — I use an electric **wheelchair** to get around.
3. cheerleader — The **cheerleader** leaped into the air.
4. newscast — Jo was interviewed on the **newscast**.
5. weekend — Dan swims both days of the **weekend**.
6. everybody — I hope that **everybody** gets to play today.
7. up-to-date — Is that story old or **up-to-date**?
8. grandparent — My father is also a **grandparent**.
9. first aid — I gave **first aid** to the hurt child.
10. wildlife — Many kinds of **wildlife** live in the woods.
11. highway — Sal drives to work on a **highway**.
12. daytime — I work only during the **daytime**.
13. whoever — I hope that **whoever** wins will be happy.
14. test tube — She wrote the date on the **test tube**.
15. turnpike — There are a lot of cars on the **turnpike**.
16. shipyard — This **shipyard** has over sixty boats.
17. homemade — The only bread I buy is **homemade**.
18. household — I have to do some **household** chores.
19. salesperson — The **salesperson** sold me track shoes.
20. brother-in-law — My **brother-in-law** is married to my sister.

Think and Write

A **compound word** is a word made up of two or more smaller words.

wheel + chair = wheelchair   **up + to + date** = up-to-date
first + aid = first aid

• What three ways can compound words be written? What words make up each compound word in the list?

Now write each Basic Word under the heading that tells how the compound word is written.

One Word	With a Hyphen	Separate Words

Review
21. afternoon
22. ninety-nine
23. everywhere
24. all right
25. breakfast

Challenge
26. extraordinary
27. self-assured
28. quick-witted
29. limelight
30. junior high school

Independent Practice

Spelling Strategy   A **compound word** is made up of two or more smaller words. To spell a compound word correctly, you must remember if it is written as one word, as a hyphenated word, or as separate words.

Word Analysis/Phonics
Write the Basic Words that include the underlined parts of these words.

1. arm<u>chair</u>
2. <u>turn</u>table
3. <u>house</u>boat
4. <u>test</u> pilot
5. home<u>sick</u>
6. <u>every</u>thing
7. mother-<u>in</u>-law
8. <u>day</u>dream

Vocabulary: Making Inferences
Write the Basic Word that fits each clue.

9. If you play this game, it is good to be tall.
10. What you build here will be used in the water.
11. A person in an accident might need this right away.
12. This person is your mother's father or mother.
13. You can listen to this on the radio many times a day.

Challenge Words Write the Challenge Word that fits each definition. Use your Spelling Dictionary.

14. confident
15. mentally alert
16. very unusual
17. the center of public attention
18. the seventh, the eighth, and sometimes the ninth grades

Spelling-Meaning Connection

Can you see *wild* in the words *wildlife* and *wilderness*? These words are related in meaning and spelling.
Think of this: Many kinds of *wildlife* live in the *wilderness*.

19–20. Write *wild*. Then write the Basic Word that is related to *wild* in spelling and meaning.

Dictionary

Stress A **syllable** is a word part that has one vowel sound. In a word with more than one syllable, one syllable is said more strongly, or with more **stress**. The dictionary pronunciation for a word shows which syllable is stressed. The stressed syllable is followed by an **accent mark (')**.

who·ev·er |hoo ĕv′ ər| *pron.* Anyone that.

Practice Look at each word and its pronunciation. Write each word in syllables. Then underline the stressed syllable.

tulip

1. tulip |too′ lĭp|
2. sorrow |sŏr′ ō|
3. neglect |nĭ glĕkt′|
4. furnish |fûr′ nĭsh|
5. dolphin |dŏl′ fĭn|
6. explain |ĭk splān′|
7. diet |dī′ ĭt|
8. destroy |dĭ stroi′|

Review: Spelling Spree

Combining Words Write Basic or Review Words by combining the words in the box with the numbered words.

yard	cast	fast	life	aid	pike
where	in-law	parent	way	person	hold
ever	made	right	tube		

9. test
10. who
11. ship
12. all
13. sales
14. news
15. turn
16. grand

17. wild
18. high
19. every
20. house
21. first
22. home
23. brother
24. break

How Are You Doing?

Write each spelling word in a sentence. Practice any misspelled spelling words with a family member.

Proofreading and Writing

Proofread for Spelling Find nine misspelled Basic or Review Words in this script for a sportscast. Write each one correctly.

WKID Radio

Marshall Arena is the setting for the exciting

weelchair baskitball championship. It seems

that every body wants to attend. The score in

the game this afternon was one hundred to

ninety nine. Guard Rob Dean seemed to be

everywhere at once. One chearleader yelled

so much that her voice was hoarse. The

games continue all weakend. This concludes

our daytim newscast. Join us this evening

for another up to date report.

Basic

1. basketball
2. wheelchair
3. cheerleader
4. newscast
5. weekend
6. everybody
7. up-to-date
8. grandparent
9. first aid
10. wildlife
11. highway
12. daytime
13. whoever
14. test tube
15. turnpike
16. shipyard
17. homemade
18. household
19. salesperson
20. brother-in-law

Review

21. afternoon
22. ninety-nine
23. everywhere
24. all right
25. breakfast

Challenge

26. extraordinary
27. self-assured
28. quick-witted
29. limelight
30. junior high school

Write a List

Make a list of the top five things you would tell a newcomer about sports at your school. Try to use five spelling words in your sentences. Read your list to a classmate.

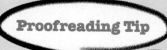

Proofreading Tip

As you check each word, put a check mark on it to show that you looked at it.

Proofreading Marks

¶   Indent
∧   Add
⌐   Delete
≡   Capital letter
/   Small letter

Expanding Vocabulary

Building Compound Words With a partner, use words in the basketball court to build a compound word for each blank line on the scoreboard. Each word you build must begin with the last half of the compound word above it. Use your Spelling Dictionary. The first two answers and the last answer are done for you.

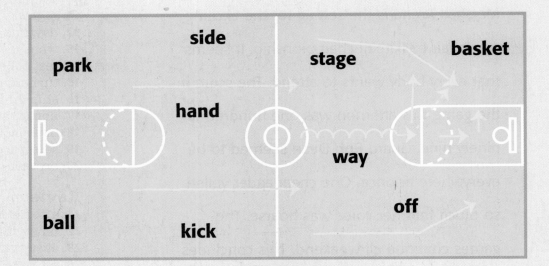

side
park   stage   basket
hand
way
off
ball   kick

SCORE BOARD

1. *basketball*
2. *ballpark*
3. ?
4. ?
5. ?
6. ?
7. ?
8. *stagehand*

Show You Know! Write a sentence for each compound word that you built.

Real-World Connection

Recreation: Wheelchair Basketball All of the words in the box relate to wheelchair basketball. Look up these words in your Spelling Dictionary. Then write the words to complete this paragraph from a sports handbook.

Spelling Word Link

basketball

referee
court
foul
dribble
forward
gymnasium
penalty
trophy

WHOOSH!

Wheelchair basketball is usually played on a regular-sized __(1)__ , often in a school __(2)__ . Any player—a center, a guard, or a __(3)__ — is allowed to push the wheels twice. Then the player must __(4)__ , or bounce, the ball at least once. If a rule is broken, the __(5)__ will call a __(6)__ , or violation. The __(7)__ can be the loss of the ball. In a tournament the winning team gets a __(8)__ .

Try This

CHALLENGE

Yes or No? Write *yes* if the underlined word is used correctly. Write *no* if it is not.

9. The player caused a <u>foul</u> and scored two points.
10. Each player got a <u>penalty</u> for winning the game.
11. The <u>referee</u> called a time-out.
12. One player made a basket from center <u>court</u>.

★★★ Fact File

The National Wheelchair Basketball Association sponsors tournaments for youths between the ages of eight and nineteen and for adults. Competitions have been held since 1949.

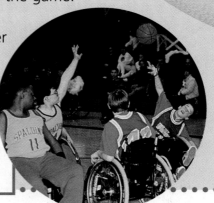

Homophones

Read and Say

berry
bury

Basic

READ the sentences. **SAY** each bold word.

1. poll	The results of the **poll** put me in the lead.
2. pole	Hang the sign on the telephone **pole**.
3. main	Where is the **main** branch of the library?
4. mane	The horse has a soft **mane**.
5. sole	I have a hole in the **sole** of my shoe.
6. soul	She sang with her heart and **soul**.
7. hall	Sarah walked down the long, dark **hall**.
8. haul	Joe will **haul** the wood in his truck.
9. peace	I felt a sense of **peace** in the quiet area.
10. piece	Do you want a **piece** of bread?
11. loan	Carl will **loan** me his bike for one day.
12. lone	I see a **lone** bright star in the sky.
13. heal	That cut should **heal** soon.
14. heel	I hurt the **heel** of my foot.
15. flea	Have you ever seen a **flea** jump?
16. flee	Some wild animals **flee** from people.
17. pore	I **pore** over my stamps for hours.
18. pour	Please **pour** us some juice.
19. berry	There is only one ripe **berry** on the bush.
20. bury	Did your dog **bury** the bone here?

Think and Write

Homophones sound alike but have different spellings and meanings.

|mān| m**ain** "most important"

|mān| m**ane** "the hair on a horse's neck"

• Does each homophone pair have the same vowel and consonant sounds? How do the spellings differ in each homophone pair? What does each word mean?

Now write each Basic Word under its vowel sound or vowel + r sounds.

|ā|	|ē|	|ō|	|ô|	Vowel + r Sounds

Review

21. wait	23. meet
22. weight	24. meat

Challenge

25. canvass	27. stationary
26. canvas	28. stationery

Independent Practice

Spelling Strategy Remember that **homophones** are words that sound alike but have different spellings and meanings.

Context Sentences Write the Basic Word in parentheses that completes each sentence correctly.

1. The _____ showed that many people have pets. (poll, pole)
2. The squirrel ran up the telephone _____. (poll, pole)
3. That horse has a beautiful black _____. (main, mane)
4. What is the _____ idea of the paragraph? (main, mane)
5. If you give the dog a bone, he may _____ it. (berry, bury)
6. A _____ is a small, juicy fruit. (berry, bury)
7. A tiny opening in the skin is a _____. (pore, pour)
8. Please _____ the milk into a glass. (pore, pour)

Vocabulary: Definitions Write the Basic Word that fits each meaning.

9. a corridor
10. freedom from war
11. to pull
12. an insect
13. to run away
14. a portion

flea

flee

Challenge Words Write the Challenge Word that fits each definition below. Use your Spelling Dictionary.

15. to poll or survey
16. not changing
17. a heavy cloth
18. writing paper

Spelling-Meaning Connection

The words *sole* and *solitary* have different vowel sounds but are related in spelling and meaning. **Think of this:** The *sole* resident of the valley led a *solitary* life.

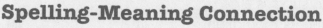

sole
solitary

19–20. Write *solitary*. Then write the Basic Word that is related in spelling and meaning to *solitary*.

Dictionary

Homophones   Because homophones sound alike, people sometimes confuse them. A dictionary entry will tell you if a word has a homophone.

> **lone** |lōn| *adj.* **1.** Without others: *A lone sailor stood watch.* **2.** By itself: *A lone tree stood in the meadow.*
> ◆ *These sound alike* **lone, loan.**

Practice   Look up the words below in your Spelling Dictionary. Write the homophone given for each word.

1. seen   **2.** hoard

Write the correct spelling for each pronunciation.

3. Have you |sēn| the results of the poll?

4. The hikers kept a |hôrd| of food in their camper.

5. Ten police officers quickly rushed to the |sēn|.

6. A |hôrd| of people gathered at the burning house.

Review: Spelling Spree

Homophone Riddles   Write a pair of Basic or Review Words to complete each statement. Write the words in the correct order. Capitalize the first word of a quotation.

7–8. A foot doctor might say to your foot, "_____ , _____."

9–10. A race between a ham and a steak is a _____ _____.

11–12. A dog might say to an insect, "_____ , _____."

13–14. A single spirit is a _____ _____.

15–16. A part of a treaty is a _____ of a _____.

17–18. A horse's most important hair is its _____ _____.

19–20. A survey of long sticks is a _____ _____.

21–22. An animal storing its food might _____ a _____.

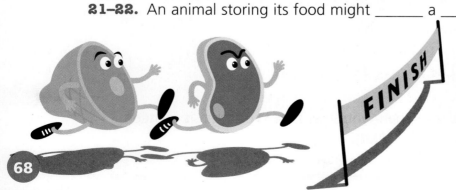

How Are You Doing?

Write your spelling words in ABC order. Practice any misspelled words with a partner.

Proofreading and Writing

Proofread for Spelling Find eight misspelled Basic or Review Words in this survey. Write each one correctly.

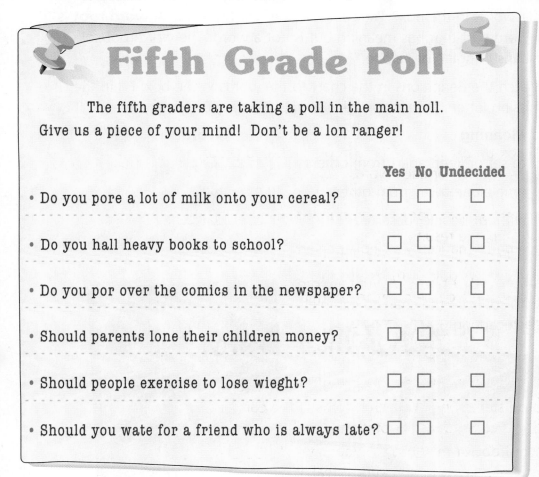

Fifth Grade Poll

The fifth graders are taking a poll in the main holl.
Give us a piece of your mind! Don't be a lon ranger!

	Yes	No	Undecided
• Do you pore a lot of milk onto your cereal?	☐	☐	☐
• Do you hall heavy books to school?	☐	☐	☐
• Do you por over the comics in the newspaper?	☐	☐	☐
• Should parents lone their children money?	☐	☐	☐
• Should people exercise to lose wieght?	☐	☐	☐
• Should you wate for a friend who is always late?	☐	☐	☐

Basic

1. poll
2. pole
3. main
4. mane
5. sole
6. soul
7. hall
8. haul
9. peace
10. piece
11. loan
12. lone
13. heal
14. heel
15. flea
16. flee
17. pore
18. pour
19. berry
20. bury

Review
21. wait
22. weight
23. meet
24. meat

Challenge
25. canvass
26. canvas
27. stationary
28. stationery

Write a Survey

POLL RESULTS

How much allowance should a fifth grader get? Should schools have a dress code? Write a list of questions for a class poll on any topic. Try to use five spelling words. Take the poll, and then graph the results.

Proofreading Tip

If you use a computer to check spelling, remember that it will not find a word that is misspelled as another word.

Proofreading Marks

¶ Indent
∧ Add
ᵍ Delete
≡ Capital letter
/ Small letter

Expanding Vocabulary

Spelling Word Link

sole

solo
isolate
solitude
desolate

The Word Root *sol* How is the spelling word *sole* related to the words in the box? They all have the word root *sol*. A **word root** is a word part that has meaning but is not a word. The word root *sol* means "single" or "alone."

Match the definitions in the chart to the words in the box. Fill in the missing letters for each word. Use your Spelling Dictionary.

Meaning	Word
to set or keep apart from others	1. __ *sol* __
time alone away from others	2. __ *sol* __
without people; deserted	3. __ *sol* __
a performance by a single person	4. __ *sol* __

Show You Know! Write a word with *sol* from the chart to complete each caption.

We had to __(7)__ the sick rabbit.

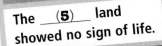

The __(5)__ land showed no sign of life.

The boy stepped forward to sing a __(6)__ .

Jean loved the quiet __(8)__ of her room.

Real-World Connection

Math: Surveys All the words in the box relate to surveys. Look up these words in your Spelling Dictionary. Then write the words to complete these directions for taking a survey.

Spelling Word Link

poll

survey
sample
data
random
predict
questionnaire
percentage
graph

Sports Day
Yes or No?
Undecided 10%
No 15%
Yes 75%

How can you ___(1)___ whether students want to have a sports day? To find out you must conduct a ___(2)___ . You can do this by handing out a printed ___(3)___ or by interviewing. Because you cannot question everyone, choose a test group, or ___(4)___ . Select a specific group, or choose people at ___(5)___ . The information, or ___(6)___ , you gather will tell you what ___(7)___ of students want a sports day. Show the results on a bar ___(8)___ or pie chart.

Try This
CHALLENGE

Yes or No? Write *yes* if the underlined word is used correctly. Write *no* if it is not.

9. A large <u>percentage</u> of the children swim daily.
10. The survey provided new <u>data</u> on the city's growth.
11. Rebecca is an excellent <u>questionnaire</u>.
12. Take a <u>survey</u> to find out if people like the product.

 Fact File

In the 1930s George Gallup developed scientific ways to take national surveys. Gallup polls provide information to businesses and other groups.

UNIT 11 — Final |ər|

Read and Say

theater
pillar
actor

Basic

READ the sentences. SAY each bold word.

1. theater — We enjoy seeing plays at the **theater**.
2. actor — The **actor** is in a movie.
3. mirror — Mike broke the bathroom **mirror**.
4. powder — Sprinkle the **powder** on the baby.
5. humor — Miguel has a good sense of **humor**.
6. anger — Only her eyes showed her **anger**.
7. banner — I hung my baseball **banner** on the wall.
8. pillar — A tall **pillar** stands on each side of the door.
9. major — I have a **major** part in the play.
10. thunder — Loud **thunder** scares me.
11. flavor — Which **flavor** of ice cream do you want?
12. finger — Kate sprained her little **finger**.
13. mayor — She was elected the **mayor** of the city.
14. polar — All **polar** bears have white fur.
15. clover — Do rabbits like to eat **clover**?
16. burglar — The **burglar** stole all our computers.
17. tractor — I rented a **tractor** to help dig up the yard.
18. matter — This is a **matter** for the police.
19. lunar — This moon rock is from the first **lunar** landing.
20. quarter — A **quarter** equals two dimes and a nickel.

Think and Write

Each word ends with the schwa sound + r. The **schwa sound** is a weak vowel sound that is often found in an unstressed syllable. It is shown as |ə|.

|ər| ang**er**, act**or**, pill**ar**

• What are three spelling patterns for the final |ər| sounds?

Now write each Basic Word under the pattern that spells its final |ər| sounds.

er	or	ar

Review
21. enter
22. honor
23. answer
24. collar
25. doctor

Challenge
26. character
27. clamor
28. tremor
29. scholar
30. chamber

72

Independent Practice

Spelling Strategy When you hear the final |ər| sounds in words of more than one syllable, think of the patterns *er*, *or*, and *ar*.

Word Analysis/Phonics Complete the exercises with Basic Words.

1–4. Write the four words that have double consonants.

5–7. Write the word that rhymes with each word below.

    5. linger   **6.** molar   **7.** chowder

Vocabulary: Definitions Write the Basic Word that fits each meaning.

  8. having to do with the moon

  9. the quality of being funny

10. a building where plays or movies are presented

11. a plant with leaves divided into three leaflets

12. the chief government officer of a city or a town

13. a rumbling noise that comes after a flash of lightning

Challenge Words Write the Challenge Word that fits each clue. Use your Spelling Dictionary.

14. a knowledgeable person

15. a room in a house

16. opposite of *silence*

17. a shaking movement

18. a person in a book, a movie, or a play

Spelling-Meaning Connection

How can you remember how to spell the final |ər| sounds in *major*? Think of the |ôr| sounds in the related word *majority*.

major
majority

19–20. Write *major* and *majority*. Then underline the two letters in *majority* that help you remember how to spell the final |ər| sounds in *major*.

Review: Spelling Spree

Letter Math Add and subtract letters from the words below to make Basic or Review Words. Write the new words.

1. c + doll − d + ar =
2. rang − r + er =
3. l + tuna − t + r =
4. cl + drove − dr + r =
5. humid − id + or =
6. pole − e + ar =
7. bent − b + er =
8. b + many − m − y + ner =
9. m + bath − b − h + ter =
10. fl + save − s − e + or =
11. d + rocket − r − ket + tor =
12. th + blunt − bl − t + der =
13. p + crowd − cr + er =
14. admire − ad − e + ror =

b+many-m-y+ner

Question Clues Write a Basic or Review Word to answer each question.

15. What *er* word is one-fourth of a dollar?
16. What *or* word is most important?
17. What *er* word responds to a question?
18. What *ar* word might hold up a bridge?
19. What *ar* word might break into a building?
20. What *er* word is part of a hand?
21. What *or* word pulls a plow?
22. What *er* word has a stage?
23. What *or* word performs onstage?
24. What *or* word governs a city?
25. What *or* word deserves respect?

How Are You Doing?

Write each spelling word as a partner reads it aloud. Did you misspell any words?

Proofreading and Writing

Proofread: Spelling and Comparing with *good* and *bad* The adjectives *good* and *bad* have special forms for making comparisons.

	good	bad
COMPARING TWO:	better	worse
COMPARING MORE THAN TWO:	best	worst

Find four misspelled Basic or Review Words and two incorrect forms of *good* or *bad* in this setting for a play. Write the setting correctly.

The Flavor of Autumn

Setting: A farm. The worse of summer is over, and best weather has arrived. The moon is about to entar its last quarter. An old tracter rests in a patch of clovar. Far away, thounder roars.

Basic

1. theater
2. actor
3. mirror
4. powder
5. humor
6. anger
7. banner
8. pillar
9. major
10. thunder
11. flavor
12. finger
13. mayor
14. polar
15. clover
16. burglar
17. tractor
18. matter
19. lunar
20. quarter

Review

21. enter
22. honor
23. answer
24. collar
25. doctor

Challenge

26. character
27. clamor
28. tremor
29. scholar
30. chamber

Write a Review

Write a short review of a movie or a television program. Include one comparison using *good* or *bad.* Try to use five spelling words. Post your review for others to read.

Proofreading Tip — Check to be sure you used the correct forms of *good* and *bad* when making comparisons.

REVIEWS

Westward Ho! is of the best week adventures to come to take in a long time. Jason Cabash, a very tough and gritty trail boss, who manages to save a few lives per episode.
Journey to Planet Zion is a super sci-fi thriller. The special effects alone are worth the price of the ticket.

ADMIT ONE

Proofreading Marks

¶ Indent
∧ Add
˞ Delete
≡ Capital letter
/ Small letter

Vocabulary Enrichment

Expanding Vocabulary

Multiple-Meaning Words Did you know that *quarter* has several meanings? Look at this dictionary entry for *quarter*.

quar·ter |kwôr′ tər| *n., pl.* **quarters** **1.** Any of four equal parts into which something can be divided: *I cut the apple into quarters.* **2.** A coin used in the United States or Canada that is worth 25 cents. **3.** One of four time periods that make up a game. **4.** A district or section of a city.

Write *1, 2, 3,* or *4* to show which meaning of *quarter* is used in each sentence.

1. The score was tied after the first quarter.
2. Two dimes and a quarter are on the table.
3. There are lots of parks in this quarter of town.
4. Only a quarter of the chicken pie is left.

Show You Know! Write a caption for each picture. Use a different meaning of *quarter* in each sentence.

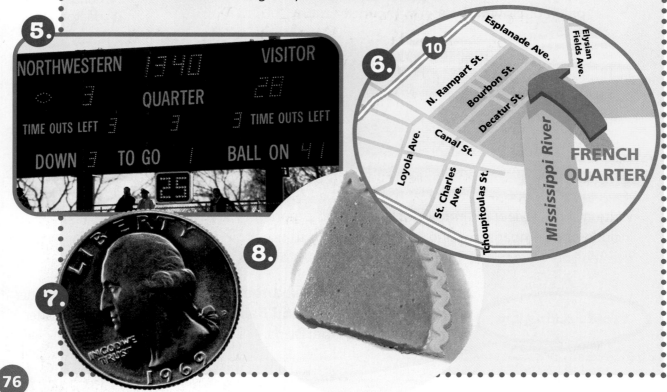

5.

6.

7.

8.

NORTHWESTERN 1340 VISITOR 28
QUARTER
TIME OUTS LEFT
DOWN TO GO BALL ON 47

10 Esplanade Ave. Elysian Fields Ave.
N. Rampart St. Bourbon St.
Decatur St.
Loyola Ave. Canal St.
St. Charles Ave. Tchoupitoulas St.
Mississippi River
FRENCH QUARTER

Real-World Connection

Performing Arts: Theater All the words in the box relate to the theater. Look up these words in your Spelling Dictionary. Then write the words to complete this interview.

Spelling Word Link

actor

audition
script
playwright
role
dialogue
cue
applause
sets

ON WITH THE SHOW

Q: How do you get a part in a Broadway show?

A: With dozens of other performers, you __(1)__ for a __(2)__ , or part. You learn your lines from the __(3)__ . At tryouts the director, the producer, and the __(4)__ are your audience. The stage is bare. There are no props and no __(5)__ . On a __(6)__ from the director, you might begin a __(7)__ with another actor. Then you listen. If you hear loud __(8)__ , you may have earned the part!

Try This CHALLENGE

Write a Bulletin Board Notice Write a notice for your school bulletin board, requesting students to sign up for the cast or the stage crew of the school play. Try to use some of the words in the box on this page.

Fact File

William Shakespeare, English playwright and poet of the 1500s, had a great understanding of people. He is considered the greatest playwright in the English language.

12 Review: Units 7–11

|ôr| |âr|
sore   **h**are

Unit 7   Spelling |ôr|, |âr|, and |är| pages 48–53

flair	harsh	soar	**warn**	**floor**
cork	carve	snare	bore	lair

Spelling Strategy

|ôr| → **or, ore, oar** |är| → **ar**
|âr| → **are, air**

Write the word that completes each sentence.

1. Please put the _____ back in the bottle.
2. The baby spilled a glass of milk all over the clean _____.
3. Kim has a _____ for designing clothes.
4. A lioness and her cubs live in a _____.
5. Long, dull stories about animals _____ me.

Write the word that is a synonym for each word below.

6. fly   8. cruel   10. cut
7. alert   9. trap

Unit 8   Spelling |ûr| and |îr| pages 54–59

germ	peer	stir	smear	**pier**
pearl	burnt	rear	worse	squirt

Spelling Strategy

|ûr| → **er, ir, ur, ear, or** |îr| → **eer, ear**

Write the word that belongs in each group.

11. ruby, jade, _____   13. spread, wipe, _____
12. front, middle, _____   14. splash, spray, _____

Write the word that fits each meaning.

15. to look closely   18. an organism that can cause disease
16. damaged by heat   19. to mix
17. a dock or wharf   20. less well

Unit 9   Compound Words   pages 60–65

| up-to-date | first aid | wildlife | wheelchair | newscast |
| homemade | whoever | brother-in-law | salesperson | test tube |

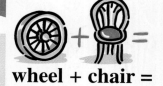

wheel + chair =

wheelchair

Spelling Strategy   A **compound word** is made up of two or more smaller words. Remember that a compound word may be written as one word, as a hyphenated word, or as separate words.

Write the compound word that has each part below.

21. person   **23.** home   **25.** in   **27.** who
22. first   **24.** chair   **26.** test

Write the compound words that complete this paragraph.

Try to watch the six o'clock ___(28)___ tonight. The town dump is polluting our water and harming the ___(29)___ in the nearby woodlands. Tune in to hear the results of an ___(30)___ government study.

Unit 10   Homophones   pages 66–71

| hall | peace | sole | berry | flea |
| haul | piece | soul | bury | flee |

berry
bury

Spelling Strategy   Remember that homophones are words that sound alike but have different spellings and meanings.

Write the words that complete these sentences.

Help me ___(31)___ this dresser down the ___(32)___. We can have no ___(33)___ until the last ___(34)___ of furniture is in place.

Write the word that fits each clue.

35. the bottom of a shoe   **38.** spirit
36. can make a dog scratch   **39.** to put in the ground
37. something you might pick   **40.** to run away
from a bush

|ər|

theater
pillar
actor

Unit 11		Final |ər|		pages 72–77

mirror	thunder	major	pillar	theater
quarter	mayor	finger	lunar	polar

Spelling Strategy   When you hear the final |ər| sounds in words of more than one syllable, think of the patterns **er**, **or**, and **ar**.

Write six words by adding the missing letters.

41. thund _ _   **44.** mirr _ _

42. theat _ _   **45.** maj _ _

43. fing _ _   **46.** quart _ _

Write the word that completes each analogy.

47. *State* is to *governor* as *city* is to _____.

48. *Sun* is to *solar* as *moon* is to _____.

49. *Heat* is to *tropical* as *cold* is to _____.

50. *Tent* is to *pole* as *building* is to _____.

Challenge Words	Units 7–11	pages 48–77

junior high school	character	folklore	dreary	stationary
extraordinary		marvelous	interpret	tremor	stationery

Write the word that fits each clue.

51. opposite of *unremarkable*

52. after elementary school

53. opposite of *terrible*

54. to explain

55. beliefs handed down through generations

Write the word that belongs in each group. Circle the words that are homophones.

56. pen, envelope, _____

57. gloomy, dismal, _____

58. actor, dialogue, _____

59. vibration, shake, _____

60. unchanging, fixed, _____

Spelling-Meaning Strategy

Vowel Changes: Long to Short Vowel Sound

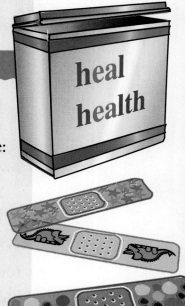

Words from the same word family are often related in both spelling and meaning. Knowing how to spell one word in the family may help you spell the other words. Read this sentence:

Although Uncle Jonathan was in very good **health** for a man of eighty, his broken leg took several months to **heal**.

Think

- How are *heal* and *health* related in meaning?
- What vowel sound do you hear in each word?
- How is each vowel sound spelled?

Here are more related words in which a long vowel sound in one word is spelled the same as a short vowel sound in the other.

dr**ea**m	c**a**ve	w**i**se
dr**ea**mt	c**a**vity	w**i**sdom

Apply and Extend

Complete these activities on a separate piece of paper.

1. Look up the words in the word box above in your Spelling Dictionary. Write six sentences, using these words.

2. With a partner list as many words as you can that are related to *heal, dream, cave,* and *wise.* Then look at the section "Vowel Changes: Long to Short Vowel Sound" beginning on page 271 of your Spelling-Meaning Index. Add any other words that you find in these word families to your list.

Summing Up

Knowing that words are related can often help you remember how to spell them, even though one word has a long vowel sound and the other has a short vowel sound.

Literature and Writing

based on

Winter Static Magic
by Doris Spaulding

If you shuffle your feet on a carpet in winter and then touch a piece of metal, you will feel a light shock. This is caused by static electricity. The following instructions are for experiments that will help you learn about static electricity. What materials are used?

It's fun to experiment with static electricity. First, place a dinner knife on a table with the blade hanging over the edge. Next, cut two pieces of thread one foot long. Make two small, rounded paper wads of dry tissue. Then tie each of these paper balls to the end of each piece of thread. Fasten both pieces of thread to the end of the knife so they hang down freely, about two inches apart. Slowly move a comb towards the paper balls.
Because there is no static electricity, nothing happens.

Then rub the comb briskly with wool. Move the comb towards the paper balls. The electrically "charged" comb attracts the paper balls.

Finally, hold the comb between the paper balls for a few seconds. When the balls touch the comb, they receive the same charge. After the paper balls become charged, the comb pushes them away.

Think and Discuss

1. What **materials** would you need to perform these experiments?

2. What is the **topic sentence** for these instructions?

3. What six **steps** are given in the first paragraph?

4. What **order words**, such as *first* or *finally,* are used?

The Writing Process
Instructions

What do you know how to do well?
Write instructions to teach someone
else how to do it. Keep the guidelines
in mind. Follow the Writing Process.

1 Prewriting
- Choose an activity that can be explained in a few steps.
- List all of the steps. Number them in order.

2 Draft
- Use an order word to begin each step.

3 Revise
- Add any missing steps or details.
- Use your Thesaurus to find exact words.
- Have a writing conference.

4 Proofread
- Did you spell each word correctly?
- Did you write possessive nouns correctly?

5 Publish
- Make a neat, final copy, and add a good title.
- Demonstrate your instructions for some classmates.

Guidelines for Writing Instructions

✓ Begin with a topic sentence that tells the main idea.
✓ List the steps in order.
✓ Use order words such as *first*, *next*, *then*, and *last*.
✓ Include details and exact words to make each step clear.

Composition Words

stir
carve
piece
household
flavor
homemade
smear
pour

Read and Say

watermelon

READ the sentences.
SAY each bold word.

Basic

1. firecracker	The **firecracker** made a loud bang.
2. sweetheart	I sent my **sweetheart** flowers.
3. touchdown	Our football team scored a **touchdown**.
4. post office	I mailed the package at the **post office**.
5. classmate	I borrowed a pen from a **classmate**.
6. baby-sit	We have to **baby-sit** my little brother.
7. flashlight	Use the **flashlight** to see in the dark.
8. grapefruit	The **grapefruit** tasted sour.
9. holiday	Thanksgiving is a **holiday**.
10. welfare	I care about your health and **welfare**.
11. warehouse	Pick up the new sofa at the **warehouse**.
12. chalkboard	Write the answers on the **chalkboard**.
13. worthwhile	It is **worthwhile** to study hard.
14. watermelon	The **watermelon** was juicy and sweet.
15. throughout	We clapped **throughout** the show.
16. furthermore	I was late. **Furthermore**, I left my lunch.
17. whereabouts	Do you know Mark's **whereabouts**?
18. masterpiece	That painting is a **masterpiece**.
19. great-grandchild	Mrs. Tang has one **great-grandchild**.
20. part of speech	A verb is a **part of speech**.

Think and Write

You have learned that a compound word is made up of two or more smaller words.

firecracker   **baby-sit**   **post office**

• What words make up each compound word in the list? How are the Elephant Words different?

Now write each Basic Word under the heading that tells how the compound word is written.

One Word	With Hyphens	Separate Words

Review
21. airport
22. homesick
23. seat belt
24. make-believe
25. however

Challenge
26. starry-eyed
27. high-spirited
28. awestruck
29. outspoken
30. halfhearted

Independent Practice

Spelling Strategy A compound word is made up of two or more smaller words. To spell a compound word correctly, you must know if it is written as one word, as a hyphenated word, or as separate words.

Word Analysis/Phonics The underlined word in each compound word is part of a Basic Word. Write the Basic Word.

1. mean<u>while</u>
2. <u>out</u>side
3. <u>class</u>room
4. <u>water</u> lily
5. <u>sweet</u> potato
6. <u>flash</u>bulb
7. car<u>fare</u>
8. every<u>where</u>

Vocabulary: Making Inferences
Write a Basic Word that fits each clue.

9. This makes a loud popping noise.
10. Labor Day is one.
11. A composer or an artist might create one.
12. This can be found on a wall in most classrooms.
13. This is a place where furniture can be kept.

Challenge Words Write the Challenge Word that fits each clue. Use your Spelling Dictionary.

14. frank and honest
15. lively
16. full of wonder
17. having little interest
18. full of youthful hope and confidence

Spelling-Meaning Connection

Did you know that *office* is related in spelling and meaning to *official*? **Think of this:** My parents talked to an *official* from the *post office*.

19–20. Write *official*. Then write the Basic Word that has one part that is related in spelling and meaning to *official*.

office
official

Review: Spelling Spree

Picture Clues Write a Basic or Review Word for each clue.

1. [image] + [image]
2. [image] + MONDAY
3. m + [image] − r + [image] + [image]
4. [image] + [image]
5. [image] + [image]
6. [image] + of + [image]
7. [image] + [image]
8. [image] + [image]
9. [image] + [image]

Compound Mix-ups Write a Basic or Review Word by matching part of the first word with part of the second word.

Example: fireworks, crackerjack *firecracker*

10. hardware, firehouse
11. lamppost, officeholder
12. flash flood, lightweight
13. airtight, porthole
14. anywhere, hereabouts
15. first class, roommate
16. anyhow, everlasting
17. worthless, meanwhile
18. great-grandparent, childlike
19. rainwater, muskmelon
20. sweet potato, heartbreak
21. mastermind, mouthpiece
22. through street, outbreak
23. welcome, thoroughfare
24. touch-and-go, downhill
25. furthermost, moreover

How Are You Doing?
Write each spelling word in a sentence. Practice any misspelled spelling words with a partner.

86

Proofreading and Writing

Proofread: Spelling and Capital Letters A **proper noun** names a specific person, place, or thing. A **proper adjective** is formed from a proper noun. Remember to capitalize these words.

PROPER NOUN	PROPER ADJECTIVE
Japan	Japanese
Mexico	Mexican
Ireland	Irish

Find four misspelled Basic or Review Words and four missing capital letters in this journal entry. Write the journal entry correctly.

tuesday, january 16

I'm in china! A classmate
met me at the arport.
Today is a holaday, the
chinese New Year, and I just
heard a firecraker. So far,
I'm not at all home sick.

Write an Invitation

Write an invitation to a friend to join you for a holiday event. What holiday is being celebrated? Why is it special? When will it take place? Try to use five spelling words and at least one proper noun or proper adjective.

Proofreading Tip **Check that you capitalized all proper nouns and proper adjectives.**

Proofreading Marks

¶ Indent
∧ Add
⌒ Delete
≡ Capital letter
/ Small letter

Vocabulary Enrichment

Expanding Vocabulary

Words That Bridge Ideas Some words bridge ideas between sentences and paragraphs. They are called **transition words**.

moreover
therefore
nevertheless
furthermore
however
thus

We will march in the parade. **Furthermore**, we will be the first in line! Ben lives next door to the school. **However**, he is always late.

Different transition words serve different purposes.

Purpose	Word
to add another point	furthermore moreover
to signal a conclusion or a result	thus therefore
to show a contrast or a limitation	however nevertheless

Write words from the word box to make transitions between the ideas in this photo strip.

Our class wants to visit the aquarium. __(1)__ , we want to buy lunch there.

We have $10 in our fund. __(2)__ , we need $200 for the trip.

__(3)__ , we plan to hold a readathon to raise money.

__(4)__ , we will have a car wash this weekend.

What if it rains?

We'll hold the car wash __(5)__ .

Can I get a discount if I bring my bicycle?

Real-World Connection

Social Studies: Holidays All the words in the box relate to holidays. Look up these words in your Spelling Dictionary. Then write the words to complete these puzzle clues.

1. This day is the first day of the year.
2. This is a day when sweethearts exchange cards.
3. This day honors the birthday of a civil rights leader.
4. This day honors workers.
5. This day honors soldiers who have died in wars.
6. This day is for giving thanks.
7. This day is observed in many areas by planting trees.
8. This day honors those who have served in the military.

Spelling Word Link

holiday

Martin Luther King Day
Thanksgiving Day
Valentine's Day
Memorial Day
Veterans Day
New Year's Day
Labor Day
Arbor Day

LOVE U

BE MINE

Try This CHALLENGE

Write an Opinion Write a paragraph telling your opinion about one of the holidays listed above. What do you like about it? What do you dislike? Why?

IN CONGRESS, JULY 4, 1776.

The unanimous Declaration of the thirteen united States of America.

Fact File

The Fourth of July, or Independence Day, celebrates the signing of the Declaration of Independence. On July 4, 1776, the American colonies broke ties with Britain.

Final |l| or |əl|

Read and Say

|əl|
ankle
shovel

Basic

READ the sentences. **SAY** each bold word.

1. *jewel* — A diamond is a **jewel**.
2. *sparkle* — The snow seems to **sparkle** in the sun.
3. *angle* — You cannot see our house from this **angle**.
4. *shovel* — Sandy will **shovel** the snow.
5. *single* — I did not eat a **single** grape.
6. *normal* — My **normal** weight is seventy pounds.
7. *angel* — My sweet little brother is an **angel**.
8. *legal* — It is not **legal** to park a car in a tow zone.
9. *whistle* — Did you hear the coach's **whistle**?
10. *fossil* — The **fossil** was an old bone.
11. *puzzle* — This **puzzle** is difficult to solve.
12. *bushel* — I picked a **bushel** of apples.
13. *local* — We watched the **local** newscast.
14. *gentle* — My dog is large but **gentle**.
15. *level* — Can you make the bumpy floor **level**?
16. *label* — Write your name on the **label**.
17. *pedal* — Put your foot on the bike **pedal**.
18. *ankle* — Did you hurt your **ankle** when you fell?
19. *needle* — I need a **needle** to sew on the button.
20. *devil* — Your frisky puppy is such a **devil**.

Think and Write

The final |l| or |əl| sounds are usually spelled with two letters.
(Some dictionaries show only the final consonant sound because
the schwa sound is so weak.)

|l| or |əl| spark**le**, jew**el**, leg**al**

• What are three patterns for the final |l| or |əl| sounds? How are the
|əl| sounds spelled in the Elephant Words?

**Now write each Basic Word under its spelling of the final
|l| or |əl| sounds.**

le	el	al

Review	23. metal	**Challenge**	28. vital
21. simple	24. nickel	26. mineral	29. neutral
22. special	25. double	27. artificial	30. kernel

Independent Practice

Spelling Strategy

When you hear the final |l| or |əl| sounds, think of the patterns *le, el,* and *al.*

Word Analysis/Phonics Complete the exercises with Basic Words.

1. Write the word that has the |k| sound spelled c.
2–5. Write the four words that have the |ĕ| sound in the first syllable.
6–7. Write the two words that have double consonants.

Vocabulary: Classifying Write the Basic Word that belongs in each group of words.

8. thread, thimble, _____
9. knee, elbow, _____
10. siren, horn, _____
11. pint, quart, _____
12. triple, double, _____
13. hoe, rake, _____

Challenge Words Write the Challenge Word that completes each sentence. Use your Spelling Dictionary.

14. Robin painted her room beige, a _____ color.
15. A natural substance such as quartz is a _____.
16. The heart and lungs are _____ organs.
17. Each yellow _____ on this ear of corn is tender and juicy.
18. These _____ pearls are made of plastic.

Spelling-Meaning Connection

How can you remember how to spell the schwa sound in *angel*? Think of the |ĕ| sound in the related word *angelic.*

angel
angelic

19–20. Write *angel* and *angelic.* Then underline the letter in *angelic* that helps you remember how to spell the schwa sound in *angel.*

Dictionary

Parts of Speech A dictionary gives the part of speech of each entry word. The part of speech is often abbreviated.

n.	noun	*adj.*	adjective	*prep.*	preposition
v.	verb	*adv.*	adverb	*pron.*	pronoun

Many words can be used as more than one part of speech. For example, *shovel* can be used as either a noun or a verb.

> **shov·el** |shŭv′əl| *n., pl.* **shovels** A tool with a long handle and a flattened scoop: *I dug out the ditch with a shovel.* *v.* **shoveled, shoveling** To pick up or move with a shovel: *Shovel the snow.*

Practice Write the two parts of speech given in your Spelling Dictionary for each word. Do not abbreviate.

1–2. sparkle   **3–4.** special   **5–6.** early   **7–8.** throughout

Review: Spelling Spree

Phrase Fillers Write the Basic or Review Word that best completes each phrase.

9. a _____ of wheat
10. a _____ and thread
11. a shrill _____
12. to tilt at an _____
13. a _____-decker bus
14. a costly _____ necklace
15. a very _____ occasion
16. the _____ driving age
17. below sea _____
18. to _____ a bicycle
19. a dinosaur _____
20. five pennies for a _____

21. a sprained _____
22. a mischievous little _____
23. a _____ body temperature
24. to _____ like a diamond

How Are You Doing?

Write your spelling words in ABC order. Practice any misspelled words with a family member.

Proofreading and Writing

Proofread for Spelling Find ten misspelled Basic or Review Words in this part of a mystery story. Write each one correctly.

I had solved the puzzel! Finding

the jewel would be simpel. The

locol sheriff told me where to find

the statue of an anjel. I got a shovle

and headed for the abandoned town.

There stood the statue. I took a singel

step and began to dig. I soon struck

metel. With a gentel tug I pulled out a

box. The lable was ripped. Through a

crack I could see something sparkel.

Basic

1. jewel
2. sparkle
3. angle
4. shovel
5. single
6. normal
7. angel
8. legal
9. whistle
10. fossil
11. puzzle
12. bushel
13. local
14. gentle
15. level
16. label
17. pedal
18. ankle
19. needle
20. devil

Review
21. simple
22. special
23. metal
24. nickel
25. double

Challenge
26. mineral
27. artificial
28. vital
29. neutral
30. kernel

Write a Fairy Tale

Suppose that a farmer planted a field of corn. Instead of corn, jewels grew on the stalks. Write a fairy tale about what happens. Try to use five spelling words. Read your tale to some classmates.

Proofreading Tip

A spell-checking program often gives choices for misspellings, such as *angel* and *angle* for *angal*. Be sure you know the spelling you want.

Proofreading Marks

¶ Indent
∧ Add
✌ Delete
≡ Capital letter
/ Small letter

Vocabulary Enrichment

Expanding Vocabulary

Spelling
Word Link

pedal

pedal
pedestrian
pedometer
pedestal
centipede

The Word Root *ped* A pedal is a lever worked by the foot. *Pedal* includes the word root *ped*, which means "foot." (A **word root** is a word part that has meaning but is not a word by itself.)

Each word in the word box has the word root *ped*. Draw the word web. Then, in the web write each word in the web next to the number that matches its meaning. Use your Spelling Dictionary.

1. a base or a support
2. a person who walks
3. an insect with many legs
4. a lever worked by the foot
5. a device worn by a walker to measure distance walked

```
        2.  ?
1.  ?              3.  ?
          ped
5.  ?              4.  ?
```

Show You Know! Write a sentence to describe each picture. Use at least one word from the web in each sentence.

6.

7.

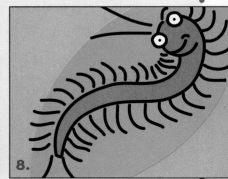

8.

⭐⭐⭐ **Fact File**

A family tree shows one's ancestors, or **pedigree**. *Pedigree* includes the word root *ped* and comes from an Anglo-Norman phrase, *pe de grue,* meaning "foot of a crane." It was thought that a family tree looked like a crane's foot!

Unit 14 BONUS

Real-World Connection

Science: Gems All the words in the box relate to gems. Look up these words in your Spelling Dictionary. Then write the words to complete this gem guide.

Spelling Word Link

jewel

topaz
sapphire
emerald
diamond
onyx
ruby
opal
jade

Precious Gems

Pale green ___(1)___ is often carved.

The blue ___(2)___ may reflect starlike rays of light.

A red ___(3)___ is found in the gravel of riverbeds.

The rare yellow ___(4)___ is mined in Brazil.

The six-sided green ___(5)___ is often found in granite.

The ___(6)___ , often dyed, is used in carving cameos.

The multicolored ___(7)___ is found in rock cavities.

The usually colorless ___(8)___ is the hardest gem.

Try This CHALLENGE

Write Similes Writers often describe colors by comparing them to gems. They may use **similes**, comparisons using *like* or *as*. Write several similes, using the gems named in the word box.

☞ The icicles were as sparkly as diamonds.

☞ The fireworks flashed like sapphires and rubies.

traf fic
VC CV

Basic

READ the sentences. **SAY** each bold word.

1. traffic	There is a lot of **traffic** on city highways.
2. permit	Please **permit** me to help you.
3. witness	I was the only **witness** who saw everything.
4. collect	We will **collect** money for the food fund.
5. tunnel	The **tunnel** goes through the mountain.
6. perhaps	Would you **perhaps** like to see this show?
7. pattern	I like the plaid **pattern** in that shirt.
8. object	Why did Maria **object** to the plan?
9. million	There must be more than a **million** stars.
10. arrive	We will **arrive** at the airport at noon.
11. barrel	The wooden **barrel** held pickles.
12. furnish	My grandmother helped us **furnish** our house.
13. shoulder	His **shoulder** hurt when he moved his arm.
14. velvet	The dress was made of soft green **velvet**.
15. effort	Make an **effort** to be on time.
16. sorrow	He felt great **sorrow** when his dog died.
17. essay	I wrote an **essay** about pollution.
18. empire	A new person will rule the **empire**.
19. publish	Who will **publish** your book?
20. subject	Math is my best **subject**.

Think and Write

A **syllable** is a word part with one vowel sound. Each word has two syllables and the vowel-consonant-consonant-vowel (VCCV) pattern.

VC | CV   VC | C V
ar | rive   **per | mit**

• Which words are divided between double consonants? between different consonants?

Now write each Basic Word. Draw a line between the syllables.

Review	23. person
21. arrow	24. mistake
22. corner	25. bottom

Challenge	28. trespass
26. collide	29. option
27. exceed	30. sincere

Independent Practice

Spelling Strategy To spell a word with the VCCV syllable pattern, divide the word between the consonants. Look for patterns you have learned, and spell the word by syllables.

Word Analysis/Phonics Complete the exercises with Basic Words.
1. Write the word that has the final |ər| sounds.
2–3. Write the two words that end with the |əl| sounds.
4–5. Write the two words that end with the |ō| or the |ā| sound.

Vocabulary: Synonyms Write the Basic Word that is a synonym for each word below.

6. maybe
7. equip
8. allow
9. observer
10. gather
11. design
12. kingdom
13. topic

Challenge Words Write the Challenge Word that fits each meaning. Use your Spelling Dictionary.

14. honest
15. a choice
16. to go beyond
17. to strike together with force
18. to go onto someone's property without permission

object
objection

Spelling-Meaning Connection

How can you remember how to spell the |sh| sound in *objection*? Think of the related word *object*. The *t* is kept in *objection,* even though the sound changes.

19–20. Write *objection*. Then write the Basic Word that helps you remember how to spell the |sh| sound in *objection*.

Dictionary

Different Pronunciations In some words the stressed syllable changes, depending on how the word is used in a sentence. Which syllable of *subject* is stressed when it is used as a noun? as a verb?

> **sub·ject** |sŭb′ jĭkt| *n., pl.* **subjects** Something thought about or discussed; topic. |səb **jĕkt′**| *v.* **subjected, subjecting** To cause to undergo: *My doctor subjected me to some tests.*

Practice Write the underlined word in each sentence. Circle the stressed syllable. Use your Spelling Dictionary.

1. Please do not <u>subject</u> us to more talk of sports.
2. I can talk about any <u>subject</u> with my best friend.
3. This zoo does not <u>permit</u> visitors to feed the animals.
4. If you must leave early, get a <u>permit</u> from the office.

Review: Spelling Spree

Word Addition Each word below has the VCCV pattern. Combine the first syllable of the first word with the second syllable of the second word to write a Basic or Review Word.

Example: patty + lantern *pattern*

5. subway + inject
6. escape + hearsay
7. misfit + intake
8. collide + elect
9. millet + trillion
10. perfect + admit
11. furnace + tarnish
12. sorry + borrow

13. barber + squirrel
14. arrange + burrow
15. witty + harness
16. ember + expire
17. perfect + lesson
18. perfume + mishaps
19. correct + manner
20. observe + inject

How Are You Doing?

Write each spelling word as a partner reads it aloud. Did you misspell any words?

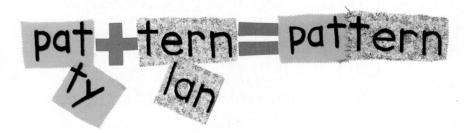

Proofreading and Writing

Proofread for Spelling Find ten misspelled Basic or Review Words in these suggestions for new drivers. Write each misspelled word correctly.

Driving Suggestions

➡ Be sure you have a learner's permit.

Make every effert to learn the trafic laws.

Your state may puplish a book of rules.

Always wear a seat belt across your sholder.

Stop and look when you arive at a cornor with a stop sign.

Turn your lights on when entering a tunel.

If you master the rules from top to botton, your driving patern will be as smooth as velvit.

Write a Traffic Report

How do you think a traffic jam would look from above? Write a traffic report, describing the traffic jam and explaining what caused it. Try to use five spelling words.

Proofreading Tip Check that you formed your *e*'s with a loop so that they do not look like *i*'s.

Basic

1. traffic
2. permit
3. witness
4. collect
5. tunnel
6. perhaps
7. pattern
8. object
9. million
10. arrive
11. barrel
12. furnish
13. shoulder
14. velvet
15. effort
16. sorrow
17. essay
18. empire
19. publish
20. subject

Review

21. arrow
22. corner
23. person
24. mistake
25. bottom

Challenge

26. collide
27. exceed
28. trespass
29. option
30. sincere

Proofreading Marks

¶   Indent
∧   Add
⌐   Delete
≡   Capital letter
/   Small letter

Vocabulary Enrichment

Expanding Vocabulary

Root	
ject = to throw	

Prefix	
ob-	= against
sub-	= under
re-	= again, back
in-	= in, into
pro-	= to, forward
e-	= out

The Word Root *ject* You see the word root *ject*, meaning "to throw," joined with different prefixes. A **prefix** is a word part added to the beginning of a word root. The meanings of the prefix and the word root can help you understand the meaning of the new word.

Write the prefix that should be added to *ject* to make a word that fits the meaning. Then write the word. Use your Spelling Dictionary, if necessary. The first row has been done.

Prefix	Word Root	Word	Meaning
sub	+ ject =	*subject*	to cause to undergo
1. ?	+ ject =	2. ?	to extend forward
3. ?	+ ject =	4. ?	to force a medicine into the body
5. ?	+ ject =	6. ?	to throw out forcefully
7. ?	+ ject =	8. ?	to be against
9. ?	+ ject =	10. ?	to refuse to accept

Work Together With a partner write a sentence for each situation. Use a word with *ject* in each one.

Example: What might a builder say to a worker about placing bricks for a wall along a path? *"Don't let any bricks project into the path."*

11. What might a doctor say to a sick person before giving a shot of medicine?

12. What might a disk jockey say to a helper about a tape in a tape player?

13. What might a parent say to a child about a messy room?

14. What might a teacher say to a student about an unreadable homework paper?

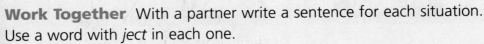
Vocabulary Enrichment

Real-World Connection

Social Studies: Traffic Safety All the words in the box relate to traffic safety. Look up these words in your Spelling Dictionary. Write the words to complete these rules from a bike rider's handbook.

Spelling Word Link

traffic

vehicle
yield
intersection
crosswalk
speedometer
caution
right of way
pedestrian

Signals

right

left

stop

BIKE RIDER'S TIPS

1. A bicycle, like any _____, must be well maintained.
2. Riders must use _____ when riding on busy streets.
3. Look both ways at the _____ of two streets.
4. When entering a road, _____ to oncoming traffic.
5. Stop for people crossing the street in a _____.
6. A green light gives you the _____.
7. Watch out for a _____ stepping out from between parked cars.
8. Watch your _____ to keep from going too fast.

Try This CHALLENGE

Yes or No? Write *yes* if the underlined word is used correctly. Write *no* if it is not.

9. The <u>speedometer</u> showed that I was lost.
10. Turn left at the <u>intersection</u> of First and L streets.
11. A green light at an intersection means <u>yield</u>.
12. Before riding your <u>vehicle</u>, check the tires.

Fact File

Familiar sayings often give wise warnings. The saying, "Better safe than sorry," is especially true in driving. It means that extra caution can prevent accidents.

IT'S THE LAW

Read and Say

dol phin

Basic

READ the sentences. **SAY** each bold word.

1. district	In which **district** do you live?
2. address	I need the **address** to find the store.
3. complain	Try not to **complain** about the bad food.
4. explain	Please **explain** how to do this job.
5. improve	If you revise this paper, you can **improve** it.
6. farther	I can throw the ball **farther** than you can.
7. simply	I **simply** do not like carrots.
8. hundred	She earns two **hundred** dollars a week.
9. although	Tony ate lunch, **although** he was not hungry.
10. laughter	Their **laughter** filled the room.
11. mischief	Our playful dog causes **mischief**.
12. complex	I cannot figure out these **complex** puzzles.
13. partner	Will you be my tennis **partner**?
14. orphan	The **orphan** had no family.
15. constant	The **constant** rain caused a flood.
16. dolphin	The **dolphin** jumped out of the sea.
17. employ	The store owner will **employ** me to clean up.
18. sandwich	Jack ate a cheese **sandwich** for lunch.
19. monster	The movie was about a scary **monster**.
20. orchard	The **orchard** has two kinds of apple trees.

Think and Write

Two-syllable words with the VCCCV pattern have two consonants that spell one sound, as in *laughter*, or that form a cluster, as in *complain*. Divide a VCCCV word into syllables before or after those consonants.

VCC | CV: **laugh | ter**   VC | CCV: **com | plain**

• Where is each word in the list divided into syllables?

Write each Basic Word under the heading that shows where it is divided.

vc	ccv	vcc	cv

Review	23. handsome	**Challenge**	28. conscience
21. empty	24. distrust	26. Congress	29. function
22. hungry	25. illness	27. abstain	30. extreme

Independent Practice

Spelling Strategy When two different consonants in a VCCCV word spell one sound or form a cluster, divide the word into syllables before or after those two consonants. Look for familiar patterns that you have learned, and spell the word by syllables.

Word Analysis/Phonics Complete the exercises with Basic Words.

1. Write the word that has a final |ō| sound.
2. Write the word that has a final |oi| sound.
3–7. Write the five words that have the |f| sound.

Vocabulary: Word Clues Write the Basic Word that fits each clue.

8. an area or region
9. synonym for *difficult*
10. someone to dance with
11. a lunch meal
12. where apples are grown
13. to express unhappiness

Challenge Words Write the Challenge Word that fits each meaning. Use your Spelling Dictionary.

14. purpose or use
15. very great
16. to hold back by choice
17. sense of right and wrong
18. U.S. Senate and House of Representatives

Spelling-Meaning Connection

Did you know that *simply* is related in spelling and meaning to *simple, simplify,* and *simplicity*? **Think of this:** These *simple* directions will get you to my house as *simply* as possible.

19–20. Write *simple*. Then write the Basic Word that is related in spelling and meaning to *simple*.

simple
simply
simplify
simplicity

Review: Spelling Spree

Syllable Match Match the syllables at the top with the numbered syllables to write Basic Words.

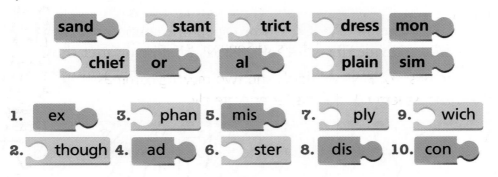

sand   stant   trict   dress mon

chief   or   al   plain sim

1. ex   3. phan 5. mis   7. ply   9. wich

2. though 4. ad   6. ster   8. dis   10. con

Contrast Clues The second part of each clue contrasts with the first part. Write a Basic or Review Word for each clue.

11. not simple, but _____
12. not nearer, but _____
13. not full, but _____
14. not tears, but _____
15. not trust, but _____
16. not health, but _____
17. not ugly, but _____
18. not worsen, but _____

19. not well fed, but _____
20. not a whale, but a _____
21. not a garden, but an _____
22. not praise, but _____
23. not alone, but with a _____
24. not a thousand, but a _____
25. not fire from a job, but _____

How Are You Doing?

List the spelling words that are hard for you. Practice them with a family member.

Proofreading and Writing

Proofread: Spelling and Commas in a Series A **series** is a list of three or more items in a sentence. Use a comma after each item except the last.

Billy, Jessie, and Luis wrote letters to Senator Barnes.

Find four misspelled Basic or Review Words and two missing commas in this part of a business letter. Write the letter correctly.

Dear Senator Barnes:

I am writing to complane about the state park in our district. I found a hundred emty bottles cans and food wrappers there today. My class is willing to help inprove the condition of the park. Can you please adress the problem?

Write a Persuasive Letter

Would you like your town to build bike paths, start a recycling program, or do something else? Write a letter to someone who might help. State your reasons. Try to use five spelling words and one series of three or more items.

BIKE ROUTE

Proofreading Tip **Check that you used commas correctly with items in a series.**

Proofreading Marks

¶ Indent
∧ Add
↝ Delete
≡ Capital letter
/ Small letter

Vocabulary Enrichment

Expanding Vocabulary

Spelling Word Link

sandwich

leotard
Dalmatian
saxophone
tangerine
magnolia

Words from Names Some words come from names of people and places. For example, the sandwich is named after the Earl of Sandwich, who liked to eat meat between two slices of bread.

Match each word in the box with its definition. Write the words.

1. a small, orangelike fruit that peels easily; first imported from Tangier, Morocco
2. a musical instrument invented by Adolphe Sax
3. a tree or shrub with large white, pink, purple, or yellow flowers and named after the French botanist Pierre Magnol
4. a spotted dog first bred in Dalmatia, an area in Croatia
5. a tight-fitting one-piece garment worn by dancers or gymnasts; invented by Jules Léotard, a French aerialist

Work Together Each word in the box is shown in the picture. With a partner write several sentences about the picture, using all the words in the box.

Fact File

The sequoia is a very large evergreen tree. It has reddish wood and can grow as high as three hundred feet. The sequoia was named in honor of Sequoya, a Cherokee who created an alphabet for the Cherokee language.

106

Vocabulary Enrichment

Real-World Connection

Social Studies: Congressional Representatives

All the words in the box relate to congressional representatives. Look up these words in your Spelling Dictionary. Then write the words to complete this paragraph from a guidebook.

U.S. Senate

The United States __(1)__ meets in the __(2)__ building. During a regular __(3)__, which lasts several months, senators discuss national issues. A new amendment might be added to the __(4)__. Some senators may work together on a small __(5)__. Because the senators __(6)__ different groups, they may disagree on an issue. They listen to each other's points of view. Often a __(7)__ might be reached before it is time to __(8)__.

Spelling Word Link

Congress

committee
Constitution
represent
Capitol
compromise
Senate
adjourn
session

Try This CHALLENGE

Questions and Answers Write the word from the box that answers each question.

9. What is one way to resolve an argument?
10. What document states our nation's basic laws?
11. What might people at a meeting do at lunchtime?
12. What is one group that represents the states?

VV Pattern

idea

Basic	READ the sentences. SAY each bold word.
1. poem	I wrote a funny **poem**.
2. idea	Use my **idea** for the story.
3. create	The cook will **create** a new meal.
4. diary	I write each day in my **diary**.
5. area	We have a big play **area** in our yard.
6. giant	The **giant** was twenty feet tall.
7. usual	What is your **usual** bedtime?
8. radio	Please turn down the **radio**.
9. cruel	Those **cruel** words hurt my feelings.
10. quiet	It was very **quiet** in the woods.
11. diet	He lost ten pounds on the **diet**.
12. liar	Is he telling the truth, or is he a **liar**?
13. fuel	A car needs **fuel** to go.
14. riot	The police tried to stop the **riot**.
15. dial	Twist the **dial** to turn on the oven.
16. lion	Is the **lion** the king of beasts?
17. ruin	That stain will **ruin** your shirt.
18. trial	The robber had a fair **trial**.
19. rodeo	The rider roped a calf at the **rodeo**.
20. science	We learned about the moon in **science** class.

Think and Write

In the VV syllable pattern, two vowel letters appear together but spell two vowel sounds. To find the syllables, divide between the vowels.

V | V   V | V
po | em   **cre | ate**

• Does the first vowel letter in the VV pattern have a long or a short vowel sound? How is the Elephant Word different?

Now write each Basic Word. Draw a line between the two vowels in each VV syllable pattern.

Review	23. wrote	**Challenge**	28. enthusiastic
21. title	24. finish	26. appreciate	29. mosaic
22. listen	25. music	27. variety	30. eventually

Independent Practice

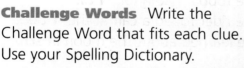

Spelling Strategy   When the two vowels in a VV pattern spell two vowel sounds, divide the word into syllables between the vowels. Look for familiar patterns that you have learned, and spell the word by syllables.

Word Analysis/Phonics   Complete the exercises with Basic Words.

1. Write the word that begins with the |kw| sounds.
2. Write the word that begins with the |j| sound.
3–6. Write the four words with the |ōō| or the |yōō| sound.

Vocabulary: Definitions   Write the Basic Word that fits each meaning.

7. a wild cat of Africa
8. to invent
9. a thought or a plan
10. a region, as of land
11. a journal
12. the face of a clock
13. a disturbance by a large crowd of people

Challenge Words   Write the Challenge Word that fits each clue. Use your Spelling Dictionary.

14. opposite of *sameness*
15. to enjoy and understand
16. synonym for *eager*
17. sooner or later
18. a design made by gluing together pieces of tile

Spelling-Meaning Connection

How can you remember how to spell the schwa sound in *poem*? Think of the |ĕ| sound in the related word *poetic*.

poem
poetic

19–20. Write *poem* and *poetic*. Then underline the letter in *poetic* that helps you remember how to spell the schwa sound in *poem*.

Review: Spelling Spree

Hint and Hunt Write the Basic or Review Word that answers
each question.

1. What should you do when someone
   is speaking?
2. Where might you write your
   private thoughts?
3. What can tell you but
   never show you the news?
4. What does a car need to run?
5. What has a tune and a beat?
6. What takes place in a courtroom?
7. What gives a hint about the subject of a book?
8. What kind of book teaches facts about our planet?
9. What kind of writing is most like a song?

Word Maze 10–25. Begin at the arrow and follow the Word Maze
to find sixteen Basic or Review Words. Write the words in order.

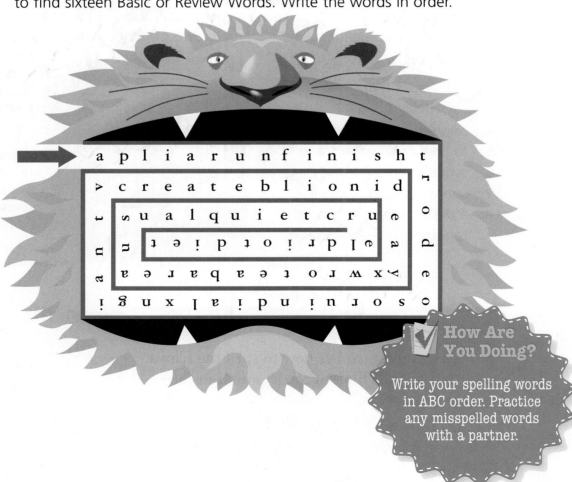

How Are You Doing?

Write your spelling words
in ABC order. Practice
any misspelled words
with a partner.

Proofreading and Writing

Proofread: Spelling and Commas **Introductory words** are words such as *yes, no, oh, well, first, next,* and *last* when they begin a sentence. Use a comma after these words.

> First, pick a theme for your poem.
> Oh, I already did.

Find four misspelled Basic or Review Words and three missing commas in these instructions. Write the instructions correctly.

> *Do you find it hard to write a pome?*
> *Well here are some hints. First lisen to*
> *your favorite kind of music. This will*
> *put you in the mood to create and will*
> *help you get an idear. Next, find a quite*
> *place. Last start to write.*

Basic

1. poem
2. idea
3. create
4. diary
5. area
6. giant
7. usual
8. radio
9. cruel
10. quiet
11. diet
12. liar
13. fuel
14. riot
15. dial
16. lion
17. ruin
18. trial
19. rodeo
20. science

Review

21. title
22. listen
23. wrote
24. finish
25. music

Challenge

26. appreciate
27. variety
28. enthusiastic
29. mosaic
30. eventually

Write a Poem

Write a poem. It could be about a special person or place, your dreams, or your feelings about something. It could even be pure nonsense! Try to use five spelling words and at least one introductory word. Read your poem to a friend.

My Poems

Private! Keep out !!!

Proofreading Tip   **Check that you used commas after introductory words.**

Proofreading Marks

¶ Indent
∧ Add
 ⌐ Delete
≡ Capital letter
/ Small letter

Expanding Vocabulary

Spelling Word Link

create

Building a Word Family for *create* You can build a family for some words by adding different suffixes. A **suffix** is a word part that can be added at the end of a word.

WORD		SUFFIX		NEW WORD
write	+	er	=	writer

Show You Know! Draw the web shown below. Add the suffixes in the web to the spelling word *create*. Then write a sentence for each new word. Use your Spelling Dictionary.
Spelling Alert! Drop the final *e* before adding each suffix.

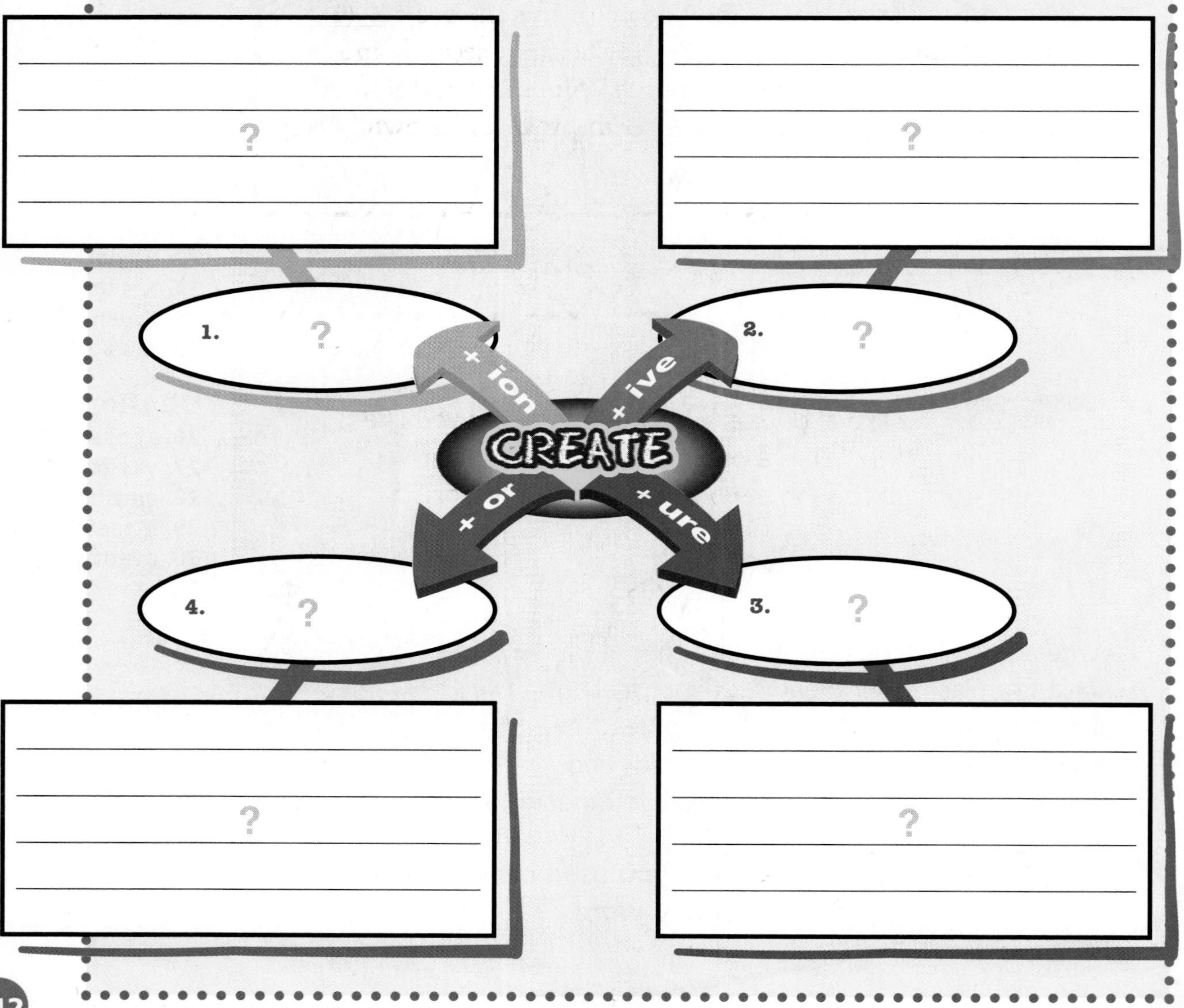

_____

?

_____

?

1.   ?

2.   ?

+ ion

+ ive

CREATE

+ or

+ ure

4.   ?

3.   ?

_____

?

_____

?

Vocabulary Enrichment

Real-World Connection

Language Arts: Poetry All the words in the box relate to poetry. Look up these words in your Spelling Dictionary. Then write the words to complete this introduction to a poetry book.

> There are many different kinds of poems. For example, a __(1)__ might write a Japanese __(2)__ , a short poem with seventeen syllables. It creates a single picture, or __(3)__ , in your mind. A story poem is called a __(4)__ . Each __(5)__ tells part of the story. A funny poem of five lines is a __(6)__ . It has a bouncing beat, or __(7)__ . The first, second, and fifth lines have the same last sounds. The third and fourth lines also __(8)__ . Each kind of poem provides its own pleasures.

Spelling Word Link

poem

poet
rhythm
haiku
stanza
limerick
rhyme
image
ballad

Try This CHALLENGE

Write an Opinion Read the haiku and the limerick. What do you like about each kind of poem? Do you like one kind better? Write a paragraph that states your opinion. Try to use some words from the word box.

Haiku
Deer, white tails blazing
Birds soaring across the sky—
Summer is coming.

Limerick
A puppy whose hair was so flowing
There really was no means of knowing
Which end was his head,
Once stopped me and said,
"Please, sir, am I coming or going?"
Oliver Herford

 Fact File

Haiku were first written in Japan about seven hundred years ago. Issa and Bashō were two Japanese poets who wrote many haiku. Most haiku focus on a topic related to nature.

113

18 Review: Units 13–17

watermelon

| Unit 13 | More Compound Words | pages 84–89 |

post office	grapefruit	holiday	welfare
firecracker	furthermore	chalkboard	throughout
warehouse	great-grandchild		

Spelling Strategy   A compound word is made up of two or more smaller words. To spell a compound word correctly, you must know if it is written as one word, as a hyphenated word, or as separate words.

Write the compound word that has each part below.

1. out **2.** more **3.** fare **4.** ware **5.** grand **6.** fire

Write the word that answers each question.

7. What is sometimes eaten for breakfast?

8. What do teachers write on when they teach a lesson?

9. What do you call a day of celebration?

10. Where can a person mail packages?

|əl|
ankle
shovel

| Unit 14 | Final \|l\| or \|əl\| | pages 90–95 |

normal	jewel	shovel	whistle	fossil
needle	local	bushel	pedal	devil

Spelling Strategy   When you hear the final |l| or |əl| sounds, think of the patterns **le**, **el**, and **al**.

Write the word that fits each meaning.

11. usual

12. a digging tool

13. a sewing tool

14. a wicked person

15. a lever that is worked by foot

16. a gem

Write the words to complete the paragraph.

While gathering a ___**(17)**___ of clams at our ___**(18)**___ beach, I picked up a pretty rock. Then I gave a ___**(19)**___ of surprise. In the rock was a perfect ___**(20)**___ of a fish.

Unit 15   VCCV Pattern   pages 96–101

permit	witness	million	perhaps	object
barrel	velvet	effort	subject	shoulder

traf fic
VC CV

Spelling Strategy   To spell a word with the VCCV syllable pattern, divide the word between the consonants. Look for patterns you have learned, and spell the word by syllables.

Write the word that fits each meaning.

21. disapprove of
22. an earnest attempt
23. possibly
24. a license
25. tells what a sentence is about

Write a word that belongs in each group.

26. hundred, thousand, _____
27. satin, silk, _____
28. trial, courtroom, _____
29. vat, keg, _____
30. wrist, elbow, _____

Unit 16   VCCCV Pattern   pages 102–107

hundred	complain	laughter	farther	although
dolphin	orchard	employ	sandwich	constant

dol phin

Spelling Strategy   When two different consonants in a VCCCV word spell one sound or form a cluster, divide the word into syllables before or after those two consonants. Look for familiar patterns that you have learned, and spell the word by syllables.

Each word below is missing a syllable. Write the word.

31. or | _____
32. _____ | though
33. em | _____
34. _____ | plain

Write the word that fits each clue.

35. 10 x 10
36. a sea animal
37. may be made with cheese
38. not changing
39. opposite of *nearer*
40. sound of happiness

115

ide a

Unit 17   VV Pattern   pages 108–113

poem	diary	create	radio	quiet
fuel	dial	science	ruin	rodeo

Spelling Strategy   When the two vowels in a VV pattern spell two vowel sounds, divide the word into syllables between the vowels. Look for familiar patterns that you have learned, and spell the word by syllables.

Write the word that completes each analogy.

41. *Television* is to *channel selector* as *radio* is to _____.

42. *Acrobat* is to *circus* as *cowhand* is to _____.

43. *Fable* is to *story* as *haiku* is to _____.

44. *Algebra* is to *math* as *biology* is to _____.

45. *Movie* is to *television* as *song* is to _____.

Write the word that is a synonym for each word below.

46. invent   **49.** silent

47. oil   **50.** wreck

48. journal

Challenge Words   Units 13–17   pages 84–113

enthusiastic	halfhearted	conscience	function	kernel
high-spirited	eventually	artificial	trespass	sincere

Write the word that fits each clue.

51. purpose   **54.** opposite of *dishonest*

52. intrude   **55.** a seed

53. opposite of *eager*

Write the word that completes each sentence.

56. The wild horse was too _____ to be easily tamed.

57. Abby's _____ would not allow her to lie.

58. These silk flowers look real even though they are _____.

59. Mario loves skating and is an _____ ice hockey player.

60. If you follow this path, you will _____ come to a pond.

Spelling-Meaning Strategy

Vowel Changes: Schwa to Short Vowel Sound

Thinking of related words may help you remember how to spell an unclear vowel sound. Read this paragraph.

A judge must often decide the **legality** of someone's actions. The judge reviews the laws to determine what is **legal** and what is not.

legal
legality

Think

- How are *legal* and *legality* related in meaning?
- What vowel sound does the letter *a* spell in each word?

Here are more related words in which the same letter spells the schwa sound in one word and the short vowel sound in the other.

local	normal	mortal
locality	normality	mortality

Apply and Extend

Complete these activities on a separate sheet of paper.

1. Look up the words in the word box above in your Spelling Dictionary, and write their meanings. Then write a short paragraph, using one pair of words.

2. With a partner list as many words as you can that are related to *legal*, *local*, *normal*, and *mortal*. Then look in the section "Vowel Changes: Schwa to Short Vowel Sound" beginning on page 272 of your Spelling-Meaning Index. Add any other words that you find in these families to your list.

Summing Up

When you do not know the spelling of the schwa sound in a word, the short vowel sound in a related word may help you figure out which vowel letter to use.

UNIT
18

Story

from

Mr. Stormalong

by Anne Malcolmson and
Dell J. McCormick

In this part of a tall tale, Stormy wants to be a cabin boy on a ship. What is unusual about Stormy?

"Excuse me, sir," said the schoolboy. "I hear you need a cabin boy."

The captain clung to the wheel to keep from slipping into the arms of the youngster who had jumped aboard. The youngster was large for his age. He stood about thirty feet tall and looked as if he weighed several tons. No wonder the *Silver Maid* was listing!

"If you don't shift your weight more to the port side, I'll need a salvage crew more than a cabin boy!" roared Captain Snard.

Stormy, the little fellow who was causing the trouble, blushed with embarrassment. "I'm sorry, sir," he stammered, and carefully placed one foot beside the port rail. The ship creaked and righted itself.

"Well!" said the captain, wiping his brow and looking up at the lad. "What makes you think you can be a cabin boy?"

Tears came to the young boy's eyes. "The sea is in my blood, sir," he said. "All my life I've wanted to join the China trade."

Think and Discuss

1. What is different about the main **character**, Stormy? What kind of person is Stormy?

2. What is the **setting** of this part of the story?

3. What might be the **plot** of the rest of this story?

The Writing Process
Story

Think of an interesting character. What might happen to that character? Write a story involving your character. Keep the guidelines in mind, and follow the Writing Process.

1 Prewriting
- Make a story map. Show what happens in the beginning, the middle, and the end.

2 Draft
- Use dialogue when the characters speak.

3 Revise
- Be sure the ending makes sense.
- Use your Thesaurus to find exact words.
- Have a writing conference.

4 Proofread
- Did you spell each word correctly?
- Did you capitalize proper nouns and adjectives?
- Did you use commas correctly?

5 Publish
- Make a neat, final copy, and add a good title.
- Invite some classmates to help you act out your story.

Guidelines for Writing a Story

✓ Introduce a problem in the beginning that your character deals with in the middle and resolves at the end.
✓ Choose characters and settings that fit the story.
✓ Use details and dialogue to bring the story to life.

Composition Words

flashlight
puzzle
jewel
giant
dolphin
tunnel
laughter
monster

The Tale of the Last Knight

Beg

VCV Pattern

ro bot

Basic

READ the sentences. **SAY** each bold word.

1. robot — Can a **robot** wash dishes?
2. behave — The twins **behave** well when I baby-sit.
3. repeat — Please **repeat** the word slowly.
4. rapid — She walked with a **rapid** stride.
5. detail — Jack told me every **detail** of his trip.
6. equal — Cut the pie into six **equal** pieces.
7. value — What is the **value** of this gold ring?
8. nation — Who makes the laws for our **nation**?
9. evil — The story is about a mean, **evil** giant.
10. closet — Your coat is hanging in the **closet**.
11. camel — A **camel** can store water in its body.
12. adore — I **adore** my cute puppy.
13. tulip — The **tulip** is my favorite flower.
14. credit — I received extra **credit** for my report.
15. aware — I am **aware** of the problem.
16. vanish — The magician made himself **vanish**.
17. shadow — I can see my dark **shadow** on the wall.
18. prefer — I **prefer** water to juice.
19. record — Listen to the song on this **record**.
20. novel — Have you finished reading the **novel**?

Think and Write

Divide a VCV word into syllables before or after the consonant.
Note the spelling of the unstressed syllable.

vc | v   v | cv
val | ue   clos | et   ro | bot   a | ware   re | peat

• Look at the first syllables in the examples. Which words have the short vowel pattern? end with a vowel sound?

Now write each Basic Word under the heading that tells where each word is divided.

After the Consonant	Before the Consonant

Review	23. basic	**Challenge**	28. device
21. human	24. amaze	26. logic	29. module
22. model	25. total	27. laser	30. nuisance

Independent Practice

Spelling Strategy

To find the syllables of a VCV word, remember to divide the word before or after the consonant. Look for spelling patterns you have learned. Note the spelling of the unstressed syllable, and spell the word by syllables.

Word Analysis/Phonics Complete the exercises with Basic Words.

1–2. Write the two words that have only the |ə| sound in the first syllable.

3–7. Write the five words that have a long vowel sound in the second syllable.

Vocabulary: Classifying Write the Basic Word that belongs in each group.

8. greater, less, _____
9. elephant, horse, _____
10. story, poem, _____
11. disk, tape, _____
12. rose, daisy, _____
13. clothes, hanger, _____

Challenge Words Write the Challenge Word that fits each clue. Use your Spelling Dictionary.

14. sound reasoning
15. astronaut's workplace
16. synonym for *pest*
17. a broom or a can opener
18. a machine that sends a powerful beam of light

Spelling-Meaning Connection

Can you see the word *nation* in the words *national, nationality,* and *international?*
These words are related in spelling and meaning.

19–20. Write *national*. Then write the Basic Word that you see in *national*.

Dictionary

Homographs   The sentence *She had a novel idea for a novel* includes two homographs. **Homographs** are words that are spelled the same but have different meanings and histories. They are numbered and listed separately in the dictionary.

> **nov·el**¹ |nŏv′ əl| *adj.* Very new, unusual, or different.
> **nov·el**² |nŏv′ əl| *n., pl.* **novels** A made-up story that is long enough to fill a book.

Practice   Write *novel¹*, *novel²*, *stalk¹*, or *stalk²* to complete each sentence. Use your Spelling Dictionary.

1. The flower _____ was covered with blossoms.
2. Emma is reading a great mystery _____ .
3. Going to the moon is no longer a _____ idea.
4. Ted heard an animal _____ past the tent.
5. I dipped the celery _____ into peanut butter.

Review: Spelling Spree

Word Clues   Write a Basic or Review Word for each clue.

6. a flower planted in fall
7. a small copy
8. a country or a people
9. to worship
10. "Buy now, pay later."
11. fast
12. wicked
13. to like better
14. knowing
15. might be read for fun
16. a shaded area
17. has one or two humps
18. where a broom is kept
19. to disappear
20. a machine with a "brain"
21. played on a phonograph
22. to fill with surprise

✔ **How Are You Doing?**

List the spelling words that are hard for you. Practice them with a family member.

Proofreading and Writing

Proofread for Spelling Find eight misspelled Basic or Review Words in this paragraph from a science article. Write each one correctly.

Modern Robots

The robot is no longer a novel machine.

The early types were very basec. They

could only reapeat the same actions over

and over. Robots have undergone a totle change. The new

robots are different in every ditail. They hardly look or behav

like people. Most robots are designed to do rapid work and

are of greatest vaule in factories. No humen can equel the

speed of these machines at their tasks. ■

Basic
1. robot
2. behave
3. repeat
4. rapid
5. detail
6. equal
7. value
8. nation
9. evil
10. closet
11. camel
12. adore
13. tulip
14. credit
15. aware
16. vanish
17. shadow
18. prefer
19. record
20. novel

Review
21. human
22. model
23. basic
24. amaze
25. total

Challenge
26. logic
27. laser
28. device
29. module
30. nuisance

Write an Ad

Suppose you are a robot for sale. Write an ad for yourself, telling what you do best. Try to use five spelling words. Read your ad to a family member.

Proofreading Tip

Circle any word that you think might be misspelled. Then look up its spelling in a dictionary.

Proofreading Marks

¶   Indent
∧   Add
⌐   Delete
≡   Capital letter
/   Small letter

Expanding Vocabulary

dahlia
rhododendron
dandelion
poinsettia
bougainvillea
daisy
gladiolus
sweet William
iris
snapdragon

Word History Flowers may be named for people or for how the flowers look. **Tulip** comes from the Turkish word *tulibend,* meaning "turban." The people of Turkey thought the flower looked like a turban, a hat worn in their country.

Write the word from the box that matches each history.

1. named for Louis Antoine de Bougainville, who discovered this vine
2. from Middle English *dayeseye,* "day's eye"
3. named for its blossoms shaped like a dragon's jaw
4. named after Iris, the Greek goddess of the rainbow
5. from the Latin *gladius,* "sword," for its sword-shaped leaves
6. named for Joel R. Poinsett, who brought it to the United States from Mexico
7. from the Latin *dens leonis,* "lion's tooth," for its jagged leaves
8. named for William, Duke of Cumberland (Scotland)
9. from the Greek *rhodon dendron,* "rose tree"
10. named in honor of Anders Dahl, an 18th-century Swedish botanist

Fact File

The joe-pye weed is an herb with groups of pink or purple flowers. Joe Pye is said to have been a Native American who cured typhus fever in New England using this weed.

Vocabulary Enrichment

Unit 19
BONUS

Real-World Connection

Science: Robots All the words in the box relate to robots. Look up each word in your Spelling Dictionary. Then write the words to complete this encyclopedia entry.

Spelling Word Link

robot

assemble
operate
computer
mechanical
circuit
remote control
sensors
command

p. 256 **ROBOT**

ROBOT A robot performs human tasks. Its "brain" is a ___(1)___ that processes information. The information is stored in a tiny electronic ___(2)___ . A robot can ___(3)___ in places where humans cannot go. A scientist can send a ___(4)___ to a robot from a distance by using ___(5)___ . A robot with ___(6)___ arms is used to explore the ocean floor. Its arms have ___(7)___ that react to pressure changes. Robots may soon be used to build, or ___(8)___ , space stations.

**Try This
CHALLENGE**

Yes or No? Write *yes* if the underlined word is used correctly. Write *no* if it is not.

9. <u>Sensors</u> can react to light and dark.
10. Thinking is a <u>mechanical</u> task.
11. Follow the instructions to <u>assemble</u> the robot.
12. Give the proper <u>command</u>, and the robot will work.

Words with -ed or -ing

Read and Say

squeeze ing

Basic

READ the sentences. **SAY** each bold word.

1. directing	A police officer is **directing** traffic.
2. amusing	I laughed at the **amusing** story.
3. delivered	The mail carrier **delivered** the package.
4. attending	She is **attending** an art show today.
5. offered	Mr. Lee **offered** me a part in the play.
6. rising	The sun will be **rising** soon.
7. deserved	My sister **deserved** the award.
8. supported	The boards **supported** the roof.
9. borrowed	He **borrowed** a dollar for lunch.
10. freezing	Wear a warm coat in **freezing** weather.
11. awaiting	I am **awaiting** my turn at bat.
12. collapsed	The bridge **collapsed** during the fire.
13. providing	Marie is **providing** the food.
14. sheltered	The hat **sheltered** her face from the sun.
15. resulting	There were floods **resulting** from the storm.
16. arrested	The police **arrested** the robber.
17. damaged	The insects **damaged** the crops.
18. seeking	I am **seeking** a job.
19. squeezing	Jamal is **squeezing** the oranges.
20. decided	I **decided** to join the art club.

Think and Write

A **base word** is a word to which endings can be added.

deserve + ed = deserv**ed**   rise + ing = ris**ing**
offer + ed = offer**ed**   direct + ing = direct**ing**

• Which words have a spelling change when the ending is added? What change occurs?

Now write each Basic Word under the heading that tells how the word is spelled when -ed or -ing is added.

Final e Dropped	No Spelling Change

Review	23. dared
21. dancing	24. traced
22. landed	25. checking

Challenge	28. dramatized
26. rehearsing	29. anticipated
27. portraying	30. entertaining

Independent Practice

Spelling Strategy When a base word ends with *e,* you usually drop the *e* when *-ed* or *-ing* is added. If a base word does not end with *e,* you usually add the ending *-ed* or *-ing* without a spelling change.

Word Analysis/Phonics Write a Basic Word that has each base word.

1. decide
2. await
3. freeze
4. damage
5. rise
6. provide
7. arrest
8. direct

Vocabulary: Context Sentences Write a Basic Word to complete each sentence.

9. We laugh when a movie is _____.
10. Return the movie you _____ from the library.
11. Tim Brown _____ an award for his role in *Raging Storm*.
12. Which letter carrier _____ mail to your house yesterday?
13. The old bridge _____ under the weight of the truck.

Challenge Words Write the Challenge Word that fits each clue. Use your Spelling Dictionary.

14. synonym for *expected*
15. opposite of *boring*
16. playing the part of
17. synonym for *practicing*
18. presented in a serious way

Spelling-Meaning Connection

Supported contains the word root *port,* meaning "to carry." A bridge is supported, or "carried," by steel towers. Knowing the root *port* can also help you spell and understand the related words *transport* and *portable.*

19–20. Write *portable.* Then write the Basic Word that has the same word root.

supported
transport
portable

Dictionary

Base Words and Endings A dictionary does not include an entry for every form of a word. To find a word that ends with *-ed, -ing, -er,* or *-est,* look up the base word. The word forms follow the part of speech.

> **squeeze** |skwēz| *v.* **squeezed, squeezing**
> **warm** |wôrm| *adj.* **warmer, warmest**

Practice Write the base word that you would look up in the dictionary to find each word below.

1. rising   **3.** offered   **5.** rarer   **7.** catcher

2. sharpest   **4.** collapsed   **6.** awaiting

Review: Spelling Spree

Meaning Match Write a Basic or Review Word that has each meaning and ending below.

Example: entertain pleasantly + ing *amusing*

8. provide with cover + ed

9. be in charge of + ing

10. bring to + ed

11. be present at + ing

12. make up one's mind + ed

13. supply + ing

14. go ashore + ed

15. move in time to music + ing

16. try to find + ing

17. be very cold + ing

18. wait for + ing

19. take prisoner + ed

20. harm + ed

21. examine + ing

22. take on loan + ed

23. press together + ing

24. follow the outline of a drawing + ed

How Are You Doing?

Write your spelling words in ABC order. Practice any misspelled words with a family member.

Proofreading and Writing

Proofread for Spelling Find eight misspelled Basic or Review Words in this movie ad. Write each one correctly.

★★★★★

Dancing in Borrowed Shoes

"Quite ammusing! I callapsed laughing!" —**Sue Critic**

"Teri Toon desirved an Oscar!" —**Ann E. Mation**

"Matt Kennett is a rizing actor. He suported the stars and offerd a new vision of today's teen." —**Ranton Rave**

"Mora Gags has daired to entertain us with two hours of nonstop fun, rezulting in a bad side ache." —**Marv L. Us**

Basic

1. directing
2. amusing
3. delivered
4. attending
5. offered
6. rising
7. deserved
8. supported
9. borrowed
10. freezing
11. awaiting
12. collapsed
13. providing
14. sheltered
15. resulting
16. arrested
17. damaged
18. seeking
19. squeezing
20. decided

Review

21. dancing
22. landed
23. dared
24. traced
25. checking

Challenge

26. rehearsing
27. portraying
28. dramatized
29. anticipated
30. entertaining

Write a Movie Review

Write a movie review. Tell why you did or did not like the movie. Try to use five spelling words in your review. Read your review to a classmate.

Proofreading Tip

If you are using a word processor, you can boldface any words that you think are misspelled. Then look them up in a dictionary.

Proofreading Marks

¶ Indent
∧ Add
⌒ Delete
≡ Capital letter
/ Small letter

129

Vocabulary Enrichment

Expanding Vocabulary

Using a Thesaurus to Find Exact Words Suppose you loaned your bike to a friend, and it came back in poor condition. Which sentence explains more clearly what the bike looked like?

My bike came back with a **damaged** frame.

My bike came back with a **dented** frame.

The second sentence is clearer because *dented* tells exactly how the bike is damaged.

Write the best word from the box to replace *damaged* in each sentence. Use your Thesaurus.

1. Cold passed through the holes in the damaged coat.
2. Chris hammered the damaged fender back into shape.
3. The paint on the old car was badly damaged.
4. Before slicing apples, cut off the damaged spots.
5. Pieces of the damaged glass lay everywhere.

Work Together Write a sentence for each picture. Use a different, more exact word for damaged in each one.

6.

7.

8.

Vocabulary Enrichment

Real-World Connection

Performing Arts: Movies All the words in the box relate to movies. Look up each word in your Spelling Dictionary. Then write the words to complete this paragraph from a newsletter.

Spelling Word Link

directing

cinema
screenplay
matinee
soundtrack
projector
stunt
reel
documentary

THE MOVIES

Last week the library showed a ___(1)___ on filmmaking. In the early 1900s, a ___(2)___, or script, was not written before a movie was made. A film had no speaking roles and no recorded ___(3)___. An actor often had to perform his or her own ___(4)___. The twenty-minute drama was made on one ___(5)___ of film. At the ___(6)___ — or the nickelodeon, as the theater was called — a ___(7)___ flashed pictures on the screen. A pianist played during the ___(8)___ and the evening show.

Try This CHALLENGE

Yes or No? Write *yes* if the underlined word is used correctly. Write *no* if it is not.

9. We attended a <u>matinee</u> last evening.
10. The actors read the new <u>screenplay</u>.
11. We saw a <u>documentary</u> on flood control.
12. The scenes were photographed with a new <u>projector</u>.

★★★ **Fact File**

Many scenes from early movies were filmed outdoors. Hollywood, California, became a film center because of its mild weather and variety of natural scenery.

131

More Words with *-ed* or *-ing*

Read and Say

drip **p** ed

Basic

READ the sentences. **SAY** each bold word.

1. whipped — Should the cream be **whipped**?
2. skimmed — I quickly **skimmed** the story.
3. dripped — Water **dripped** from the faucet.
4. covered — I **covered** the baby with a soft blanket.
5. gathering — He went to a family **gathering**.
6. bragging — Lee was **bragging** about his new bike.
7. visiting — I like **visiting** my aunt.
8. planned — Our class **planned** a picnic in the park.
9. winning — Which team is **winning** the game?
10. mixed — Jan has **mixed** feelings about moving.
11. stunned — Mary was **stunned** by how tall I was.
12. hitting — I have been **hitting** the ball well.
13. begged — The dog **begged** for a bone.
14. shipped — We **shipped** the package yesterday.
15. ordered — My dad **ordered** six new books.
16. slammed — The door **slammed** shut.
17. swimming — We went **swimming** in the pond.
18. suffering — She is **suffering** from a cold.
19. wandered — We **wandered** through the woods.
20. spotted — I **spotted** my friend in the line.

Think and Write

Each word has *-ed* or *-ing* added to a base word. Each base word ends with a vowel and a consonant.

whip + ed = whip**ped**   cover + ed = cover**ed**

• How many syllables are in *whip*? in *cover*? In which word is the final consonant doubled when *-ed* is added? How is the Elephant Word different?

Now write each Basic Word under the heading that shows what happens to the base word when *-ed* or *-ing* is added.

Final Consonant Doubled	Final Consonant Not Doubled

Review
21. flipped
22. rubbing
23. snapping
24. dimmed
25. stripped

Challenge
26. catering
27. shredded
28. layered
29. scalloped
30. whirred

Independent Practice

Spelling Strategy When a one-syllable word ends with one vowel and a single consonant, you usually double the consonant when *-ed* or *-ing* is added. When a two-syllable word ends with one vowel and a single consonant, you often do not double the consonant when *-ed* or *-ing* is added.

Word Analysis/Phonics Write six Basic Words by combining each base word and ending.

1. visit + ing
2. slam + ed
3. beg + ed
4. mix + ed
5. skim + ed
6. hit + ing

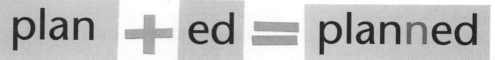

plan + ed = planned

Vocabulary: Synonyms Write the Basic Word that is a synonym for each word below.

7. located
8. boasting
9. collecting
10. commanded
11. dazed
12. roamed
13. sent

Challenge Words Write the Challenge Word that fits each meaning. Use your Spelling Dictionary.

14. providing food for a party
15. baked with sauce
16. placed several thicknesses on top of each other
17. cut into small strips
18. moved quickly with a buzzing sound

Spelling-Meaning Connection

Can you see *win* in *winner* and *winning?* Different endings can be added to base words to form new words that are related in spelling and meaning.

win
winner
winning

19–20. Write *win*. Then write the Basic Word that is related in spelling and meaning to *win*.

Review: Spelling Spree

Crack the Code Use the following code to find a Basic or Review Word in each item below. Write each word correctly.

CODE	z	y	x	w	v	u	t	s	r	q	p	o	j	i	h	g	f	e	d	c	b	a
LETTER	a	b	c	d	e	f	g	h	i	k	l	m	n	o	p	r	s	t	u	v	w	x

Example: widypvw *doubled*

1. fegrhhvw
2. fjzhhrjt
3. fqroovw
4. bzjwvgvw
5. fduuvgrjt
6. oravw
7. sreerjt
8. igwvgvw
9. hpzjjvw
10. yvttvw
11. xicvgvw
12. fpzoovw
13. uprhhvw
14. fedjjvw
15. bsrhhvw

Book Titles Write a Basic or Review Word to complete each funny book title. Remember to use capital letters.

16. *The Tale of the _____ Coat* by Leo Pard
17. *Where the Water _____* by Lee Key Faucet
18. *Diving and _____ in the Ocean* by C. Otter
19. *Making a Fire by _____ Sticks Together* by Frick Shun
20. *Get Ahead by _____ About Your Achievements* by Bo Sting
21. *Is _____ Everything?* by Kaymen Last
22. *Finding and _____ Plants You Can Eat* by Herb Cole Ecter
23. *Where Were You When the Lights _____?* by Flash Bulb
24. *Shaped Up and _____ Out* by C. Goer
25. *Talking and _____ with the Queen* by Roy L. Guest

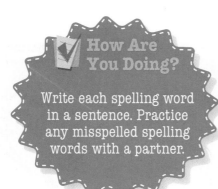

How Are You Doing?

Write each spelling word in a sentence. Practice any misspelled spelling words with a partner.

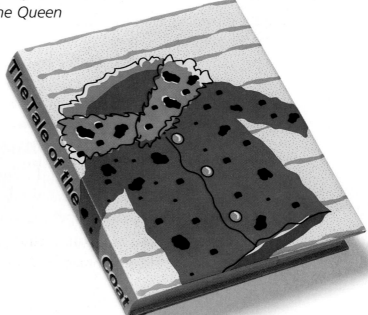

Proofreading and Writing

Proofread for Spelling and Commas Whenever you speak to a person by name, you are using a noun in direct address. Use a comma or commas to set off the noun.

Angie, are you hungry?   No, Bert, I just ate dinner.

Find four misspelled Basic or Review Words and three missing commas in this script for a TV cooking show. Write the script correctly.

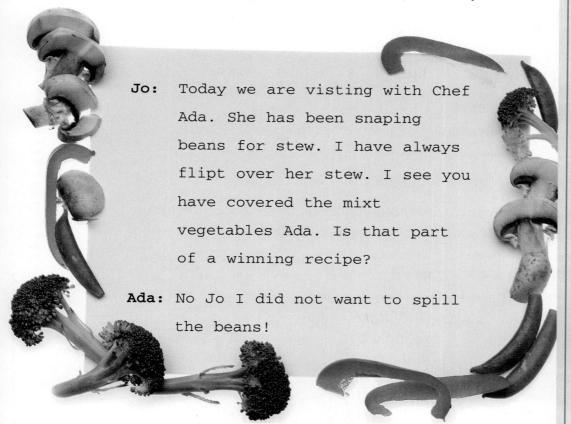

Jo: Today we are visting with Chef Ada. She has been snaping beans for stew. I have always flipt over her stew. I see you have covered the mixt vegetables Ada. Is that part of a winning recipe?

Ada: No Jo I did not want to spill the beans!

Basic

1. whipped
2. skimmed
3. dripped
4. covered
5. gathering
6. bragging
7. visiting
8. planned
9. winning
10. mixed
11. stunned
12. hitting
13. begged
14. shipped
15. ordered
16. slammed
17. swimming
18. suffering
19. wandered
20. spotted

Review

21. flipped
22. rubbing
23. snapping
24. dimmed
25. stripped

Challenge

26. catering
27. shredded
28. layered
29. scalloped
30. whirred

Write a Conversation

Melissa, where is your homework?

I think my dog ate it.

Write a conversation between you and a friend. Try to use five spelling words and one noun in direct address in your conversation.

Proofreading Tip

Be sure you included commas when writing nouns in direct address.

Proofreading Marks

¶ Indent
∧ Add
⌿ Delete
≡ Capital letter
/ Small letter

Expanding Vocabulary

Multiple-Meaning Words: *spot* Did you know that *spot* has several meanings? Look at this dictionary entry for *spot*.

> **spot** |spŏt| *n., pl.* **spots 1.** A small mark or stain.
> **2.** An area that is different, as in color, from the area around it: *My dog has brown fur with white spots.*
> **3.** A place or location.

Write *1*, *2*, or *3* to show which meaning of *spot* is used in each sentence.

1. The cow was white with large black <u>spots</u>.

2. The library is a good <u>spot</u> to read a book.

3. The blue ink <u>spot</u> on my shirt won't rub off.

Show You Know! Write three sentences about the picture below. Use a different meaning of *spot* in each sentence.

Real-World Connection

Home Economics: Cooking All the words in the box relate to cooking. Look up these words in your Spelling Dictionary. Then write the words to complete this lunch menu.

> ### TODAY'S LUNCH SPECIAL
>
> Today's special starts with a mixed-greens salad, topped with a dressing of oil and __(1)__ and fresh minced __(2)__ cloves.
>
> Next, there's Chef Marie's famous tuna-noodle __(3)__ —a huge mound of homemade egg noodles, smothered in a light cream sauce flavored with a thinly sliced yellow __(4)__ , the __(5)__ basil, and lots of pepper to make it extra __(6)__ .
>
> A flaky, fresh-baked buttermilk __(7)__ and a mug of hot apple cider with a __(8)__ stick are also included.

Spelling Word Link

whipped

- casserole
- biscuit
- herb
- spicy
- garlic
- vinegar
- onion
- cinnamon

Try This CHALLENGE

Write Couplets Write rhyming couplets about food on another sheet of paper. Try to use some of the words in the box. Here's one to get you started:

> This pasta has a spicy taste,
> But I won't let it go to waste.

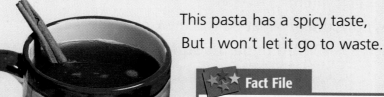

★★★ Fact File

Most spices come from plants. For example, cinnamon comes from tree bark, and the mustard we spread on sandwiches comes from the seeds of the mustard plant.

137

Words with Suffixes

Read and Say

READ the sentences.
SAY each bold word.

watchful

Basic

1. dreadful — The storm was **dreadful**.
2. enjoyment — We showed our **enjoyment** by clapping.
3. safely — He arrived at the house **safely**.
4. watchful — The **watchful** dog kept an eye on us.
5. speechless — The news left us **speechless**.
6. paleness — The **paleness** of her skin makes her look ill.
7. breathless — He was **breathless** after he ran.
8. government — Who heads the local **government**?
9. cheerful — Carol is **cheerful** and always smiling.
10. actively — She is **actively** running for mayor.
11. closeness — I love the **closeness** of my family.
12. lately — Ben has been busy **lately**.
13. goodness — She enjoyed the **goodness** of the fresh juice.
14. retirement — Mom is planning her **retirement**.
15. forgetful — I am very **forgetful**.
16. basement — Our **basement** is flooded.
17. softness — Velvet is known for its **softness**.
18. delightful — This is a **delightful** party.
19. settlement — That was the first **settlement** in this area.
20. countless — Roy had done **countless** favors for me.

Think and Write

Each word has a base word and a **suffix**, a word part added to the end of a base word. A suffix adds meaning.

safe + ly = safe**ly**   cheer + ful = cheer**ful**
pale + ness = pale**ness**   speech + less = speech**less**
enjoy + ment = enjoy**ment**

• What suffixes do you see? What do you think each suffix means?
Now write each Basic Word under its suffix.

-ly	-ment or -ness	-ful or -less

Review
21. fearful   23. careless
22. movement   24. lonely
                25. powerful

Challenge
26. suspenseful   28. defenseless
27. suspiciously 29. seriousness
                  30. contentment

Independent Practice

Spelling Strategy A **suffix** is a word part added to the end of a base word. A suffix adds meaning to the word. The word parts *-ly, -ful, -ness, -less,* and *-ment* are suffixes. The spelling of the base word is usually not changed when the suffix begins with a consonant.

Word Analysis/Phonics Complete the exercises with Basic Words.

1–4. Write the four words that have the |ā| sound spelled *a*-consonant-*e*.

5–8. Write the word that has the same base word as each word below.

   5. closely   **6.** speeches   **7.** settler   **8.** enjoyable

Vocabulary: Antonyms Write the Basic Word that is an antonym, or a word that means the opposite, of each word below.

   9. unhappy
   10. hardness
   11. wonderful
   12. badness
   13. few

Challenge Words Write the Challenge Word that fits each meaning. Use your Spelling Dictionary.

   14. helpless   **16.** full of uncertainty   **18.** happiness and
   15. importance   **17.** distrustfully   satisfaction

Spelling-Meaning Connection

govern
govern ment
govern or

Can you see *govern* in these words: *government, governor?* These words are all related in spelling and meaning.
Think of this: The *government* could not *govern* without laws.

19–20. Write *govern*. Then write the Basic Word that is related in spelling and meaning to *govern*.

Dictionary

Suffixes Dictionaries list suffixes in alphabetical order among the entry words. A hyphen is shown before a suffix.

> **-ness** A suffix that forms nouns and means "condition" or "quality." Kindness is the condition or quality of being kind.

You will not find a dictionary entry for every word with a suffix, but you can always look up the base word and the suffix separately. Then you can figure out their combined meaning.

Practice Look up each base word and suffix below in your Spelling Dictionary. Write the meaning of each word below.

1. quietly
2. useless
3. sweetness
4. swiftly

Review: Spelling Spree

Syllable Scramble Rearrange the syllables to write a Basic or Review Word. One syllable in each item is extra.

Example: ful ion watch *watchful*

5. tire al ment re
6. get for ous ful
7. less plore speech
8. er ence pow ful

9. ness able good
10. ment ern ly gov
11. pale re ness
12. ful fear tive
13. close ceed ness
14. tle ing set ment
15. ture ly lone
16. light sion ful de

17. ac ly tive ed
18. ness ure soft
19. cheer ic ful
20. joy ment tion en

How Are You Doing?

List the spelling words that are hard for you. Practice them with a family member.

Proofreading and Writing

Proofread for Spelling Find nine misspelled Basic or Review Words in this detective's log. Write each one correctly.

Tuesday, March 12

What a dredful assignment! I spend contless hours in the basment of this apartment building keeping a wachful eye on the residents. There has been a lot of movment in one of the apartments latly. I wait, brethless, because I can't afford to be carless. Powerful people may have their headquarters here, and the government wants the criminals safly behind bars.

Write a Book Jacket Blurb

Write a book jacket blurb for an imaginary book. Write a few exciting sentences about the book. Try to use five spelling words.

Proofreading Tip

Read your paper from right to left. This will make you focus on each word by itself.

Proofreading Marks

¶ Indent
∧ Add
⌒ Delete
≡ Capital letter
/ Small letter

Expanding Vocabulary

Spelling Word Link

basement

goober
porch
tap
firefly
attic
basement
drinking fountain
milk shake

Regional Differences People from various regions of the United States call some things by different names. What is this sandwich called?

HERO   submarine   bomber   hoagie   GRINDER   WEDGE

Write a word from the box that has the same meaning as each numbered word. Use your Spelling Dictionary.

1. veranda
2. lightning bug
3. faucet
4. bubbler
5. garret
6. peanut
7. cellar
8. frappe

Fact File

Most of the names for this long sandwich are found in the northeast United States. In Maine it is called an "Italian" sandwich. Upstate New Yorkers call it a "bomber," while downstate speakers call it a "wedge."

Real-World Connection

Language Arts: Mysteries All the words in the box relate to mysteries. Look up these words in your Spelling Dictionary. Then write the words to complete this book jacket blurb.

Spelling Word Link

suspenseful

mystery
suspect
baffle
solve
motive
weapon
guilty
evidence

Miss Jane Marple and Hercule Poirot are fictional detectives, creations of the famous __(1)__ writer Agatha Christie. No crime will ever __(2)__ these two! They always find the __(3)__ person. How do they __(4)__ a case? They examine every bit of __(5)__ . They find out which __(6)__ was used to commit the crime. They question every __(7)__ to determine who had a __(8)__ , or reason, for committing the crime.

ONE SPY TOO MANY

Try This CHALLENGE

Yes or No? Write *yes* if the underlined word is used correctly. Write *no* if it is not.

9. The prosecutor submitted the shoes as <u>evidence</u>.
10. The innocent person was <u>guilty</u>.
11. A <u>motive</u> was used to commit the crime.
12. The gun was the <u>weapon</u> found at the crime scene.

Final |n| or |ən|, |chər|, |zhər|

Read and Say

|zhər|
treasure

Basic

READ the sentences. **SAY** each bold word.

1.	mountain	We will climb the **mountain**.
2.	treasure	Where did he bury the **treasure**?
3.	culture	We are studying African **culture**.
4.	fountain	Let's sit near the water **fountain**.
5.	creature	A dolphin is a smart sea **creature**.
6.	captain	The **captain** gave an order.
7.	future	I plan to grow corn in the **future**.
8.	adventure	Jon likes exciting **adventure** stories.
9.	moisture	This dry plant needs **moisture**.
10.	surgeon	A **surgeon** removed my tonsils.
11.	lecture	She gave a **lecture** on wildlife.
12.	curtain	Please hang the **curtain**.
13.	pasture	The cows are grazing in the **pasture**.
14.	measure	Erin will **measure** one yard of cloth.
15.	fixture	This light **fixture** has a loose wire.
16.	feature	A radio is a **feature** of most cars.
17.	furniture	We bought new bedroom **furniture**.
18.	pleasure	Working in a garden can be a **pleasure**.
19.	mixture	The paint is a **mixture** of red and blue.
20.	luncheon	I ate chicken at the **luncheon**.

Think and Write

Each word has the final |n|, |ən|, |chər|, or |zhər| sounds:

|n| or |ən| capt**ain** |chər| cul**ture** |zhər| trea**sure**

• What is one pattern for the final |n| or |ən| sounds? What is one pattern for the final |chər| sounds? What is one pattern for the final |zhər| sounds? How are the |ən| sounds spelled in the Elephant Words? **Now write each Basic Word under its final sounds.**

|n| or |ən|	|chər|	|zhər|

Review		Challenge	
Review	23. capture	**Challenge**	28. architecture
21. nature	24. bridge	26. departure	29. texture
22. picture	25. climb	27. leisure	30. villain

Independent Practice

Spelling Strategy

When you hear these final sounds, think of these patterns: |n| or |ən| *ain*, |chər| *ture*, |zhər| *sure*.

Word Analysis/Phonics Complete the exercises with Basic Words.

1–2. Write the two words that have the |ē| sound spelled *ea*.

3–5. Write the three words that have the |ĕ| sound spelled *ea*.

6–7. Write the two words that have the |ou| sound.

Vocabulary: Analogies Write a Basic Word to complete each analogy.

8. *Chicken* is to *meat* as *chair* is to _____.

9. *Morning* is to *breakfast* as *afternoon* is to _____.

10. *Day* is to *night* as *past* is to _____.

11. *Sew* is to *tailor* as *operate* is to _____.

12. *Lamp* is to *shade* as *window* is to _____.

13. *Airplane* is to *pilot* as *ship* is to _____.

Challenge Words Write the Challenge Word that fits each clue. Use your Spelling Dictionary.

14. free time

15. antonym of *hero*

16. a style of building

17. antonym of *arrival*

18. the feel of a surface

Spelling-Meaning Connection

To remember to spell the |ch| sound in *moisture* with a *t*, think of the *t* in the related word *moist*.

19–20. Write *moisture*. Then write the word that helps you remember how to spell the |ch| sound in *moisture*.

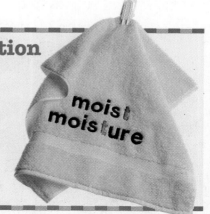

145

Review: Spelling Spree

Jobs Match Write a Basic or Review Word that names something each person makes or something or someone each person works with.

1. carpenter
2. chef
3. photographer
4. chemist
5. architect
6. tailor
7. nurse
8. zookeeper
9. sailor

Word Clues Write a Basic or Review Word to fit each clue.

10. This is where cows graze.
11. This is a speech that gives information about something.
12. You might see this hanging from the ceiling.
13. This is taller than a hill.
14. This is not the past or the present.
15. You must do this to get to the top of a cliff.
16. Trees, plants, and animals are part of this.
17. You will find this in a wet basement.
18. This is a full-length film.
19. You do this to find out how tall a person is.
20. This is a good place to get a drink of water.
21. A sheriff must do this when a prisoner escapes.
22. This is an exciting, dangerous experience.
23. This is something that is valued highly.
24. Customs, beliefs, and ways of life are part of this.

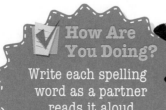

How Are You Doing?

Write each spelling word as a partner reads it aloud. Did you misspell any words?

Proofreading and Writing

Proofread: Spelling and Quotation Marks Set off a speaker's exact words with **quotation marks**. Capitalize the first word of the quotation. Put end marks inside the quotation marks.

Juan said, "The explorer Paul Cohen gave a talk."
"What did he talk about?" asked Kim.

Find four misspelled Basic or Review Words, one word that needs a capital letter, and two missing quotation marks in this part of a school newspaper article. Write the article correctly.

Famous Explorer Visits

"Mr. Cohen, who is the captian of an exploration team, spoke to our class last week,"said student council president Juan Varela. "He showed a picher of some tresure he found in a cave on a mountain.

"What an adventure he had! said Nicole. "his talk did capure the thrill of the discovery."

Basic
1. mountain
2. treasure
3. culture
4. fountain
5. creature
6. captain
7. future
8. adventure
9. moisture
10. surgeon
11. lecture
12. curtain
13. pasture
14. measure
15. fixture
16. feature
17. furniture
18. pleasure
19. mixture
20. luncheon

Review
21. nature
22. picture
23. capture
24. bridge
25. climb

Challenge
26. departure
27. leisure
28. architecture
29. texture
30. villain

Write Quotations

Write sentences that different people might say. Try to use five spelling words. Be sure to use quotation marks.

The hiker said, "Please hand me the rope."

Proofreading Tip

Check that you used punctuation marks and capital letters correctly when writing quotations.

Proofreading Marks
¶ Indent
∧ Add
⌐ Delete
≡ Capital letter
/ Small letter

147

Vocabulary Enrichment

Expanding Vocabulary

The Word Root *ven* or *vent* *Adventure* has the word root *vent*, meaning "to come." *Adventure* is related to *advent*, which means "the coming or arrival of something important." (The word root *vent* is sometimes spelled *ven*.)

Match the definitions in the chart to the words in the box. Fill in the missing letters for each word. Use your Spelling Dictionary.

Spelling Word Link

adventure

convention
invent
circumvent
event
prevent

Meaning	Word
a gathering of people for a meeting	1. _____? _____ *ven* _____?_____
to make up or create	2. _____?_____ *vent*
a happening	3. _____?_____ *vent*
to go around	4. _____?_____ *vent*
to keep from happening	5. _____?_____ *vent*

Work Together With a partner, write a caption for each picture. Use a word with *ven* or *vent* from the chart in each sentence.

6.

7.

Real-World Connection

Social Studies: Exploration All of the names in the box relate to exploration. Look up these names in your Spelling Dictionary. Then write the names to complete the time line.

| A.D. 1000 | 1254–1324 | 1492 | 1497 | 1521 | 1540–1596 | 1774–1809 | 1909 |

The Viking __(1)__ reached America around A.D. 1000.

A merchant who made trips to China was __(2)__ .

In 1492 __(3)__ reached America.

In 1497 __(4)__ claimed America for England.

While trying to sail around the world, __(5)__ died.

The English explorer __(6)__ was also a naval hero.

The Pacific Northwest was explored by __(7)__ .

The North Pole was first reached by __(8)__ in 1909.

Spelling Word Link

adventure

Marco Polo
Leif Ericson
John Cabot
Sir Francis Drake
Ferdinand Magellan
Christopher Columbus
Robert Peary
Meriwether Lewis

Try This CHALLENGE

Clue Match Write a word from the box to match each clue.

9. He sailed for the Indies but found America instead.
10. He followed the caravan routes to China.
11. He made several Arctic expeditions.
12. He led the British navy under Queen Elizabeth I.

 Fact File

In 1924–1925 Delia Akeley crossed undeveloped parts of Africa from east to west all by herself. During her trip she lived with and studied Pygmy tribes. She later published her studies.

24 Review: Units 19–23

Unit 19   VCV Pattern   pages 120–125

behave	rapid	equal	closet	robot
novel	aware	camel	shadow	record

Spelling Strategy   To find the syllables of a VCV word, remember to divide the word before or after the consonant. Look for spelling patterns you have learned. Note the spelling of the unstressed syllable, and spell the word by syllables.

Each word below is missing a syllable. Write the word.

1. clos | _____
2. ro | _____
3. shad | _____
4. rap | _____
5. cam | _____
6. nov | _____

Write the word that fits each meaning.

7. the same
8. conscious of something
9. to act in a certain way
10. to set down in writing

squeeze**ing**

Unit 20   Words with *-ed* or *-ing*   pages 126–131

delivered	amusing	directing	attending	deserved
resulting	squeezing	collapsed	providing	arrested

Spelling Strategy

amuse - e + ing = amus**ing**

direct + ing = direct**ing**

Write the word that rhymes with each word below.

11. freezing
12. shivered
13. swerved
14. consulting
15. tested
16. mending

Write the word that is a synonym for each word below.

17. toppled
18. managing
19. supplying
20. entertaining

150

Unit 21   More Words with *-ed* or *-ing*   pages 132–137

winning	gathering	covered	planned	mixed
ordered	suffering	begged	swimming	spotted

drip p **ed**

Spelling Strategy

ONE-SYLLABLE WORDS:
spot + t + ed = spot**ted**

TWO-SYLLABLE WORDS:
cover + ed = cover**ed**

Write the word that completes each analogy.

21. *Zebra* is to *striped* as *leopard* is to _____.
22. *Polite* is to *courteous* as *hurting* is to _____.
23. *Finished* is to *incomplete* as *losing* is to _____.
24. *Court* is to *basketball* as *pool* is to _____.

Write the word that fits each meaning.

25. arranged in sequence   27. intended   29. blended
26. bringing together   28. pleaded   30. put over

Unit 22   Words with Suffixes   pages 138–143

actively	cheerful	paleness	government	speechless
softness	lately	countless	forgetful	settlement

watchful

Spelling Strategy   A **suffix** is a word part added to the end of
a base word. A suffix adds meaning to the word. The word parts **-ly**,
-ful, **-ness**, **-less**, and **-ment** are suffixes. The spelling of the base word
is usually not changed when the suffix begins with a consonant.

Write the word that fits each clue.

31. antonym of *few*   33. recently   35. unable to speak
32. antonym of *gloomy*   34. busily   36. lack of color

Write the word that completes each sentence.

37. The President is the highest _____ official.
38. Jamestown was the first permanent English _____ in America.
39. Tina cannot remember anything. She is so _____.
40. Surprised by its _____, Joseph stroked the kitten's fur.

|zhər|
treasure

Unit 23 Final |n| or |ən|, |chər|, |zhər| pages 144–149

culture	creature	mountain	treasure	surgeon
curtain	mixture	pleasure	furniture	luncheon

Spelling Strategy

|n| or |ən| → **ain** |chər| → **ture** |zhər| → **sure**

Write the word that belongs in each group. Then circle the words that have the final |chər| sounds.

41. beast, animal, _____
42. joy, delight, _____
43. blend, combination, _____

44. river, valley, _____
45. shade, blind, _____

Write the word that fits each clue.

46. a way of life
47. a doctor
48. chairs and tables

49. a midday meal
50. a precious object

Challenge Words Units 19–23 pages 120–149

module	entertaining	catering	anticipated	nuisance
leisure	suspiciously	scalloped	architecture	seriousness

Write the word that fits each meaning.

51. providing food and drink
52. baked in a casserole with sauce
53. the art of designing buildings
54. relaxation
55. someone who is annoying

Write the word that fits each clue. Then circle the word in which a final e is dropped before -ed or -ing is added.

56. antonym of *humor*
57. synonym for *amusing*
58. antonym of *unexpected*

59. antonym of *trustfully*
60. synonym for *unit*

Spelling-Meaning Strategy

Consonant Changes: The Sound of *t*

create
creature

You know that some words in a word family often have the same spellings for different sounds. Read this paragraph.

> I love to **create** animals from things I find outdoors. Yesterday I made a funny **creature** from moss, leaves, and sticks.

Think

- What does *create* mean? What does *creature* mean? How are they related in meaning?
- What sound does the letter *t* spell in each word?

Here are more related words in which the spelling remains the same even though the sound of the **t** changes.

depar**t**	habi**t**	fac**t**
depar**t**ure	habi**t**ual	fac**t**ual

Apply and Extend

Complete these activities on a separate sheet of paper.

1. Look up the meanings of the words in the word box above in your Spelling Dictionary. Then write six sentences, using one of the words in each sentence.

2. With a partner list as many words as you can that are related to *create, depart, habit,* and *fact*. Then look in the section titled "Consonant Changes: The Sound of *t*" beginning on page 270 of your Spelling-Meaning Index. Add any other words that you find in these families to your list.

Summing Up

The sound of a final *t* may change when an ending or a suffix is added. Thinking of a related word can help you remember that the |ch| sound can be spelled *t*.

Description

from

A Zillion Stars

by Yoshiko Uchida

Rumi, a city child, is visiting a farm. Which of your five senses does this description appeal to?

The barn was nice and cool, and it smelled of fresh hay and animals. I looked for the mules and found them outside standing in the hot sun, swishing flies with their tails. I lured them over to the fence with some weeds I pulled from the ground, but when they got close and sniffed the weeds, they just bared their huge yellow teeth at me.

I finally found Rick, the old collie, lying in the shade of the walnut tree, and he gave me a friendly wag of his tail. His nose felt cool and wet even in all that heat, and when I scratched his head, he thumped his tail again.

I walked out a little way after that, right up to the edge of the vineyards. They looked as though they went on forever, curving clear around the entire world, and I could feel the sun beating down on them and on my head like a silent drum. There were no sounds of streetcars or rumbling delivery trucks. I felt as though somebody had put a huge glass bowl over my head that cut out all the sounds of the world.

Think and Discuss

1. What **sense words**, such as *huge yellow teeth*, tell what Rumi saw, heard, smelled, and felt?

2. What **exact words** did the author use to name the dog, a tree, and the fields on the farm?

3. To what did the author **compare** the heat of the sun?

4. How are the **details** organized?

The Writing Process
Description

Choose something interesting that you can use at least three senses (sight, sound, smell, taste, and touch) to describe. Write a description, keeping the guidelines in mind. Follow the Writing Process.

1 Prewriting
- Make a word web of the five senses. List words that describe how your subject looks, sounds, smells, feels, or tastes.

2 Draft
- Write something interesting about your subject in your first sentence.

3 Revise
- Use your Thesaurus to find exact words.
- Have a writing conference. Ask your partner to draw your subject. Do you need to add any details?

4 Proofread
- Did you spell each word correctly?
- Did you use capital letters, end marks, and commas correctly?

5 Publish
- Make a neat, final copy, and add a good title.
- Make a poster to share your description.

···· Guidelines for Writing a Description

✓ Open with an interesting topic sentence.
✓ Use details to create a clear picture.
✓ Use sense words, exact words, and comparisons.
✓ Put the details in an easy-to-follow order.

Composition Words

freezing
slammed
breathless
softness
watchful
shadow
amusing
vanish

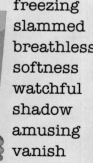

The Forest

Final |ĭj|, |ĭv|, and |ĭs|

Read and Say

luggage

Basic

READ the sentences. **SAY** each bold word.

1. voyage	The sea **voyage** took five days.
2. baggage	Did you take much **baggage** on your trip?
3. luggage	I try to limit my **luggage** to one suitcase.
4. native	My mother is a **native** of this area.
5. language	Can you speak more than one **language**?
6. postage	This letter needs fifty cents **postage**.
7. notice	Did you **notice** the color of her eyes?
8. creative	Liz is a very **creative** artist.
9. practice	I **practice** the flute every day.
10. knowledge	He has no **knowledge** of the surprise.
11. captive	The pirate hid the **captive** in a cave.
12. average	Pepper is just an **average** dog.
13. justice	I believe in equal **justice** for all.
14. bandage	Put a **bandage** on that cut.
15. message	Did you read my **message**?
16. service	Our bus **service** is good.
17. shortage	There was a **shortage** of food at the party.
18. passage	The **passage** between the buildings is narrow.
19. detective	The **detective** found a clue.
20. relative	My grandfather is my oldest **relative**.

Think and Write

Each word has the final |ĭj|, |ĭv|, or |ĭs| sounds.

|ĭj| voy**age** |ĭv| nat**ive** |ĭs| not**ice**

• What is one pattern for the final |ĭj| sounds? What is one pattern for the final |ĭv| sounds? What is one pattern for the final |ĭs| sounds? How is the Elephant Word different?

Now write each Basic Word under its final sounds.

|ĭj|	|ĭv|	|ĭs|

Review	23. manage	**Challenge**	28. apprentice
21. village	24. cottage	26. heritage	29. superlative
22. package	25. marriage	27. cooperative	30. primitive

Independent Practice

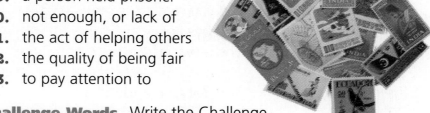

Spelling Strategy When you hear the final |ĭj|, |ĭv|, or |ĭs| sounds, think of these patterns:

|ĭj| *age* |ĭv| *ive* |ĭs| *ice*

Word Analysis/Phonics Complete the exercise with Basic Words.

1–5. Write the words with these base words.

1. pass   **2.** bag   **3.** detect   **4.** relate   **5.** create

Vocabulary: Definitions Write a Basic Word that fits each meaning.

6. the charge for mailing
7. a covering for a wound
8. facts and ideas
9. a person held prisoner
10. not enough, or lack of
11. the act of helping others
12. the quality of being fair
13. to pay attention to

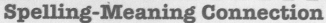

Challenge Words Write the Challenge Word that completes each sentence. Use your Spelling Dictionary.

14. The tourists explored the ruins of a _____ civilization.
15. We went to Jamestown to learn about our nation's _____.
16. The actor received an award for his _____ performance.
17. To work well with others, you must be _____.
18. Amelia, a carpenter's _____, enjoys learning her new trade.

Spelling-Meaning Connection

How can you remember how to spell the |s| sound in *practice*? Think of the related word *practical*. The sound of the *c* changes, but the spelling remains the same.

19–20. Write *practice* and *practical*. Then underline the letter in *practical* that helps you spell the |s| sound in *practice*.

practice
practical

Review: Spelling Spree

Picture Clues Write a Basic or Review Word for each clue.

1.  + t + age   6. + age

2. + g + age   7. − e + ice

3. + age   8. + age

4. + age   9. − e + ice

5. + age   10. + t + ive

Ending Match Write Basic or Review Words by matching word parts and endings. Be sure to write each ending correctly.

|ĭj| |ĭv| |ĭs|

11. lugg
12. relat
13. creat
14. just
15. aver
16. marri
17. nat
18. detect

19. knowl
20. short
21. vill
22. langu
23. pract
24. pass
25. voy

How Are You Doing?

Write your spelling words in ABC order. Practice any misspelled words with a family member.

Proofreading and Writing

Proofread: Spelling and Titles A person's title is often abbreviated. The abbreviation begins with a capital letter and ends with a period. (See also page 247 in your Student's Handbook.)

Mister **Mr.**   Doctor **Dr.**   Junior **Jr.**

Find four misspelled Basic or Review Words, two missing periods, and one missing capital letter in this announcement. Write the announcement correctly.

Mr John Kurt and his son, John Kurt, jr, will speak to the Travel Club about their voage to the African country of Ghana. They will share their knowlege of the native languge, the villige life, and the creative crafts of Ghana.

Basic

1. voyage
2. baggage
3. luggage
4. native
5. language
6. postage
7. notice
8. creative
9. practice
10. knowledge
11. captive
12. average
13. justice
14. bandage
15. message
16. service
17. shortage
18. passage
19. detective
20. relative

Review
21. village
22. package
23. manage
24. cottage
25. marriage

Challenge
26. heritage
27. cooperative
28. apprentice
29. superlative
30. primitive

Write a Post Card

Write a post card from a place you have been, a place you would like to go, or an imaginary place. Address the post card. Try to use five spelling words and one abbreviation for a person's title. Share your post card.

Proofreading Tip

Check that you used capital letters and periods correctly when abbreviating titles for people.

Proofreading Marks

¶ Indent
∧ Add
⌐ Delete
≡ Capital letter
/ Small letter

159

Unit 25 BONUS

Spelling Word Link

passage

Multiple-Meaning Words: *passage* You can read a passage about a ship's passage through a narrow passage. *Passage* has many meanings!

pas·sage |păs′ ĭj| *n., pl.* **passages** **1.** The act or process of passing: *The river is deep enough for safe passage.* **2.** A journey. **3.** A narrow path or channel. **4.** Approval of law by a legislative body. **5.** A part of a written work or piece of music.

Write *1, 2, 3, 4,* or *5* to show which meaning of *passage* is used in each sentence.

1. The underground <u>passage</u> was dark and scary. _____

2. The senator thinks that <u>passage</u> of the bill is certain. _____

3. Is this your first <u>passage</u> across the ocean? _____

4. Lynn was unaware of the <u>passage</u> of time. _____

5. Let me read you a <u>passage</u> from my favorite story. _____

Show You Know! Look up *staff* in your Spelling Dictionary. Then write a caption for each picture, using a different meaning for *staff* in each one.

6.

7.

8.

9.

Vocabulary Enrichment

Real-World Connection

Social Studies: Travel All the words in the box relate to travel. Look up these words in your Spelling Dictionary. Then write the words to complete this entry in a travel diary.

Spelling Word Link

voyage

region
porter
customs
schedule
scenic
sightseer
berth
passport

The movement of the train woke me, and I sat up in my __(1)__. My curiosity about new places made me an eager __(2)__. I pulled aside the curtain to enjoy the __(3)__ countryside. I had never seen this __(4)__ of the world. We arrived at the Swiss border at 7:55 A.M.—right on __(5)__. The train had to wait while the __(6)__ officer examined each person's __(7)__. When I arrived in Bern, I found a __(8)__ to help carry my bags.

Try This CHALLENGE

Yes or No? Write *yes* if the underlined word is used correctly. Write *no* if it is not.

9. Many artists have painted this <u>scenic</u> countryside.
10. Next summer we will tour the northern <u>berth</u>.
11. According to my <u>passport</u>, the train is late.
12. At the border you must pass a <u>customs</u> inspection.

★★★ Fact File

The Great Wall of China, constructed to prevent invasion, winds more than fifteen hundred miles across mountains and desert. Built by hand, it is the world's longest structure.

Spelling Unstressed Syllables

Read and Say

spinach   carrot

Basic

READ the sentences. **SAY** each bold word.

1.	pilgrim	The **pilgrim** will visit the famous place.
2.	worship	This church is a place of **worship**.
3.	forbid	The rules **forbid** running in the hall.
4.	distance	Measure the **distance** between the rows.
5.	hidden	The money is **hidden** in a safe place.
6.	repair	My dad will **repair** the broken toy.
7.	dozen	There are twelve eggs in a **dozen**.
8.	destroy	Did a fire **destroy** these homes?
9.	carrot	Add a chopped **carrot** to the soup.
10.	entry	She wrote a new **entry** in her diary.
11.	wisdom	My grandmother has a lot of **wisdom**.
12.	crystal	This vase is made of **crystal**.
13.	respond	Please **respond** to the question.
14.	program	Did you see the **program** about bears?
15.	solid	Is this door **solid** or hollow?
16.	salute	The troops **salute** the flag.
17.	spinach	I grew **spinach** in my garden.
18.	ashamed	Do not be **ashamed** to ask for help.
19.	blossom	This plant has a bright red **blossom**.
20.	neglect	The dog will starve if you **neglect** it.

Think and Write

Each two-syllable word has the VCCV, VCCCV, or VCV syllable pattern. Study the unstressed syllable, as the vowel sound is often unclear.

re | pair |rĭ pâr′| **dis | tance** |dĭs′ təns|

• Where is each Basic Word divided into syllables? Which syllable is unstressed?

Now write each Basic Word under its syllable pattern. Underline the unstressed syllable.

VCCV	VCCCV	VCV

Review		**Challenge**	
21. harvest	23. allow	26. refuge	28. somber
22. honest	24. whether	27. charter	29. exert
	25. middle		30. adapt

Independent Practice

Spelling Strategy To spell a two-syllable word, divide the word into syllables. Spell the word by syllables, noting carefully the spelling of the unstressed syllable.

Word Analysis/Phonics Complete the exercises with Basic Words.

1–3. Write the three words that have double consonants.

4–8. Write the words that have the underlined syllables below.

    4. <u>for</u>get **5.** <u>spin</u>ner **6.** <u>wor</u>ry **7.** <u>dis</u>like **8.** a<u>gree</u>

Vocabulary: Analogies Write the Basic Word that completes each analogy.

  9. *Two* is to *pair* as *twelve* is to _____.
10. *Question* is to *ask* as *answer* is to _____.
11. *Beautiful* is to *beauty* as *wise* is to _____.
12. *Metal* is to *silver* as *glass* is to _____.
13. *Reduce* is to *increase* as *break* is to _____.

Challenge Words Write the Challenge Word that fits each meaning. Use your Spelling Dictionary.

14. apply effort
15. serious
16. protection
17. to change for a certain purpose
18. a written formal document granting certain rights

Spelling-Meaning Connection

Did you know that the words *enter, entry,* and *entrance* are related in meaning? They all come from a Latin word meaning "within." **Think of this:** *Enter* the building through the *entry.*

| enter |
| enter |
| entry |
| entrance |

19–20. Write *enter*. Then write the Basic Word that is related to *enter*.

Review: Spelling Spree

Finding Words Each word below is hidden in a Basic or Review Word. Write the Basic or Review Word.

Example: is *wisdom*

1. pond
2. vest
3. gram
4. bid
5. hid
6. nest
7. pin
8. grim
9. lid
10. ship
11. pair
12. shame

Questions Write the Basic or Review Word that answers each of these questions.

13. What do military officers do when they meet?
14. What helps you make good decisions?
15. Which word rhymes with *together*?
16. What could cause a garden to fill up with weeds?
17. What does a yardstick measure?
18. What is a stronger word for *damage*?
19. What is a solid with a regular pattern, such as a snowflake?
20. What is halfway between two points?
21. What is another word for a flower?
22. What does every room have?
23. What is a set of twelve called?
24. What is a synonym for *permit*?
25. What is a vegetable that is popular with rabbits?

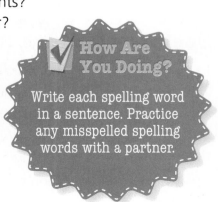

How Are You Doing?

Write each spelling word in a sentence. Practice any misspelled spelling words with a partner.

Proofreading and Writing

Proofread: Spelling and Titles Capitalize the first, the last, and all important words in a title. Underline the titles of books, magazines, newspapers, and movies. Put quotation marks around the titles of short stories, songs, articles, book chapters, and most poems.

BOOK: <u>At Home in a New Land</u>   POEM: "The Promise"

Find four misspelled Basic or Review Words, two missing capital letters, and two missing quotation marks in this book report. Write the book report correctly.

Title: <u>a Salute to america</u>

Author: Beth Ray

About the Book: This book

includes a dosen stories about the American

Colonies. One story titled The Harvest is about an English

girl who sails the long distants to America in the midle

of winter. Bad storms almost distroy the ship.

Basic

1. pilgrim
2. worship
3. forbid
4. distance
5. hidden
6. repair
7. dozen
8. destroy
9. carrot
10. entry
11. wisdom
12. crystal
13. respond
14. program
15. solid
16. salute
17. spinach
18. ashamed
19. blossom
20. neglect

Review

21. harvest
22. honest
23. allow
24. whether
25. middle

Challenge

26. refuge
27. charter
28. somber
29. exert
30. adapt

Write a Book List

Write the titles for five books, stories, or poems that you would recommend. Add a sentence telling why you like each one. Try to use five spelling words. Post your list.

Proofreading Tip

Check that you used capital letters and underlines or quotation marks correctly in each title.

Proofreading Marks

¶ Indent
∧ Add
 ⌐ Delete
≡ Capital letter
/ Small letter

Expanding Vocabulary

Antonyms This child tried to *repair* the kite, but he accidentally *destroyed* it. *Repair* and *destroy* are **antonyms**, or words that have opposite meanings.

Spelling Word Link

repair
destroy

hollow
ignorance
proud
allow
visible
exit

Write the word from the box that is an antonym for each word in the circle. Use your Spelling Dictionary.

hidden	1. ?
forbid	2. ?
entry	3. ?
solid	4. ?
wisdom	5. ?
ashamed	6. ?

Work Together Work with a partner to write six sentences, using the pairs of antonyms above.

Example: The people will come into the room through the <u>entry</u> on the left, and they will leave through the <u>exit</u> on the right.

Real-World Connection

Social Studies: The Pilgrims All the words in the box relate to the Pilgrims. Look up these words in your Spelling Dictionary. Then write the words to complete this paragraph from a social studies book.

Spelling Word Link

pilgrim

freedom
Mayflower
Puritans
Plymouth
hardships
governor
treaty
prosper

The Pilgrims

The Pilgrims belonged to a religious group known as __(1)__. Seeking religious __(2)__, the Pilgrims sailed to America on the __(3)__ and settled __(4)__ Colony. John Carver was the first __(5)__ of the colony. During their first winter the Pilgrims suffered many __(6)__. In the spring they signed a peace __(7)__ with the Wampanoag Indians. The Wampanoags showed the Pilgrims where to fish and how to grow crops, and the colony started to __(8)__.

Yes or No? Write *yes* if the underlined word is used correctly. Write *no* if it is not.

9. The Pilgrims came to America on <u>hardships</u>.
10. The Pilgrims chose a governor to lead the <u>colony</u>.
11. A <u>treaty</u> was served at the harvest feast.
12. The Pilgrims worked hard in order to <u>prosper</u>.

 Fact File

According to legend, the first thing the Pilgrims stepped on when they landed in America was Plymouth Rock. This rock is on display in Plymouth, Massachusetts.

Words with Prefixes

Read and Say

in crease

		READ the sentences. **SAY** each bold word.

Basic

1. *disaster* — The forest fire was a **disaster**.
2. *unknown* — The cause of her illness is **unknown**.
3. *discover* — Did you **discover** what happened?
4. *unable* — The baby is **unable** to walk yet.
5. *inform* — Please **inform** me of any change.
6. *increase* — The cost of milk will **increase** by ten cents.
7. *report* — She wrote a science **report**.
8. *dispute* — Will the losing team **dispute** the score?
9. *insist* — I **insist** that you come to the party.
10. *remind* — **Remind** me to water the plants if I forget.
11. *insult* — You will **insult** him if you go home now.
12. *regard* — She holds her sister in high **regard**.
13. *install* — Did you **install** a new radio in your car?
14. *dismiss* — Mr. Lee will **dismiss** us early for recess.
15. *relax* — We like to **relax** at the beach.
16. *unaware* — I was **unaware** of the change in plans.
17. *disagree* — People with different ideas may **disagree**.
18. *unskilled* — The **unskilled** worker will need training.
19. *revenge* — We must win this game to **revenge** our loss.
20. *display* — The artist will **display** his paintings.

Think and Write

A **base word** can stand alone. A **prefix** and a **word root** are word parts. They cannot stand alone. A prefix is added to the beginning of a base word or a word root. It adds meaning to a word.

PREFIX + BASE WORD: **un**able   **dis**agree

PREFIX + WORD ROOT: **in**sist   **re**port

• What four prefixes do you see?

Now write each Basic Word under its prefix.

un-	dis-	in-	re-

Review	23. rebuild
21. unsure	24. disorder
22. dislike	25. uneven

Challenge	28. unnecessary
26. inquiry	29. inflate
27. unfortunate	30. responsible

Independent Practice

Spelling Strategy   A **prefix** is a word part added to the beginning of a base word or a word root. A prefix adds meaning. *Un-*, *in-*, *dis-*, and *re-* are prefixes. Find the prefix and the base word or the word root. Spell the word by parts.

Word Analysis/Phonics   Complete the exercise with Basic Words.

1–5.   Write five words by changing the underlined prefixes.

1. <u>im</u>port
2. <u>dis</u>able
3. <u>re</u>cover
4. <u>re</u>sult
5. <u>de</u>crease

Vocabulary: Definitions   Write a Basic Word that fits each meaning.

6. to send away
7. to fail to agree
8. to cause to remember
9. not familiar
10. to show
11. to make less tense
12. lacking skills or training
13. to argue or debate

Challenge Words   Write the Challenge Word that completes each sentence. Use your Spelling Dictionary.

14. The boating accident was due to _____ circumstances.
15. Strong winds and high waves were _____ for the accident.
16. The passengers were able to _____ their life raft.
17. Would the Coast Guard conduct an _____?
18. As no other boat was involved, an investigation is _____.

Spelling-Meaning Connection

Insist contains the Latin word root *sist*, meaning "to stand." To insist is to "stand on" your wish or request. Other words with this root are *assist*, *resist*, and *consist*.

19–20.   Write *resist*. Then write the Basic Word that also has the word root *sist*.

in**sist**
as**sist**
re**sist**
con**sist**

Dictionary

Word History English has borrowed words from many languages. As words pass from one language to another, they often change in meaning. Read the history of *disaster*.

History

Disaster was formed from the Latin prefix *dis-*, meaning "away from," and the Greek word *ast*, meaning "star." *Disastro* meant "bad luck brought by the stars." When *disaster* came into English, it meant simply "something that causes destruction."

Practice Read the history of each word below in your Spelling Dictionary. Write the earlier form of the word, the language it came from, and what it meant.

1. robot   **2.** clue

Review: Spelling Spree

Alphabet Puzzler Write the Basic or Review Word that fits alphabetically between the two words in each group.

3. unpack, _____, unsound
4. inside, _____, inspect
5. under, _____, unit
6. reason, _____, recover
7. displace, _____, dispose
8. reject, _____, relay
9. dimple, _____, disappear
10. disk, _____, dismay
11. remember, _____, rent
12. inspire, _____, instead
13. disobey, _____, disorganize

14. instrument, _____, interest
15. dispose, _____, dissolve
16. rest, _____, review
17. unarmed, _____, unbroken
18. repair, _____, rescue
19. unsteady, _____, untie
20. dislike, _____, disorder

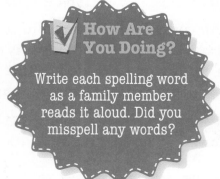

How Are You Doing?

Write each spelling word as a family member reads it aloud. Did you misspell any words?

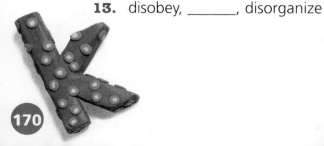

Proofreading and Writing

Proofread for Spelling Find eight misspelled Basic Words in this report. Write the words correctly.

News Bulletin

We just received this riport about a disastar that was avoided

today. Unaware of a patch of thin ice, a young girl fell into

Saw Pond. Without reguard for his own safety, an unnown

man crawled out on the ice. He threw his coat toward her and

pulled her to safety. When more help arrived, the rescuer left.

The child's parents have been unabel to discuver who he is.

If you know him, please informe the police. As a result of this

accident, Mayor Ames said that all parents must increese

their children's understanding of the danger of thin ice.

Basic

1. disaster
2. unknown
3. discover
4. unable
5. inform
6. increase
7. report
8. dispute
9. insist
10. remind
11. insult
12. regard
13. install
14. dismiss
15. relax
16. unaware
17. disagree
18. unskilled
19. revenge
20. display

Review

21. unsure
22. dislike
23. rebuild
24. disorder
25. uneven

Challenge

26. inquiry
27. unfortunate
28. unnecessary
29. inflate
30. responsible

Write a News Report

Write a short news report. Answer the questions *Who? What? When? Where? Why?* and *How?* Try to use five spelling words. "Broadcast" your news to classmates.

Proofreading Tip

Read your paper aloud to a partner to help you find missing words.

Proofreading Marks

¶   Indent
∧   Add
℘   Delete
≡   Capital letter
/   Small letter

Vocabulary Enrichment

Expanding Vocabulary

Spelling Word Link
uneven
disorder

Building Words with Prefixes and Suffixes You can add different prefixes and suffixes to base words to build new words. Look at the words you can build with *even*.

PREFIX	SUFFIX	BOTH
uneven	even**ly**	**un**even**ly**
	even**ness**	**un**even**ness**

Look at the diagram. Add different prefixes and suffixes to *order* and *complete* to write new words. To make most of the new words, add one prefix <u>or</u> one suffix. For some words, add one prefix <u>and</u> one suffix. For two new words, you must add <u>two</u> suffixes. Use your Spelling Dictionary.

PREFIXES
in-
dis-
re-

BASE WORDS
order
complete

SUFFIXES
-ly
-ness
-less

order

1. ?
2. ?
3. ?
4. ?
5. ?
6. ?

complete

7. ?
8. ?
9. ?
10. ?
11. ?

Work Together With a partner write five sentences, using any five of the words you built with *order* and *complete*.

Vocabulary Enrichment

Real-World Connection

Social Studies: The *Titanic* All the words in the box relate to the *Titanic*. Look up these words in your Spelling Dictionary. Then write the words to complete this paragraph.

TITANIC THOUGHT UNSINKABLE!

The *Titanic* was so well built that it was thought to be ___(1)___. It featured every kind of ___(2)___ for the pleasure of its ___(3)___. No one could have imagined that the *Titanic* would strike a floating body of ice, or ___(4)___, and sink into the ___(5)___ on its first voyage. An SOS, the ___(6)___ signal for help, was sent; but the rescue ship arrived too late. Some people managed to escape by ___(7)___, but those who died far outnumbered the ___(8)___.

The *Titanic*

Spelling Word Link

disaster

iceberg
passengers
luxury
survivors
lifeboat
emergency
Atlantic Ocean
unsinkable

Try This CHALLENGE

Yes or No? Write *yes* if the underlined word is used correctly. Write *no* if it is not.

9. Lianne put an <u>iceberg</u> in her juice.
10. The siren alerted everyone to the <u>emergency</u>.
11. The diamond necklace was a <u>luxury</u>.
12. The accident's <u>survivors</u> had been frightened.

 Fact File

Icebergs are huge bodies of ice that float in the sea. Most of the iceberg lies below the water. Icebergs are very dangerous to ships.

Changing Final *y* to *i*

Read and Say

scar**y**
scar**i**est

Basic

READ the sentences. **SAY** each bold word.

1.	liberties	Freedom of speech is one of our **liberties**.
2.	victories	Our team had two **victories** and one loss.
3.	countries	We visited five **countries** on our trip.
4.	spied	I **spied** a mouse in the field.
5.	enemies	The kind man has no **enemies**.
6.	armies	The **armies** trained for battle.
7.	scariest	The roller coaster is the **scariest** ride.
8.	dirtier	My muddy shoes are **dirtier** than his.
9.	happiness	Her children bring her **happiness**.
10.	abilities	We trust his cooking **abilities**.
11.	pitied	I **pitied** the runner who fell in the race.
12.	ladies	The **ladies** wore blue dresses.
13.	busier	The store is **busier** today than yesterday.
14.	duties	My **duties** are dusting and mopping.
15.	lilies	Plant the **lilies** near the tulips.
16.	worthiness	Do you question my **worthiness** for the job?
17.	tiniest	This puppy is the **tiniest** of the three dogs.
18.	emptiness	I had a feeling of **emptiness** when I left.
19.	replies	Your **replies** to my questions puzzle me.
20.	dizziness	Beth felt some **dizziness** after falling.

Think and Write

Each word has an ending or a suffix added to a base word.

army + es = arm**ies**   scary + est = scar**iest**
dirty + er = dirt**ier**   happy + ness = happ**iness**

• How does each base word change when an ending or a suffix is added? Does a vowel or a consonant come before the *y*?

Now write each Basic Word. Underline the letter that replaced the final *y* when the ending or the suffix was added.

Review   23. families
21. cities   24. studied
22. easier   25. angriest

Challenge   28. colonies
26. unified   29. rivalries
27. levied   30. strategies

Independent Practice

Spelling Strategy When a word ends with a consonant and *y*, change the *y* to *i* when adding *-es, -ed, -er, -est,* or *-ness*.

Word Analysis/Phonics Complete the exercises with Basic Words.

1–4. Write the plural of each word below.

    1. duty   **2.** army   **3.** enemy   **4.** liberty

5–7. Write the three words that have the |ī| sound.

Vocabulary: Making Inferences Write the Basic Word that fits each clue.

  8. These appear on a map.

  9. A winning team has these.

10. Your mother and aunt are examples of these.

11. This is what you feel when you get an A on a test.

12. People often experience this after spinning around.

13. You might find some of these in a field or a garden.

Challenge Words Write the Challenge Word that fits each definition. Use your Spelling Dictionary.

14. settled territories

15. made into a whole

16. plans of action

17. ordered something to be paid

18. fierce competitions

Spelling-Meaning Connection

How can you remember how to spell the schwa sound in *abilities*? Think of the |ā| sound in the related word *able*. **Think of this:** If you are *able* to draw, you have artistic *abilities*.

19–20. Write *able*. Then write the Basic Word that is related to *able* in spelling and meaning.

abilities
able

Review: Spelling Spree

Syllable Rhymes Write the Basic or Review Word that has a first syllable that rhymes with each word below.

1. ham
2. rib
3. slap
4. mud

5. when
6. tic
7. quiz

8. peas
9. star
10. shirt

Puzzle Play Write a Basic or Review Word to fit each clue. Circle the letter that would appear in the box.

Example: less difficult _ ☐ _ _ _ _ e(a)sier

11. nations _ _ _ _ _ _ _ ☐
12. very large towns _ _ ☐ _ _ _
13. the most angry ☐ _ _ _ _ _ _ _
14. answers ☐ _ _ _ _ _ _
15. most frightening _ _ _ _ _ _ ☐ _
16. women _ ☐ _ _ _ _
17. value _ _ _ _ _ _ ☐ _ _ _
18. watched secretly _ _ _ _ ☐
19. trumpet-shaped flowers _ _ _ _ _ _ ☐
20. felt sorry for _ _ ☐ _ _ _
21. having more to do _ _ _ _ _ _ ☐
22. the smallest _ ☐ _ _ _ _ _
23. nothing inside _ _ ☐ _ _ _ _ _ _
24. skills _ _ _ _ _ _ _ ☐ _
25. responsibilities _ _ _ _ _ ☐

Now write the circled letters in order below. They will spell three mystery words that are a nickname for the United States flag.

Mystery Words:

_ _ _ _ _ _ _ _
　　?　　　?

_ _ _ _ _ _ _
　　?

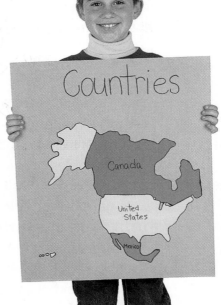

Proofreading and Writing

Proofread: Spelling and Business Letters Use a colon after the greeting in a business letter. Use a comma after the closing.

GREETING: Dear Mr. Armando**:**   CLOSING: Sincerely**,**

Find four misspelled words and two mistakes in punctuation in this part of a business letter. Write the letter correctly.

Dear Ms. Kaplan,

Welcome to your new dutys as the organizer of

our Community Volunteer Program. We are busyer

than ever, but I am sure that your abilites will make

our task easyier. With your leadership, our volunteers

will bring happiness to many more people in our town.

Sincerely
Paul Martinez
Paul Martinez

Basic

1. liberties
2. victories
3. countries
4. spied
5. enemies
6. armies
7. scariest
8. dirtier
9. happiness
10. abilities
11. pitied
12. ladies
13. busier
14. duties
15. lilies
16. worthiness
17. tiniest
18. emptiness
19. replies
20. dizziness

Review

21. cities
22. easier
23. families
24. studied
25. angriest

Challenge

26. unified
27. levied
28. colonies
29. rivalries
30. strategies

Write a Business Letter

★ I am ★
proud
★
to be a volunteer

How could volunteers make life easier or happier in your town? Share your ideas in a letter to the editor of your newspaper. Try to use five spelling words.

Proofreading Tip   **Check that you used a colon after the greeting and a comma after the closing.**

Proofreading Marks

¶ Indent
∧ Add
ꝰ Delete
≡ Capital letter
/ Small letter

Expanding Vocabulary

Thesaurus: Exact Words for *small* If you were given a hamburger the size of a quarter, you might say, "This hamburger is tiny!" Using the exact word *tiny* would make your point clearly.

Write the best word from the box to replace *small* in each sentence. Use your Thesaurus.

1. Jess carved a <u>small</u> model of a soldier.
2. The <u>small</u> infant was one hour old.
3. The human eye cannot see the <u>small</u> red blood cells.
4. The plan was perfect except for one <u>small</u> problem.
5. The plants were <u>small</u> this year because of dry weather.

Show You Know! Write a caption for each picture. Use the best word for *small* that fits the picture.

6.

7.

Vocabulary Enrichment

Unit 28
BONUS

Real-World Connection

Social Studies: The American Revolution All the words in the box relate to the American Revolution. Look up these words in your Spelling Dictionary. Then write the words to complete this paragraph from a social studies book.

Spelling Word Link

liberties

revolution
rebel
boycott
battleground
patriot
taxation
allegiance
independence

LESSON 2

Problems with Britain

By 1773 many American colonists felt no __(1)__ to Britain. When the British decided to tax tea and other basic products, the colonists thought that this __(2)__ was unfair. They chose to __(3)__ these products rather than pay the tax. These taxes and other problems led the colonists to __(4)__ and declare their __(5)__ from Britain. This caused a __(6)__, which turned America into a __(7)__. Every __(8)__ fought for the new country.

The Stamp Act created a new tax.

Try This CHALLENGE

Yes or No? Write *yes* if the underlined word is used correctly. Write *no* if it is not.

9. The colonists stopped buying tea as part of a <u>boycott</u>.
10. The government pays <u>taxation</u> to the people.
11. A <u>patriot</u> supports and protects his or her country.
12. He showed his <u>allegiance</u> by fighting for his country.

⭐⭐ **Fact File**

Powerful speeches helped spark the American Revolution. One of the most powerful was given by Patrick Henry, a Virginian, who said, "Give me liberty, or give me death."

179

Adding *-ion*

Read and Say

correction

Basic

READ the sentences. **SAY** each bold word.

1. *televise* — They plan to **televise** the program.
2. *television* — .Can we watch a movie on **television**?
3. *act* — I am going to **act** in the play.
4. *action* — The game was filled with **action**.
5. *regulate* — The lights **regulate** traffic.
6. *regulation* — The **regulation** forbids fishing here.
7. *locate* — I cannot **locate** my keys.
8. *location* — He lives in a good **location**.
9. *elect* — We will vote to **elect** a leader.
10. *election* — She won the **election** by ten votes.
11. *react* — How did he **react** to winning the award?
12. *reaction* — What was your **reaction** to the news?
13. *tense* — The big crowd made us feel **tense**.
14. *tension* — Changing schools can create **tension**.
15. *populate* — What animals **populate** this forest?
16. *population* — This town has a **population** of 890 people.
17. *convict* — Will the judge **convict** her of a crime?
18. *conviction* — We heard about the **conviction** of the thief.
19. *correct* — Are the answers wrong or **correct**?
20. *correction* — Make this **correction** to fix the mistake.

Think and Write

Each pair of words includes a verb and a noun. The noun is formed by adding the suffix *-ion* to the verb.

VERB:	elect	locat**e**
NOUN:	elect**ion**	locat**ion**

• What happens to the final *e* when *-ion* is added?

Now write each pair of Basic Words under the heading that tells what happens to the spelling of the verb when *-ion* is added.

No Spelling Change	Final *e* Dropped

Review
21. camera
22. movie
23. famous
24. minute
25. question

Challenge
26. animate   28. fascinate
27. animation 29. fascination

Independent Practice

Spelling Strategy Remember that the suffix *-ion* can change verbs into nouns. When a verb ends with *e*, drop the *e* before adding *-ion*.

Word Analysis/Phonics Complete the exercises with Basic Words.

1–2. Write the word pair with the prefix *con-*.

3–6. Write *act* and *action*. Then write the word pair that has a prefix added to *act* and *action*.

7–8. Write the two words that have double consonants.

Vocabulary: Context Sentences Write a Basic Word to complete each sentence.

9. Our local station will _____ the high school football game.
10. The show was filmed on _____ in Quebec, Canada.
11. How many hours of _____ do you watch every week?
12. If you are old enough, you should vote in every _____.
13. I cannot seem to _____ Tim's street on the map.
14. During the last five years, the town's _____ has increased.

Five years ago ✦✦✦✦✦
Today ✦✦✦✦✦✦✦✦   ✦ =1,000 people

Challenge Words Write a Challenge Word for each verb definition. Then write the related noun form. Use your Spelling Dictionary.

15–16. to attract the interest of   **17–18.** to bring to life

regulation
regulate

Spelling-Meaning Connection

To remember how to spell the |sh| sound in *regulation*, think of the *t* in *regulate*. The *t* is kept in *regulation* even though the sound changes.

19–20. Write *regulate* and *regulation*. Underline the letter in *regulate* that helps you spell the |sh| sound in *regulation*.

Dictionary

Primary and Secondary Stress You know that the syllables in a word are said with different levels of stress.

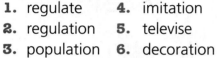

pop·u·late |pŏp′ yə lāt′|

The first syllable in *populate* is shown in dark print with a dark accent mark (′). It has **primary stress** and is said more strongly. The last syllable has **secondary stress**. It has a light accent mark (′) and is said with less stress.

Practice Write each word below in syllables. Underline the syllable with primary stress. Circle the syllable with secondary stress. Use your Spelling Dictionary.

1. regulate
2. regulation
3. population
4. imitation
5. televise
6. decoration

Review: Spelling Spree

Syllable Scramble Rearrange the syllables to write a Basic or Review Word. One syllable in each item is extra.

7. re er act
8. ness vict con
9. la reg al u tion
10. ly lect e
11. vic tion ex con
12. ic ac tion
13. lo de cate
14. cor tion rec less

15. late u en pop
16. e ful vise tel
17. cor er rect
18. sion ten vent
19. pre fa mous
20. reg u ist late
21. lec val e tion
22. u pop pro la tion

How Are You Doing?

Write each spelling word as a family member reads it aloud. Did you misspell any words?

Proofreading and Writing

Proofread for Spelling Find ten misspelled Basic or Review Words in this magazine interview. Write the words correctly.

Reporter: I know that you've been asked this qustion before, Tillie. How does it feel to be a famos star?

Tillie Burbanks: I love the riaction of my adoring fans. They won't leave me alone for a minite.

Reporter: You will soon begin filming a moovie for telavision. What's it about? Are you tenss?

Tillie Burbanks: It's a Western. The action will take place in New Mexico, and most scenes will be shot on loction. I can't wait to akt in front of the camra again!

Basic

1. televise
2. television
3. act
4. action
5. regulate
6. regulation
7. locate
8. location
9. elect
10. election
11. react
12. reaction
13. tense
14. tension
15. populate
16. population
17. convict
18. conviction
19. correct
20. correction

Review

21. camera
22. movie
23. famous
24. minute
25. question

Challenge

26. animate
27. animation
28. fascinate
29. fascination

Write a TV Schedule

Write a television schedule that you would like for one hour. Include times, channels, and one sentence about each program. Try to use five spelling words. Post your schedule.

Proofreading Tip

When using a word processor, highlight any words you think are misspelled. Then check them in a dictionary.

Proofreading Marks

¶   Indent
∧   Add
  Delete
≡   Capital letter
/   Small letter

Vocabulary Enrichment

Expanding Vocabulary

The Greek Word Part *tele* When the Greek word part *tele* is combined with other word parts, its meaning becomes part of the meaning of the new word.

ROOT	MEANING	WORD	MEANING
tele	far off, distant	**tele**vise	to see images broadcast from a distance

The chart shows the meanings for the five words in the box. Write the letters to complete each word. Then write the word.

Spelling Word Link

televise

telephone
telescope
telecast
telegram
television

Meaning	Word Part	Whole Word
an instrument that reproduces and receives distant sounds	1. *tele* _____ ?	2. _____ ?
a device that receives and reproduces images and sounds from a distance	3. *tele* _____ ?	4. _____ ?
a message sent by wire or radio	5. *tele* _____ ?	6. _____ ?
a device that makes distant objects appear closer	7. *tele* _____ ?	8. _____ ?
a broadcast on television	9. *tele* _____ ?	10. _____ ?

Show You Know! Write the word from the box that completes each sentence. Use your Spelling Dictionary.

11. Peter looked at the North Star through a _____.
12. Every Sunday I call my grandmother on the _____.
13. Eva's favorite _____ program is shown on Tuesday.
14. Send a _____ to contact someone far away quickly.
15. The dolphin show was _____ from the aquarium.

Real-World Connection

Performing Arts: Television All the words in the box relate to television. Look up these words in your Spelling Dictionary. Then write the words to complete this script for a TV ad.

NBS is the national TV __(1)__ for action-packed shows this season. *The Spartans* has surprised everyone with its success. The show is so popular that each __(2)__ pays a fortune to air a thirty-second __(3)__. *The Spartans* is __(4)__ every Monday at 8:00 P.M. Check TV listings for the NBS __(5)__ in your area. The last __(6)__ of the ten-part __(7)__ will air in April. If you missed any parts, a __(8)__ of the entire program will soon be available.

Spelling Word Link

television

broadcast
network
sponsor
channel
commercial
series
video
episode

Try This CHALLENGE

Write a Plan If you were the president of a TV station, what would your station be like? What kinds of shows would you have? Who would you like the sponsors to be? Write a paragraph that presents a plan for your TV station. Try to use some of the words from the word box on this page.

★★★ Fact File

The Nielsen Survey helps a network keep track of a show's popularity. The viewing choices of the 5,000 families who participate supposedly reflect the choices of the nation.

30 Review: Units 25–29

Unit 25   Final |ĭj|, |ĭv|, and |ĭs| pages 156–161

creative	baggage	notice	language	knowledge
justice	service	average	relative	detective

Spelling Strategy

|ĭj| → **age** |ĭv| → **ive** |ĭs| → **ice**

Write the word that fits each clue.

1. ordinary
2. English or Spanish
3. carried when traveling
4. facts and ideas
5. inventive
6. to pay attention to

Write the word that completes each sentence.

7. The courts make sure that _____ is carried out.
8. Rosa Martinez, the new _____, solved the crime.
9. My cousin Sammy is my favorite _____.
10. We thanked the waiter for his excellent _____.

Unit 26   Unstressed Syllables   pages 162–167

dozen	worship	pilgrim	forbid	repair
salute	crystal	neglect	respond	spinach

Spelling Strategy   To spell a two-syllable word, divide the word into syllables. Spell the word by syllables, noting carefully the spelling of the unstressed syllable.

Write the word that fits each meaning.

11. to mend
12. a set of twelve
13. to honor and love
14. a traveler to a sacred place
15. to fail to care for
16. to order not to do something

Write the word that completes each group.

17. answer, reply, _____
18. silver, china, _____
19. cabbage, lettuce, _____
20. handshake, wave, _____

Unit 27   Words with Prefixes   pages 168–173

in|crease

| dispute | insist | increase | discover | unknown |
| install | dismiss | regard | unskilled | revenge |

Spelling Strategy   A **prefix** is a word part added to the beginning of a base word or a word root. A prefix adds meaning. **Un-**, **in-**, **dis-**, and **re-** are prefixes. Find the prefix and the base word or the word root. Spell the word by parts.

Write the word that fits each meaning.

21. to place in service   **23.** to argue   **25.** to demand
22. to think highly of   **24.** to get even   **26.** growth

Write the word that completes each analogy.

27. *Ordinary* is to *unusual* as *familiar* is to _____.
28. *Melt* is to *dissolve* as *release* is to _____.
29. *Perfect* is to *imperfect* as *skilled* is to _____.
30. *Observe* is to *see* as *learn* is to _____.

Unit 28   Changing Final *y* to *i*   pages 174–179

**scary
scariest**

| abilities | happiness | dirtier | scariest | spied |
| dizziness | tiniest | pitied | replies | busier |

Spelling Strategy   When a word ends with a consonant and **y**, change the **y** to **i** when adding **-es**, **-ed**, **-er**, **-est**, or **-ness**.

Write the word formed by adding each base word to the ending or suffix.

31. dizzy + ness   **33.** pity + ed   **35.** spy + ed
32. reply + es   **34.** scary + est   **36.** dirty + er

Write the words that complete the paragraph.

Ice-skating keeps Anna __(37)__ than most children, and it brings her great __(38)__. She practices hard to improve her __(39)__. Even the __(40)__ improvement takes hours of work.

187

Unit 29   Adding -ion   pages 180–185

televise	elect	locate	react	populate
television	election	location	reaction	population

Spelling Strategy   Remember that the suffix **-ion** can change verbs into nouns. When a verb ends with **e**, drop the **e** before adding **-ion**.

Write the noun that fits each meaning.

41. the number of people who live in a particular place
42. a device that receives and reproduces sounds and images
43. selection by vote
44. a position
45. a response

Write the verb form of each noun.

46. reaction   48. television   50. election
47. location   49. population

Challenge Words   Units 25–29   pages 156–185

cooperative	charter	strategies	fascinate
unfortunate	refuge	apprentice	fascination
responsible	unified		

Write the word that fits each meaning. Circle the word that begins with the |yo͞o| sound.

51. joined   54. a person who is learning a job
52. to attract   55. having a certain obligation
53. plans of action   56. a strong attraction

Write the word that completes each group. Circle the word that has the base word *operate*.

57. document, contract, _____
58. protection, shelter, _____
59. unlucky, unhappy, _____
60. willing, helpful, _____

Spelling-Meaning Strategy

The Greek Word Part *ast*

Did you know that *disaster*, *asterisk*, and *astronomer* are related in meaning? Each word has the Greek word part *ast*, meaning "star."

A Greek word part affects the meaning of each word that contains it. You have learned that many years ago *disaster* meant "bad luck brought by the stars." An *asterisk* is a symbol shaped like a star. An *astronomer* is someone who studies the stars. Knowing the meaning of *ast* can help you spell and understand other words with this same word part.

Here is a list of words that contain the Greek word part *ast*.

asterisk	**ast**ronomer	**ast**ronomy
aster	**ast**eroid	**ast**ronaut

Think
- Look up each word above in your Spelling Dictionary. How does the word part *ast* affect the meaning of each word?

Apply and Extend

Complete these activities on a separate sheet of paper.

1. Write six sentences, using one word from the word box above in each sentence. Can you make the words' meanings clear?

2. With a partner list as many other words as you can that include the word part *ast*. Then look in the section titled "Greek Word Parts" on page 275 of your Spelling-Meaning Index. Add any other words that you find with this word part to your list.

Summing Up

The Greek word part *ast* means "star." Words that have the same Greek word part are often related in spelling and meaning. Knowing the meaning of the word part can help you understand and spell the words in that family.

asteroid

astronaut

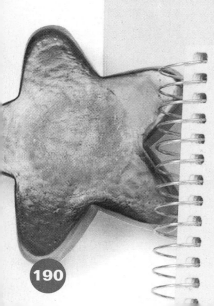

Rachel's grandfather has the same problem as the grandfather in *Gramp* by Joan Tate. Rachel wrote this business letter to her building manager. What does she ask him to do?

205 Dana St., Apt. 1006
Bridgeport, CT 06608
August 22, 1998

Mr. John Cohan, Manager
205 Dana St., Apt. 1
Bridgeport, CT 06608

Dear Mr. Cohan:

My grandfather needs a place in the basement where he can keep his workbench and use his tools. If you gave him a place to work, he would help you make repairs, if you wish. He repairs everything that gets broken in our home. He is also neat and friendly and would work around your schedule. He would work in the evening after you go home. Do you have a spot that he could use?

Sincerely yours,

Rachel Kaplan

Rachel Kaplan

Think and Discuss

1. What did Rachel want to persuade Mr. Cohan to do? Which sentence states her **opinion**?

2. What **reasons** did Rachel give? What **facts** and **examples** support her reasons?

3. Explain the **six parts** of this letter. See page 253 for a model if you need help.

The Writing Process
Persuasive Letter

What would you like to persuade someone to do? Write a business letter to that person. Use the guidelines for persuading. Follow the Writing Process.

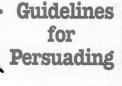

• • • • Guidelines for Persuading

✓ Introduce the problem or your goal. State your goal or problem clearly.
✓ Support strong reasons with facts or examples.
✓ Answer possible objections.
✓ Conclude by encouraging an action.

1 Prewriting
- List two or three reasons that your audience might find persuasive.
- Role-play your argument with some classmates. What worked? What didn't?

2 Draft
- Support each reason with at least one fact or example.

3 Revise
- Be sure each reason is followed by the facts or examples that support it.
- Use your Thesaurus to find exact words.
- Have a writing conference.

4 Proofread
- Did you spell each word correctly?
- Did you write people's titles correctly?
- Did you use punctuation marks and capital letters correctly?

5 Publish
- Mail a neat final copy of your letter.

Composition Words

repair
respond
action
notice
neglect
inform
disagree
regulate

More Words with -ion

Read and Say

pollution
pollute   –ion

Basic

READ the sentences. SAY each bold word.

1. pollute — Do not **pollute** the river with trash.
2. pollution — Our class learned about air **pollution**.
3. protect — Animals **protect** their young.
4. protection — The knight wore a helmet for **protection**.
5. inspect — I will **inspect** the tires before my trip.
6. inspection — The car passed **inspection**.
7. impress — Do these tall buildings **impress** you?
8. impression — What is your **impression** of the city?
9. migrate — Some birds **migrate** south.
10. migration — When does the **migration** of robins begin?
11. promote — I gave a speech to **promote** my book.
12. promotion — Tim's boss gave him a **promotion**.
13. imitate — My friends like to **imitate** my laugh.
14. imitation — Is the ruby real or an **imitation**?
15. decorate — We will **decorate** the den with flowers.
16. decoration — She made a colorful **decoration**.
17. confess — Did the thief **confess** to the crime?
18. confession — Her **confession** of the crime was forced.
19. express — He could not **express** his feelings well.
20. expression — Meg has a sad **expression** on her face.

Think and Write

Each pair of words is made up of a verb and a noun. The noun is formed by adding the suffix -ion to the verb.

VERB:	impress	pollute
NOUN:	impression	pollution

• How do the spellings of *impress* and *pollute* change when -ion is added?

Now write each Basic Word under the heading that shows what happens to the verb when -ion is added.

No Spelling Change	Final *e* Dropped

Review
21. garbage
22. health
23. dirty
24. ocean
25. awful

Challenge
26. contaminate
27. contamination
28. irritate
29. irritation

Independent Practice

Spelling Strategy The suffix *-ion* can change verbs to nouns. When a verb ends with *e*, drop the *e* when adding *-ion*. If a verb does not end with *e*, just add *-ion*.

Word Analysis/Phonics Complete the exercise with Basic Words.

1–7. Add *-ion* to each verb to write a Basic Word.
1. pollute
2. protect
3. promote
4. confess
5. imitate
6. impress
7. express

Vocabulary: Definitions Write the Basic Word that fits each definition.
8. an ornament
9. to make dirty or impure
10. to copy the actions of
11. to move from one region to another
12. to keep safe from harm
13. to put into words
14. to furnish with something attractive

Challenge Words Write the Challenge Word that fits each meaning. Use your Spelling Dictionary.
15. an impurity
16. to annoy
17. an annoyance
18. to make impure

Simon says, "Put your hands on your shoulders."

Spelling-Meaning Connection

Inspect and *inspection* share the word root *spect,* meaning "to look." To inspect is to look at closely. Remembering the root *spect* will help you spell and understand the related words *spectacle* and *spectator.*

19–20. Write *inspect* and *inspection.* Underline the root in each word.

inspect
inspection
spectacle
spectator

Review: Spelling Spree

Syllable Addition Combine the first syllable of the first word with the final syllable of the second word to write a Basic or Review Word.

1. excellent + compress =
2. provide + demote =
3. open + crustacean =
4. garden + cabbage =
5. important + depress =

6. increase + respect =
7. provide + detect =
8. continue + profess =
9. dirtier + tasty =
10. minor + integrate =

Book Titles Write a Basic or Review Word to complete each funny book title. Begin each word with a capital letter.

11. *Don't Dirty or _____ Our Water* by Crystal Kleer
12. *How to _____ a Cake* by F. Ross Ting
13. *Bird _____* by Duck E. Overhead
14. *How to Make a Positive _____* by Look N. Goode
15. *Physical Fitness and Your _____* by Bea Vita Min
16. *How to _____ Bird Calls* by Ma Kingbird
17. *The Terrible, Horrible, _____ Day* by Mona Growner
18. *A Criminal's _____* by Gil T. Pardee
19. *How to Speak with Enthusiasm and _____* by Hammett Up
20. *How to Earn a _____ to a Higher Position* by Getta Head
21. *The Care and _____ of Your Belongings* by Lock N. Keye
22. *Apartment Design and _____* by D. Zina Pad
23. *Cleaning Up Environmental _____* by Ernest Scrubber
24. *How to Get Your Car to Pass _____* by Fussy Checker
25. *Making _____ Pearls Look Real* by Kop E. Kat

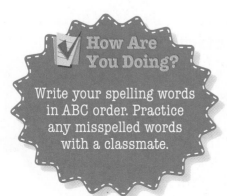

How Are You Doing?

Write your spelling words in ABC order. Practice any misspelled words with a classmate.

Proofreading and Writing

Proofread: Spelling and Commas in Letter Headings Use a comma between the city and the state and between the day and the year.

Columbus, OH 43229   October 12, 1991

Find four misspelled Basic or Review Words and two missing commas in this part of a friendly letter. Write the letter correctly.

Save Our Wildlife

1414 Tidewater Dr.

Baton Rouge LA 70811

April 10 1997

Dear Ms. Sanchez,

I want to exspress my thanks to you

for coming to my helth class. Your

talk about polution and the protection

of wildlife made a strong impreshion

on me.

Basic
1. pollute
2. pollution
3. protect
4. protection
5. inspect
6. inspection
7. impress
8. impression
9. migrate
10. migration
11. promote
12. promotion
13. imitate
14. imitation
15. decorate
16. decoration
17. confess
18. confession
19. express
20. expression

Review
21. garbage
22. health
23. dirty
24. ocean
25. awful

Challenge
26. contaminate
27. contamination
28. irritate
29. irritation

Write a Letter

Write a letter asking someone, such as a safety officer, to speak at your school on Career Day. Try to use five spelling words. Be sure to use commas in the heading of your letter.

Proofreading Tip **Check that you used commas correctly when writing a letter.**

Proofreading Marks
¶ Indent
∧ Add
⌐ Delete
≡ Capital letter
/ Small letter

Expanding Vocabulary

Spelling
Word Link
impress
impression

Building Words with *impress* Draw the web below. Then add each suffix to make a form of *impress*. Write the new word in the circle.

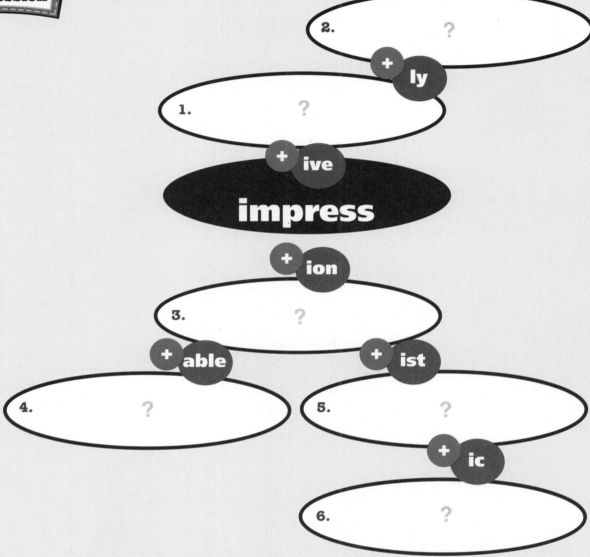

2. ?

+ ly

1. ?

+ ive

impress

+ ion

3. ?

+ able

+ ist

4. ?

5. ?

+ ic

6. ?

Work Together With a partner choose three new words that you built, and use each one in a sentence. Use your Spelling Dictionary to find the meaning of each word.

Real-World Connection

Health: Pollution All the words in the box are related to pollution. Look up these words in your Spelling Dictionary. Then write the words to complete this student report.

Spelling Word Link

pollution

chemicals
recycle
environment
waste
litter
smog
fumes
toxic

STOP POLLUTION

Keeping our __(1)__ clean is important. We try not to __(2)__ public areas with bottles and paper, but more care is required. Laws now regulate the use of acids and other __(3)__ because they are __(4)__, or poisonous. New auto exhaust systems reduce the __(5)__ from cars, which contribute to __(6)__ in the air. Rather than bury or dump leftover __(7)__ materials, some companies __(8)__ them for use in other products.

Try This
CHALLENGE

Yes or No? Write *yes* if the underlined word is used correctly. Write *no* if it is not.

9. <u>Smog</u> blanketed the city of Los Angeles.
10. The desert is a dry <u>environment</u>.
11. The fresh, unpolluted air was <u>toxic</u> to my health.
12. The <u>fumes</u> filled the room with a pleasant odor.

★ Fact File

The Air Quality Index tells the amount of harmful particles and chemicals in the air. An index above 100 indicates unhealthy air. An index above 400 indicates a health emergency.

Air Quality Index

Hazardous	
Very unhealthy	
Unhealthy	
Moderate	
Good	

50 100 200 300 400 500

More Words with Prefixes

com-
con-
en-
ex-
pre-
pro-

Basic

READ the sentences. **SAY** each bold word.

1. propose   Roberto will **propose** a new law.
2. convince   Can Maria **convince** you to vote for her?
3. concern   Did Dad show **concern** about the problem?
4. enforce   The police **enforce** the laws.
5. compare   Let's **compare** your notes with mine.
6. excuse   Please **excuse** me for being late.
7. conduct   Who will **conduct** the meeting?
8. preserve   Some laws try to **preserve** wildlife.
9. contain   What does the box **contain**?
10. excite   Do not **excite** the baby.
11. extend   We need to **extend** the road by two miles.
12. prefix   The word *extend* has the **prefix** *ex-*.
13. engage   Did the army **engage** in battle?
14. pronoun   The word *you* is a **pronoun**.
15. consist   What does the mixture **consist** of?
16. enclose   A fence will **enclose** the yard.
17. consent   Did they **consent** to your plan?
18. proverb   A **proverb** is a short saying.
19. compound   The word *doorknob* is a **compound** word.
20. exchange   We should **exchange** addresses.

Think and Write

Each word begins with a prefix. A **prefix** is a word part that is added to the beginning of a base word or a word root, a word part that cannot stand alone.

     compare   **con**vince   **en**force   **ex**cite   **pre**serve   **pro**pose

• What six prefixes do you see? *Com-* is a form of the prefix *con-*. Before which letter is *con-* spelled *com*?

Now write each Basic Word under its prefix.

en-, ex-	con-, com-	pre-, pro-

Review	23. exit
21. compose	24. common
22. exact	25. expert

Challenge	28. convene
26. enactment	29. preamble
27. procedure	30. concise

Independent Practice

Spelling Strategy

Com-, con-, en-, ex-, pre-, and *pro-* are prefixes. Because you know how to spell the prefix, pay special attention to the spelling of the base word or the word root. Spell the word by parts.

Word Analysis/Phonics Complete the exercises with Basic Words.

1–4. Write the four words with the |s| sound spelled c or ce.

5–6. Write the word that rhymes with each word below.

    5. spare   **6.** pretend

Vocabulary: Synonyms

Write the Basic Word that is a synonym for each word below.

    7. protect   **11.** permission
    8. trade   **12.** surround
    9. behavior **13.** pardon
   10. hold

Challenge Words Write the Challenge Word that fits each meaning. Use your Spelling Dictionary.

   14. an introduction to a document
   15. a way of doing something
   16. to come together
   17. passage of a law
   18. brief and to the point

Spelling-Meaning Connection

How can you remember how to spell the first schwa sound in *proposition*? Think of the |ō| sound in the related word *propose*.

proposition
propose

19–20. Write *propose* and *proposition*. Underline the letter in *propose* that helps you spell the schwa sound in *proposition*.

Dictionary

Different Pronunciations Some words have different pronunciations when used as different parts of speech. *Excuse* is pronounced with a final |z| sound when used as a verb and with a final |s| sound when used as a noun.

> **ex·cuse** |ĭk skyōōz′| *v.* **excused, excusing 1.** To forgive: *Please excuse me for what I did.* **2.** To release from a duty or promise. |ĭk skyōōs′| *n., pl.* **excuses** Something given as a reason for excusing: *a written excuse for an absence.*

Practice Write the part of speech for each underlined word. Use your Spelling Dictionary.

1. Lauren has a good <u>excuse</u> for being late.
2. Mr. Stern will <u>excuse</u> David from gym today.
3. Please <u>excuse</u> me for interrupting you.
4. Ushers in theaters <u>conduct</u> people to their seat.
5. Ms. Yazzi praised the team for their good <u>conduct</u>.

Please **excuse** my late homework. My dog ate my first paper.

A classic **excuse**!

Review: Spelling Spree

Changing Prefixes Change the underlined prefix in each word to write a Basic or Review Word.

6. <u>pre</u>pare
7. <u>in</u>tend
8. <u>ac</u>cuse
9. <u>dis</u>close
10. <u>re</u>act
11. <u>de</u>serve
12. <u>in</u>sist
13. <u>re</u>sent
14. <u>im</u>pound
15. <u>de</u>tain
16. <u>dis</u>cern
17. <u>re</u>cite
18. <u>suf</u>fix
19. <u>de</u>duct
20. <u>in</u>terchange

How Are You Doing?

List the spelling words that are hard for you. Practice them with a family member.

Proofreading and Writing

Proofread for Spelling Find ten misspelled Basic or Review Words in this speech. Write each one correctly.

A provirb says, "Actions speak louder than words." Our comman sense tells us that now is the time for action! We—I emphasize the pronun—must preserve our historic buildings. We have to convience Congress to pass and inforce a law to protect these landmarks. I.M.A. Saver, an expirt on colonial architecture, will compos a bill. She will also ingage Senator Hy Rise in debate. I perpose that everyone support her efforts. Near the exsit you will find more information about the debate.

Basic

1. propose
2. convince
3. concern
4. enforce
5. compare
6. excuse
7. conduct
8. preserve
9. contain
10. excite
11. extend
12. prefix
13. engage
14. pronoun
15. consist
16. enclose
17. consent
18. proverb
19. compound
20. exchange

Review
21. compose
22. exact
23. exit
24. common
25. expert

Challenge
26. enactment
27. procedure
28. convene
29. preamble
30. concise

Write a List of Rules

Book of Classroom Rules

Schools have laws called rules. List some new rules for your school. Try to use five spelling words in your list. Discuss your rules with some classmates.

Proofreading Tip **Check that you did not switch any letters, such as *per* for *pre*.**

Proofreading Marks

¶ Indent
∧ Add
ℛ Delete
≡ Capital letter
/ Small letter

Expanding Vocabulary

Spelling
Word Link

propose

Building New Words with Prefixes The spelling word
propose is made up of the prefix *pro-* and the word root *pose*.
The meaning of *propose* is taken from the meaning of its parts.

pro + pose = propose
("before") ("put") ("to suggest or put forth")

You can make other words simply by using different prefixes with *pose*.
The meaning of *pose* will be kept in each word.

op = against	**ex** = out	**trans** = change	**com** = together, with

For each picture, add a prefix from the box to *pose* to write a new word
that matches the meaning of the picture. Use your Spelling Dictionary.

1.

2.

3.

4.

Show You Know! Use each word you created in a sentence.

Real-World Connection

Social Studies: Making Laws All the words in the box relate to making laws. Look up these words in your Spelling Dictionary. Then write the words to complete this page.

Spelling Word Link

preamble

veto
amendment
legislation
majority
statute
bill
lobbyist
filibuster

How does a __(1)__ become a law?
It is debated in Congress. If a member of Congress wants to make changes, he or she attaches an __(2)__ or stages a __(3)__ to delay passage.

Often a __(4)__ for a special-interest group will try to influence votes.

If a __(5)__ of the members vote for the proposed law, it is sent to the President, who can sign the piece of __(6)__ or __(7)__ it. Once the President signs the proposal, it becomes a __(8)__ .

Try This CHALLENGE

Yes or No? Write *yes* if the underlined word is used correctly. Write *no* if it is not.

9. Congress quickly passed the <u>filibuster</u>.
10. The <u>statute</u> on auto insurance never became law.
11. The President may <u>veto</u> any bill.
12. The <u>majority</u> of senators, 75 to 25, voted *yes*.

 Fact File

The first ten amendments to the Constitution are known as the Bill of Rights. They guarantee such basic rights as freedom of speech and freedom of religion.

203

Suffixes *-ent, -ant; -able, -ible*

Read and Say

Basic

READ the sentences. **SAY** each bold word.

1.	fashionable	My old coat is still **fashionable**.
2.	comfortable	The soft chair is **comfortable**.
3.	different	Mexico and Spain are **different** countries.
4.	suitable	Wear clothes **suitable** for a picnic.
5.	merchant	The **merchant** sold me a hat.
6.	profitable	Selling our house was **profitable**.
7.	student	The **student** worked hard in class.
8.	possible	Is it **possible** to land on Mars?
9.	resident	Are you our new town **resident**?
10.	terrible	The flood was **terrible**.
11.	absent	I was **absent** from school yesterday.
12.	vacant	Is that old house **vacant**?
13.	servant	A police officer is a public **servant**.
14.	valuable	Her diamond pin is **valuable**.
15.	accident	I met Jack by **accident**.
16.	horrible	That plant has a **horrible** skunk smell.
17.	honorable	Leah behaved in an **honorable** way.
18.	reasonable	Two dollars for markers is **reasonable**.
19.	remarkable	You did a **remarkable** job.
20.	laughable	That excuse is **laughable**.

Think and Write

Each word ends with the suffix *-ent, -ant, -able,* or *-ible.* Because these suffixes begin with a schwa sound, their spellings must be remembered.

|ənt| stud**ent**, merch**ant**
|ə bəl| suit**able**, poss**ible**

• What are two spelling patterns for the suffix |ənt|? What are two patterns for the suffix |ə bəl|?

Now write each Basic Word under its suffix.

–ent	–ant	–able	–ible

Review	23. moment
21. current	24. silent
22. important	25. parent

Challenge	28. extravagant
26. elegant	29. durable
27. prominent	30. reversible

Independent Practice

Spelling Strategy   The suffixes *-ent* and *-ant* and the suffixes *-able* and *-ible* sound alike but are spelled differently. You have to remember the spellings of these suffixes.

Word Analysis/Phonics   Complete the exercise with Basic Words.

1–6. Write the Basic Word that has each base word below.

1. profit	**3.** differ	**5.** honor
2. fashion	**4.** laugh	**6.** value

Vocabulary: Word Clues   Write the Basic Word that fits each clue.

7. at ease
8. not occupied
9. extraordinary
10. proper
11. an unexpected event
12. sensible
13. capable of being done

Challenge Words   Write the Challenge Word that fits each meaning. Use your Spelling Dictionary.

14. wasteful
15. able to take hard wear
16. marked by good taste
17. widely known
18. able to be worn or used with either side out

Spelling-Meaning Connection

Resident and *reside* have different vowel sounds but are related in spelling and meaning. **Think of this**: You must *reside* within the Tampa city limits to be a *resident* of Tampa.

19-20. Write *reside*. Then write the Basic Word that is related in spelling and meaning to *reside*.

Review: Spelling Spree

Suffix Clues Write the Basic or Review Word that fits each clue.

1. What *ent* word studies hard?
2. What *ent* word is not the same as something else?
3. What *ent* word is part of the present?
4. What *able* word is very funny?
5. What *ent* word has no sound?
6. What *ant* word will serve you?
7. What *ent* word lives in a particular place?
8. What *ant* word sells goods?
9. What *ent* word has children?
10. What *ent* word is not present?
11. What *able* word makes money?
12. What *able* word is never out of style?

Syllable Scramble Rearrange the syllables to write a Basic or Review Word. One syllable in each item is extra.

13. ri hor pre ble
14. a son ble en rea
15. tant cap por im
16. ble fort ion a com
17. u ble trans a val
18. ment cre mo
19. cant pre va
20. a hon tion or ble
21. ble fer pos si
22. a suit de ble
23. in re a ble mark
24. ble ate ri ter
25. ci dent com ac

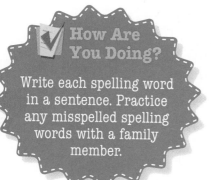

How Are You Doing?

Write each spelling word in a sentence. Practice any misspelled spelling words with a family member.

Proofreading and Writing

Proofread: Spelling and Using *I* and *me* Use *I* as the subject of a sentence or after forms of *be*. Use *me* after action verbs or prepositions. When using *I* or *me* with nouns or other pronouns, name yourself last.

Pat and **I** bought jeans.   These jeans look good on **me**.

Find four misspelled Basic or Review Words and three errors in using *I* and *me* in this ad. Write the ad correctly.

1

I am Mike Mars, speaking for

Jax jeans. You and me are no

diffrent when it comes to jeans.

2

It's importent for I and you to be

comfertable and fashonable.

Try these remarkable jeans now!

Write a Song

A shoe company is making a fancy new sneaker. Write a catchy song for the product. Use a tune that you already know, such as "Happy Birthday." Try to use five spelling words and *I* and *me* in your song.

Proofreading Tip   **Check that you used *I* and *me* correctly.**

Proofreading Marks

¶ Indent
∧ Add
⌇ Delete
≡ Capital letter
/ Small letter

207

Expanding Vocabulary

The Word Root *vac* A vacant house is not occupied. A vacuum has nothing in it. *Vacant* and *vacuum* each have the word root *vac*.

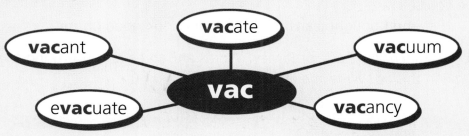

Write the word from the word web that completes each sentence. Underline the Latin root. Use your Spelling Dictionary.

1. We played baseball on a _____ lot.
2. There is nothing in a _____ , not even air.
3. We must either sign a lease or _____ our apartment.
4. The residents had to _____ the burning building.
5. We could not stay at the hotel because it had no _____ .

Show You Know! Write a headline for each picture below. Use a word from the web in each headline.

Daily News
Volume 1

?

?

6.

FiRE

School

7.

Room for Rent

Real-World Connection

Business: Fashion All the words in the box are related to fashion. Look up these words in your Spelling Dictionary. Then write the words to complete this interview.

Spelling Word Link

fashionable

fad
tailor
garment
designer
fabric
boutique
modeling
alteration

Fashion Review

Q: How is a dress, a suit, or any stylish ___(1)___ made?

A: A fashion ___(2)___ creates the style. He or she also chooses the type of ___(3)___ from which to make a sample. The sample is sewn by a ___(4)___, who may suggest a change, or ___(5)___, in the design.

Q: What happens next?

A: The next step is ___(6)___ the sample in a fashion show. If the buyers at the show like the sample, you may soon see the style in a clothing store or a ___(7)___. If the style is popular, it may start a ___(8)___!

Try This CHALLENGE

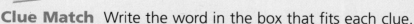

Clue Match Write the word in the box that fits each clue.

9. This job may be done in front of a camera.
10. Expensive perfumes might be sold here.
11. This is chosen for its pattern and texture.
12. This is here today but gone tomorrow.

⭐ **Fact File**

Long ago in Japan a belted robe called a kimono was the fashion for both men and women. Today kimonos are worn mainly for special events and ceremonies, such as weddings.

Three-Syllable Words

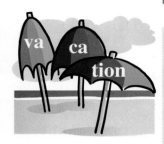

Basic	READ the sentences. SAY each bold word.
1. *wilderness*	I hiked in the **wilderness**.
2. *vacation*	She took a **vacation** to China.
3. *president*	Jed is **president** of the Chess Club.
4. *popular*	Everyone reads that **popular** magazine.
5. *memory*	An actor needs a good **memory**.
6. *monument*	Will we visit a historical **monument**?
7. *educate*	A teacher's job is to **educate** students.
8. *general*	Where is the **general** location of the store?
9. *regular*	Lunch today will be at the **regular** time.
10. *avenue*	Do you live on a road or an **avenue**?
11. *canary*	Sam gave his **canary** some birdseed.
12. *potato*	Sue ordered a baked **potato** for lunch.
13. *energy*	Exercise increases my **energy**.
14. *deposit*	I made a large **deposit** in my bank account.
15. *period*	Should I use a **period** or a question mark?
16. *industry*	He has a job in the steel **industry**.
17. *uniform*	The officer wore a navy blue **uniform**.
18. *condition*	My bike is in good **condition**.
19. *romantic*	I saw a **romantic** play on Valentine's Day.
20. *attention*	Mrs. Dasho tried to get our **attention**.

Think and Write

To spell the three-syllable words, divide them into syllables. Note the spelling of the two syllables that are unstressed or have secondary stress.

va | ca | tion |vā kā′ shən| **ed | u | cate** |ĕj′ ə kāt′|

• Where is each word divided into syllables? What familiar patterns do you see?

Now write each Basic Word under the heading that names its stressed syllable. Use your Spelling Dictionary.

Stressed First Syllable	Stressed Second Syllable

Review		Challenge	
21. beautiful	23. library	26. majestic	28. astonish
22. remember	24. another	27. reverence	29. stimulate
	25. enemy		30. obvious

Independent Practice

Spelling Strategy A three-syllable word has one stressed syllable and two syllables with less stress. To help you spell the word, divide the word into syllables. Note the spelling of the syllables that have less stress.

Word Analysis/Phonics Complete the exercises with Basic Words.

1–4. Write the four words that end with the |ē| sound spelled *y*.

5–7. Write the three words that end with the suffix *-ion*.

Vocabulary: Analogies Write the Basic Word that completes each analogy.

8. *Doctor* is to *heal* as *teacher* is to _____.
9. *Navy* is to *admiral* as *army* is to _____.
10. *Fruit* is to *apple* as *vegetable* is to _____.
11. *Team* is to *captain* as *government* is to _____.
12. *Keen* is to *sharp* as *well-liked* is to _____.
13. *Actor* is to *costume* as *police officer* is to _____.

Challenge Words Write the Challenge Word that fits each meaning. Use your Spelling Dictionary.

14. deep respect
15. to make active
16. easy to see
17. stately
18. to surprise

Spelling-Meaning Connection

How can you remember how to spell the final |ər| sounds in *regular*? Think of the |ăr| sounds in the related word *regularity*.

19–20. Write *regular* and *regularity*. Then underline the two letters in *regularity* that help you remember how to spell the final |ər| sounds in *regular*.

regular
regularity

Dictionary

Prefixes Dictionaries list prefixes in alphabetical order among the entry words. A hyphen follows the prefix.

> **uni-** A prefix that means "one, single": *unicycle*.

You will not find a dictionary entry for every word with a prefix, but you can look up the base word and the prefix separately. Then you can combine their meanings.

Practice Look up the prefix and the base word of each word below in your Spelling Dictionary. Then write the meaning of each word listed below.

1. preview   **2.** reship   **3.** inexact   **4.** dissimilar

Review: Spelling Spree

Hidden Words Write the Basic or Review Word that is hidden in each row of letters. Don't let the other words fool you!

Example: c a m p e r i o d d l y *period*

5. g a m e m o r y o l e
6. l i p o t a t o m i c
7. w i n d u s t r y o u t
8. t r o p i c a n a r y e
9. l i m p o p u l a r g e
10. f u n i f o r m a l l y
11. w h e n e r g y r o
12. f a r e m e m b e r b

13. e c o n d i t i o n y
14. r e d u c a t e r i n
15. m e n e m y p u m
16. h e r o m a n t i c h
17. t a n o t h e r m o s
18. c r a v e n u e t t a
19. d r e g u l a r v a
20. s p r e s i d e n t i

How Are You Doing?

Write each spelling word as a partner reads it aloud. Did you misspell any words?

Proofreading and Writing

Proofread for Spelling Find nine misspelled Basic or Review Words in this article. Write each one correctly.

The Dinosaur Quarry

Visitors to the Dinosaur Quarry, a popular national monewment and vakation spot, can watch workers dig up dinosaur fossils from an ancient time peroid. Dinosaur skeletons in perfect condition have been found in this beutiful wildaness, which is located in Colorado and Utah. The quarry, with its amazing deposite of fossils, has drawn attenshun from scientists and the genaral public. Books about the area are available in any libary.

Basic
1. wilderness
2. vacation
3. president
4. popular
5. memory
6. monument
7. educate
8. general
9. regular
10. avenue
11. canary
12. potato
13. energy
14. deposit
15. period
16. industry
17. uniform
18. condition
19. romantic
20. attention

Review
21. beautiful
22. remember
23. library
24. another
25. enemy

Challenge
26. majestic
27. reverence
28. astonish
29. stimulate
30. obvious

Write a Personal Story

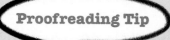

Write a story about a visit you made to a national park or another park. What did you see there? What did you do? Try to use five spelling words.

Proofreading Tip Check that you have not capitalized any words incorrectly.

Proofreading Marks

¶ Indent
∧ Add
℘ Delete
≡ Capital letter
/ Small letter

Vocabulary Enrichment

Expanding Vocabulary

Antonyms and Synonyms Many words have both synonyms and antonyms.

Spelling Word Link

uniform

reduce
enthusiastic
frisky
flawed
uninterested
amusing
sluggish
serious
extend
model

uniform

same

Synonym

different

Antonym

Write a synonym and an antonym for each word in the arrows. Use words from the box. Use your Spelling Dictionary to help you.

SYNONYMS   **ANTONYMS**

SYNONYMS		ANTONYMS
1. ?	lively	2. ?
3. ?	perfect	4. ?
5. ?	funny	6. ?
7. ?	eager	8. ?
9. ?	increase	10. ?

Work Together Work with a partner to write five sentences. In each sentence use one synonym–antonym pair above. Write on another sheet of paper.

Example: I am *enthusiastic* about our vacation to Jewel Cave National Monument, but my sister is *uninterested*.

Vocabulary Enrichment

Real-World Connection

Social Studies: National Parks All the names in the box relate to national parks. Look up these words in your Spelling Dictionary. Then write the words to complete this travel poster.

Explore Our National Parks!

See the colored, mile-deep walls of the __(1)__ .

Admire the Blue Ridge Mountains in Virginia's __(2)__ National Park.

Walk the Maine coast in __(3)__ National Park.

See fossils in the cliffs of South Dakota's __(4)__ .

See alligators in Florida's __(5)__ , a vast swamp.

Walk on rivers of ice in __(6)__ National Park.

Time the eruptions of Old Faithful in __(7)__ .

Don't forget the spectacular waterfalls in __(8)__ !

Try This CHALLENGE

Clue Match Write the word from the box that fits each clue.

9. The Colorado River runs through this park.
10. This park lies in Montana and borders Canada.
11. Established in 1872, this was the first national park.
12. Granite mountains line the seashores of this park.

★★★ Fact File

Petrified Forest National Park in Arizona contains the stonelike fossil remains of thousands of trees. These giant trees lived about one hundred and fifty million years ago.

More Three-Syllable Words

stadium

Basic

READ the sentences. **SAY** each bold word.

1. *champion* — Pablo is a hockey **champion**.
2. *stadium* — We saw the ball game at the **stadium**.
3. *history* — I'm studying the **history** of popular music.
4. *dangerous* — Swimming alone is **dangerous**.
5. *slippery* — The wet floor is **slippery**.
6. *favorite* — Dan tore his **favorite** shirt.
7. *personal* — Don't ask me any **personal** questions.
8. *continue* — The game will **continue** later today.
9. *division* — The **division** of chores was not fair.
10. *apartment* — Grandma rented a small **apartment**.
11. *violet* — Carolyn has **violet** eyes.
12. *emotion* — The actor showed no **emotion**.
13. *typical* — What is your **typical** day like?
14. *imagine* — I can't **imagine** a better movie.
15. *grocery* — My dad shops at this **grocery** store.
16. *consider* — Will you **consider** my offer?
17. *property* — This seaside **property** belongs to me.
18. *festival* — We attended the music **festival**.
19. *companion* — Liza's favorite **companion** is her poodle.
20. *sensitive* — My skin is **sensitive** to the sun.

Think and Write

To spell each three-syllable word, divide the word into syllables. Note the spelling of the two unstressed syllables.

cham | pi | on |chăm′ pē ən| **di | vi | sion |dĭ vĭzh′ ən|**

• Where is each word divided into syllables? What familiar spelling patterns do you see?

Now write each Basic Word under the heading that shows its stressed syllable. Use your Spelling Dictionary.

Stressed First Syllable	Stressed Second Syllable

Review	23. yesterday	**Challenge**	28. amateur
21. magazine	24. tomorrow	26. Olympics	29. spectator
22. together	25. hospital	27. muscular	30. ovation

Independent Practice

Spelling Strategy To spell a three-syllable word, divide the word into syllables. Note carefully the spelling of the unstressed syllables, and spell the word by syllables.

Word Analysis/Phonics Complete the exercises with Basic Words.

1–2. Write the two words that begin with the prefix *con-*.

3–8. Write the Basic Word that is formed from each base word below.

    3. slip **4.** favor **5.** person **6.** sense **7.** danger **8.** image

Vocabulary: Classifying Write the Basic Word that belongs in each group.

  9. rose, lily, _____
 10. friend, buddy, _____
 11. house, cabin, _____
 12. shop, market, _____
 13. addition, subtraction, _____

Challenge Words Write the Challenge Word that fits each clue. Use your Spelling Dictionary.

 14. someone in the audience
 15. having strong muscles
 16. a big round of applause
 17. antonym of *professional*
 18. athletic competition originating in Greece

Spelling-Meaning Connection

How can you remember how to spell the schwa sound in *history*? Think of the |ôr| sounds in the related word *historical*.

history
historical

19–20. Write *historical*. Then write the Basic Word that is related to *historical*.

Review: Spelling Spree

Puzzle Play Write a Basic or Review Word to fit each clue. Circle the letter that would appear in the box.

Example: risky _ _ _ _ _ □ _ _ _ *dangerous*

1. like best _ □ _ _ _ _ _ _
2. sore _ _ _ □ _ _ _ _ _
3. keep up _ _ _ _ □ _ _ _
4. slick _ □ _ _ _ _ _ _
5. 10 ÷ 5 _ _ □ _ _ _ _ _
6. think of _ _ _ _ _ _ □ _

7. with _ _ _ _ _ _ _ □
8. pretend _ □ _ _ _ _ _
9. feeling □ _ _ _ _ _ _ _
10. arena _ _ _ □ _ _ _
11. pal _ _ _ _ □ _ _ _ _
12. ordinary _ _ _ _ _ _ □

Write the circled letters in order to spell three mystery words that name an award.

Mystery Words: ? _ ? _ _ _ _ _ _ ? _ _ _ _ _

Using Clues Write a Basic or Review Word to fit each clue.

13. This is another name for land or real estate.
14. The things sold here are canned, frozen, or fresh.
15. Doctors and nurses work here.
16. This is a school subject.
17. This is the day after today.
18. This is the day before today.
19. These kinds of thoughts might be written in a diary.
20. This publication may contain articles and short stories.
21. You get this color when you mix red and blue.
22. This is another name for a winner.
23. This usually has a bedroom, a bathroom, and a kitchen.
24. Driving over the speed limit is this.
25. This might include a parade and special foods.

✓ How Are You Doing?

Write each spelling word in a sentence. Practice any misspelled spelling words with a partner.

Proofreading and Writing

Proofread: Spelling and Contractions A **contraction** is a shortened form of two words, usually a verb and *not* or a pronoun and a verb. An apostrophe replaces the dropped letters. (See page 250 in your Student's Handbook for other contractions.)

would not = wouldn't   cannot = can't   she is = she's

Find four misspelled Basic or Review Words and add two missing apostrophes in this school notice. Write the notice correctly.

REMINDER

The track events start tomorow and continnue all week. Its your personel responsibility to get to the stadeum on time. Dont be late. Have a companion remind you of your schedule.

Basic
1. champion
2. stadium
3. history
4. dangerous
5. slippery
6. favorite
7. personal
8. continue
9. division
10. apartment
11. violet
12. emotion
13. typical
14. imagine
15. grocery
16. consider
17. property
18. festival
19. companion
20. sensitive

Review
21. magazine
22. together
23. yesterday
24. tomorrow
25. hospital

Challenge
26. Olympics
27. muscular
28. amateur
29. spectator
30. ovation

Write a Character Sketch

Write a paragraph describing the ideal champion. Try to use five spelling words in your paragraph.

Proofreading Tip

If you use a computer to check spelling, remember that it will not find a word that is misspelled as another word.

Proofreading Marks

¶ Indent
∧ Add
⌇ Delete
≡ Capital letter
/ Small letter

Expanding Vocabulary

Spelling Word Link

dangerous

adventure
glory
mountain
poison
space

The Suffix -ous "Danger! Thin Ice!" These words warn skaters that a lake is a dangerous, or unsafe, place to skate. *Dangerous* has the base word *danger* and the suffix *-ous*, meaning "full of" or "having." Notice that the spelling of a base word may change when *-ous* is added.

BASE WORD	SUFFIX	NEW WORD	MEANING
danger	+ ous	= danger**ous**	"full of danger"
fame	+ ous	= fam**ous**	"having fame"
vary	+ ous	= vari**ous**	"having variety"

Tina loves to go hiking in the mountains. Read what Tina said about her last hike. Then complete each sentence with a word from the box plus the suffix *-ous*. Use your Spelling Dictionary.

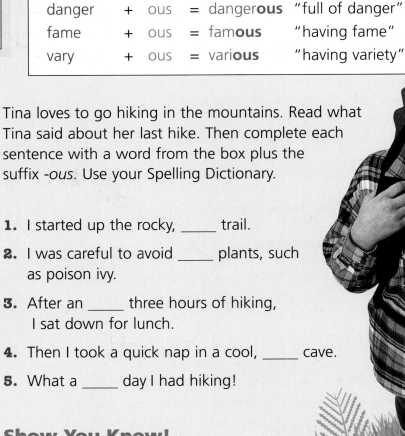

1. I started up the rocky, _____ trail.

2. I was careful to avoid _____ plants, such as poison ivy.

3. After an _____ three hours of hiking, I sat down for lunch.

4. Then I took a quick nap in a cool, _____ cave.

5. What a _____ day I had hiking!

Show You Know!
Choose three words that you made and use each one in a sentence.

Real-World Connection

Recreation: Summer Olympic Games All the words in the box are related to the Summer Olympic Games. Look up these words in your Spelling Dictionary. Then write the words to complete this sports magazine article.

Spelling Word Link

champion

gymnastics
marathon
discus
javelin
fencing
decathlon
vault
kayak

GOING FOR THE GOLD

   The Summer Olympic Games include a variety of events, such as paddling a __(1)__ over a 1,000-meter course, __(2)__ with a sword, running a 26-mile __(3)__ , and performing acrobatic tricks in __(4)__ . The toughest event is the __(5)__ , which actually includes ten events. As part of this contest an athlete must use a pole to __(6)__ over a high crossbar, throw a spear called a __(7)__ , hurl a round __(8)__ , and compete in track events.

Try This
CHALLENGE

Yes or No? Write *yes* if the underlined word is used correctly. Write *no* if it is not.

9. The runners were exhausted after the <u>marathon</u>.
10. An athlete gripped the <u>decathlon</u> with his fingers.
11. The <u>kayak</u> cut through the water like a knife.
12. The pointed tip of the <u>discus</u> pierced the earth.

★★★ **Fact File**

The Olympic Games began in ancient Greece as a festival to honor the Greek god Zeus. The word *Olympic* comes from Mount Olympus, where Zeus was believed to live.

Entranceway to the stadium at Olympia

36 Review: Units 31–35

Unit 31   More Words with *-ion*   pages 192–197

impress	pollute	migrate	express	imitate
impression	pollution	migration	expression	imitation

Spelling Strategy   The suffix **-ion** can change verbs to nouns. When a verb ends with **e**, drop the **e** when adding **-ion**. If a verb does not end with **e**, just add **-ion**.

Write the verb that fits each clue.

1. to have an effect on
2. to make known
3. what car fumes do
4. what many birds do
5. to copy

Write the noun form of each verb.

6. migrate
7. imitate
8. pollute
9. impress
10. express

Unit 32   More Words with Prefixes   pages 198–203

concern	excite	preserve	enforce	propose
compound	consent	prefix	enclose	extend

Spelling Strategy   **Com-, con-, en-, ex-, pre-,** and **pro-** are prefixes. Because you know how to spell the prefix, pay special attention to the spelling of the base word or the word root. Spell the word by parts.

Write the word that belongs in each group.

11. spread, expand, _____
12. suggest, present, _____
13. agree, approve, _____
14. worry, trouble, _____

Write the word that fits each clue.

15. rhymes with *suffix*
16. a word such as *baseball*
17. to surround
18. to freeze, can, or pickle
19. to make others obey
20. rhymes with *ignite*

Unit 33 Suffixes -ent, -ant; -able, -ible   pages 204–209

| terrible | comfortable | different | merchant | resident |
| absent | horrible | reasonable | laughable | vacant |

Spelling Strategy

|ənt| → -ent, -ant |ə bəl| → -able, -ible

Write the words to complete the sentences.

21. In our neighborhood we have a _____ lot for playing ball.

22. Tammy has been a _____ of Georgia for two years.

23. Lila loves to curl up in a _____ chair and read a book.

24. A local _____ is having a sale on blue jeans.

25. John is _____ from school today.

Write the words that are forms of the words below.

26. terror   **28.** laugh   **30.** differ

27. horror   **29.** reason

Unit 34   Three-Syllable Words   pages 210–215

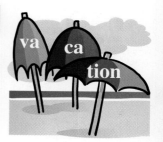

| popular | memory | vacation | wilderness | monument |
| potato | canary | industry | condition | energy |

Spelling Strategy   A three-syllable word has one stressed
syllable and two syllables with less stress. To help you spell the word,
divide the word into syllables. Note the spelling of the syllables that
have less stress.

Write the words to complete the sentences.

31. Coal mining is an important _____ in West Virginia.

32. Elk living in the _____ travel in herds.

33. This summer we will spend our _____ in the mountains.

34. In honor of the soldiers, the town built a _____.

Write the word that fits each meaning.

35. well-liked   **37.** the ability to remember   **39.** a songbird

36. power   **38.** working order   **40.** a vegetable

UNIT
36

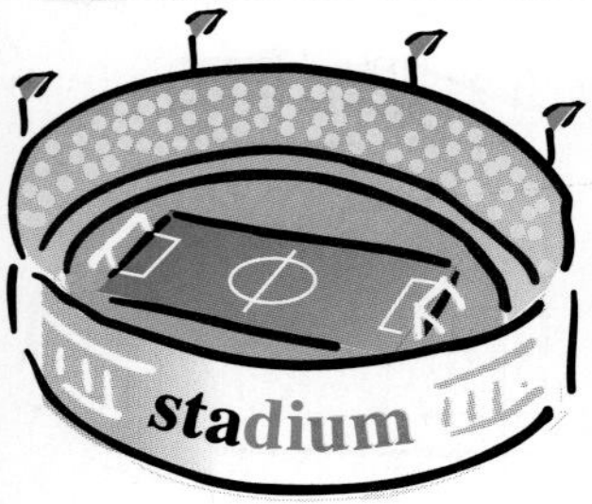

Unit 35 More Three-Syllable Words pages 216–221

stadium	division	slippery	champion	dangerous
emotion	property	grocery	typical	companion

Spelling Strategy To help you spell a three-syllable word, divide the word into syllables. Look for familiar spelling patterns. Note carefully the spelling of the unstressed syllables, and spell the word by syllables.

Write the word that completes each analogy.

41. *Numerous* is to *few* as *unusual* is to ______.
42. *Hockey* is to *rink* as *football* is to ______.
43. *Safe* is to *secure* as *risky* is to ______.
44. *Sandpaper* is to *rough* as *oil* is to ______.

Write the word that fits each clue.

45. love, sorrow, joy
46. possessions
47. a hero
48. separation
49. a market
50. friend

Challenge Words Units 31–35 pages 192–221

enactment	astonish	contaminate	extravagant
reversible	muscular	contamination	procedure
spectator	stimulate		

Write the word that fits each clue.

51. excite
52. strong
53. impurity
54. viewer
55. amaze

Write a word that can replace each underlined word or phrase.

56. This jacket is <u>wearable on both sides</u>.
57. This outfit is much too <u>expensive</u> for me to buy.
58. Control the fumes so that they do not <u>pollute</u> the air.
59. To assemble the tent, follow this simple <u>series of steps</u>.
60. The <u>passage</u> of the new law will change the length of the school year.

Spelling-Meaning Strategy

The Latin Word Root *spect*

Did you know that *inspect* and *spectator* are related in meaning? Each word has the Latin word root *spect,* meaning "to look." When you inspect something, you look at it carefully. A spectator is someone who looks at an event. Knowing the meaning of *spect* can help you spell and understand other words with this same word root.

Here is a list of words that contain the Latin word root *spect.*

inspect
spectator

in**spect**	**spect**ator	su**spect**
spectrum	in**spect**or	**spect**acle

Think

- Look up each word in the word box above in your Spelling Dictionary. How does the word root *spect* affect the meaning of each word?

Apply and Extend

Complete these activities on a separate sheet of paper.

1. Write six sentences, using one word from the word box above in each sentence. Can you make the meaning of each word clear?

2. With a partner, list as many other words as you can that include the Latin root *spect.* Then look in the section titled "Word Parts" beginning on page 274 of your Spelling-Meaning Index. Add any other words that you find with this word root to your list.

Summing Up

The Latin word root *spect* means "to look." Words that have the same Latin word root are related in spelling and meaning. Knowing the meaning of the word root *spect* can help you understand and spell the words in that family.

from

Nature's Champions
by Alvin and Virginia Silverstein

Electric eels have unusual abilities. What part of the electric eel produces electricity?

The electric eel uses its electricity in several ways. When it swims, a small "battery" in its tail sends out weak electric pulses at a rate of twenty to fifty a second. The eel uses these electric pulses to find its way. They bounce off objects and come back to special pits in the eel's head. The eel uses electricity in much the same way that bats use sound to find their way around. Scientists think that the electric eel may also use electricity to communicate with other eels.

Think and Discuss

1. What part of the electric eel sends out electric pulses?

2. What is the **main idea** of this paragraph? What is the **topic sentence**?

3. What **facts** did you learn about how the electric eel uses its electricity?

The Writing Process
Research Report

What topics really interest you? Choose one to research, and write a short report about it. Use the guidelines, and follow the Writing Process.

1 Prewriting
- Make a K-W-L chart. List what you know, what you want to know, and what you learned from your research.
- Organize your research notes into an outline.

2 Draft
- Follow your outline. State each main idea in a topic sentence.

3 Revise
- Put all the facts about one main idea together.
- Use your Thesaurus to find exact words.
- Have a writing conference.

4 Proofread
- Did you spell each word correctly?
- Did you use capital letters and punctuation marks correctly ?

5 Publish
- Add a title.
- Display a neat, final copy with books about the topic.

Guidelines for Writing a Research Report

✓ Write topic sentences that state the main ideas.
✓ Support each main idea with facts and details.
✓ Put paragraphs in an order that makes sense.
✓ Include an introduction and a conclusion.

Composition Words

protection
president
pollution
different
remarkable
popular
history
dangerous

The Hermit Crab

Student's Handbook

Extra Practice and Review   229

Writer's Resources

Capitalization and Punctuation Guide
Abbreviations   247
Titles   248
Quotations   248
Capitalization   249
Punctuation   250

Letter Models
Friendly Letter   252
Business Letter   253

Thesaurus

Using the Thesaurus   254
Thesaurus Index   256
Thesaurus   261

Spelling-Meaning Index

Consonant Changes   270
Vowel Changes   271
Word Parts   274

Spelling Dictionary

Spelling Table   276
How to Use a Dictionary   278
Spelling Dictionary   279

Handwriting Models   341
Words Often Misspelled   342

Extra Practice and Review   Cycle 1

Unit 1   Short Vowels   pages 12–17

swift	mist	dock	bunk	stuck
dwell	crush	fund	swept	split

|ŭ| |ĕ|
bunk   **slept**

Spelling Strategy   Remember that a short vowel sound is usually spelled by a single vowel and followed by a consonant sound.

|ă| → **a** |ĕ| → **e** |ĭ| → **i** |ŏ| → **o** |ŭ| → **u**

Write the word that fits each meaning.

1. a source of supply
2. a fine spray
3. to crumple
4. unable to move
5. a platform for loading
6. past tense of *sweep*

Write the word that belongs in each group.

7. live, reside, _____
8. quick, speedy, _____
9. divide, break, _____
10. bed, cot, _____

Unit 2   Spelling |ā| and |ē| pages 18–23

deal	claim	raise	greet	leaf
laid	lease	seal	waist	praise

|ā| |ē|
stray   **leaf**

Spelling Strategy

|ā| → **a-consonant-e, ai, ay** |ē| → **ea, ee**

Write the word that fits each meaning.

11. to rent
12. to state as a fact
13. to close tightly
14. a business agreement
15. approval
16. to welcome
17. placed or set down

Write the word that fits each clue.

18. A belt can go around this.
19. This may change color in autumn.
20. This is an increase in pay.

sign   slope

Unit 3   Spelling |ī| and |ō| pages 24–29

thrown	strike	sign	stole	boast
code	slope	slight	flow	hose

Spelling Strategy

|ī| → **i-consonant-e, igh, i** |ō| → **o-consonant-e, oa, ow, o**

Combine the underlined letters in the first word with the underlined letters in the second word. Write the new word.

21. st<u>raw</u> + <u>bi</u>ke   **24.** <u>st</u>em + m<u>ole</u>
22. <u>fl</u>ing + m<u>ow</u>   **25.** <u>three</u> + sh<u>own</u>
23. <u>sl</u>im + <u>ho</u>pe   **26.** <u>sl</u>ick + n<u>ight</u>

Write the word that fits each clue.

27. stockings or socks   **29.** secret writing
28. what a proud person may do   **30.** to write one's name

proof
clue

Unit 4   Spelling |o͞o| and |yo͞o| pages 30–35

choose	proof	route	troop	rule
bruise	rude	scoop	flute	loop

Spelling Strategy

|o͞o| and |yo͞o| → **u-consonant-e, ue, ew, oo, ui, ou**

Two vowels are missing from each word. Write the words.

31. pr _ _ f   **33.** r _ _ te   **35.** ch _ _ se
32. br _ _ se   **34.** sc _ _ p

Write the word that fits each meaning.

36. not considerate of others
37. a group of soldiers
38. a circular path or pattern
39. a musical instrument
40. a statement or principle that controls behavior

Cycle 1

Unit 5   Spelling |ou|, |ô|, and |oi| pages 36–41

| hawk | tower | bald | claw | prowl |
| coward | haunt | drown | fault | royal |

|oi| |ou|
royal tower

Spelling Strategy

|ou| → **ou, ow** |ô| → **aw, au, a** before **l** |oi| → **oi, oy**

Change the underlined letter in each word to a different letter. Write the new word.

41. b̲old   **43.** g̲awk   **45.** v̲ault   **47.** f̲law

42. b̲rown   **44.** power̲   **46.** l̲oyal

Write the word that completes each sentence.

48. At night cats like to _____ around my neighborhood.

49. Choosing not to fight does not mean one is a _____.

50. Kay loved to win, but a defeat would _____ her for days.

Challenge Words   Units 1–5   pages 12–41

nominate	reproach	plight	presume	trek
campaign	pursuit	mascot	awkward	site
intrude	grouse	poise	rustic	cease

Write the word that fits each meaning.

51. the act of chasing

52. countrylike

53. a slow, hard journey

54. not graceful

55. organized activity to gain a goal

56. to suppose to be true

57. blame or disapproval

58. to select as a candidate

59. a position or a location

60. someone or something believed to bring good luck

Write the word that belongs in each group.

61. trespass, invade, _____

62. problem, difficulty, _____

63. sureness, confidence, _____

64. stop, halt, _____

65. turkey, quail, _____

Unit 7	Spelling |ôr|, |âr|, and |är|		pages 48–53	
hare	scar	lord	sore	torch
tore	flare	fare	rare	barge

\|ôr\| \|âr\|
sore   **hare**

Spelling Strategy

\|ôr\| → **or, ore, oar**   \|âr\| → **are, air**   \|är\| → **ar**

Write a word by changing the underlined letter in each word.

1. <u>b</u>lare
3. s<u>t</u>ar
2. <u>p</u>orch
4. <u>l</u>arge

Write the word that completes each analogy.

5. *Ordinary* is to *common* as *unusual* is to _____.
6. *Wear* is to *wore* as *tear* is to _____.
7. *Burro* is to *donkey* as *jack rabbit* is to _____.
8. *Puffy* is to *swollen* as *painful* is to _____.
9. *Museum* is to *fee* as *bus* is to _____.
10. *Boss* is to *chief* as *nobleman* is to _____.

Unit 8	Spelling |ûr| and |îr|		pages 54–59	
blur	squirm	nerve	early	worth
term	steer	thirst	stern	hurl

Squirt
\|ûr\|

Spelling Strategy

\|ûr\| → **er, ir, ur, ear, or**   \|îr\| → **eer, ear**

Two letters are missing from each word. Write the words.

11. n _ _ ve
13. h _ _ l
15. squ _ _ m
12. th _ _ st
14. bl _ _
16. w _ _ th

Write the word that completes each sentence.

17. The governor was elected to a second _____ in office.
18. We left before sunrise to get an _____ start on our hike.
19. The propeller of a boat is in the _____, or rear.
20. Try to _____ your bicycle away from potholes.

Unit 9   Compound Words   pages 60–65

basketball	cheerleader	weekend	everybody	grandparent
highway	shipyard	daytime	turnpike	household

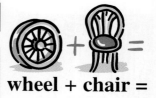

wheel + chair =

wheelchair

Spelling Strategy   A **compound word** is made up of two or more smaller words. Remember that a compound word may be written as one word, as a hyphenated word, or as separate words.

Write the word that fits each clue.

21. Saturday and Sunday
22. home and its activities
23. one who leads a cheering section
24. where boats are built
25. a wide road that drivers pay a toll to use

Write the word that contains part of each word below.

26. baseball
27. grandchild
28. nighttime
29. everyone
30. highlight

Unit 10   Homophones   pages 66–71

poll	main	loan	heal	pore
pole	mane	lone	heel	pour

berry
bury

Spelling Strategy   Remember that **homophones** are words that sound alike but have different spellings and meanings.

Write the word that completes each sentence.

31. I asked my sister to _____ me one of her sweaters.
32. Al stumbled when he caught his _____ on a root.
33. The only shade on the farm came from a _____ cottonwood.
34. A good scrubbing cleans every _____ of your skin.

Write the word that is a synonym for each word below.

35. rod
36. flow
37. chief
38. survey
39. mend
40. hair

|ər|

theater
pillar
actor

Unit 11	The Final |ər|	pages 72–77

actor	powder	humor	anger	banner
matter	flavor	clover	burglar	tractor

Spelling Strategy   When you hear the final |ər| sounds in words of more than one syllable, think of the patterns **er**, **or**, and **ar**.

Two letters are missing from each word. Write the words.

41. ang _ _

42. powd _ _

43. flav _ _

44. clov _ _

45. matt _ _

Write the word that belongs in each group.

46. stage, script, _____

47. comedy, joke, _____

48. flag, sign, _____

49. plow, thresher, _____

50. robber, thief, _____

Challenge Words	Units 7–11	pages 48–77

self-assured	unicorn	ordeal	clamor	canvas
quick-witted	scholar	emerge	yearn	canvass
limelight	chamber	career	hoard	

Write the word that belongs in each group.

51. uproar, racket, _____

52. arise, appear, _____

53. attention, publicity, _____

54. employment, occupation, _____

55. collect, save, _____

56. desire, want, _____

57. trial, hardship, _____

Write the word that fits each clue.

58. This person studies.

59. An artist paints on this.

60. People who take polls do this.

61. This is a synonym for *clever*.

62. This animal is not real.

63. This is a synonym for *self-confident*.

64. A bedroom or a living room is one.

Unit 13 More Compound Words pages 84–89

flashlight	classmate	baby-sit	sweetheart
touchdown	watermelon	masterpiece	whereabouts
worthwhile	part of speech		

watermelon

Spelling Strategy A compound word is made up of two or more smaller words. To spell a compound word correctly, you must know if it is written as one word, as a hyphenated word, or as separate words.

Write the compound word that has each underlined part below.

1. <u>down</u>town
2. time<u>piece</u>
3. part-<u>time</u>
4. <u>sit</u>-up
5. room<u>mate</u>
6. <u>water</u>fall

Write the compound word that belongs in each group.

7. place, location, _____
8. lamp, lantern, _____
9. valuable, useful, _____
10. darling, valentine, _____

Unit 14 Final |l| or |əl| pages 90–95

| sparkle | angle | single | legal | angel |
| level | gentle | label | puzzle | ankle |

|əl|
ankle
shovel

Spelling Strategy When you hear the final |l| or |əl| sounds, think of the patterns **le, el,** and **al.**

Write the word that means the opposite of each word below.

11. illegal
12. harsh
13. married
14. tilted
15. devil

Write the word that completes each sentence.

16. Leah put gold paint on her valentine to make it _____.
17. Would you like to help me put together this jigsaw _____?
18. The contents of this box are listed on the _____.
19. A high-top sneaker supports your _____.
20. The view of the canyon is best from this _____.

traf fic
VC CV

Unit 15   VCCV Pattern   pages 96–101

pattern	tunnel	collect	arrive	traffic
essay	publish	furnish	empire	sorrow

Spelling Strategy   To spell a word with the VCCV syllable pattern, divide the word between the consonants. Look for patterns you have learned, and spell the word by syllables.

Each word below is missing a syllable. Write the words.
21. tun | ___   **23.** em | ___   **25.** ___ | rive
22. ___ | lect   **24.** traf | ___   **26.** pub | ___

Write the word that is a synonym for each underlined word.
27. A store offered to <u>supply</u> the team with uniforms.
28. The fabric had a bright red polka dot <u>design</u>.
29. Kris proofread her <u>composition</u> about her trip.
30. A play about <u>sadness</u> is called a tragedy.

Unit 16   VCCCV Pattern   pages 102–107

improve	simply	explain	address	district
partner	monster	complex	mischief	orphan

Spelling Strategy   When two different consonants in a VCCCV word spell one sound or form a cluster, divide the word into syllables before or after those two consonants. Look for familiar patterns that you have learned, and spell the word by syllables.

Write the word that has each underlined syllable below.
31. cor<u>ner</u>   **32.** <u>ex</u>cite   **33.** amp<u>ly</u>   **34.** <u>mis</u>take

Write the word that fits each clue.
35. synonym for *area*   **38.** a child without parents
36. 217 Baker Street   **39.** a frightening imaginary creature
37. to become better   **40.** difficult to understand

Unit 17   VV Pattern   pages 108–113

giant	cruel	usual	idea	area
riot	diet	trial	lion	liar

ide a

Spelling Strategy   When the two vowels in a VV pattern spell two vowel sounds, divide the word into syllables between the vowels. Look for familiar patterns that you have learned, and spell the word by syllables.

Write the word that completes each analogy.

41. *Irregular* is to *strange* as *regular* is to _____.
42. *Classroom* is to *lesson* as *courtroom* is to _____.
43. *Mild* is to *harsh* as *kind* is to _____.
44. *Small* is to *little* as *huge* is to _____.

Two vowels are missing from each word. Write the words.

45. l _ _ r   **47.** r _ _ t   **49.** d _ _ t
46. id _ _   **48.** ar _ _   **50.** l _ _ n

Challenge Words   Units 13–17   pages 84–113

appreciate	outspoken	extreme	abstain	vital
starry-eyed	exceed	Congress	neutral	mosaic
collide	mineral	awestruck	option	variety

Write the word that fits each meaning.

51. not to do   **54.** go beyond   **57.** to be thankful for
52. important   **55.** full of awe   **58.** not taking sides
53. farthest   **56.** crash   **59.** bold in speech

Write the word that completes each sentence.

60. The Romans mined copper, a _____ with many uses.
61. The President spoke to both houses of _____.
62. Jo had the _____ of seeing a movie or a play.
63. The artist used colorful stone chips to form the _____.
64. A salad can include a _____ of different vegetables.
65. Chen had youthful hope and confidence. He was _____.

Unit 19   VCV Pattern   pages 120–125

evil	detail	value	repeat	nation
vanish	credit	prefer	adore	tulip

Spelling Strategy   To find the syllables of a VCV word, remember to divide the word before or after the consonant. Look for spelling patterns you have learned. Note the spelling of the unstressed syllable, and spell the word by syllables.

Each word below is missing a syllable. Write the word.

1. tu l ___
2. van l ___
3. e l ___
4. ___ l dore
5. ___ l fer
6. na l ___

Write the word that fits each meaning.

7. to say or do again
8. what something is worth
9. a small part of a whole
10. belief or confidence in the truth of something

squeeze**ing**

Unit 20   Words with -ed or -ing   pages 126–131

borrowed	rising	supported	offered	freezing
awaiting	sheltered	seeking	decided	damaged

Spelling Strategy

rise – e + ing = ris**ing**   shelter + ed = shelter**ed**

Write the word that fits each clue.

11. expecting
12. kept from falling
13. very cold
14. volunteered
15. injured
16. going up

Write the word that completes each sentence.

17. The jury finally _____ that the man on trial was innocent.
18. The doghouse Toni made _____ her pet comfortably.
19. I hope Klaus finds the kind of job he is _____.
20. Dana wore a baggy shirt she had _____ from her brother.

Unit 21   More Words with *-ed* or *-ing*   pages 132–137

bragging	skimmed	whipped	dripped	visiting
slammed	wandered	shipped	stunned	hitting

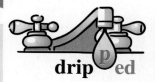

dripp**ed**

Spelling Strategy

ONE-SYLLABLE WORDS: whip + p + ed = whip**ped**
TWO-SYLLABLE WORDS: visit + ing = visit**ing**

Write the word that has each base word below.

21. whip   **23.** wander   **25.** drip
22. ship   **24.** brag   **26.** stun

Write the word that completes each sentence.

27. Margarita quickly _____ the short story.
28. Nina spent the holiday _____ with her relatives.
29. A gust of wind _____ the screen door shut.
30. Henry Aaron is famous for _____ the most home runs.

Unit 22   Words with Suffixes   pages 138–143

watchful	safely	dreadful	enjoyment	breathless
basement	goodness	closeness	delightful	retirement

watchful

Spelling Strategy

A **suffix** is a word part added to the end of a base word. A suffix adds meaning to the word. The word parts **-ly, -ful, -ness, -less,** and **-ment** are suffixes. The spelling of the base word is usually not changed when the suffix begins with a consonant.

Write a spelling word by changing each ending or suffix.

31. delighting   **33.** safety   **35.** closer
32. watched   **34.** breathy   **36.** goodly

Write the word that completes each analogy.

37. *Pain* is to *suffering* as *pleasure* is to _____.
38. *Wonderful* is to *excellent* as *terrible* is to _____.
39. *Faucet* is to *tap* as *cellar* is to _____.
40. *Pay* is to *payment* as *retire* is to _____.

|zhər|
treasure

Unit 23   Final |n| or |ən|, |chər|, |zhər| pages 144–149

| adventure | captain | moisture | fountain | future |
| lecture | feature | pasture | fixture | measure |

Spelling Strategy

|n| or |ən| → **ain** |chər| → **ture** |zhər| → **sure**

Write the word that fits each meaning.

41. the time that is to come
42. something that stays in place
43. one of the parts of the face
44. dampness
45. leader of a group
46. to find the size of

Write the word that completes each sentence.

47. The dentist gave Pepe a _____ about brushing his teeth.
48. I often get a drink of cool water at the _____.
49. A cow and her calf were grazing in the green _____.
50. Kate's camping trip in Alaska was a great _____.

Challenge Words   **Units 19–23**   pages 120–149

contentment	departure	rehearsing	shredded	device
portraying	laser	suspenseful	villain	layered
dramatized	whirred	defenseless	logic	texture

Write the word that fits each clue.

51. acted out
52. uncertain
53. hummed
54. light beam
55. practicing
56. torn in strips
57. arranged in sheets
58. clear reasoning
59. playing the part of

Write the word that completes each analogy.

60. *Sadness* is to *gloominess* as *satisfaction* is to _____.
61. *Yo-yo* is to *toy* as *can opener* is to _____.
62. *Loud* is to *sound* as *rough* is to _____.
63. *Safe* is to *secure* as *unprotected* is to _____.
64. *Greeting* is to *arrival* as *farewell* is to _____.
65. *Good* is to *hero* as *evil* is to _____.

Cycle 5

Unit 25   Final |ĭj|, |ĭv|, and |ĭs| pages 156–161

practice	native	luggage	postage	voyage
bandage	message	captive	shortage	passage

luggage

Spelling Strategy

|ĭj| → **age** |ĭv| → **ive** |ĭs| → **ice**

Write the word that fits each clue.

1. This covers a wound.
2. This is a scarcity.
3. A ship or an airplane can take you on this.
4. This is a communication.
5. This is shown by a stamp.
6. This includes suitcases.

Write the word that belongs in each group. Underline the letters that spell the final |ĭv|, |ĭj|, or |ĭs| sounds.

7. resident, citizen, _____
8. path, channel, _____
9. rehearsal, training, _____
10. trapped, imprisoned, _____

Unit 26   Unstressed Syllables   pages 162–167

carrot	hidden	entry	destroy	distance
blossom	ashamed	program	wisdom	solid

spinach   carrot

Spelling Strategy
To spell a two-syllable word, divide the word into syllables. Spell the word by syllables, noting carefully the spelling of the unstressed syllable.

Write the word that has each underlined syllable.

11. milli<u>gram</u>   12. gar<u>den</u>   13. par<u>rot</u>   14. pan<u>try</u>

Write the word that fits each meaning.

15. feeling guilt
16. to bloom
17. strong and firm
18. to ruin completely
19. intelligence and good judgment
20. the amount of space between two places

in crease

Unit 27   Words with Prefixes   pages 168–173

report	unable	inform	remind	disaster
unaware	disagree	relax	display	insult

Spelling Strategy   A **prefix** is a word part added to the beginning of a base word or a word root. A prefix adds meaning. **Un-, in-, dis-,** and **re-** are prefixes. Find the prefix and the base word or the word root. Spell the word by parts.

Add a prefix to each base word or word root. Write the words.

21. ___ | lax   **23.** ___ | form   **25.** ___ | aware
22. ___ | aster   **24.** ___ | port   **26.** ___ | sult

Write the word that completes each sentence.

27. Since I sprained my ankle, I am _____ to run very fast.
28. Tomas saw the book he wanted in the window _____.
29. These photos from last summer _____ me of the fun we had.
30. I will not vote for Smith because I _____ with his views.

scary
scariest

Unit 28   Changing Final *y* to *i*   pages 174–179

enemies	victories	armies	liberties	countries
ladies	emptiness	duties	lilies	worthiness

Spelling Strategy   When a word ends with a consonant and **y**, change the **y** to **i** when adding **-es, -ed, -er, -est,** or **-ness**.

Write the word formed by adding each base word and ending or suffix below.

31. empty + ness   **33.** enemy + es   **35.** worthy + ness
32. army + es   **34.** lily + es

Write the word that is a synonym for each word below.

36. nations   **39.** responsibilities
37. successes   **40.** freedoms
38. women

Unit 29   Adding *-ion*   pages 180–185

regulate	act	correct	tense	convict
regulation	action	correction	tension	conviction

correction

Spelling Strategy   Remember that the suffix **-ion** can change verbs into nouns. When a verb ends with **e**, drop the **e** before adding **-ion**.

Write the word that completes each sentence.

41. The hero came onstage in the second _____ of the play.

42. My paper will have no errors after I make this _____.

43. Rather than complain, Jo took _____ to solve the problem.

44. Facts proved the man's innocence, so there was no _____.

Write the word that fits each meaning.

45. accurate   **48.** anxious

46. stress   **49.** a rule

47. criminal   **50.** to control

Challenge Words   Units 25–29   pages 156–185

superlative	primitive	levied	exert	animate
unnecessary	colonies	adapt	inflate	animation
rivalries	heritage	inquiry	somber	

Write the word that belongs in each group.

51. change, adjust, _____

52. brighten, energize, _____

53. simple, crude, _____

54. dark, gloomy, _____

Write the word that fits each clue.

55. synonym for *settlements*

56. antonym of *needed*

57. synonym for *liveliness*

58. being the very best

59. imposed a tax

60. the act of asking in order to find out

61. synonym for *apply*

62. synonym for *competitions*

63. to fill with gas and expand

64. something handed down from earlier generations

Unit 31   More Words with *-ion*   pages 192–197

inspect	protect	promote	confess	decorate
inspection	protection	promotion	confession	decoration

Spelling Strategy   The suffix **-ion** can change verbs to nouns. When a verb ends with **e**, drop the **e** when adding **-ion**. If a verb does not end with **e**, just add **-ion**.

Write a word by changing each underlined prefix.

1. <u>re</u>spect
2. <u>de</u>tect
3. <u>pro</u>fession
4. <u>re</u>mote

Write the word that fits each clue.

5. synonym for *admit*
6. an official examination
7. something put up for a party or a celebration
8. a synonym for *beautify*
9. advancement in rank
10. what a guard provides

Unit 32   More Words with Prefixes   pages 198–203

conduct	excuse	convince	contain	compare
exchange	consist	proverb	engage	pronoun

Spelling Strategy   **Com-, con-, en-, ex-, pre-,** and **pro-** are prefixes. To spell a word with a prefix, find the prefix and the base word or the word root. Spell the word by parts.

Write the word that fits each clue.

11. needed if you are late
12. synonym for *persuade*
13. takes the place of a noun
14. to swap
15. "Better late than never," for example

Write the word that rhymes with each word below.

16. insist
17. retain
18. prepare
19. deduct
20. enrage

Cycle 6

Unit 33 Suffixes *-ent, -ant; -able, -ible* pages 204–209

student	profitable	possible	suitable	fashionable
honorable	accident	remarkable	valuable	servant

Spelling Strategy

|ənt| → **-ent, -ant** |ə bəl| → **-able, -ible**

Write a word to replace each underlined word.

21. a <u>stylish</u> coat

22. a <u>precious</u> jewel

23. an <u>honest</u> person

24. a public <u>employee</u>

25. a straight-A <u>pupil</u>

26. <u>proper</u> behavior

Write the word that completes each sentence.

27. Without advanced rockets, space travel would not be _____.

28. I did not mean to tear the page. It was an _____!

29. My money-making plan was more _____ than I had hoped.

30. Abby's great musical talent is _____ for one so young.

Unit 34 Three-Syllable Words pages 210–215

general	president	avenue	regular	educate
uniform	deposit	attention	period	romantic

Spelling Strategy
A three-syllable word has one stressed syllable and two syllables with less stress. To help you spell the word, divide the word into syllables. Note the spelling of the syllables that have less stress.

Write a word to complete each phrase. Underline the word that has the |yo͞o| sound in the first syllable.

31. a _____ novel

32. get _____ checkups

33. not paying _____

34. a bank _____ slip

35. a nurse's white _____

36. a five-star _____

Write the word that belongs in each group.

37. street, road, _____

38. teach, tutor, _____

39. secretary, treasurer, _____

40. comma, question mark, _____

245

stadium

Unit 35   More Three-Syllable Words   pages 216–221

continue	personal	favorite	apartment	history
sensitive	consider	festival	violet	imagine

Spelling Strategy   To help you spell a three-syllable word, divide the word into syllables. Look for familiar spelling patterns. Note carefully the spelling of the unstressed syllables, and spell the word by syllables.

Write a word by adding two syllables to each syllable below.

41. ___ | sid | ___   **43.** his | ___ ___   **45.** fa | ___ ___

42. ___ | mag | ___   **44.** ___ | tin | ___   **46.** sen | ___ ___

Write the word that completes each analogy.

47. *Fruit* is to *strawberry* as *flower* is to _____.

48. *Lone* is to *single* as *private* is to _____.

49. *Gathering* is to *meeting* as *celebration* is to _____.

50. *Fare* is to *airplane* as *rent* is to _____.

Challenge Words   Units 31–35   pages 192–221

preamble	Olympics	convene	durable	irritate
reverence	majestic	ovation	obvious	irritation
prominent	concise	elegant	amateur	

Write the word that is a synonym for each word below.

51. sturdy   **53.** respect   **55.** annoy   **57.** applause

52. brief   **54.** dignified **56.** assemble

Write the word that completes each sentence.

58. The purpose of a document may be stated in the _____.

59. The new principal is a _____ citizen.

60. Speed skating is my favorite event of the Winter _____.

61. Buzzing mosquitoes were a constant _____ on the hike.

62. Unlike a professional athlete, an _____ is not paid.

63. The decorations for the party were tasteful and _____.

64. I found an _____ spelling error in my essay.

Writer's Resources

Capitalization and Punctuation Guide

Abbreviations

Abbreviations are shortened forms of words. Most abbreviations begin with a capital letter and end with a period. Use abbreviations only in special kinds of writing, such as addresses and lists.

Titles	Mr. *(Mister)* Mr. Juan Albano Sr. *(Senior)* John Helt, Sr.
	Mrs. *(Mistress)* Mrs. Frances Wong Jr. *(Junior)* John Helt, Jr.
	Ms. Leslie Clark Dr. *(Doctor)* Dr. Janice Dodd
	Note: *Miss* is not an abbreviation and does not end with a period.

Words used in addresses

St. *(Street)*   Blvd. *(Boulevard)*   Pkwy. *(Parkway)*
Rd. *(Road)*   Rte. *(Route)*   Mt. *(Mount or Mountain)*
Ave. *(Avenue)*   Apt. *(Apartment)*   Expy. *(Expressway)*
Dr. *(Drive)*

Words used in business

Co. *(Company)*   Inc. *(Incorporated)*
Corp. *(Corporation)*   Ltd. *(Limited)*

Other abbreviations

Some abbreviations are written in all capital letters, with a letter standing for each important word.

P.D. *(Police Department)*   P.O. *(Post Office)*
J.P. *(Justice of the Peace)*   R.N. *(Registered Nurse)*

The United States Postal Service uses two capital letters and no period in each of its state abbreviations.

AL	*(Alabama)*	IN	*(Indiana)*	NE	*(Nebraska)*
AK	*(Alaska)*	IA	*(Iowa)*	NV	*(Nevada)*
AZ	*(Arizona)*	KS	*(Kansas)*	NH	*(New Hampshire)*
AR	*(Arkansas)*	KY	*(Kentucky)*	NJ	*(New Jersey)*
CA	*(California)*	LA	*(Louisiana)*	NM	*(New Mexico)*
CO	*(Colorado)*	ME	*(Maine)*	NY	*(New York)*
CT	*(Connecticut)*	MD	*(Maryland)*	NC	*(North Carolina)*
DE	*(Delaware)*	MA	*(Massachusetts)*	ND	*(North Dakota)*
FL	*(Florida)*	MI	*(Michigan)*	OH	*(Ohio)*
GA	*(Georgia)*	MN	*(Minnesota)*	OK	*(Oklahoma)*
HI	*(Hawaii)*	MS	*(Mississippi)*	OR	*(Oregon)*
ID	*(Idaho)*	MO	*(Missouri)*	PA	*(Pennsylvania)*
IL	*(Illinois)*	MT	*(Montana)*		

(continued)

Other abbreviations *(continued)*

RI	*(Rhode Island)*	TX	*(Texas)*	WA	*(Washington)*
SC	*(South Carolina)*	UT	*(Utah)*	WV	*(West Virginia)*
SD	*(South Dakota)*	VT	*(Vermont)*	WI	*(Wisconsin)*
TN	*(Tennessee)*	VA	*(Virginia)*	WY	*(Wyoming)*

Initials are abbreviations that stand for a person's first or middle name. Some names have both a first and a middle initial.

E. B. White *(Elwyn Brooks White)*
T. James Carey *(Thomas James Carey)*
Mr. John M. Gordon *(Mister John Morris Gordon)*

Titles

Underlining

The important words and the first and last words in a title are capitalized. Titles of books, magazines, TV shows, movies, and newspapers are underlined.

Oliver Twist *(book)*   Treasure Island *(movie)*
Cricket *(magazine)*   The Phoenix Express *(newspaper)*
Nova *(TV show)*

Quotation marks with titles

Titles of short stories, songs, articles, book chapters, and most poems are set off by quotation marks.

"The Necklace" *(short story)*   "The Human Brain" *(chapter)*
"Home on the Range" *(song)*   "Deer at Dusk" *(poem)*
"Three Days in the Sahara" *(article)*

Quotations

Quotation marks with commas and periods

Quotation marks are used to set off a speaker's exact words. The first word of a quotation begins with a capital letter. Punctuation belongs *inside* the closing quotation marks. Commas separate a quotation from the rest of the sentence.

"Where," asked the stranger, "is the post office?"
"Please put away your books now," said Mr. Emory.
Linda whispered, "What time is it?"
"It's late," replied Bill. "Let's go!"

Capitalization

Rules for capitalization

Capitalize the first word of every sentence.

What an unusual color the roses are!

Capitalize the pronoun *I*.

What should I do next?

Capitalize proper nouns. If a proper noun is made up of more than one word, capitalize each important word.

Emily G. Messe   District of Columbia   Lincoln Memorial

Capitalize titles or their abbreviations when used with a person's name.

Governor Bradford   Senator Smith   Dr. Ling

Capitalize proper adjectives.

We ate at a French restaurant.
She is French.
That is a North American custom.

Capitalize the names of days, months, and holidays.

My birthday is on the last Monday in March.
We watched the parade on the Fourth of July.

Capitalize the names of buildings and companies.

Empire State Building
Central School
Able Supply Company

Capitalize the first, last, and all important words in a title. Do not capitalize words such as *a, in, and, or,* and *the* unless they begin or end a title.

From Earth to the Moon   "The Rainbow Connection"
The New York Times   "Growing Up"

Rules for capitalization
(continued)

Capitalize the first word of each main topic and subtopic in an outline.

I. Types of libraries
   A. Large public library
   B. Bookmobile

Capitalize the first word in the greeting and the closing of a letter.

Dear Marcia,   Yours truly,

Punctuation

End marks

There are three end marks. A period (.) ends a declarative or imperative sentence. A question mark (?) follows an interrogative sentence. An exclamation point (!) follows an exclamatory sentence.

The scissors are on my desk. *(declarative)*
Look up the spelling of that word. *(imperative)*
How is the word spelled? *(interrogative)*
This is your best poem so far! *(exclamatory)*

Apostrophe

To form the possessive of a singular noun, add an apostrophe and *s*.

doctor's   teacher's   grandmother's   family's

For a plural noun that ends in *s*, add only an apostrophe.

sisters'   families'   Smiths'   hound dogs'

For a plural noun that does not end in *s*, add an apostrophe and *s* to form the plural possessive.

women's   mice's   children's   geese's

Use an apostrophe in contractions in place of dropped letters. Do not use contractions in formal writing.

isn't *(is not)*   don't *(do not)*   wasn't *(was not)*
can't *(cannot)*   won't *(will not)*   we're *(we are)*
it's *(it is)*   they've *(they have)*   could've *(could have)*
I'm *(I am)*   they'll *(they will)*   would've *(would have)*

Colon	Use a colon after the greeting in a business letter.
	Dear Mrs. Trimby: Dear Realty Homes:

Comma	A comma tells your reader where to pause. For words in a series, put a comma after each item except the last. Do not use a comma if only two items are listed.
	Clyde asked if we had any apples, peaches, or grapes.
	Use commas to separate two or more adjectives that are listed together unless one adjective tells how many.
	The fresh, ripe fruit was placed in a bowl.
	One red apple was especially shiny.
	Use a comma before the conjunction in a compound sentence.
	Some students were at lunch, but others were studying.
	Use commas after introductory words such as *yes, no, oh,* and *well* when they begin a sentence.
	Well, it's just too cold out. No, it isn't six yet.
	Use a comma to separate a noun in direct address.
	Jean, help me fix this tire.
	How was your trip, Grandpa?
	Can you see, Joe, where I left my glasses?
	Use a comma between the names of a city and a state.
	Chicago, Illinois Miami, Florida
	Use a comma after the greeting in a friendly letter.
	Dear Deena, Dear Uncle Rudolph,
	Use a comma after the closing in a letter.
	Your nephew, Sincerely yours,

Letter Models

Friendly Letter

Use correct letter format, capitalization, and punctuation in a friendly letter. A friendly letter has **five** parts.

1. The **heading** contains your complete address and the date.

2. The **greeting** usually includes the word *Dear* and the name of the person to whom you are writing.

3. The **body** is the main part of the letter. It includes all the information that you want to tell your reader.

4. The **closing** says "good-bye." Use closings such as *Your friend* or *Love.*

5. The **signature** is your first name. Sign it under the closing.

Study this model.

1201 Ridge Road
Austin, TX 78768   ◄---- **Heading**
October 5, 1998

Dear Jerry, ◄········· **Greeting**

Body

   It seems funny to be writing to you instead of just running next door. I hope you feel at home in your new school by now. Make lots of new friends, but don't forget your old friends in Austin!

   Carmen and I have great plans for the class trip, but we miss your neat ideas.

   Write soon and tell us about Iowa!

Closing ·········► Your friend,
                      Tony

Signature ·········►

Letter Models

Business Letter

Use correct letter format, capitalization, and punctuation in a business letter. A business letter has **six** parts.

1 The **heading** is the same as in a friendly letter.

2 The **inside address** includes the name and address of the person or business that will receive the letter.

3 The **greeting** follows the inside address. If you do not know whom to address, use *Dear Sir or Madam* or the company's name. Use a colon (:) after the greeting.

4 The **body** is your message. Be direct and polite.

5 The **closing** is formal. Use *Yours truly,* for example.

6 The **signature** is your full name. Write it under the closing. Print or type your name under your signature.

Study this model.

> **Heading** →
> 38 Spruce Street
> East Lansing, MI 48823
> September 28, 1998
>
> **Inside address** →
> Royal Stamp Company
> 2102 North Avenue
> Chicago, IL 60607
>
> Dear Sir or Madam: ← **Greeting**
>
> **Body** →
> I would like to be on your mailing list. I want to collect stamps from around the world that mark the birthdays of famous people.
>
> Please send me any of your catalogs that list this kind of stamp.
>
> Sincerely, ← **Closing**
> *Daniel Hayes* ← **Signature**
> Daniel Hayes

Using the Thesaurus

Why Use a Thesaurus?

A **thesaurus** is a reference that can help you make your writing clearer and more interesting. Use it to find a word to replace an overused word or to find an exact word to say what you mean.

How to Use This Thesaurus

This thesaurus includes main entries for words you often use. The **main entry words** appear in blue and are in alphabetical order. The main entry for *same* is shown below. Each main entry includes

- the **part of speech,** a **definition,** and a **sample sentence** for the main entry word;

- several **subentry words** that could be used in place of the main entry word, with a definition and a sample sentence for each one;

- **antonyms,** or opposites, for the main entry word.

> **For example** How would you decide which subentry to use to replace *same* in this sentence?

> ### The twins look the **same.**

1. Find each subentry word given for *same.* They are *equal, identical,* and *uniform.*
2. Read the definition and the sample sentence for each subentry. Decide which subentry fits the meaning of the sentence most closely.

> ### The twins look **identical.**

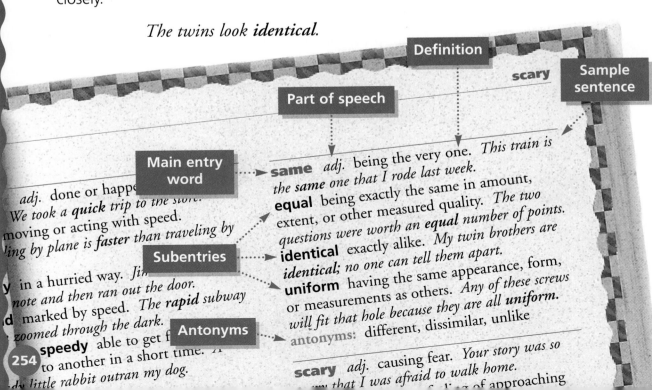

Definition

scary

Part of speech

Main entry word

adj. done or happe...
We took a **quick** *trip to the store.*
moving or acting with speed.
ling by plane is **faster** *than traveling by*

Subentries

y in a hurried way. *Ji*
note and then ran out the door.
d marked by speed. *The* **rapid** *subway*
zoomed through the dark.

Antonyms

254 **speedy** able to get f
to another in a short time. *A*
little rabbit outran my dog.

Sample sentence

same *adj.* being the very one. *This train is the same one that I rode last week.*
equal being exactly the same in amount, extent, or other measured quality. *The two questions were worth an* **equal** *number of points.*
identical exactly alike. *My twin brothers are identical; no one can tell them apart.*
uniform having the same appearance, form, or measurements as others. *Any of these screws will fit that hole because they are all* **uniform.**
antonyms: different, dissimilar, unlike

scary *adj.* causing fear. *Your story was so ... that I was afraid to walk home.*
... of approaching

Using the Thesaurus Index

The Thesaurus Index will help you find a word in this Thesaurus. The Thesaurus Index lists **all** of the main entry words, the subentries, and any antonyms included in the Thesaurus. The words in the Thesaurus Index are in alphabetical order.

When you look in the Thesaurus Index, you will see that words are shown in three ways.

Main entry words are shown in blue. For example, the word *same* is a main entry word.

Subentries are shown in dark print. For example, *satisfactory* is a subentry.

Antonyms are shown in regular print. For example, *secure* is an antonym.

S

sadness **happiness** *n.*
safe **dangerous** *adj.*
same *adj.*
sanitary **dirty** *adj.*
satisfactory good *adj.*
scary *adj.*
scatter **gather** *v.*
scorn **praise** *n.*
scratched damaged *adj.*
second-rate **good** *adj.*
secure **dangerous** *adj.*
see *v.*
separate different *adj.*

Practice Look up each word below in the Thesaurus Index. Write the main entry word for each word.

1. spotless   **2.** haul   **3.** alarming   **4.** hurl   **5.** extend

Use the Thesaurus to choose a more exact word to replace each underlined word. Rewrite each sentence, using the new word.

6. It was a <u>normal</u> spring day.

7. I decided to <u>walk</u> to a nearby park.

8. A small crowd had <u>gathered</u> near the bandstand.

9. I stopped and heard two performers telling <u>funny</u> stories.

10. I did not <u>think</u> that I could laugh so hard!

Thesaurus Index

A

abnormal **normal** *adj.*
accept **give** *v.*
acceptable good *adj.*
accumulate gather *v.*
acquire get *v.*
active lively *adj.*
address speech *n.*
adept good *adj.*
adequate good *adj.*
admirable good *adj.*
admirable worthy *adj.*
admiration praise *n.*
agitated **peaceful** *adj.*
agreeable **angry** *adj.*
alarm warning *n.*
alarming scary *adj.*
alert warning *n.*
amusing funny *adj.*
angry *adj.*
antiseptic **dirty** *adj.*
anxious **peaceful** *adj.*
approval praise *n.*
arrangement order *n.*
assemble gather *v.*
average normal *adj.*
aware educated *adj.*
awareness knowledge *n.*
awful **good** *adj.*

B

bad **good** *adj.*
believe think *v.*
blend mixture *n.*
blossom grow *v.*
boast *v.*
bored **eager** *adj.*

boring *adj.*
brag boast *v.*
bruised damaged *adj.*
bunch gather *v.*
bury hide *v.*
buy get *v.*

C

calm **angry** *adj.*
calm peaceful *adj.*
careful *adj.*
cast throw *v.*
cause **effect** *n.*
caution warning *n.*
cautious careful *adj.*
changeable **faithful** *adj.*
cheer happiness *n.*
chief *adj.*
chipper lively *adj.*
choose decide *v.*
chuck throw *v.*
clean **dirty** *adj.*
cluster gather *v.*
collect gather *v.*
comforting **scary** *adj.*
comical funny *adj.*
command order *n.*
common regular *adj.*
competent good *adj.*
conceal hide *v.*
connect join *v.*
consequence effect *n.*
consider think *v.*
constant faithful *adj.*
contaminated dirty *adj.*
cover hide *v.*
create *v.*
criticism **praise** *n.*
cross angry *adj.*
crow boast *v.*

D

damaged *adj.*
dangerous *adj.*
decency justice *n.*
decide *v.*
decline **grow** *v.*
decrease increase *v.*
delight happiness *n.*
demolish **create** *v.*
demonstration display *n.*
dented damaged *adj.*
deposit put *v.*
depression **happiness** *n.*
deserve *v.*
design create *v.*
desirable good *adj.*
destroy **create** *v.*
determine decide *v.*
develop grow *v.*
devoted faithful *adj.*
different *adj.*
different **same** *adj.*
dingy dirty *adj.*
dirty *adj.*
disapproval **praise** *n.*
disinfected **dirty** *adj.*
disloyal **faithful** *adj.*
display *n.*
display **hide** *v.*
dissimilar **same** *adj.*
distressed **peaceful** *adj.*
double-crossing **faithful** *adj.*
drag pull *v.*
dreadful **good** *adj.*
dream think *v.*
dreary boring *adj.*
dry boring *adj.*
dull boring *adj.*
dull **lively** *adj.*
dusty dirty *adj.*
dwindle **grow** *v.*

E

eager *adj.*
earn deserve *v.*
earn get *v.*
earnest **funny** *adj.*
edgy **peaceful** *adj.*
educated *adj.*
effect *n.*
endanger **protect** *v.*
energetic lively *adj.*
enjoyment happiness *n.*
enlarge increase *v.*
enormous **small** *adj.*
enthusiastic eager *adj.*
equal same *adj.*
equality justice *n.*
establish create *v.*
excellent perfect *adj.*
exciting **boring** *adj.*
exhibit display *n.*
exhibit **hide** *v.*
expand increase *v.*
expose **hide** *v.*
extend increase *v.*
extraordinary **normal** *adj.*

F

fairness justice *n.*
faithful *adj.*
faithless **faithful** *adj.*
false **faithful** *adj.*
fast **quick** *adj.*
faulty **perfect** *adj.*
filthy dirty *adj.*
fine **good** *adj.*
fire throw *n.*
flavor taste *n.*
flawed **perfect** *adj.*

fling throw *v.*
flip throw *v.*
flourish grow *v.*
foolhardy **careful** *adj.*
forbidding scary *adj.*
forfeit **get** *v.*
forgiving **angry** *adj.*
frightening scary *adj.*
frisky lively *adj.*
funny *adj.*
furious angry *adj.*
furnish give *v.*

G

gather *v.*
general normal *adj.*
get *v.*
giant **small** *adj.*
give *v.*
good *adj.*
grave **funny** *adj.*
grimy dirty *adj.*
grow *v.*
grungy dirty *adj.*
guard protect *v.*

H

happiness *n.*
harmless **dangerous** *adj.*
harmonious peaceful *adj.*
hasty quick *adj.*
haul pull *v.*
hazardous dangerous *adj.*
heave throw *v.*
heedful careful *adj.*
hide *v.*
honorable worthy *adj.*
horrible **good** *adj.*

huge **small** *adj.*
humorous funny *adj.*
hurl throw *v.*
hygienic **dirty** *adj.*

I

ideal perfect *adj.*
identical same *adj.*
idle **lively** *adj.*
ignorant **educated** *adj.*
ignore **see** *v.*
imagine think *v.*
immaculate **dirty** *adj.*
impure dirty *adj.*
inactive **lively** *adj.*
increase *v.*
indifferent **eager** *adj.*
inequality justice *n.*
inferior **good** *adj.*
informed educated *adj.*
injustice **justice** *n.*
interesting **boring** *adj.*
invent create *v.*

J

join *v.*
jumble mixture *n.*
justice *n.*

K

keen eager *adj.*
knowledge *n.*
knowledgeable educated *adj.*

Thesaurus Index

L

laughable **funny** *adj.*
launch **throw** *v.*
lay **put** *v.*
lazy **lively** *adj.*
leading **chief** *adj.*
learned **educated** *adj.*
lecture **speech** *n.*
leisurely **quick** *adj.*
lifeless **lively** *adj.*
limp **walk** *v.*
lively *adj.*
lively **boring** *adj.*
lob **throw** *v.*
locate **put** *v.*
lose **get** *v.*
loyal **faithful** *adj.*

M

magnify **increase** *v.*
main **chief** *adj.*
major **chief** *adj.*
major **small** *adj.*
march **walk** *v.*
marvelous **good** *adj.*
mask **hide** *v.*
menace **protect** *v.*
merit **deserve** *v.*
messy **dirty** *adj.*
microscopic **small** *adj.*
miniature **small** *adj.*
minor **chief** *adj.*
minor **small** *adj.*
misery **happiness** *n.*
miss **see** *v.*
mixture *n.*
model **perfect** *adj.*
monotonous **boring** *adj.*

morality **justice** *n.*
muddy **dirty** *adj.*
murky **dirty** *adj.*

N

neglectful **careful** *adj.*
nervous **peaceful** *adj.*
normal *adj.*
notice **see** *v.*

O

observe **see** *v.*
obtain **get** *v.*
offer **give** *v.*
order *n.*
outcome **effect** *n.*
outstanding **good** *adj.*
overhauled **damaged** *adj.*
overlook **see** *v.*

P

participate **join** *v.*
patched **damaged** *adj.*
peaceful *adj.*
pelt **throw** *v.*
perfect *adj.*
perilous **dangerous** *adj.*
place **put** *v.*
placid **peaceful** *adj.*
pleased **angry** *adj.*
pleasure **happiness** *n.*
polluted **dirty** *adj.*
ponder **think** *v.*
poor **good** *adj.*
poor **perfect** *adj.*
praise *n.*

preference **taste** *n.*
present **give** *v.*
principal **chief** *adj.*
produce **create** *v.*
propel **throw** *v.*
protect *v.*
provide **give** *v.*
pull *v.*
pure **dirty** *adj.*
push **pull** *v.*
put *v.*

Q

quick *adj.*
quiet **peaceful** *adj.*

R

rapid **quick** *adj.*
rare **normal** *adj.*
rate **deserve** *v.*
reason **effect** *n.*
reassuring **scary** *adj.*
receive **give** *v.*
reckless **careful** *adj.*
reduce **increase** *v.*
regard **see** *v.*
regular *adj.*
regular **normal** *adj.*
relaxed **peaceful** *adj.*
remarkable **normal** *adj.*
remove **put** *v.*
repaired **damaged** *adj.*
resentful **angry** *adj.*
resolve **decide** *v.*
restful **peaceful** *adj.*
restless **peaceful** *adj.*
result **effect** *n.*
reveal **hide** *v.*
risky **dangerous** *adj.*
routine **regular** *adj.*

S

sadness **happiness** *n.*
safe **dangerous** *adj.*
same *adj.*
sanitary **dirty** *adj.*
satisfactory good *adj.*
scary *adj.*
scatter **gather** *v.*
scorn **praise** *n.*
scratched damaged *adj.*
second-rate **good** *adj.*
secure **dangerous** *adj.*
see *v.*
separate different *adj.*
separate **gather** *v.*
serene peaceful *adj.*
serious **funny** *adj.*
set put *v.*
settle decide *v.*
shattered damaged *adj.*
shield protect *v.*
shoddy **good** *adj.*
shoot throw *v.*
shove **pull** *v.*
show **hide** *v.*
shrink **increase** *v.*
signal warning *n.*
slack **quick** *adj.*
sling throw *v.*
slow **quick** *adj.*
sluggish **lively** *adj.*
small *adj.*
smudged dirty *adj.*
soiled dirty *adj.*
soothing peaceful *adj.*
soothing **scary** *adj.*
sooty dirty *adj.*
sorrow **happiness** *n.*
source **effect** *n.*

speech *n.*
speedy quick *adj.*
spirited lively *adj.*
splendid good *adj.*
spot see *v.*
spotless **dirty** *adj.*
sprout grow *v.*
stained dirty *adj.*
sterile **dirty** *adj.*
strange **normal** *adj.*
stride walk *v.*
stroll walk *v.*
stunt **grow** *v.*
stunted small *adj.*
substandard **good** *adj.*
suffering **happiness** *n.*
sufficient good *adj.*
suitable good *adj.*
superb good *adj.*
supply give *v.*
swift quick *adj.*

T

take **give** *v.*
take away **put** *v.*
tarnished dirty *adj.*
taste *n.*
tattered damaged *adj.*
tense **peaceful** *adj.*
terrible **good** *adj.*
terrific good *adj.*
terrifying scary *adj.*
think *v.*
threaten **protect** *v.*
throw *v.*
thrust **pull** *v.*
tiny small *adj.*
tiptoe walk *v.*
tolerable good *adj.*

toss throw *v.*
tow pull *v.*
tranquil peaceful *adj.*
treacherous dangerous *adj.*
tremendous **small** *adj.*
troubled **peaceful** *adj.*
true faithful *adj.*
tug pull *v.*
typical normal *adj.*

U

unaware **educated** *adj.*
unclean dirty *adj.*
undeserving **worthy** *adj.*
undisturbed peaceful *adj.*
undo **create** *v.*
uneasy **peaceful** *adj.*
unenthusiastic **eager** *adj.*
uniform same *adj.*
unimportant **chief** *adj.*
unimportant **worthy** *adj.*
uninterested **eager** *adj.*
unlike **same** *adj.*
unruffled peaceful *adj.*
unsanitary dirty *adj.*
unschooled **educated** *adj.*
unsettled peaceful *adj.*
unsterile dirty *adj.*
unthreatening **dangerous** *adj.*
untroubled peaceful *adj.*
unusual different *adj.*
unusual **normal** *adj.*
upset angry *adj.*
upset **peaceful** *adj.*
upshot effect *n.*
useless **worthy** *adj.*
usual normal *adj.*

V

valuable worthy *adj.*
varied **boring** *adj.*
view see *v.*

W

walk *v.*
wander walk *v.*
warning *n.*
wary careful *adj.*
washed **dirty** *adj.*
watchful careful *adj.*
win get *v.*
wisdom knowledge *n.*
witness see *v.*
wonderful good *adj.*
worried **peaceful** *adj.*
worthless **worthy** *adj.*
worthy *adj.*
worthy good *adj.*
wrong **justice** *n.*

Thesaurus

A

angry *adj.* feeling or showing displeasure. *I was **angry** when I broke my shoelace.*

cross in a bad mood; grumpy. *I get **cross** if I don't get enough sleep.*

furious feeling or showing rage. *After missing his train, Ted was so **furious** that he tore up his ticket.*

resentful feeling or showing anger or bitterness over something that is thought to be unfair. *Beth was **resentful** when no one thanked her for her help.*

upset sad or worried. *Joy was **upset** until her lost cat returned.*

antonyms: agreeable, calm *adj.*, forgiving *adj.*, pleased *adj.*

B

boast *v.* to praise oneself, one's belongings, or one's actions. *Sara always **boasts** about how fast she can run.*

brag to speak with too much pride about oneself in an attempt to show off. *Leroy **bragged** to everyone about his new bike.*

crow to utter a cry of delight or victory. *We all smiled when Pat **crowed**, "I won! I won!"*

---

boring *adj.* not interesting. *The television program was so **boring** that I fell asleep.*

dreary boring; dull. *Cleaning my room was a **dreary** task.*

dry tiresome. *It was hard to finish reading the long, **dry**, government report.*

dull lacking excitement. *Neither team scored during the **dull** soccer match.*

monotonous not interesting because of being always the same. ***Monotonous** songs just repeat the same words over and over.*

antonyms: exciting *adj.*, interesting *adj.*, lively, varied *adj.*

C

careful *adj.* using caution or care. *Looking for clues, the detective made a **careful** search of the room.*

cautious not taking chances. *Kim is too **cautious** to try the dangerous climb to the top.*

heedful paying close attention. *The campers were **heedful** of the forest ranger's warnings about campfires.*

wary on one's guard against danger. *He was **wary** of skiing down such a steep and icy slope.*

watchful on the lookout; alert. *The **watchful** dog barked at every passer-by.*

antonyms: foolhardy, neglectful, reckless

---

chief *adj.* highest in rank or importance. *My sister was appointed **chief** architect for her company.*

leading most important. *Paris, France, is one of the **leading** cities for fashion.*

main most important. *The **main** library is bigger than its branches.*

major larger, greater, or more important. *High winds caused some destruction, but flooding was the **major** cause of damage.*

principal leading all others. *Did you know that the panda's **principal** food is a kind of bamboo?*

antonyms: minor *adj.*, unimportant

---

create *v.* to bring into being. *Spiders **create** webs to trap insects.*

design to make a plan or drawing for something. *An art student **designed** the school's new sign.*

establish to begin or set up. *The settlers soon **established** a small town.*

invent to make something that did not exist before. *No one is sure who really **invented** the camera.*

produce to manufacture. *How many cars a year does Japan **produce**?*

antonyms: demolish, destroy, undo

D

damaged *adj.* harmed or injured. *That door will not shut because the hinge is **damaged**.*

bruised made discolored as a result of an injury that does not break the skin. *Gregory's leg was **bruised** from a bad fall.*

dented having a hollow in the surface caused by pressure or a blow. *The tin pan would not lie flat because the bottom was **dented**.*

scratched having a thin, shallow cut or mark made by or as if by a sharp tool. *We sanded and waxed the **scratched** wooden floor.*

shattered broken suddenly into many small pieces; smashed. *Pieces of the **shattered** window lay on the floor.*

tattered having torn and hanging pieces; shredded; ragged. *The **tattered** dress could no longer be mended.*

antonyms: overhauled *adj.*, patched *adj.*, repaired *adj.*

dangerous *adj.* full of danger; risky. *Riding a bicycle on a busy street is **dangerous**.*

hazardous able or likely to cause harm. *Breathing polluted air can be **hazardous** to your health.*

perilous very dangerous. *Climbing the steep, icy mountain was a **perilous** adventure.*

risky involving the possibility of suffering harm or loss. *Crossing the shaky old bridge was **risky**, but we had no choice.*

treacherous not to be trusted; dangerous. *Driving was difficult on the **treacherous** roads.*

antonyms: harmless, safe *adj.*, secure *adj.*, unthreatening.

decide *v.* to make up one's mind. *I **decided** to buy the red bike instead of the blue one.*

choose to pick out, especially on the basis of what one wants and thinks best. *I **chose** to spend my vacation with my grandmother.*

determine to make a firm decision. *Dr. Tsao **determined** to do all that he could to save the injured cat.*

resolve to make a firm plan. *I **resolve** to eat a good breakfast every day from now on.*

settle to arrange or decide by agreement. *They finally **settled** on a place to have the picnic.*

deserve *v.* to be worthy of or have a right to. *An animal lover like Paul **deserves** a pet of his own.*

earn to deserve as a result of effort or behavior. *The hard-working crew had **earned** a good long rest.*

merit to be worthy of; deserve. *June's courage **merits** the highest praise.*

rate to be good or valuable enough to receive. *The television show was too silly to **rate** much interest from the viewers.*

different *adj.* not identical. *David and Emily live in **different** parts of the country.*

separate individual or independent. *Each of the cats eats from a **separate** bowl.*

unusual not usual, common, or ordinary. *Maura wears her hair in a very **unusual** style.*

Shades of Meaning

dirty *adj.*

1. full of or covered with dirt; not clean:

dingy	messy	soiled
dusty	muddy	sooty
filthy	murky	stained
grimy	smudged	tarnished
grungy		

2. polluted:

contaminated	unclean	unsterile
impure	unsanitary	

antonyms: **1.** clean *adj.*, immaculate, spotless, washed *adj.* **2.** antiseptic *adj.*, disinfected *adj.*, hygienic, pure, sanitary, sterile

display *n.* a public showing. *The science fair included a display of lovely seashells.*

demonstration a show and explanation of the operation of something for sale. *The salesperson gave us a demonstration of what the computer can do.*

exhibit something put on display, as at a museum or gallery. *At the crafts shop Mario saw an exhibit of Indian pottery.*

E

eager *adj.* full of strong desire; impatient. *Carly was eager to read the new book by her favorite author.*

enthusiastic full of or showing strong interest or eagerness. *Our performance got an enthusiastic response from the audience.*

keen full of enthusiasm and interest. *Alice has a keen interest in windsurfing.*

antonyms: bored *adj.*, indifferent, unenthusiastic, uninterested.

educated *adj.* provided with formal instruction. *All college professors are highly educated people.*

aware having knowledge. *One purpose of a newspaper is to make the public aware of world events.*

informed having, displaying, or using information. *Informed shoppers judge a product before making a purchase.*

knowledgeable well-informed. *Since the speaker was knowledgeable, he was able to answer all of our questions.*

learned having or showing much knowledge or learning. *The learned professor had read every book ever written on Greek and Roman history.*

antonyms: ignorant, unaware, unschooled

effect *n.* something brought about by a cause. *The effect of too much eating can be a stomachache.*

consequence a direct outcome of something. *The musicians' fine performance was a consequence of their hard work.*

outcome something that happens as a result. *The outcome of the trial was a surprise to everyone.*

result something that happens because of something else. *The broken branches are the result of last night's storm.*

upshot the final result; outcome. *The upshot of our meeting was that we decided to have a party.*

antonyms: cause *n.*, reason *n.*, source

F

faithful *adj.* worthy of trust. *Theresa was a faithful friend who stood by her promises.*

constant firm in loyalty and affection; faithful. *Jonah and Dan have been constant friends since the day they met.*

devoted having or showing loyalty and affection. *My dog is my devoted companion and would follow me anywhere.*

loyal firm in supporting a person, country, or cause. *Ben was a loyal customer at his neighborhood market.*

true trustworthy and devoted. *Ariel was a true friend when I needed her.*

antonyms: changeable, disloyal, double-crossing, faithless, false

funny *adj.* causing laughter or amusement. *Sal told such a funny story that my sides hurt from laughing.*

amusing pleasantly entertaining. *The juggler on stilts was amusing.*

comical producing much laughter. *Three-legged races are always comical to watch.*

humorous causing a smile or a laugh. *Ron told a humorous story about a chicken.*

laughable causing or likely to cause laughter or amusement. *Maria did a laughable imitation of a cow.*

antonyms: earnest, grave *adj.*, serious

G

gather *v.* to bring or come together into one place. *They **gathered** around the campfire and sang songs.*

accumulate to gather together; pile up. *Chen has **accumulated** stacks of science fiction magazines.*

assemble to bring or come together as a group. *The band members must **assemble** in the auditorium at noon.*

bunch to gather into or form a group of things. *The puppies **bunched** together in a corner of the room.*

cluster to grow or gather in a group. *The fans **clustered** around the singer to ask for her autograph.*

collect to bring or come together in a group. *Drops of dew **collect** on our lawn each morning.*

antonyms: scatter, separate *v.*

---

get *v.* to receive. *Did you **get** any payment for your work in the garden?*

acquire to gain by one's own efforts. *Ed worked many hours to **acquire** his skill in typing.*

buy to gain by paying a price for. *Ana used her allowance to **buy** a gift for her mother.*

earn to gain by working or supplying a service. *Jason **earns** money by baby-sitting for families in his neighborhood.*

obtain to gain by means of planning or effort. *Dara wants to know how she can **obtain** a driver's license in this state.*

win to receive as a prize or reward. *Did Joe **win** a prize in the school essay contest?*

antonyms: forfeit, lose

---

give *v.* to hand over to another. *Sara **gave** her sister a beautiful music box for her birthday.*

furnish to supply; give. *A hardware store **furnished** hoses and buckets for the fifth-grade car wash.*

offer to put forward to be accepted or refused. *Katie **offered** Ina half of a turkey sandwich.*

present to make a gift or award to. *Coach Hart **presented** a trophy to our basketball team.*

provide to give something needed or useful. *The City Hotel **provides** breakfast for its guests.*

supply to make available something that is needed. *The blood **supplies** oxygen to the brain.*

antonyms: accept, receive, take

Shades of Meaning

good *adj.* having positive or desirable qualities.

1. good enough:

acceptable	satisfactory	suitable
adequate	sufficient	tolerable

2. very good:

adept	competent	fine
admirable	desirable	worthy

3. extremely good:

marvelous	splendid	terrific
outstanding	superb	wonderful

antonyms: **1.** inferior, second-rate, substandard **2.** bad, poor, shoddy **3.** awful, dreadful, horrible, terrible

---

grow *v.* to become or cause to become larger. *Lots of rain helped the plants **grow** tall.*

blossom to develop gradually. *Emily's artistic talent **blossomed** with practice.*

develop to grow or cause to grow. *Exercise **develops** strong muscles.*

flourish to grow very well; thrive. *Tomatoes **flourish** in hot, sunny weather.*

sprout to produce or appear as new growth. *New leaves **sprouted** from the dogwood tree.*

antonyms: decline *v.*, dwindle, stunt *v.*

H

happiness *n.* pleasure or joy. *Marta smiled with **happiness** as she told me the news.*
cheer good spirits; happiness. *The holiday celebration filled us with **cheer**.*
delight great pleasure. *The playful kittens made him laugh with **delight**.*
enjoyment a form or source of pleasure; joy. *Reading brings Kris great **enjoyment**.*
pleasure a feeling of happiness or enjoyment; delight. *Josh gazed at the lovely scene with **pleasure**.*
antonyms: depression, misery, sadness, sorrow, suffering *n.*

hide *v.* to keep or put out of sight. *The cat **hid** under the bed until the company left.*
bury to hide by placing in the ground and covering with earth. *The dog **buried** another bone under the rosebush.*
conceal to keep from being seen or known. *Allen **concealed** his sadness behind a happy face.*
cover to put something over or on. *The turtle **covered** her eggs with sand.*
mask to cover or hide. *They used vines and branches to **mask** the opening of the cave.*
antonyms: display *v.*, exhibit *v.*, expose, reveal, show *v.*

I

increase *v.* to make or become greater or larger. *The thin cattle were given extra food to **increase** their weight.*
enlarge to make or become larger. *The photographer **enlarged** the snapshots.*
expand to make or become larger in size, volume, or amount. *The Dashos **expanded** their house by adding a second floor.*
extend to make greater or larger. *Road workers **extended** the road another mile.*

magnify to enlarge the appearance of. *The microscope **magnified** the cells so that they could be seen by the human eye.*
antonyms: decrease *v.*, reduce, shrink

J

join *v.* to bring or come together, as by fastening. *Liz **joined** the two short poles to form one long one.*
connect to link or come together. *Electrical tape was used to **connect** the two wires.*
participate to join with others in being active; take part. *Carlos **participated** in the discussion.*

justice *n.* the quality of being just or fair. *Everyone was satisfied with the **justice** of the judge's decision.*
decency the quality of being proper or moral. *Abby found a purse and had the **decency** to call the owner.*
equality the condition of being equal, especially the condition of enjoying equal rights. *According to the Constitution, everyone has **equality** under the law.*
fairness the quality of being free of bias. *Listening to both sides of the argument was Catherine's way of showing **fairness**.*
morality the quality of being good and just. *A person of high **morality** can usually be trusted.*
antonyms: inequality, injustice, wrong *n.*

K

knowledge *n.* understanding; awareness. *Philip's **knowledge** of animal behavior comes from raising many kinds of pets over the years.*
awareness consciousness of something. *Her trip to Asia gave Ann a new **awareness** of other ways of life.*

wisdom intelligence and good judgment in knowing what to do and being able to tell the difference between good and bad and right and wrong. *People often ask my aunt for advice because she is known for her **wisdom**.*

L

lively *adj.* full of energy; active. *The **lively** baby kept climbing out of the crib.*
active busy. *My baby sister is very **active**.*
chipper full of cheer. *Ike felt **chipper** on this lovely morning.*
energetic full of energy; vigorous. *I've been watching those **energetic** children on the swings.*
frisky energetic, lively, and playful. *The **frisky** colt leaped around the pasture.*
spirited full of life. *Our team put on a **spirited** performance.*
antonyms: dull *adj.*, idle, inactive, lazy, lifeless, sluggish

M

mixture *n.* any combination of different ingredients, things, or kinds. *The sand was a **mixture** of crushed rocks and shells.*
blend a mixture in which the parts are combined. *The sauce was a **blend** of spices.*
jumble a group of things mixed together without any order. *The toolbox contained a **jumble** of nails, screws, nuts, and bolts.*

N

normal *adj.* of the usual or regular kind. *The guest speaker provided a break from our **normal** school schedule.*

average typical, usual, or ordinary. *The **average** person needs eight hours of sleep nightly.*
general widespread. *The students had a **general** feeling of excitement before the game.*
regular usual or normal; standard. *Because our **regular** teacher is ill, we had a substitute.*
typical showing the special traits or characteristics of a group, kind, or class; ordinary. *A **typical** circus includes clowns, acrobats, and wild animals.*
usual happening at regular intervals or all of the time; customary. *Nicole took a shortcut instead of going to school the **usual** way.*
antonyms: abnormal, extraordinary, rare, remarkable, strange, unusual

O

order *n.* a command or rule. *The patient was careful to follow the doctor's **orders**.*
arrangement a set of things that have been put in order. *The pins and earrings were displayed in an attractive **arrangement**.*
command an order or direction. *The soldiers obeyed the general's **command**.*

P

Word Bank

peaceful *adj.* marked by peace and calmness.

calm	relaxed	tranquil
harmonious	restful	undisturbed
placid	serene	unruffled
quiet	soothing	untroubled

antonyms: agitated *adj.*, anxious, distressed *adj.*, edgy, nervous, restless, tense *adj.*, troubled *adj.*, uneasy, unsettled, upset *adj.*, worried *adj.*

perfect *adj.* having no errors, flaws, or defects. *It's a **perfect** day for sailing when the weather is sunny and slightly breezy.*
excellent of the highest quality. *The chef made our **excellent** meal from the freshest ingredients.*
ideal thought of as being the best possible. *Casey had an **ideal** vacation riding horses on a ranch.*
model worthy of imitation. *Carlos studies hard and is a **model** student.*
antonyms: faulty, flawed, poor

praise *n.* approval or admiration. *The teacher's words of **praise** made Alex beam with pride.*
admiration an expression of pleasure, wonder, and approval. *Lisa's singing won the **admiration** of her classmates.*
approval favorable judgment. *Pablo's suggestion met with everyone's **approval**.*
antonyms: criticism, disapproval, scorn *n.*

protect *v.* to keep safe from harm, attack, or injury. *Calvin wears a helmet to **protect** his head when he rides his bike.*
guard to defend or keep safe from danger. *The police **guarded** the museum against theft.*
shield to protect or cover. *Cowhands used kerchiefs to **shield** their faces from the dust.*
antonyms: endanger, menace *v.*, threaten

pull *v.* to apply force to in order to draw someone or something in the direction of the force. *I **pulled** the door toward me as hard as I could.*
drag to draw along the ground by force. *Jim **dragged** the heavy trash barrel across the lawn.*
haul to pull or carry with effort. *The horses **hauled** the wagon up the mountain.*
tow to draw along behind with a chain or rope. *Two small boats **towed** the enormous barge into the harbor.*
tug to pull at strongly. *She **tugged** at the knot until it finally came loose.*
antonyms: push *v.*, shove *v.*, thrust *v.*

put *v.* to cause to be in a particular position. *Put your bike in the shed.*
deposit to lay or put down. *I **deposited** a package on your front steps.*
lay to put or set down. *Be gentle when you **lay** the baby in the crib.*
locate to place or situate. *A sunny spot is certainly the best place to **locate** your garden.*
place to lay something in a certain space. *Place your hands on your hips.*
set to cause to be in a particular location. *Set the books on the kitchen table before you go to your room.*
antonyms: remove, take away

Q

quick *adj.* done or happening without delay. *We took a **quick** trip to the store.*
fast moving or acting with speed. *Traveling by plane is **faster** than traveling by car.*
hasty in a hurried way. *Jim scribbled a **hasty** note and then ran out the door.*
rapid marked by speed. *The **rapid** subway train zoomed through the dark.*
speedy able to get from one place to another in a short time. *A **speedy** little rabbit outran my dog.*
swift moving or able to move very fast. *Charlie is very **swift** on his feet.*
antonyms: leisurely, slack, slow *adj.*

R

regular *adj.* appearing again and again. *Exercise should be a **regular** part of one's life.*
common found or occurring often. *Blizzards are **common** in North Dakota.*
routine done as part of a regular procedure. *Amanda made an appointment for a **routine** eye examination.*

S

same *adj.* being the very one. *This train is the **same** one that I rode last week.*

equal being exactly the same in amount, extent, or other measured quality. *The two questions were worth an **equal** number of points.*

identical exactly alike. *My twin brothers are **identical**; no one can tell them apart.*

uniform having the same appearance, form, or measurements as others. *Any of these screws will fit that hole because they are all perfectly **uniform**.*

antonyms: different, dissimilar, unlike

scary *adj.* causing fear. *Your story was so **scary** that I was afraid to walk home.*

alarming causing a feeling of approaching danger. *The police siren was **alarming** to the drivers on the highway.*

forbidding threatening, dangerous, or unfriendly in nature or appearance; frightening. *Brian trembled as he entered the dark, **forbidding** forest.*

frightening causing sudden, great fear. *He told us that the **frightening** crash was only thunder.*

terrifying causing overpowering fright. *The **terrifying** noise made me freeze in my tracks.*

antonyms: comforting *adj.*, reassuring *adj.*, soothing *adj.*

see *v.* to take in with the eyes. *Julie stared at the tree, but she could not **see** the bird.*

notice to take note of; pay attention to. *Noah entered quietly, but everyone **noticed** that he was late.*

observe to watch carefully. *The cat **observed** the bird in the tree.*

regard to look at. *The artist stood back from the easel to **regard** her work.*

spot to find or locate. *The sunbathers **spotted** dolphins not far from shore.*

view to look at. *We **viewed** the entire city from the top of the skyscraper.*

witness to be a witness of; see. *Several passers-by had **witnessed** the accident.*

antonyms: ignore, miss *v.*, overlook *v.*

small *adj.* little in size, amount, or extent. *A **small** dog sat on the girl's lap.*

microscopic capable of being seen only through a microscope. *The book contained an enlarged photograph of a **microscopic** plant cell.*

miniature much smaller than the usual size. *I gave my sister a **miniature** living room set for her dollhouse.*

minor smaller in amount, size, extent, or importance. *The hurricane that had been forecast turned out to be only a **minor** storm.*

stunted being smaller than normal due to an interference with growth. *The **stunted** growth of the trees was the result of poor soil.*

tiny extremely small. *He could hold the **tiny** baby rabbit in the palm of his hand.*

antonyms: enormous, giant *adj.*, huge, major *adj.*, tremendous

speech *n.* a public talk. *The writer gave a **speech** at the high school.*

address a formal speech. *We listened to the President's **address**.*

lecture a speech providing information on a subject, given before a class. *The class heard a **lecture** about the planets.*

T

taste *n.* a sensation produced by a substance taken into the mouth; flavor. *Coconut milk has a sweet **taste**.*

flavor the quality that causes something to have a certain taste. *The spices gave the stew a delicious **flavor**.*

preference a liking for one person or thing over another. *He likes string beans, but his **preference** is for broccoli.*

think *v.* to use one's mind to form ideas and make decisions. *You should think carefully before you answer the question.*

believe to expect or suppose. *I believe that it is going to rain.*

consider to think about before deciding. *Ellie considered moving to the city.*

dream to think or believe possible. *Daniel never dreamed that he could be so lucky.*

imagine to form a mental picture or idea of. *Try to imagine what life was like a hundred years ago.*

ponder to think about carefully. *Max had pondered the problem for hours but still had found no solution.*

Word Bank

throw *v.* to send through the air with a fast motion of the arm.

cast	heave	propel
chuck	hurl	shoot
fire	launch	sling
fling	lob	toss
flip	pelt	

W

---

walk *v.* to move or cause to move on foot at an easy, steady pace. *The smooth path made it easy for us to walk the trail.*

limp to walk in an uneven way. *Marcia got a blister on her foot and had to limp home.*

march to walk with regular and measured steps, often in a group. *The baton twirlers marched in the parade.*

stride to walk with long steps. *Tim strode across the stage to receive his diploma.*

stroll to walk around in a slow, relaxed way. *At lunch hour the office workers strolled around the mall.*

tiptoe to walk softly, as if on the tips of one's toes. *Kevin tiptoed behind Julie and said, "Surprise!"*

wander to move from place to place without a special purpose or destination; roam. *Since our flight was delayed, we wandered around the airport to pass the time.*

---

warning *n.* something that urges one to watch out for danger. *The sign was a warning to drivers about a curve ahead.*

alarm a bell or light that alerts one to danger. *The fire alarm clanged as smoke filled the attic.*

alert a warning signal of attack or danger. *When a tornado is coming, the weather station sends out a special alert.*

caution a warning against possible trouble or danger. *The label on the can included a caution against improper use.*

signal a sign, gesture, or device that gives a command, a warning, or other information. *As the traffic signal turned from yellow to red, the cars came to a stop.*

---

worthy *adj.* having worth, merit, or value. *A cleanup drive for the park is a worthy cause.*

admirable deserving of respect. *Her hard work and devotion are most admirable.*

honorable deserving honor or respect. *The firefighter was awarded for his years of honorable service.*

valuable of great importance, use, or service. *A hammer is a valuable tool to a carpenter.*

antonyms: undeserving, unimportant, useless, worthless

Spelling-Meaning Index

This Spelling-Meaning Index contains words related in spelling and meaning. The Index has three sections: Consonant Changes, Vowel Changes, and Word Parts. The first two sections contain related word pairs and other words in the same word families. The last section contains a list of Latin word roots, Greek word parts, and words that contain these word parts. The words in each section of this Index are in alphabetical order.

Consonant Changes

The letters in dark print show that the spelling stays the same even though the sound changes.

Consonant Changes: Silent to Sounded

Sometimes you can remember how to spell a word with a silent consonant by thinking of a related word in which the letter is pronounced.

bomb-bombard

bombarded, bombarder, bombardier, bombarding, bombardment, bombards, bombed, bomber, bombing, bombs

column-columnist

columnar, columned, columnists, columns

heir-inherit

disinherit, heirless, heirs, heritage, inheritance, inherited, inheriting, inherits

moist-moisten

moistened, moistening, moistens, moister, moistest, moistness

muscle-muscular

muscled, muscles, muscling, musculature

receipt-reception

receipts, receptacle, receptionist, receptions, receptive

sign-signal

signaled, signaler, signaling, signals, signature, signed, signer, signify, signing, signs

Consonant Changes: The Sound of c

The |k| sound spelled c may change to the |s| sound in some words. Thinking of a related word can help you remember that the |s| sound is spelled c.

critic-criticize

critical, critically, criticism, criticized, criticizer, criticizes, criticizing, critics, uncritical

practical-practice

impractical, impracticality, impractically, practicality, practically, practiced, practices, practicing, unpracticed

Consonant Changes: The Sound of t

The sound of a final t may change to the |sh| or the |ch| sound when an ending or a suffix is added. Thinking of a related word can help you remember that those sounds are spelled t.

affect-affection

affected, affecting, affectionate, affectionately, affective, affects, disaffected, unaffected

create-creature

created, creates, creating, creation, creative, creatively, creativity, creator, creatures, noncreative, re-create

depart-departure

departed, departing, departs, departures, undeparted

except-exception

excepted, excepting, exceptional, exceptionally, exceptions, excepts, unexceptional, unexceptionally

fact-factual

facts, factually

graduate-graduation

graduated, graduates, graduating, graduations, postgraduate, undergraduate

habit-habitual

habits, habitually

instruct-instruction

instructed, instructing, instructional, instructions, instructive, instructor, instructorship, instructs, uninstructive

invent-invention

invented, inventing, inventions, inventive, inventively, inventiveness, inventor, invents

moist-moisture

moister, moistest, moistness, moisturize, moisturizer

object-objection

objected, objecting, objectionable, objectionably, objects

part-partial

parted, partially, particle, parting, partition, partly, parts

regulate-regulation

regulated, regulates, regulating, regulations, regulator, regulatory, unregulated

suggest-suggestion

suggested, suggestible, suggesting, suggestions, suggestive, suggests

Vowel Changes

The letters in dark print show that the spelling stays the same even though the sound changes.

Vowel Changes:
Long to Short Vowel Sound

Words that are related in meaning are often related in spelling, even though one word has a long vowel sound and the other word has a short vowel sound.

breathe-breath

breathable, breathed, breather, breathes, breathily, breathiness, breathing, breathless, breathlessly, breathlessness, breaths, breathtaking

cave-cavity

caved, cavern, cavernous, caves, caving, cavities

clean-cleanse

cleanable, cleaned, cleaner, cleanest, cleaning, cleanliness, cleanly, cleanness, cleans, cleansed, cleanser, cleanses, cleansing, unclean, uncleanable

271

Spelling-Meaning Index

cycle-bicycle

bicycled, bicycles, bicycling, bicyclist, cycled, cycler, cycles, cyclical, cycling, cyclist, recycle, tricycle, unicycle, unicyclist

deal-dealt

dealer, dealership, dealing, deals

dream-dreamt

dreamed, dreamer, dreamily, dreaminess, dreaming, dreamless, dreamlike, dreams, dreamy

heal-health

healed, healer, healing, heals, healthful, healthfully, healthfulness, healthily, healthiness, healthy, unhealthy

mean-meant

meaning, meaningful, meaningless, means, unmeant

minus-minimum

minimal, minimize, minimums, minuscule

mute-mutter

muted, mutely, muteness, mutes, muting, muttered, muttering, mutters

nation-national

denationalize, international, nationalism, nationalist, nationalistic, nationality, nationalize, nationally, nationals, nationhood, nationwide

page-paginate

paged, pages, paginated, paginates, paginating, pagination, paging

pale-pallid

paled, paleness, paler, pales, palest, paling, pallor

sole-solitary

solely, solitarily, solitariness, solitude, solo, soloist

unite-unity

reunite, unit, united, uniting

wise-wisdom

wisely, wiser, wisest

Vowel Changes:
Schwa to Long Vowel Sound

You can remember how to spell the schwa sound in some words by thinking of a related word with a long vowel sound spelled the same way.

ability-able

abilities, abler, ablest, ably, disability, disable, inability, unable

equaled-equation

equal, equaling, equality, equalize, equals, equate, equations, equator, inequality, unequal

proposition-propose

proposal, proposed, proposer, proposes, proposing, propositions

Vowel Changes:
Schwa to Short Vowel Sound

You can remember how to spell the schwa sound in some words by thinking of a related word with a short vowel sound spelled the same way.

angel-angelic

angelical, angelically, angels

compete-competition

competed, competes, competing, competitions, competitive, competitively, competitiveness, competitor

democracy-democratic

democracies, democrat, democratically, democratization, democratize, undemocratic

formal-formality

form, formalism, formalist, formalities, formalize, formally, format, formula, informal, informality, informally

general-generality

generalist, generalities, generalization, generalize, generally, generalness

history-historical

historian, historic, historically, histories, prehistory

individual-individuality

individualism, individualist, individualistic, individualities, individualize, individually, individuals

legal-legality

illegal, illegality, illegally, legalese, legalism, legalities, legalize, legally

local-locality

locale, localism, localities, localize, locally

major-majority

majorities

medal-medallion

medalist, medallions, medals

mental-mentality

mentalities, mentally

metal-metallic

metallically, metallography, metallurgy, metals

method-methodical

methodic, methodically, methodicalness, methods

moral-morality

immoral, morale, moralism, moralist, moralistic, moralities, moralize, morally, morals

mortal-mortality

immortal, mortalities, mortally, mortals

normal-normality

abnormal, abnormalities, norm, normalcy, normalize, normally

personal-personality

impersonal, interpersonal, person, personalism, personalities, personalize, personally

poem-poetic

poems, poet, poetical, poetically, poetics, poetry

regular-regularity

irregular, regularities, regularize, regularly

reside-resident

resided, residence, residency, residential, residentially, resides, residing

similar-similarity

dissimilar, dissimilarity, similarities, similarly

total-totality

totaled, totaling, totalitarian, totalities, totally, totals

Spelling-Meaning Index

Word Parts

Words with the same Latin word root or the same Greek word part are related in spelling and meaning. Knowing the meaning of a word part can help you understand and spell the words in that family. The letters in dark print highlight the word part.

Latin Word Roots

aud, "to hear"

audible	**aud**it
audience	**aud**ition
audio	**aud**itorium
audio-visual	**aud**itory

dict, "to tell"

contra**dict**	**dict**ionary
dictate	pre**dict**
dictator	vale**dict**orian
diction	ver**dict**

ject, "to throw"

ad**ject**ive	pro**ject**
de**ject**	pro**ject**or
in**ject**	re**ject**
inter**ject**	sub**ject**
ob**ject**	sub**ject**ive
ob**ject**ive	

loc, "place"

al**loc**ate	**loc**ate
dis**loc**ate	**loc**ation
local	**loc**omotion
locale	**loc**omotive
locality	re**loc**ate

mit, "to send"

ad**mit**	per**mit**
com**mit**	sub**mit**
com**mit**tee	trans**mit**

ped, "foot"

centi**ped**e	**ped**estrian
milli**ped**e	**ped**igree
pedal	**ped**ometer
pedestal	

port, "to carry"

de**port**	**port**er
ex**port**	re**port**
im**port**	sup**port**
im**port**ant	trans**port**
portable	

pose, "to put"

com**pose**	**pos**itive
de**pose**	**pos**ture
dis**pose**	pro**pose**
ex**pose**	re**pose**
op**pose**	sup**pose**
op**pos**ite	trans**pose**
position	

scribe or **script**, "to write"

de**scribe**	de**script**ion
in**scribe**	de**script**ive
pre**scribe**	in**script**ion
scribble	manu**script**
scribe	pre**script**ion
sub**scribe**	sub**script**ion
tran**scribe**	tran**script**ion

sist, "to stand"

as**sist**	irre**sist**ible
as**sist**ance	per**sist**
con**sist**	per**sist**ent
con**sist**ent	re**sist**
in**sist**	re**sist**ance
in**sist**ence	

sol, "alone"

de**sol**ate	**sol**itary
i**sol**ate	**sol**itude
i**sol**ation	**sol**o
sole	**sol**oist

spect, "to look"

a**spect**	re**spect**
circum**spect**	re**spect**able
in**spect**	**spect**acle
in**spect**ion	**spect**acles
in**spect**or	**spect**ator
per**spect**ive	**spect**er
pro**spect**	**spect**rum
pro**spect**or	su**spect**

tract, "to pull"

abs**tract**	ex**tract**
at**tract**	pro**tract**
at**tract**ion	re**tract**
at**tract**ive	sub**tract**
con**tract**	**tract**
de**tract**	**tract**ion
dis**tract**	**tract**or

vac, "to be empty"

e**vac**uate	**vac**ate
vacancy	**vac**uum
vacant	

ven, "to come"

ad**vent**	**even**tual
ad**ven**ture	inter**vene**
a**ven**ue	inter**ven**tion
circum**vent**	in**vent**
con**vene**	in**ven**tion
con**ven**tion	pre**vent**
e**ven**t	pre**ven**tion

vis, "to see"

ad**vise**	**vis**ible
audio-**vis**ual	**vis**ion
impro**vise**	**vis**it
pro**vis**ion	**vis**or
re**vise**	**vis**ta
super**vise**	**vis**ual
tele**vise**	**vis**ualize
visa	

Greek Word Parts

ast, "star"

aster	**ast**ronaut
asterisk	**ast**ronomer
asteroid	**ast**ronomy
astrology	dis**ast**er

phys, "nature"

physical	**phys**ics
physician	**phys**ique

poli, "city" or "government"

Acro**poli**s	**poli**ce
cosmo**poli**tan	**poli**cy
megalo**poli**s	**poli**tician
metro**poli**s	**poli**tics
metro**poli**tan	

tele, "far off; distant"

telecast	**tele**scope
telegram	**tele**thon
telegraph	**tele**vise
telepathy	**tele**vision
telephone	

Spelling Dictionary

Spelling Table

This Spelling Table shows many of the letter combinations that spell the same sounds in different words. Use this table for help in looking up words that you do not know how to spell.

Sounds	Spellings	Sample Words	Sounds	Spellings	Sample Words
|ă|	a, au	bat, have, laugh	|îr|	ear, eer, eir, ier	near, deer, weird, pier
|ā|	a, ai, ay, ea	made, later, rain, play, great	|j|	dge, g, ge, j	judge, gem, range, jet
|âr|	air, ar, are, eir, ere	fair, scarce, care, their, where	|k|	c, ch, ck, k	picnic, school, tick, key
|ä|	a, al	father, calm	|kw|	qu	quick
|är|	ar, ear	art, heart	|l|	l, ll	last, all
|b|	b, bb	bus, rabbit	|m|	m, mb, mm, mn	mop, bomb, summer, column
|ch|	ch, tch, tu	chin, match, culture	|n|	gn, kn, n, nn	sign, knee, no, inn
|d|	d, dd	dark, sudden	|ng|	n, ng	think, ring
|ĕ|	a, ai, ay, e, ea, ie	any, said, says, went, head, friend	|ŏ|	a, ho, o	was, honor, pond
|ē|	e, ea, ee, ei, ey, i, ie, y	these, we, beast, fleet, receive, honey, ski, magazine, chief, bumpy,	|ō|	o, oa, ough, ow	most, hope, float, though, row
|f|	f, ff, gh	funny, off, enough	|ô|	a, al, au, aw, o, ough	wall, talk, haunt, lawn, soft, brought
|g|	g, gg, gu	get, egg, guide	|ôr|	oar, oor, or, ore, our	roar, door, storm, store, court
|h|	h, wh	hat, who			
|hw|	wh	when	|oi|	oi, oy	join, toy
|ĭ|	a, e, ee, i, ia, u, ui, y	cottage, before, been, mix, give, carriage, busy, build, gym	|ou|	ou, ough, ow	loud, bough, now
|ī|	ei, i, ie, igh, y	height, time, mind, pie, fight, try, type	|o͝o|	oo, ou, u	good, could, put

(continued)

Sounds	Spellings	Sample Words	Sounds	Spellings	Sample Words
|oo|	ew, o, oe, oo, ou, u, ue, ui	flew, do, lose, shoe, spoon, you, truth, blue, juice	|ŭ|	o, oe, oo, ou, u	front, come, does, flood, tough, sun
|p|	p, pp	paint, happen	|yoo|	eau, ew, iew, u, ue	beauty, few, view, use, cue
|r|	r, rh, rr, wr	rub, rhyme, borrow, write	|ûr|	ear, er, ir, or, ur	learn, herd, girl, word, turn
|s|	c, ce, ps, s, sc, ss	city, fence, psychology, same, scent, lesson	|v|	f, v	of, very
|sh|	ce, ch, ci, s, sh, ss, ti	ocean, machine, special, sure, sheep, mission, nation	|w|	o, w	one, way
			|y|	i, y	million, yes
|t|	ed, t, tt	stopped, talk, little	|z|	s, z, zz	rise, zoo, fizz
|th|	th	they, other	|zh|	ge, s	garage, usual
|th|	th	thin, teeth	|ə|	a, ai, e, eo, i, o, ou, u	about, captain, silent, surgeon, pencil, lemon, famous, circus

Spelling Dictionary

How to Use a Dictionary

Finding an Entry Word

Guide Words

The word you want to find in a dictionary is listed in alphabetical order. To find it quickly, use the guide words at the top of each page. Guide words name the first and last entries on the page.

Base Words

To find a word ending in **-ed** or **-ing**, you usually must look up its base word. To find **imitated** or **imitating**, for example, look up the base word **imitate**.

Homographs

Homographs have separate, numbered entries. For example, **sole** meaning "the bottom of a shoe, boot, or slipper" is listed as **sole¹**. **Sole** meaning "being the only one; single" is **sole²**.

Reading an Entry

Read the dictionary entry below. Note the purpose of each part.

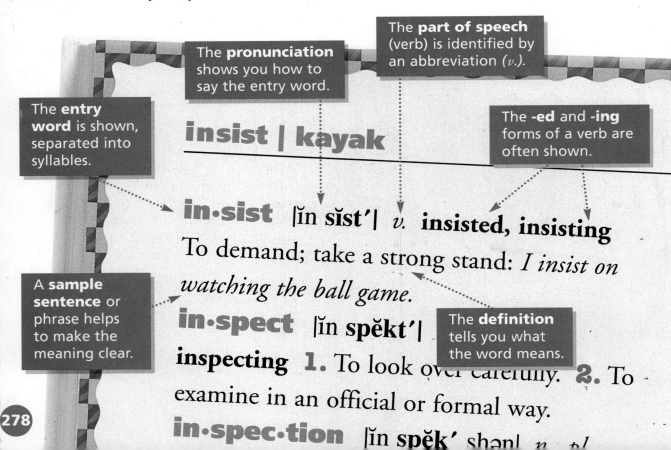

The **pronunciation** shows you how to say the entry word.

The **part of speech** (verb) is identified by an abbreviation (*v.*).

The **entry word** is shown, separated into syllables.

The **-ed** and **-ing** forms of a verb are often shown.

insist | kayak

A **sample sentence** or phrase helps to make the meaning clear.

The **definition** tells you what the word means.

in·sist |ĭn sĭst′| *v.* **insisted, insisting**
To demand; take a strong stand: *I insist on watching the ball game.*

in·spect |ĭn spĕkt′|
inspecting **1.** To look over carefully. **2.** To examine in an official or formal way.

in·spec·tion |ĭn spĕk′ shən| *n.*

Spelling Dictionary

A

a·bil·i·ty |ə **bĭl′** ĭ tē| *n., pl.* **abilities**
1. The quality of being able to do something; power: *Most people have the ability to dance.*
2. Power to do something, especially as a result of practice; skill: *You have real ability as a dancer.*

-able A suffix that forms adjectives and means: **1.** Capable of; able to: *breakable.*
2. Worthy of: *lovable.*

a·ble |**ā′** bəl| *adj.* **abler, ablest** Having the power or ability to do something: *I will be able to see you tomorrow.*

ab·sent |**ăb′** sənt| *adj.* Not present in a place or with someone: *Two students are absent today.*

ab·stain |ăb **stān′**| *v.* **abstained, abstaining** To keep oneself from doing by choice; hold back: *We abstained from eating too much.*

A·ca·di·a Na·tion·al Park |ə **kā′** dē ə| A scenic area with rugged granite mountains along the coast of Maine.

Acadia National Park

ac·cent |**ăk′** sĕnt′| *n., pl.* **accents** A mark showing the stress given to one or more syllables in pronouncing a word.

ac·ci·dent |**ăk′** sĭ dənt| *n., pl.* **accidents**
1. Something that happens without being planned ahead of time: *Our meeting was a lucky accident.* **2.** An unexpected and undesirable event: *An accident held up traffic for miles.*

ac·cuse |ə **kyōōz′**| *v.* **accused, accusing** To blame for wrongdoing: *They were accused of stealing.*

act |ăkt| *v.* **acted, acting 1.** To conduct oneself; behave: *You act as if you are tired.*
2. To perform a part, especially in a play or movie: *I want to act in the movies. n., pl.* **acts**
1. A thing done: *It was a brave act to rescue the drowning child.* **2.** One of the main divisions, especially of a play: *The first act takes place in a factory.*

ac·tion |**ăk′** shən| *n., pl.* **actions 1.** A thing done; act: *Take responsibility for your actions.* **2.** The activities or events of a play, story, or movie.

ac·tive |**ăk′** tĭv| *adj.* Full of energy; busy.
—*adv.* **actively** *My grandfather, who is eighty-seven, still lives quite actively.*

ac·tor |**ăk′** tər| *n., pl.* **actors** A person who performs a part, especially in a play or motion picture.

Pronunciation Key

ă	pat	ō	go	th	thin
ā	pay	ô	paw, for	hw	which
â	care	oi	oil	zh	usual
ä	father	ŏŏ	book	ə	ago,
ĕ	pet	ōō	boot		item,
ē	be	yōō	cute		pencil,
ĭ	pit	ou	out		atom,
ī	ice	ŭ	cut		circus
î	near	û	fur	ər	butter
ŏ	pot	*th*	the		

Abbreviation Key

n.	noun	*prep.*	preposition
v.	verb	*interj.*	interjection
adj.	adjective	*sing.*	singular
adv.	adverb	*pl.*	plural
pron.	pronoun	*p.*	past
conj.	conjunction	*p. part.*	past participle

a·dapt |ə **dăpt′**| v. **adapted, adapting**
To change so as to be suitable for a different
condition or purpose: *We put legs on a large
tray to adapt it for use as a table.*

ad·dress |ə **drĕs′**| or |**ăd′** rĕs′| n., pl.
addresses 1. The place where someone lives,
works, or receives mail: *What is your home
address?* **2.** A formal speech. v. |ə **drĕs′**|
addressed, addressing To direct one's efforts
or attention toward: *We addressed ourselves to
our homework.*

ad·journ |ə **jûrn′**| v. **adjourned,
adjourning** To bring or come to a close
until later: *Our meeting was adjourned until
next week.*

ad·mit |ăd **mĭt′**| v. **admitted, admitting**
1. To make known that something is true.
2. To allow or permit to enter.

ad·dore |ə **dôr′**| v. **adored, adoring**
1. To worship as a divine being. **2.** To love
with deep devotion: *I adore my sisters.*

ad·ven·ture |əd **vĕn′** chər| n., pl.
adventures 1. A bold, dangerous, or risky
undertaking: *They set out on a daring space
adventure.* **2.** An unusual or exciting experience:
The storm made our hike a real adventure.

ad·ven·tur·ous |əd **vĕn′** chər əs| adj.
Willing to risk danger in order to have exciting
adventures.

af·ter·noon |ăf′ tər **noon′**| n., pl.
afternoons The part of the day from noon
until the sun sets.

air |âr| n. The colorless, odorless, tasteless
mixture of gases that surrounds the earth.
◇ *Idiom* **walk on air** To feel very happy.

air·port |âr′ pôrt′| n., pl. **airports** A place
with marked, open spaces where aircraft can
take off and land.

al·le·giance |ə **lē′** jəns| n., pl. **allegiances**
Faithful devotion to one's country, a person, or
a cause; loyalty: *Martin had a deep allegiance to
his family and always helped them.*

al·low |ə **lou′**| v. **allowed, allowing**
1. To let do or happen; permit: *No ball playing
allowed!* **2.** To permit to have; let have: *Please
allow me to explain our project.*

all right |ôl′ **rīt′**| adj. and adv. Satisfactory
but not excellent; good enough: *These peaches
are all right, but they could be fresher.*

al·ter·a·tion |ôl′ tə **rā′** shən| n., pl.
alterations A change: *We made alterations to
the house by adding a den and a garage.*

al·though |ôl **thō′**| conj. Even though.

am·a·teur |**ăm′** ə chər| or |**ăm′** ə tər| n.,
pl. **amateurs** A person who engages in an art,
science, or sport for enjoyment rather than for
money. adj. Not professional.

a·maze |ə **māz′**| v. **amazed, amazing**
To fill with surprise or wonder; astonish: *The
idea of water carving a deep canyon out of solid
rock amazes me.*

a·mend·ment |ə **mĕnd′** mənt| n., pl.
amendments A change made to improve,
correct, or add something: *An amendment
to the United States Constitution limits the
President to two full terms in office.*

a·muse |ə **myooz′**| v. **amused, amusing**
1. To give enjoyment to; entertain pleasantly:
Playing checkers always amuses me. **2.** To cause to
laugh or smile: *The clown's tricks amused us all.*

a·nal·o·gy |ə **năl′** ə jē| n., pl. **analogies**
An explanation of something by comparing it
with something similar: *The author uses the
analogy of a beehive when describing the city.*

an·gel |**ān′** jəl| n., pl. **angels 1.** A spiritual
being. **2.** A person who is like an angel, for
example, by being kind or innocent.

an·gel·ic |ăn **jĕl′** ĭk| adj. Of or like angels:
She has an angelic voice.

an·ger |**ăng′** gər| A strong feeling of not
being pleased with someone or something; rage.

an·gle |**ăng′** gəl| n., pl. **angles 1.** The
figure made by two lines that begin at the
same point. **2.** A way of looking at something;
point of view.

an·gry |**ăng′** grē| adj. **angrier, angriest**
Feeling, showing, or resulting from anger: *I am
angriest when you are late.*

an·i·mate |**ăn′** ə māt′| v. **animated,
animating 1.** To give life to or make so as
to seem alive. **2.** To produce as an animated
cartoon: *Walt Disney animated stories, such as
"Snow White."*

an·i·ma·tion |ăn′ ə **mā′** shən| n. **1.** The
condition or quality of being alive; liveliness;
vitality. **2.** The process or processes by which
an animated cartoon is prepared. **3.** An
animated cartoon.

an·kle |ăng′ kəl| *n., pl.* **ankles** The joint between the foot and leg.

an·oth·er |ə nŭth′ ər| *adj.* Being a second or an additional one: *I'd love another helping.* *pron.* An additional person or thing: *First one left and then another.*

an·swer |ăn′ sər| *n., pl.* **answers** Something said or written in return to a question, statement, request, or letter; reply.

-ant A suffix that forms nouns and adjectives: *occupant.*

an·tic·i·pate |ăn tĭs′ ə pāt′| *v.* **anticipated, anticipating** To look forward to; expect: *We anticipate a fine weekend.*

an·to·nym |ăn′ tə nĭm′| *n., pl.* **antonyms** A word meaning the opposite of another word. For example, **dirty** is an antonym of **clean**.

a·part·ment |ə pärt′ mənt| *n., pl.* **apartments** One or more rooms usually used as a place to live.

ap·plause |ə plôz′| *n.* Enjoyment or approval expressed especially by the clapping of hands: *The actors loved the loud applause at the end of the play.*

ap·pre·ci·ate |ə prē′ shē āt′| *v.* **appreciated, appreciating** **1.** To enjoy and understand: *I appreciate books.* **2.** To be thankful for: *I appreciated your help.*

ap·pren·tice |ə prĕn′ tĭs| *n., pl.* **apprentices** A person who is learning a craft or trade by working for a skilled worker.

Ar·bor Day |är′ bər| *n.* A holiday, often in the spring, observed in many areas by planting trees.

arch·er·y |är′ chə rē| *n.* The sport or skill of shooting with a bow and arrows: *He loves the sport of archery, and all of his arrows hit the target.*

ar·chi·tec·ture |är′ kĭ tĕk′ chər| *n.* **1.** The art of designing buildings. **2.** A style of building.

ar·e·a |âr′ ē ə| *n., pl.* **areas** A region, as of land: *The family moved from the city to a farming area.*

ar·my |är′ mē| *n., pl.* **armies** A large body of men and women organized and trained for land warfare.

ar·rest |ə rĕst′| *v.* **arrested, arresting** To seize and hold by authority of law; take prisoner: *The detective arrested the thief.*

ar·rive |ə rīv′| *v.* **arrived, arriving** To reach a place: *They arrived early.*

ar·row |ăr′ ō| *n., pl.* **arrows** A straight, thin shaft that is shot from a bow. An arrow has a pointed head at one end and feathers at the other.

ar·ti·fi·cial |är′ tə fĭsh′ əl| *adj.* **1.** Made by humans rather than occurring in nature: *artificial pearls.* **2.** Not genuine or natural; pretended: *an artificial smile.*

a·shamed |ə shāmd′| *adj.* Feeling shame or guilt; not proud.

as·sem·ble |ə sĕm′ bəl| *v.* **assembled, assembling** To put together the parts of; build: *The mechanic assembled the engine.*

as·sist |ə sĭst′| *v.* **assisted, assisting** To give help; aid.

as·ter |ăs′ tər| *n., pl.* **asters** A plant whose white, pink, purple, or yellow flowers have petals arranged in a starlike pattern.

aster

as·ter·isk |ăs′ tə rĭsk| *n., pl.* **asterisks** A symbol (*) used in printing to direct the reader to another part of the page.

as·ter·oid |ăs′ tə roid′| *n., pl.* **asteroids**
One of the thousands of small planets that
orbit the sun.

as·ton·ish |ə stŏn′ ĭsh| *v.* **astonished,
astonishing** To surprise greatly; amaze: *The
brilliant sunrise astonished us.*

a·stound |ə stound′| *v.* **astounded,
astounding** To astonish: *Her brilliant
performance astounded the audience.*

as·tro·naut |ăs′ trə nôt′| *n., pl.* **astronauts**
A person trained to travel in a spacecraft.

astronaut

as·tron·o·mer |ə strŏn′ ə mər| *n., pl.*
astronomers An expert in astronomy.

as·tron·o·my |ə strŏn′ ə mē| *n.* The
scientific study and observation of the part of
the universe beyond the earth, including stars,
planets, comets, and galaxies.

At·lan·tic O·cean |ăt lăn′ tĭk ō′ shən|
The second largest of the oceans, extending
from the Arctic to the Antarctic between the
Americas on the west and Europe and Africa
on the east.

at·tend |ə tĕnd′| *v.* **attended, attending**
To be present at: *I will attend Teri's party.*

at·ten·tion |ə tĕn′ shən| *n., pl.* **attentions**
1. The ability to concentrate: *The story held
our attention for more than an hour.* **2.** The act
of noticing or giving careful thought: *Your
letter has come to our attention.*

au·di·tion |ô dĭsh′ ən| *n., pl.* **auditions**
A short performance to test the ability of
a musician, singer, dancer, or actor. *v.*
auditioned, auditioning To test or perform
in an audition: *Have you auditioned for the lead
in the school play?*

av·e·nue |ăv′ ə nōō′| or |ăv′ ə nyōō′|
n., pl. **avenues** A usually wide street.

av·er·age |ăv′ ər ĭj| *adj.* Typical, usual,
or ordinary: *The average two-year-old loves
teddy bears.*

a·wait |ə wāt′| *v.* **awaited, awaiting** To
wait for; expect: *We are awaiting our test scores.*

a·ware |ə wâr′| *adj.* Conscious of
something: *We are aware of the time.*

awe·struck |ô′ strŭk′| *adj.* Full of or
exhibiting awe or wonder.

aw·ful |ô′ fəl| *adj.* Very bad; horrible.

awk·ward |ôk′ wərd| *adj.* Not graceful;
clumsy: *Seals are awkward when out of water.*

B

ba·by-sit |bā′ bē sĭt′| *v.* **baby-sat, baby-
sitting** To take care of a child or children
when the parents are not at home.

bac·te·ri·a |băk tîr′ ē ə| *pl. n.* Tiny one-
celled organisms. Some bacteria help digest
food; other bacteria cause diseases.

badge |băj| *n., pl.* **badges** Something
worn to show that a person belongs to a
certain group, such as a police force: *Every
police officer carries a badge.*

Bad·lands Na·tion·al Park
|băd′ lăndz′| *pl. n.* A scenic area in South
Dakota characterized by eroded ridges, peaks,
and mesas. The area contains fossil remains.

baf·fle |băf′ əl| *v.* **baffled, baffling** To
be too difficult or confusing to understand or
solve: *These strange events baffle me.*

bag·gage |băg′ ĭj| *n.* The suitcases and
other containers that one carries when traveling.

bald |bôld| *adj.* **balder, baldest 1.** Lacking
hair on the top of the head. **2.** Lacking
natural or usual covering; bare: *The fire left a
bald spot in the lawn.*

bal·lad |băl′ əd| *n., pl.* **ballads** A poem or
song that has a plot and characters and tells a
story, usually about love.

ball bear·ing |bôl′ bâr′ ĭng| *n., pl.* **ball
bearings** A bearing in which the moving part
slides on a number of loose steel balls in a
groove. Ball bearings reduce friction between
machine parts.

ball game |bôl′ gām| A game, especially baseball, that is played with a ball.

ball·room |bôl′ rōōm′| or |bôl′ rōōm′| n., pl. **ballrooms** A large room for dancing.

bal·lot |băl′ ət| n., pl. **ballots** A piece of paper on which a voter marks a choice or choices: *She went into the voting booth and marked her ballot.*

band·age |băn′ dĭj| n., pl. **bandages** A strip of cloth or other material used to bind, cover, or protect a wound or other injury.

ban·ner |băn′ ər| n., pl. **banners** A flag or similar piece of material with words or a special design on it.

barge |bärj| n., pl. **barges** A large boat with a flat bottom, used to carry freight on rivers and canals.

bar·rel |băr′ əl| n., pl. **barrels** A large container with bulging sides and round, flat ends. Barrels are usually made of narrow strips of wood held together by hoops.

base·ment |bās′ mənt| n., pl. **basements** The lowest floor of a building, usually below ground level; cellar.

base word |bās wûrd| n., pl. **base words** A word to which other word parts may be added. For example, in *filled, refill,* and *filling, fill* is the base word.

ba·sic |bā′ sĭk| adj. Main, essential, primary: *Her basic chores were mopping and emptying the trash.*

bas·ket·ball |băs′ kĭt bôl′| n., pl. **basketballs** 1. A game played by two teams of five players each on a court with a raised basket at each end. Players score by throwing the ball through the basket defended by the other team. 2. The large, round ball used in this game.

bas·ket weave |băs′ kĭt wēv′| n., pl. **basket weaves** A pattern of weaving in which double threads are woven together to produce a plain, regular effect.

bat·tle·ground |băt′ l ground′| n., pl. **battlegrounds** A place of fighting or conflict; battlefield.

beast |bēst| n., pl. **beasts** An animal other than a human, especially a large, four-footed animal.

Pronunciation Key

ă	pat	ō	go	th	thin
ā	pay	ô	paw, for	hw	which
â	care	oi	oil	zh	usual
ä	father	ōō	book	ə	ago,
ĕ	pet	ōō	boot		item,
ē	be	yōō	cute		pencil,
ĭ	pit	ou	out		atom,
ī	ice	ŭ	cut		circus
î	near	û	fur	ər	butter
ŏ	pot	th	the		

beau·ti·ful |byōō′ tə fəl| adj. Being very pleasing to the senses or mind: *Beautiful music filled the air.*

beg |bĕg| v. **begged, begging** To ask earnestly as a favor; plead.

be·have |bĭ hāv′| v. **behaved, behaving** 1. To function in a certain way: *The car behaves well in snow.* 2. To act in a given way: *You behaved badly.*

ber·ry |bĕr′ ē| n., pl. **berries** A usually small, juicy fruit that has many seeds.
♦ *These sound alike* **berry, bury.**

berth |bûrth| n., pl. **berths** A bunk, as on a ship or railroad sleeping car: *She slept on the top berth as the train sped along.*

be·ware |bĭ wâr′| v. To be careful; look out: *Beware of the dog.*

bill |bĭl| n., pl. **bills** A draft of a law presented for approval to a legislature: *The bill passed by only three votes.*

bis·cuit |bĭs′ kĭt| n., pl. **biscuits** A small cake of baked bread dough: *We ate the biscuits while they were still hot.*

blew |blōō| v. Past tense of **blow:** *The wind blew John's hat off.*

blos·som |blŏs′ əm| n., pl. **blossoms** A flower, especially of a fruit-bearing plant. v. **blossomed, blossoming** To come into flower; bloom.

blur |blûr| n., pl. **blurs** Something that is dim or hard to see.

board |bôrd| v. **boarded, boarding** To go aboard: *We boarded the plane.*

boast |bōst| v. **boasted, boasting** To praise oneself, one's belongings, or one's actions; brag.

283

bore |bôr| *v.* **bored, boring** To cause to feel that one has had enough, as by seeming dull or uninteresting.
◆ *These sound alike* **bore, boar.**

bor·row |bŏr′ ō| *v.* **borrowed, borrowing** To get from someone else with the understanding that what is gotten will be returned or replaced; to take on loan: *The book I borrowed from the library is due today.*

bot·tom |bŏt′ əm| *n., pl.* **bottoms 1.** The lowest part of something. **2.** The land under a body of water: *At the bottom of the lake I found buried treasure.*

bou·tique |bo͞o tēk′| *n., pl.* **boutiques** A shop or store that sells such things as gifts or clothes: *She bought a very stylish dress at the boutique.*

boy·cott |boi′ kŏt′| *v.* **boycotted, boycotting** To refuse as part of an organized group to use, buy from, or deal with a store, company, person, or nation. Boycotting may be an act of protest or punishment: *boycott a store; boycott an airline.*

brag |brăg| *v.* **bragged, bragging** To speak with too much pride about oneself in an attempt to show off; boast.

brain |brān| *n., pl.* **brains** The main organ of the nervous system in humans and other animals with backbones. The brain controls voluntary actions such as speaking and many involuntary actions such as breathing. In humans the brain is the center of memory, learning, and emotion.

break·fast |brĕk′ fəst| *n., pl.* **breakfasts** The first meal of the day.

breath |brĕth| *n., pl.* **breaths** The air taken into the lungs and forced out when a person breathes.

breathe |brēth| *v.* **breathed, breathing** To take air into the lungs and force it out; inhale and exhale: *All mammals breathe air.*

breath·less |brĕth′ lĭs| *adj.* **1.** Out of breath; panting: *We were breathless after running up the stairs.* **2.** Holding the breath from excitement or suspense.

bridge |brĭj| *n., pl.* **bridges** A structure built over a river, railroad, or other obstacle so that people or vehicles can cross from one side to the other.

broad·cast |brôd′ kăst′| *v.* **broadcast** *or* **broadcasted, broadcasting** To send out over a wide area by radio or television: *All the networks will broadcast the governor's speech.*

broke |brōk| *v.* Past tense of **break:** *He ran faster than anyone else ever had, and he broke the record for the fifty-meter dash.*

broth·er-in-law |brŭth′ ər in lô′| *n., pl.* **brothers-in-law 1.** The brother of one's husband or wife. **2.** The husband of one's sister.

bruise |bro͞oz| *n., pl.* **bruises** An injury that leaves a mark on the skin but does not break it.

bub·bler |bŭb′ lər| *n., pl.* **bubblers** A drinking fountain in which the water flows upward through a small nozzle.

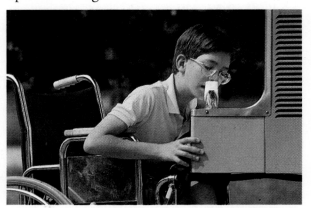

bubbler

bunch |bŭnch| *n., pl.* **bunches** A group of things of the same kind that are growing, fastened, or placed together: *I put the bunch of keys in my pocket.*

bunk |bŭngk| *n., pl.* **bunks 1.** A narrow bed built like a shelf against a wall. **2.** A double-decker bed.

bur·glar |bûr′ glər| *n., pl.* **burglars** A person who breaks into a building in order to steal; a thief.

burnt |bûrnt| *v.* A past tense and past participle of **burn.** Damaged by heat; scorched: *We burnt the roast by leaving it in the oven too long.*

bur·y |bĕr′ ē| *v.* **buried, burying** To hide by placing in the ground and covering with earth: *The dog buried the bone in the garden.*
◆ *These sound alike* **bury, berry.**

bush·el |bŏŏsh′ əl| *n., pl.* **bushels** A unit of measure for dry things, such as fruit or grain, equal to 4 pecks or 32 quarts.

bus·y |bĭz′ ē| *adj.* **busier, busiest**
1. Engaged in work or other activity: *I am busy studying for an important exam.*
2. Crowded with activity: *Today I had a busy morning.*

C

Cab·ot |kăb′ ət|, **John** 1450–1498. Italian explorer in the service of England; explored the mainland of North America in 1497.

cam·el |kăm′ əl| *n., pl.* **camels** A large animal with a long neck and one or two humps. Camels are found in northern Africa and western Asia.

cam·er·a |kăm′ ər ə| *n., pl.* **cameras**
1. A device for taking photographs or motion pictures. **2.** A device that receives an image and changes it into electrical signals for television.

cam·paign |kăm pān′| *n., pl.* **campaigns** Organized activity to gain a goal, as electing a candidate to office.

camp·fire |kămp′ fīr′| *n., pl.* **campfires** An outdoor fire used for warmth or cooking: *The children sat around the campfire and roasted potatoes.*

camp·site |kămp′ sīt′| *n., pl.* **campsites** An area used for camping.

ca·nar·y |kə nâr′ ē| *n., pl.* **canaries** A songbird, often yellow in color, that can be kept as a pet.

can·di·date |kăn′ dĭ dāt′| *n., pl.* **candidates** A person who seeks or is put forward by others for an office or honor.

ca·noe |kə nōō′| *n., pl.* **canoes** A light, slender boat with pointed ends that is propelled by paddles: *The campers paddled their canoes across the lake.*

can·vas |kăn′ vəs| *n., pl.* **canvases** A heavy coarse cloth of cotton, hemp, or flax that is used for making tents and sails and is the material on which artists make paintings.
♦ *These sound alike* **canvas, canvass.**

can·vass |kăn′ vəs| *v.* **canvassed, canvassing** To visit (a person or region) to get votes, hear opinions, or make sales; to poll or survey.
♦ *These sound alike* **canvass, canvas.**

Cap·i·tol |kăp′ ĭ tl| *n.* The domed building in Washington, D.C., in which the Congress of the United States meets.

cap·tain |kăp′ tən| *n., pl.* **captains**
1. The leader of a group; chief. **2.** The person in command of a ship. **3.** An Army, Air Force, or Marine Corps officer ranking above a lieutenant.

cap·tive |kăp′ tĭv| *adj.* Held prisoner or kept under the control of another. *n., pl.* **captives** A person or animal held captive.

cap·ture |kăp′ chər| *v.* **captured, capturing 1.** To seize and hold, as by force or skill: *The team captured the trophy.* **2.** To hold or preserve in permanent form: *capture the excitement.*

car·di·nal |kär′ dn əl| *n., pl.* **cardinals** A North American songbird with a crest on its head and bright red feathers.

ca·reer |kə rîr′| *n., pl.* **careers** A profession that a person chooses as a life's work; occupation: *My cousin has a career as a scientist.*

care·less |kâr′ lĭs| *adj.* Not taking the necessary care: *a careless mistake.*

car·rot |kăr′ ət| *n., pl.* **carrots** The long, tapering, yellow-orange edible root of a garden plant.

carve |kärv| *v.* **carved, carving** To make by cutting: *I carved a clown from a bar of soap.*

Spelling Dictionary

cas·se·role |kăs′ ə rōl′| *n., pl.* **casseroles** Food baked and served in a dish made of pottery or glass: *a shrimp casserole.*

ca·ter |kā′ tər| *v.* **catered, catering** To provide food, supplies, and sometimes service and entertainment, as for a party.

cause |kôz| *n., pl.* **causes** Someone or something that makes something happen: *What was the cause of the fire?*

cau·tion |kô′ shən| *n., pl.* **cautions** Great care so as to avoid possible danger or trouble: *Use caution when you climb the rocky cliff.*

cave |kāv| *n., pl.* **caves** A hollow area in the earth, usually on the side of a hill or mountain, with an opening to the outside.

cav·i·ty |kăv′ ĭ tē| *n., pl.* **cavities** A hollow place or area; hole: *The dentist filled two cavities in my teeth.*

cease |sēs| *v.* **ceased, ceasing** To come or bring to an end; stop: *The storm ceased at daybreak.*

cell |sĕl| *n., pl.* **cells** The smallest and most basic part of a plant or animal. Most cells consist of protoplasm, have a small mass called a nucleus near the center, and are enclosed by a thin membrane.

cel·lar |sĕl′ ər| *n., pl.* **cellars** A room or rooms under a building where things are stored; basement.

cen·te·nar·i·an |sĕn′ tə nâr′ ē ən| *n., pl.* **centenarians** A person who is 100 years old or older.

cen·ten·nial |sĕn tĕn′ ē əl| *adj.* Happening once every 100 years: *Our town had its centennial celebration last year.*

cen·ti·pede |sĕn′ tə pēd′| *n., pl.* **centipedes** A wormlike animal that has many pairs of legs.

centipede

chalk·board |chôk′ bôrd′| *n., pl.* **chalkboards** A panel, usually green or black, for writing on with chalk; a blackboard.

cham·ber |chām′ bər| *n., pl.* **chambers** A room in a house, especially a bedroom.

cham·pi·on |chăm′ pē ən| *n., pl.* **champions** The winner of a game or contest, accepted as the best of all.

chan·nel |chăn′ əl| *n., pl.* **channel**s A band of radio waves used for broadcasting, as on television: *Change the channel so I can watch my favorite TV show.*

char·ac·ter |kăr′ ĭk tər| *n., pl.* **characters** A person in a book, play, or movie.

char·ter |chär′ tər| *n., pl.* **charters** A formal written document from an authority, as a ruler or government, granting rights or privileges.

check |chĕk| *v.* **checked, checking** To test or examine to find out if something is correct or in good condition: *Check your answers after doing the math problems.*

cheer·ful |chîr′ fəl| *adj.* Showing or full of cheer; happy; not gloomy.

cheer·lead·er |chîr′ lē′ dər| *n., pl.* **cheerleaders** A person who starts and leads the cheering of spectators at a game.

chem·i·cal |kĕm′ ĭ kəl| *n., pl.* **chemicals** Any of the substances classed as elements or the compounds formed from them: *Oxygen and hydrogen are chemicals.*

choose |chooz| *v.* **chose, chosen, choosing** To pick out, especially on the basis of what one wants and thinks best: *I chose four games to take on my trip.*

cin·e·ma |sĭn′ ə mə| *n., pl.* **cinemas** A motion-picture theater: *We saw a movie at the cinema.*

cin·na·mon |sĭn′ ə mən| *n.* A spice made from the dried or ground bark of a tropical tree: *She sprinkled cinnamon on her toast.*

cir·cuit |sûr′ kĭt| *n., pl.* **circuits** A device that can store information and through which electricity can flow.

cir·cum·vent |sûr′ kəm vĕnt′| *v.* **circumvented, circumventing** To avoid by going around: *Take side roads to circumvent the road work.*

cit·y |sĭt′ ē| *n., pl.* **cities** A place where many people live close to one another. Cities are larger than towns and are usually centers of business activity.

cit·y hall |sĭt′ ē hôl′| *n., pl.* **city halls** The building in which the offices of a city or local government are located.

claim |klām| *n., pl.* **claims** A right to something. *v.* **claimed, claiming** To state to be true; assert: *I claim that I can run faster than you.*

clam·or |klăm′ ər| *n., pl.* **clamors** A loud noise, as of a crowd shouting; a great uproar: *Instead of silence a great clamor filled the kitchen.*

class·mate |klăs′ māt′| *n., pl.* **classmates** A member of the same class in school.

claw |klô| *n., pl.* **claws** A sharp, often curved nail on the toe of an animal or bird. *v.* **clawed, clawing** To dig, scratch, or scrape with or as if with claws: *The kitten clawed the couch.*

cleanse |klĕnz| *v.* **cleansed, cleansing** To make clean.

climb |klīm| *v.* **climbed, climbing** To go in various directions, such as up, down, or over, often by use of the hands and feet.

close |klōs| *adj.* **closer, closest 1.** Near in space or time: *The airport is close to town.* **2.** Near in relationship; intimate: *She is my close friend.* —*n.* **closeness** *There was a fond closeness between Cheryl and her grandfather.*

clos·et |klŏz′ ĭt| *n., pl.* **closets** A small room in which clothes or household supplies can be kept.

clo·ver |klō′ vər| *n., pl.* **clovers** Any of several plants with leaves divided into three leaflets and rounded heads of small flowers.

clue |kloō| *n., pl.* **clues** Something that helps to solve a problem or mystery: *I'll give you one more clue to the riddle.*

History

Clue comes from an Old English word *clewe,* meaning a "ball of thread."

---

code |kōd| *n. pl.* **codes** A system of signals, symbols, or letters given special meanings and

---

Pronunciation Key

ă	pat	ō	go	th	thin
ā	pay	ô	paw, for	hw	which
â	care	oi	oil	zh	usual
ä	father	ŏŏ	book	ə	ago,
ĕ	pet	ōō	boot		item,
ē	be	yōō	cute		pencil,
ĭ	pit	ou	out		atom,
ī	ice	ŭ	cut		circus
î	near	û	fur	ər	butter
ŏ	pot	*th*	*the*		

used in sending messages and especially in keeping them secret.

col·lapse |kə lăps′| *v.* **collapsed, collapsing** To fall down suddenly; cave in; topple: *Part of the roof collapsed under the weight of the snow.*

col·lar |kŏl′ ər| *n., pl.* **collars** The part of a garment that fits around the neck.

col·lect |kə lĕkt′| *v.* **collected, collecting 1.** To bring or come together in a group; accumulate: *We collected wood to build a campfire.* **2.** To gather as a hobby or for study: *I collect stamps.*

col·lide |kə līd′| *v.* **collided, colliding** To strike together with force; crash: *The kites collided high in the air.*

col·o·ny |kŏl′ ə nē| *n., pl.* **colonies 1.** A group of people who settle in a distant land but remain citizens of their native country; settlement. **2. Colonies** The 13 British colonies that became the United States.

Co·lum·bus |kə lŭm′ bəs|, **Christopher** 1451–1506. Italian navigator and explorer; opened the New World to exploration. He sailed for the Indies but instead reached America in 1492.

col·umn |kŏl′ əm| *n., pl.* **columns** An article that appears regularly in a newspaper or magazine: *the sports column.*

col·um·nist |kŏl′ əm nĭst| or |kŏl′ ə mĭst| *n., pl.* **columnists** One who writes a column for a newspaper or magazine.

com- *See* con-.

com·fort·a·ble |kŭm′ fər tə bəl| *adj.* **1.** Giving comfort: *Every living room needs a comfortable couch.* **2.** In a state of comfort; at ease: *We tried to make our guests comfortable.*

com·mand |kə **mănd′**| n., pl. **commands**
A signal that tells a computer to start, stop, or continue a specific operation: *Type your command on the computer keyboard.*

com·mer·cial |kə **mûr′** shəl| n., pl. **commercials** An advertisement on television or radio: *Who is the actor in that toothpaste commercial?*

com·mit·tee |kə **mĭt′** ē| n., pl. **committees** A group of people chosen to do a particular job: *Please join the committee to raise money for a new hospital.*

com·mon |**kŏm′** ən| adj. **commoner, commonest 1.** Belonging to or shared equally by everybody: *The swamp was drained for common use.* **2.** Found or occurring often; widespread: *Cats are common pets.*

com·pan·ion |kəm **păn′** yən| n., pl. **companions** A person who often accompanies or associates with another person; friend.

com·pare |kəm **pâr′**| v. **compared, comparing 1.** To represent as similar; liken: *We can compare the wings of a bird to those of an airplane.* **2.** To study in order to note similarities and differences: *We compared the habits of bees and spiders.*

com·plain |kəm **plān′**| v. **complained, complaining** To express unhappiness or discontent: *Don't complain about the food.*

com·plete |kəm **plēt′**| adj. Having all necessary parts: *A complete chess set has thirty-two pieces and a board.* —adv. **completely** *Ray ate the meal completely.* —n. **completeness** *She did her homework with completeness.*

com·plex |kəm **plĕks′**| or |**kŏm′** plĕks′| adj. Difficult to understand; not simple: *Computers are used to help solve complex mathematical problems.*

com·pose |kəm **pōz′**| v. **composed, composing** To make or create by putting parts or elements together: *An artist composes a picture by arranging forms and colors.*

com·pound |**kŏm′** pound′| n., pl. **compounds** A word made by combining two or more other words. *Basketball, up-to-date,* and *test tube* are compounds.

com·pro·mise |**kŏm′** prə mīz′| n., pl. **compromises** A settlement of an argument or dispute reached by each side giving up some of its claims or demands: *The children compromised by taking turns.*

com·pu·ter |kəm **pyoo′** tər| n., pl. **computers** A complex electronic machine that can accept information, work on the information to solve a problem, and produce an answer or result.

con- A prefix that means "together"; "with": *contain.*

con·cern |kən **sûrn′**| n., pl. **concerns** A worry: *The doctor saw the parents' concern for their sick child.* v. **concerned, concerning** To worry or trouble: *The rain clouds concern the hikers.*

con·cise |kən **sīs′**| adj. Saying much in a few words; brief and to the point: *Write a concise book report.*

con·di·tion |kən **dĭsh′** ən| n., pl. **conditions 1.** The way someone or something is: *The house was in poor condition after the flood.* **2.** Working order: *Our car is in good condition.*

con·dor |**kŏn′** dər| n., pl. **condors** A large bird, a vulture, that lives in the mountains of California and South America.

condor

con·duct |kən **dŭkt′**| v. **conducted, conducting 1.** To lead, guide, or direct: *The guide conducts daily tours.* **2.** To behave in a certain way. n. |**kŏn′** dŭkt′| The way a person acts; behavior.

con·fess |kən **fĕs′**| v. **confessed, confessing** To admit that one has done something bad or illegal: *I confess that I broke the window.*

con·fes·sion |kən **fĕsh′** ən| n., pl. **confessions** The act of confessing or admitting guilt.

Con·gress |kŏng′ grĭs| *n.* The United States Senate and House of Representatives, the assemblies that make laws.

con·science |kŏn′ shəns| *n., pl.* **consciences** Inner feelings and ideas that tell a person what is right and what is wrong: *My conscience tells me to be honest.*

con·sent |kən sĕnt′| *v.* **consented, consenting** To give permission: *My parents consented to my plans.* *n., pl.* **consents** Permission; approval: *I have my teacher's consent to go to the library.*

con·sid·er |kən sĭd′ ər| *v.* **considered, considering** 1. To think about before deciding: *Chen is considering a new job in Ohio.* 2. To think of as; believe to be: *I consider you the best player on the team.*

con·sist |kən sĭst′| *v.* **consisted, consisting** To be made up: *A week consists of seven days.*

con·stant |kŏn′ stənt| *adj.* Always remaining the same; not changing: *We kept a constant speed of 55 mph.*

Con·sti·tu·tion |kŏn stĭ tōō′ shən| or |kŏn stĭ tyōō′ shən| *n.* The written laws and principles by which the United States is governed, adopted in 1787 and put into effect in 1789.

con·tain |kən tān′| *v.* **contained, containing** 1. To have within itself; hold: *Orange juice contains vitamins.* 2. To consist of or include: *A gallon contains four quarts.*

con·tam·i·nate |kən tăm′ ə nāt′| *v.* **contaminated, contaminating** To make impure or unfit for use by mixture or contact; pollute.

con·tam·i·na·tion |kən tăm′ ə nā′ shən| *n.* 1. The act or process of contaminating, or the condition of being contaminated. 2. An impurity: *Fumes from cars contaminate the air.*

con·tent·ment |kən tĕnt′ mənt| *n.* Happiness and satisfaction; peace of mind.

con·tin·ue |kən tĭn′ yōō| *v.* **continued, continuing** 1. To keep on or persist in: *The rain continued for days.* 2. To begin again after stopping; resume: *Our program will continue after a word from our sponsor.*

con·trac·tion |kən trăk′ shən| *n., pl.* **contractions** The shortened form of one

or more words. An apostrophe replaces the missing letter or letters. For example, *isn't* is a contraction of *is not.*

con·vene |kən vēn′| *v.* **convened, convening** To assemble or cause to assemble; come together: *Congress will convene next month.*

con·ven·tion |kən vĕn′ shən| *n., pl.* **conventions** A formal assembly or meeting: *A convention was held to select a presidential candidate.*

con·vict |kən vĭkt′| *v.* **convicted, convicting** To find or prove guilty. *n.* |kŏn′ vĭkt′|, *pl.* **convicts** A person serving a prison sentence; criminal.

con·vic·tion |kən vĭk′ shən| *n., pl.* **convictions** The act or process of finding or proving guilty.

con·vince |kən vĭns′| *v.* **convinced, convincing** To persuade to do or believe: *Can you convince your parents to let you go on the trip?*

co·op·er·a·tive |kō ŏp′ ər ə tĭv| or |kō ŏp′ ə rā′ tĭv| *adj.* 1. Done in cooperation or by working together with others: *The team made a cooperative effort.* 2. Willing to help or cooperate: *The nurse said you are a cooperative patient.*

cork |kôrk| *n., pl.* **corks** A cork, rubber, or plastic stopper for a bottle or jug.

cor·ner |kôr′ nər| *n., pl.* **corners** 1. The point or place at which two lines or surfaces meet: *a corner of the room.* 2. The place where two roads or streets meet.

cor·rect |kə rĕkt′| *adj.* Free from error; accurate: *Your addition is correct.*

Spelling Dictionary

cor·rec·tion |kə **rĕk′** shən| *n., pl.*
corrections 1. The act or process of removing errors or mistakes. **2.** Something that replaces a mistake.

cot·tage |**kŏt′** ĭj| *n., pl.* **cottages** A small house in the country.

coun·sel·or |**koun′** sə lər| *n., pl.*
counselors A person who supervises children at a summer camp: *The counselor told the campers to get ready for swimming.*

count·less |**kount′** lĭs| *adj.* Too many to count: *The stars are not few, but countless.*

coun·try |**kŭn′** trē| *n., pl.* **countries** A land in which people live under a single government; nation: *We studied several countries.*

court |kôrt| *n., pl.* **courts** A level area marked for playing a game, as tennis or basketball: *Jill is the best player on the court.*

cov·er |**kŭv′** ər| *v.* **covered, covering** To put something over or on: *I covered my ears with my hands.*

cow·ard |**kou′** ərd| *n., pl.* **cowards** A person who has no courage.

craft |krăft| *n., pl.* **crafts** An occupation, trade, or hobby that requires special skill, especially with the hands: *We learned the craft of pottery at camp.*

cre·ate |krē **āt′**| *v.* **created, creating** To bring into being; invent: *Thomas Edison created hundreds of useful devices.*

cre·a·tion |krē **ā′** shən| *n., pl.* **creations** The act or process of creating: *The creation of a poem requires imagination.*

cre·a·tive |krē **ā′** tĭv| *adj.* Having the ability to create things; having original ideas.

cre·a·tor |krē **ā′** tər| *n., pl.* **creators** One who creates.

crea·ture |**krē′** chər| *n., pl.* **creatures** A living being, especially an animal.

cred·it |**krĕd′** ĭt| *n., pl.* **credits 1.** Belief or confidence in the truth of something; trust: *I gave full credit to what you told me.* **2.** A system of buying things and paying for them later.

creep |krēp| *v.* **crept, creeping** To move slowly or quietly.

crim·i·nal |**krĭm′** ə nəl| *n., pl.* **criminals** A person who has committed a crime or been convicted of one; a convict: *The criminal was sentenced to two years in prison.*

cross·walk |**krôs′** wôk′| *n., pl.*
crosswalks A specially marked path for people walking across a street: *Cross the street only at a crosswalk.*

cru·el |**krōō′** əl| *adj.* **crueler, cruelest** Liking to cause pain or suffering; unkind.

cruise |krōōz| *n., pl.* **cruises** A sea voyage for pleasure. *v.* **cruised, cruising** To drive about in an area without having a definite destination.

crush |krŭsh| *v.* **crushed, crushing** To press, squeeze, or bear down on with enough force to break or injure; crumple: *The tree fell on the car and crushed it.*

crys·tal |**krĭs′** təl| *n., pl.* **crystals**
1. A solid piece of matter that has a regular pattern of flat surfaces and angles between the surfaces. Water vapor forms ice crystals, or snow. **2.** Glass that is clear, colorless, and of high quality.

crystal

cue |kyōō| *n., pl.* **cues** A word or signal given to remind a performer to begin a speech or movement: *The actor waited for a cue before going on-stage.*

cul·ture |**kŭl′** chər| *n., pl.* **cultures** The customs, beliefs, laws, ways of living, and all other results of human work and thought that belong to a people: *ancient Egyptian culture.*

cun·ning |**kŭn′** ĭng| *n.* The quality or condition of being sly: *His cunning helped him find a way to get what he wanted.*

cur·rent |**kûr′** ənt| *adj.* Belonging to the present time: *Newspapers and weekly magazines report on current events.*

cur·tain |**kûr′** tn| *n., pl.* **curtains** A piece of material hanging in a window or other opening.

curve |kûrv| *n., pl.* **curves** A line or surface that keeps bending smoothly without sharp angles.

cus·toms |kŭs′ təmz| *n. (used with a singular verb)* **1.** A tax that must be paid on goods brought in from another country: *We had to pay customs on the jewelry we bought in Italy.* **2.** The inspection of goods and baggage entering a country, as for a tax.

D

dam·age |dăm′ ĭj| *v.* **damaged, damaging** To harm or injure: *The plants were damaged by insects.*

dance |dăns| *v.* **danced, dancing** To move with rhythmic steps and motions, usually in time to music.

dan·ger·ous |dān′ jər əs| *adj.* Full of danger; risky.

dare |dâr| *v.* **dared, daring** **1.** To be brave or bold enough: *The explorer dared to sail alone across the ocean.* **2.** To challenge: *My friend dared me to climb over the fence.*

da·ta |dā′ tə| or |dăt′ ə| *pl. n.* Facts and figures, especially for use in making decisions: *The scientists examined the data on measles and recommended immunization for every child.*

dawn |dôn| *n., pl.* **dawns** The time each morning when the sun comes up.

day·time |dā′ tīm′| *n.* The time between dawn and dark.

deaf |děf| *adj.* **deafer, deafest** Unable to hear or to hear well.

deal |dēl| *v.* **dealt, dealing** **1.** To hand out (cards) to players in a card game. **2.** To act toward; treat: *Deal fairly with your friends.* *n., pl.* **deals** **1.** A bargain: *I got a deal on some used books.* **2.** A business agreement.

dealt |dělt| *v.* Past tense and past participle of **deal**: *Lisa dealt with her money wisely.*

de·cath·lon |dĭ kăth′ lən| or |dĭ kăth′ lŏn′| *n., pl.* **decathlons** An athletic contest in which each contestant participates in ten different track and field events.

de·cide |dĭ sīd′| *v.* **decided, deciding** To make up one's mind: *I decided to become a mechanic.*

dec·o·rate |děk′ ə rāt′| *v.* **decorated, decorating** To furnish with something attractive or beautiful; beautify; adorn: *We decorated the room with flowers.*

dec·o·ra·tion |děk′ ə rā′ shən| *n., pl.* **decorations** **1.** The act or process of decorating. **2.** Something that decorates; ornament.

de·fense |dĭ fĕns′| *n., pl.* **defenses** Something that protects: *Storm windows are a good defense against winter winds.* —*adj.* **defenseless** *Newly hatched turtles are quite defenseless.*

de·light·ful |dĭ līt′ fəl| *adj.* Very pleasing: *I had a delightful visit with you.*

de·liv·er |dĭ lĭv′ ər| *v.* **delivered, delivering** To take and turn over to the proper person or at the proper destination; bring to: *The mail carrier delivered a package today.*

Dem·o·crat |děm′ ə krăt′| *n., pl.* **Democrats** A member of the Democratic Party: *The Democrats held their convention in Atlanta, Georgia.*

de·part |dĭ pärt′| *v.* **departed, departing** To go away or away from: *We departed for our vacation.*

de·par·ture |dĭ pär′ chər| *n., pl.* **departures** The act of going away: *The train's departure will be at 1 P.M. Its arrival in New York will be at 5:30 P.M.*

de·pend·a·ble |dĭ pěn′ də bəl| *adj.* Capable of being depended on; reliable.

de·pos·it |dĭ pŏz′ ĭt| *n., pl.* **deposits** **1.** An amount of money deposited in a bank account. **2.** A mass of material, as a mineral, that builds up by a natural process: *Prospectors looked for gold deposits.*

depth |dĕpth| *n., pl.* **depths** Distance from top to bottom or front to back.

dep·u·ty |dĕp′ yə tē| *n., pl.* **deputies** A person appointed to act for or as an assistant to another: *The sheriff asked his deputy to help with the investigation.*

de·serve |dĭ zûrv′| *v.* **deserved, deserving** To be worthy of or have a right to: *You deserved the reward.*

de·sign·er |dĭ zī′ nər| *n., pl.* **designers** A person who creates ideas for clothing and stage settings.

des·o·late |dĕs′ ə lĭt′| *adj.* Without people; deserted: *The beach is desolate in winter.*

de·stroy |dĭ stroi′| *v.* **destroyed, destroying** To completely ruin: *The explosion destroyed several homes.*

de·tail |dĭ tāl′| or |dē′ tāl′| *n., pl.* **details** A small part of a whole; item: *Give me all the details of your plan.*

de·tec·tive |dĭ tĕk′ tĭv| *n., pl.* **detectives** A person whose work is to get information about crimes and try to solve them.

de·vice |dĭ vīs′| *n., pl.* **devices** A piece of equipment that is made for a particular purpose: *A broom is a device for sweeping.*

dev·il |dĕv′ əl| *n., pl.* **devils** A wicked, evil, or mischievous person.

dew |doo| or |dyoo| *n.* Moisture that condenses and collects on cool surfaces, usually at night.

di·al |dī′ əl| *n., pl.* **dials** 1. A control that chooses the setting on a radio or television set. 2. The face of a clock.

di·a·logue |dī′ ə lôg′| *n., pl.* **dialogues** The words spoken in conversation by the characters of a written work, as a play: *Susan had to learn her lines for a ten-minute dialogue in the third act.*

di·a·mond |dī′ ə mənd| *n., pl.* **diamonds** An extremely hard, usually colorless, mineral that is a crystal form of carbon. Diamonds are used for cutting and grinding and as jewelry.

di·a·ry |dī′ ə rē| *n., pl.* **diaries** A daily written record of a person's thoughts, activities, opinions, and experiences; a journal: *I write my private thoughts in my diary.*

di·et |dī′ ĭt| *n., pl.* **diets** 1. The usual food and drink taken in by a person or an animal: *a balanced diet.* 2. Special foods eaten especially to cause one to lose weight or to improve the health.

dif·fer·ent |dĭf′ ər ənt| *adj.* 1. Partly or completely unlike another: *The sea horse is different from any other fish.* 2. Not identical; separate: *I visited you on two different days.*

dim |dĭm| *adj.* **dimmer, dimmest** 1. Somewhat dark: *The cat lay in a dim corner of the hall.* 2. Giving off little light: *Don't try to read by a dim lamp.* *v.* **dimmed, dimming** To make or become dim.

di·rect |dĭ rĕkt′| *v.* **directed, directing** 1. To aim, point, or guide to or toward: *Please direct me to the post office.* 2. To be in charge of; manage: *My sister is directing her class play.*

dirt·y |dûr′ tē| *adj.* **dirtier, dirtiest** Full of or covered with dirt; not clean.

dis- A prefix that means: 1. Not; opposite: *dishonest.* 2. Not having; lack of: *discomfort; disagreement.*

dis·a·gree |dĭs′ ə grē′| *v.* **disagreed, disagreeing** To fail to agree; be different: *Your answer disagrees with mine.*

dis·as·ter |dĭ zăs′ tər| *n., pl.* **disasters** Something, such as a flood, that causes great destruction.

dis·cov·er |dĭ skŭv′ ər| *v.* **discovered, discovering** To find out; learn: *I looked down and discovered that my shoelace was untied and ripped.*

dis·cus |dĭs′ kəs| *n., pl.* **discuses** A disk of wood and metal that is hurled for distance in athletic contests.

discus

dis·like |dĭs līk′| *v.* **disliked, disliking**
To have a feeling of not liking: *I dislike having to get up early.*

dis·lo·cate |dĭs′ lō kāt′| *v.* **dislocated, dislocating** To put or force out of a normal position: *The football player dislocated his shoulder when he fell.*

dis·miss |dĭs mĭs′| *v.* **dismissed, dismissing** **1.** To allow or ask to leave; send away: *At two o'clock our teacher dismissed the class.* **2.** To put out of one's mind; ignore.

dis·or·der |dĭs ôr′ dər| *n., pl.* **disorders** Lack of order; confusion: *The kitchen is in disorder.*

dis·or·der·ly |dĭs ôr′ dər lē| *adj.* Not neat or tidy: *My brother has a disorderly room.* —**disorderliness,** *n.*

dis·play |dĭ splā′| *v.* **displayed, displaying** To put on view; exhibit; show: *The store displayed suits in the window. n., pl.* **displays** An advertisement designed to catch the eye: *The store made a display for all the items on sale.*

dis·pute |dĭ spyo͞ot′| *v.* **disputed, disputing** To argue about; debate: *In the debate the students disputed the question of a dress code.*

dis·tance |dĭs′ təns| *n., pl.* **distances** The amount of space between two places, things, or points.

dis·trict |dĭs′ trĭkt| *n., pl.* **districts** **1.** A part, as of a city, that is set aside for a particular purpose: *Our town is divided into three school districts.* **2.** An area or region that has a certain use or character: *The city has several shopping districts.*

dis·trust |dĭs trŭst′| *n.* Lack of trust; suspicion. *v.* **distrusted, distrusting** To doubt.

ditch |dĭch| *n., pl.* **ditches** A long, narrow trench; hole; pit.

di·vi·sion |dĭ vĭzh′ ən| *n., pl.* **divisions** **1.** The mathematical process of dividing. **2.** The act of dividing or the condition of being divided; separation.

diz·zy |dĭz′ ē| *adj.* **dizzier, dizziest** Having a sensation of whirling or feeling a tendency to fall. —*n.* **dizziness** *Spinning around causes dizziness.*

Pronunciation Key

ă	pat	ō	go		th	thin
ā	pay	ô	paw, for		hw	which
â	care	oi	oil		zh	usual
ä	father	o͞o	book		ə	ago,
ě	pet	o͞o	boot			item,
ē	be	yo͞o	cute			pencil,
ĭ	pit	ou	out			atom,
ī	ice	ŭ	cut			circus
î	near	û	fur		ər	butter
ŏ	pot	*th*	**the**			

---

dock |dŏk| *n., pl.* **docks** **1.** A group of piers that serves as a landing area for ships and boats; a wharf. **2.** A platform for loading or unloading.

doc·tor |dŏk′ tər| *n., pl.* **doctors** A physician, dentist, or veterinarian who is trained in and licensed to practice a healing art.

doc·u·men·ta·ry |dŏk′ yə měn′ tə rē| *n., pl.* **documentaries** A motion picture giving a factual account of some subject and often showing actual events: *We saw a documentary about the heart.*

dol·phin |dŏl′ fĭn| *n., pl.* **dolphins** A sea animal that is related to the whale but is smaller and has a snout that looks like a beak.

dou·ble |dŭb′ əl| *adj.* **1.** Twice as much in size, strength, number, or amount. **2.** Made up of two parts: *double doors.*

dough |dō| *n., pl.* **doughs** A soft, thick mixture of flour or meal and liquids that is used to make bread and baked goods.

doz·en |dŭz′ ən| *n., pl.* **dozens** *or* **dozen** A set of twelve.

Drake |drāk|, **Sir Francis** 1540?–1596. English naval hero and explorer. He led the British navy under Queen Elizabeth I, and was the first Englishman to sail around the world.

dram·a·tize |drăm′ ə tīz′| *or* |drăm′ ə tīz′| *v.* **dramatized, dramatizing** **1.** To make a play of; act out. **2.** To present or portray in a serious way.

dread·ful |drĕd′ fəl| *adj.* **1.** Causing great fear; terrible. **2.** Very unpleasant, bad, or shocking: *The snowstorm turned a wonderful day into a dreadful one.*

dream |drēm| *v.* **dreamed** *or* **dreamt,**
dreaming To have a series of pictures,
thoughts, or emotions occurring during sleep.

dreamt |drĕmt| *v.* Past tense and past
participle of **dream**: *Last night I dreamt of
a flying horse.*

drear·y |drîr′ ē| *adj.* **drearier, dreariest**
Gloomy; dismal; not cheerful: *Winter can be
a dreary time.*

drib·ble |drĭb′ əl| *v.* **dribbled, dribbling**
To move a ball along by bouncing or kicking,
as in basketball: *She dribbled the basketball
down the court.*

drip |drĭp| *v.* **dripped, dripping** To
fall or let fall in drops: *Water dripped from
the faucet.*

drought |drout| *n., pl.* **droughts** A period
of little or no rain.

drown |droun| *v.* **drowned, drowning** To
be loud enough to overpower: *The lawnmower
drowned out my voice.*

duke |dōōk| *or* |dyōōk| *n., pl.* **dukes**
A member of the highest level of the British
nobility.

du·ra·ble |dōōr′ ə bəl| *or* |dyōōr′ ə bəl|
adj. Capable of withstanding hard wear or
long use; sturdy.

du·ty |dōō′ tē| *or* |dyōō′ tē| *n., pl.* **duties**
1. Something that a person ought to do;
responsibility: *It is my duty to clean my room.*
2. Action that a person's occupation or job
requires; task: *The duties of a police officer are
to enforce the laws.*

dwell |dwĕl| *v.* **dwelt** *or* **dwelled, dwelling**
To live as a resident; reside: *A monarch often
dwells in a palace.*

E

ea·ger |ē′ gər| *adj.* **eagerer, eagerest**
Having or showing keen interest or desire;
enthusiastic.

ear·ly |ûr′ lē| *adj.* **earlier, earliest**
1. Of or happening near the beginning: *We
ate breakfast in the early morning.* **2.** Coming
or happening before the usual or expected

time: *We ate an early dinner. adv.* **earlier,**
earliest At or near the beginning: *We always
get up early in the morning.*

eas·y |ē′ zē| *adj.* **easier, easiest** Needing
very little effort; not hard.

ed·u·cate |ĕj′ ə kāt′| *v.* **educated,**
educating To provide with formal instruction;
teach.

ef·fort |ĕf′ ərt| *n., pl.* **efforts** An earnest
attempt; try: *Please make an effort to arrive on
time.*

e·ject |ĭ jĕkt′| *v.* **ejected, ejecting** To
throw out forcefully: *The machine ejects the
finished product.*

e·lect |ĭ lĕkt′| *v.* **elected, electing** To
choose by vote: *We elected a class president in
September.*

e·lec·tion |ĭ lĕk′ shən| *n., pl.* **elections**
The act or process of electing, or the condition
of being elected: *Did you vote in the
presidential election?*

el·e·gant |ĕl′ ĭ gənt| *adj.* Marked by good
taste and refinement: *We had dinner last night
in an elegant restaurant.*

em·er·ald |ĕm′ ər əld| *n., pl.* **emeralds**
A bright-green stone, often found in granite,
that is used as a gem. An emerald is six-sided.

emerald

e·merge |ĭ mûrj′| *v.* **emerged, emerging**
To come into view; appear: *The butterfly
emerged from the cocoon.*

e·mer·gen·cy |ĭ mûr′ jən sē| *n., pl.*
emergencies A situation that develops
suddenly and unexpectedly and calls for
immediate action.

e·mo·tion |ĭ mō′ shən| *n., pl.* **emotions**
A strong feeling, as love, sorrow, hate, or joy.

em·pire |ĕm′ pīr′| *n., pl.* **empires** A group
of territories or nations headed by a single
ruler; a kingdom.

em·ploy |ĕm **ploi**′| *v.* **employed,
employing** To engage the services of; hire:
*The construction company employed many
workers to build the skyscraper.*

emp·ty |ĕmp′ tē| *adj.* **emptier, emptiest**
1. Containing nothing: *The gas tank is empty,
so the car will not start.* **2.** Vacant; unoccupied.
—n. **emptiness** *Astronauts have experienced
emptiness in outer space.*

en- A prefix that means "to put or go in,
into, or on": *endanger.*

en·act |ĕn **ăkt**′| *v.* **enacted, enacting**
To establish by passing a law; decree: *The
Senate enacted legislation to stop pollution.*
—n. **enactment** *The enactment of a bill
depends on the President.*

en·close |ĕn **klōz**′| *v.* **enclosed, enclosing**
To close in on all sides; surround: *A high fence
encloses the garden.*

en·e·my |ĕn′ ə mē| *n., pl.* **enemies**
A person, animal, or group that hates or
wishes harm to another; foe.

en·er·gy |ĕn′ ər jē| *n., pl.* **energies** Heat
or electric power usable for doing physical
work, such as moving or lifting objects.

en·force |ĕn **fôrs**′| *v.* **enforced, enforcing**
To force others to obey: *Police officers have the
power to enforce the laws.*

en·gage |ĕn **gāj**′| *v.* **engaged, engaging**
To draw into; involve: *engage someone in debate.*

en·joy·ment |ĕn **joi**′ mənt| *n., pl.*
enjoyments A form or source of pleasure:
We work in the garden for enjoyment.

-ent A suffix that forms adjectives and
nouns: *different, resident.*

en·ter |ĕn′ tər| *v.* **entered, entering**
1. To come or go in or into: *The ship entered
the harbor.* **2.** To become a member of; join:
to enter the army. **3.** The act of including an
item in a record, as a diary or list.

en·ter·tain |ĕn′ tər **tān**′| *v.* **entertained,
entertaining** To hold the attention of in an
agreeable way; amuse: *We entertained them
with stories about our trip to Hawaii.*

en·thu·si·as·tic |ĕn thoō′ zē **ăs**′ tĭk| *adj.*
Full of or showing strong interest or eagerness;
eager: *My parents are enthusiastic skiers.*

en·trance |ĕn′ trəns| *n., pl.* **entrances**
1. The act or example of entering: *The

Pronunciation Key

ă	pat	ō	go	th	thin
ā	pay	ô	paw, for	hw	which
â	care	oi	oil	zh	usual
ä	father	oͦo	book	ə	ago,
ĕ	pet	oͦo	boot		item,
ē	be	yoͦo	cute		pencil,
ĭ	pit	ou	out		atom,
ī	ice	ŭ	cut		circus
î	near	û	fur	ər	butter
ŏ	pot	*th*	the		

audience applauded the singer's entrance.
2. A door or passageway; entry.

en·try |ĕn′ trē| *n., pl.* **entries 1.** The act or
right of entering: *You need a passport for entry
into the country.* **2.** A place, as a passage or
door, through which to enter. **3.** The act of
including an item in a record, as a diary or list.

en·vi·ron·ment |ĕn **vī**′ rən mənt| *n., pl.*
environments Surroundings and conditions
that affect natural processes and the growth
and development of living things: *Protecting
Earth's environment from pollution is a major
challenge for everyone.*

ep·i·sode |ĕp′ ĭ sōd′| *n., pl.* **episodes**
A distinct part of a story or a separate part of
a continuing story: *We saw the first episode of
a ten-part mystery series.*

e·qual |ē′ kwəl| *adj.* Being exactly the
same in amount, extent, or other measured
quality: *Three feet are equal to one yard. v.*
equaled, equaling To be the same as: *Two
pints equal one quart.*

Er·ic·son |ĕr′ ĭk sən|, **Leif** Norwegian
navigator, believed to have landed in North
America in about the year A.D. 1000.

es·say |ĕs′ ā′| *n., pl.* **essays** A short piece
of writing that gives the author's opinions on a
certain subject; composition.

e·vac·u·ate |ĭ **văk**′ yoō āt′| *v.* **evacuated,
evacuating** To leave or send away from a
dangerous place: *The residents quickly evacuated
the burning building.*

e·vent |ĭ **vĕnt**′| *n., pl.* **events** Something
that happens: *The holiday celebration will include
many events, such as a parade and fireworks.*

e·ven·tu·al |ĭ **vĕn**′ chōō əl| *adj.*
Occurring in the near or far future; to happen
sooner or later: *He never lost hope of eventual
victory.* —*adv.* **eventually** *We will arrive at
the park eventually.*

Ev·er·glades Na·tion·al Park
|**ĕv**′ ər glādz′| Area enclosing a swampy
region in southern Florida, abundant in
wildlife and tropical plants.

Everglades National Park

eve·ry·bod·y |**ĕv**′ rē bŏd′ ē| *pron.* Every
person; everyone: *Everybody makes a mistake
sometimes.*

eve·ry·where |**ĕv**′ rē hwâr′| *adv.* In
every place; in all places: *I looked everywhere for
my lost keys.*

ev·i·dence |**ĕv**′ ĭ dəns| *n.* Facts or signs
that help one find out the truth or come to a
conclusion: *The broken window was evidence
that a burglary had taken place.*

e·vil |**ē**′ vəl| *adj.* **eviler, evilest** Bad,
wrong, or wicked.

ex- A prefix that means: **1.** Out; out of:
exchange. **2.** Former: *ex-president.*

ex·act |ĭg **zăkt**′| *adj.* Accurate in every
detail: *The exact amount was $5.03.*

ex·ceed |ĭk **sēd**′| *v.* **exceeded, exceeding**
To go beyond: *Be careful not to exceed the speed
limit.*

ex·change |ĭks **chānj**′| *v.* **exchanged,
exchanging** To give one thing for another;
trade: *The traders exchanged cheap trinkets for
valuable furs.*

ex·cite |ĭk **sīt**′| *v.* **excited, exciting** **1.** To
stir up; arouse: *News of the party excited the
children.* **2.** To make more active; stimulate:
Do not excite the bees.

ex·cuse |ĭk **skyōōz**′| *v.* **excused, excusing**
1. To forgive: *Please excuse me for what I
did.* **2.** To release from a duty or promise.
|ĭk **skyōōs**′| *n., pl.* **excuses** Something given
as a reason for excusing: *a written excuse for
an absence.*

ex·ert |ĭg **zûrt**′| *v.* **exerted, exerting** To
put into use; apply effort: *I exerted all my
strength to move the stone.*

ex·haust |ĭg **zôst**′| *v.* **exhausted,
exhausting** To wear out completely; tire:
The long swim exhausted me.

ex·it |**ĕg**′ zĭt| or |**ĕk**′ sĭt| *n., pl.* **exits** **1.** A
way out. **2.** The act of going away or out: *We
made a hasty exit from the room.*

ex·per·i·ment |ĭk **spĕr**′ ə mĕnt′| *n., pl.*
experiments A test used to find out or prove
something: *The scientists did an experiment to
learn more about blood cells.*

ex·pert |**ĕk**′ spûrt′| *n., pl.* **experts** A person
who has great knowledge or skill in a special
area: *My teacher is an expert on American history.*

ex·plain |ĭk **splān**′| *v.* **explained,
explaining** To make clear or understandable;
clarify: *The science teacher explained atoms to us.*

ex·pose |ĭk **spōz**′| *v.* **exposed, exposing**
To leave without cover or protection; put out
in the open.

ex·press |ĭk **sprĕs**′| *v.* **expressed,
expressing** **1.** To make known; reveal: *This
story expresses the writer's love of animals.* **2.** To
put into words; state: *I must express my opinion
to the teacher.*

ex·pres·sion |ĭk **sprĕsh**′ ən| *n., pl.*
expressions **1.** A look that shows mood or
feeling. **2.** A lively manner of speaking: *The
lecturer spoke with great expression.*

ex·tend |ĭk **stĕnd**′| *v.* **extended,
extending** To make greater or larger; expand:
The empire sought to extend its boundaries.

ex·traor·di·nar·y |ĭk **strôr**′ dn ĕr′ ē| or
|ĕk′ strə **ôr**′ dn ĕr′ ē| *adj.* Very unusual;
remarkable: *Landing on the moon was an
extraordinary accomplishment.*

ex·trav·a·gant |ĭk **străv**′ ə gənt| *adj.*
1. Costing or spending too much; expensive;
wasteful. **2.** Going beyond the limits of
reason; excessive.

ex·treme |ĭk **strēm′**| *adj.* **1.** Very great or intense: *The Arctic explorers suffered from the extreme cold.* **2.** The farthest possible: *the extreme end of the island.*

eye·ball |ī′ bôl| *n., pl.* **eyeballs** The ball-shaped part of the eye, enclosed by the sockets and eyelids.

F

fab·ric |făb′ rĭk| *n., pl.* **fabrics** A material that is produced by joining fibers together, as by weaving; cloth.

fact |făkt| *n., pl.* **facts** Something that has really happened or really exists: *It is a fact that the sun is a star.*

fac·tu·al |făk′ chōō əl| *adj.* Of or based on facts: *Just give a factual account of what happened.*

fad |făd| *n., pl.* **fads** Something that is very popular for a short time; craze: *Silly shoelaces were a fad last month.*

fal·con |făl′ kən| or |fôl′ kən| *n., pl.* **falcons** A hawk with long wings and hooked claws, especially one that is trained to hunt small animals and birds.

false |fôls| *adj.* **falser, falsest** Not true, real, honest, or correct: *Is that conclusion false?*

fam·i·ly |făm′ ə lē| *n., pl.* **families** **1.** A group consisting of parents and their children. **2.** A group of persons related by blood; relatives.

fa·mous |fā′ məs| *adj.* Very well known.

fare |fâr| *n., pl.* **fares** The money a person pays to travel, as on a plane, train, or bus. ◆ *These sound alike* **fare, fair.**

far·ther |fär′ thər| *adv.* To or at a greater distance: *The drive to the beach was farther than we thought. adj.* More distant: *We docked the boat on the farther shore.*

fas·ci·nate |făs′ ə nāt′| *v.* **fascinated, fascinating** To attract and hold the interest of.

fas·ci·na·tion |făs′ ə **nā′** shən| *n.* **1.** The condition of being fascinated: *Everyone watched in fascination.* **2.** The power of fascinating; a strong attraction: *The sea has always held fascination for me.*

ă	pat	ō	go	th	thin
ā	pay	ô	paw, for	hw	which
â	care	oi	oil	zh	usual
ä	father	ŏŏ	book	ə	ago,
ĕ	pet	ōō	boot		item,
ē	be	yōō	cute		pencil,
ĭ	pit	ou	out		atom,
ī	ice	ŭ	cut		circus
î	near	û	fur	ər	butter
ŏ	pot	th	the		

fash·ion·a·ble |făsh′ ə nə bəl| *adj.* Following the current style or latest fashion; stylish.

fau·cet |fô′ sĭt| *n., pl.* **faucets** A device for controlling the flow of liquid, as from a pipe; tap.

fault |fôlt| *n., pl.* **faults** **1.** Responsibility for a mistake or offense: *Failing the test was my own fault.* **2.** A mistake; error: *I found many faults in spelling and grammar in my report.*

fa·vor·ite |fā′ vər ĭt| *n., pl.* **favorites** Someone or something that is preferred above all others. *adj.* Preferred above all others; liked.

fawn |fôn| *n., pl.* **fawns** A young deer, especially one that is less than a year old.

fear·ful |fîr′ fəl| *adj.* Feeling fear; afraid: *I was fearful of losing my way in the forest.*

feat |fēt| *n., pl.* **feats** An act or accomplishment that shows skill, strength, or bravery: *The gymnasts performed remarkable feats.*

fea·ture |fē′ chər| *n., pl.* **features** **1.** One of the distinct parts, as the chin or nose, of the face. **2.** A full-length movie.

fenc·ing |fĕn′ sĭng| *n.* The sport of fighting with long, slender swords: *Helmets and padded jackets are worn for fencing.*

fes·ti·val |fĕs′ tə vəl| *n., pl.* **festivals** **1.** A day or period of celebrating; holiday. **2.** A series of special cultural events, such as parades, films, concerts, or exhibitions.

fil·i·bus·ter |fĭl′ ə bŭs tər| *n., pl.* **filibusters** An example of the tactic, used especially in the United States Senate, of delaying or trying to prevent the passage of legislation by making extremely long speeches: *The senator's filibuster against the bill failed in every respect.*

fin·ger |fĭng′ gər| *n., pl.* **fingers** One of the five extensions of the hand.

fin·ish |fĭn′ ĭsh| *v.* **finished, finishing** **1.** To bring or come to an end; get done: *I have finished my lunch.* **2.** To use all of.

fire·crack·er |fīr′ krăk′ ər| *n., pl.* **firecrackers** A small explosive charge in a paper tube. Firecrackers are set off to make loud noise during celebrations.

firm |fûrm| *adj.* **firmer, firmest** Not giving way when pressed or pushed; solid: *The firm ground of the track was ideal for running.*

first aid |fûrst′ ād′| *n.* Emergency care given to an injured or sick person before a doctor comes.

fix·ture |fĭks′ chər| *n., pl.* **fixtures** Something fixed or attached permanently in a place: *There are two light fixtures on the ceiling.*

flair |flâr| *n., pl.* **flairs** A natural talent or aptitude.

◆ *These sound alike* **flair, flare.**

fla·min·go |flə mĭng′ gō| *n., pl.* **flamingos** *or* **flamingoes** A tropical wading bird that has long legs, a long neck, and reddish or pinkish feathers.

flamingo

flare |flâr| *n., pl.* **flares** Something that produces a bright flame for signaling or lighting. *v.* **flared, flaring** To burn with a sudden or unsteady flame: *The candle flared just before going out.*

◆ *These sound alike* **flare, flair.**

flash·light |flăsh′ līt′| *n., pl.* **flashlights** A lamp or lantern powered by batteries that is small enough to be carried around.

fla·vor |flā′ vər| *n., pl.* **flavors** **1.** The quality that causes something to have a certain taste: *The sauce had a burnt flavor.* **2.** A quality felt to be characteristic of a thing: *the mysterious flavor of the Orient.*

flaw |flô| *n., pl.* **flaws** A defect or blemish. *v.* **flawed** To make or become defective.

flea |flē| *n., pl.* **fleas** A small, wingless insect that sucks blood from animals and humans.

◆ *These sound alike* **flea, flee.**

flee |flē| *v.* **fled, fleeing** To run away.

◆ *These sound alike* **flee, flea.**

fleet |flēt| *n., pl.* **fleets** A number of boats, ships, or vehicles that form a group: *The company owns a fleet of cars.*

flip |flĭp| *v.* **flipped, flipping** **1.** To move or turn by tossing in the air: *Let's flip a coin to decide who goes first.* **2.** Slang. To be overwhelmed: *I flipped when I saw the high grade on my test.*

floor |flôr| *n., pl.* **floors** **1.** The bottom surface of a room, on which one stands. **2.** The ground or lowest surface, as of a forest or ocean.

◇ *Idioms* **get in on the ground floor** Be part of something from the beginning. **take the floor** Rise to give a formal speech.

flow |flō| *v.* **flowed, flowing** To move or run freely in or as if in a stream: *Air flowed in through the window.*

flute |flōōt| *n., pl.* **flutes** A pipe-shaped musical instrument played by blowing across or into a hole near one end.

fo·cus |fō′ kəs| *n., pl.* **focuses** The adjustment of a lens, an eye, or a camera that gives the best image: *The camera was out of focus, so the picture was blurred.*

folk·lore |fōk′ lôr′| *n.* The beliefs, legends, fables, myths, customs, and other traditions handed down by a people from generation to generation.

fond |fŏnd| *adj.* **fonder, fondest** **1.** Loving or affectionate. **2.** Having a liking for: *My cousin is very fond of skiing.*

foot·ball |fŏŏt′ bôl′| *n.* A team game played with an inflated oval ball on a long field with goals at either end.

for·bid |fər **bĭd′**| *v.* **forbade** or **forbad,
forbidden, forbidding 1.** To order against
with authority; not allow: *The rules forbid
running in the hallways.* **2.** To order not to
do something: *I forbid you to go.*

for·get·ful |fər **gĕt′** fəl| *adj.* Apt to
forget; likely not to remember: *I am so forgetful
I often leave my keys at home.*

for·ward |**fôr′** wərd| *n., pl.* **forwards** A
player in certain games, as basketball, who is
part of the front line: *The forward scored ten
baskets in the first half of the game.*

fos·sil |**fŏs′** əl| *n., pl.* **fossils** The remains
or traces of a plant or animal of an earlier
age. Fossils are embedded in rock or in the
earth's crust.

foul |foul| *n., pl.* **fouls** A violation of a rule
of play in a game or sport: *The game stops
when a foul is called.*

foun·tain |**foun′** tən| *n., pl.* **fountains**
A stream or jet of water, as for drinking or
for decoration.

frappe |frăp| *n., pl.* **frappes** A drink made
with ice cream; a milk shake.

free |frē| *adj.* **freer, freest** Given or
provided at no cost: *We won a free meal at a
fancy restaurant.*

free·dom |**frē′** dəm| *n., pl.* **freedoms** The
right to use or enjoy something freely: *Freedom
of speech and religion are guaranteed by the
Constitution.*

freeze |frēz| *v.* **froze, frozen, freezing
1.** To change from a liquid to a solid by loss
of heat: *The pond froze over during the cold
night.* **2.** To be uncomfortably cold: *I forgot
my gloves, and my hands are freezing.*

fresh |frĕsh| *adj.* **fresher, freshest** Just
made, grown, or gathered: *We ate warm, fresh
bread with our salad.*

frisk·y |**frĭs′** kē| *adj.* **friskier, friskiest**
Lively and playful; energetic.

fruit |fro͞ot| *n., pl.* **fruit** *or* **fruits** A seed-
bearing plant part that is fleshy or juicy, eaten
as food. Apples, oranges, grapes, strawberries,
and bananas are fruits.

fu·el |**fyo͞o′** əl| *n., pl.* **fuels** A substance
that is burned to give off heat or produce
energy. Coal, wood, oil, gas, and gasoline are
fuels.

Pronunciation Key

ă	pat	ō	go	th	thin
ā	pay	ô	paw, for	hw	which
â	care	oi	oil	zh	usual
ä	father	o͞o	book	ə	ago,
ĕ	pet	o͞o	boot		item,
ē	be	yo͞o	cute		pencil,
ĭ	pit	ou	out		atom,
ī	ice	ŭ	cut		circus
î	near	û	fur	ər	butter
ŏ	pot	th	the		

-ful A suffix that forms adjectives and
means: **1.** Full of: *beautiful.* **2.** Able or apt
to: *forgetful.* **3.** An amount that fills: *cupful;
handful.*

fume |fyo͞om| *n., pl.* **fumes** An irritating
or strong-smelling smoke; vapor, or gas: *The
fumes from the car were making me sick.*

func·tion |**fŭngk′** shən| *n., pl.* **functions**
The proper activity; purpose or use: *The
function of a knife is to cut.*

fund |fŭnd| *n., pl.* **funds 1.** A sum of
money raised or kept for a certain purpose:
The family has a vacation fund. **2.** A source of
supply; stock: *A library is a fund of information.*

fun·ny |**fŭn′** ē| *adj.* **funnier, funniest**
Causing amusement or laughter.

fur·nish |**fûr′** nĭsh| *v.* **furnished,
furnishing 1.** To equip with furniture: *We
are furnishing a new home.* **2.** To supply; give:
*The company furnishes the bats and balls for our
baseball league.*

fur·ni·ture |**fûr′** nə chər| *n.* The movable
objects that are needed to make a room or
office fit for living or working. Chairs, tables,
and beds are pieces of furniture.

fur·ther·more |**fûr′** thər môr′| *adv.*
In addition; moreover: *Fresh vegetables are
nutritious; furthermore, they are cheaper than
frozen ones.*

fu·ry |**fyo͝or′** ē| *n., pl.* **furies** Violent
anger; rage.

fu·ture |**fyo͞o′** chər| *n., pl.* **futures** The
time that is to come: *We must plan now for the
future.* *adj.* Occurring in time that is to come:
We will meet at some future date.

G

gain |gān| *v.* **gained, gaining** To get, achieve, or obtain by effort: *We gained experience by working in a number of jobs.*

gar·bage |gär′ bĭj| *n.* Food and trash to be thrown away, as from a kitchen.

gar·lic |gär′ lĭk| *n.* A plant that is related to the onion. Cloves of the strong-tasting bulb of garlic are used to flavor food.

garlic

gar·ment |gär′ mənt| *n., pl.* **garments** An article of clothing: *That shop makes shirts, pants, and other garments.*

gar·ret |gär′ ĭt| *n., pl.* **garrets** A room or space in a house, directly under a sloping roof; attic.

gath·er |găth′ ər| *v.* **gathered, gathering** **1.** To bring or come together into one place; collect: *I gathered the papers together.* **2.** To pick up from many sources: *Squirrels gather nuts.*

gen·er·al |jĕn′ ər əl| *adj.* Of or involving all: *a general election.* *n., pl.* **generals** An Army, Air Force, or Marine Corps officer ranking above a colonel.

gen·tle |jĕn′ tl| *adj.* **gentler, gentlest** **1.** Mild and soft; not harsh: *a gentle breeze.* **2.** Thoughtful: *a gentle nature.*

germ |jûrm| *n., pl.* **germs** A very tiny organism that can cause disease.

gi·ant |jī′ ənt| *n., pl.* **giants** A huge, very strong, imaginary creature resembling a human. *adj.* Extremely large; huge.

gla·cier |glā′ shər| *n., pl.* **glaciers** A large mass of ice that moves very slowly down a mountain or through a valley. Glaciers are formed from snow on the tops of huge mountains.

Gla·cier Na·tion·al Park |glā′ shər| A scenic area in Montana, containing many small glaciers. The park borders Canada.

glor·i·ous |glôr′ ē əs| *adj.* Having great beauty; magnificent: *We saw a glorious sunset.*

goal |gōl| *n., pl.* **goals** Something wanted or worked for; purpose: *My goal in life is to help other people.*

good·ness |good′ nĭs| *n.* The quality or condition of being good.

gov·ern |gŭv′ ərn| *v.* **governed, governing** To direct the public affairs of a country or state: *Congress and the President govern the United States.*

gov·ern·ment |gŭv′ ərn mənt| *n., pl.* **governments** **1.** The act or process of governing, especially the direction of the public affairs of a country, state, or city. **2.** A form or system by which a political unit, as a country, is governed: *In a democratic government elected representatives make the laws.*

gov·er·nor |gŭv′ ər nər| *n., pl.* **governors** **1.** A person who is appointed to govern a colony or territory. **2.** The person elected as head of state in the United States.

Grand Can·yon |grănd′ kăn′ yən| A huge gorge, four to eighteen miles wide and one mile deep, formed by the Colorado River in northern Arizona.

grand·par·ent |grănd′ pâr′ ənt| *n., pl.* **grandparents** A parent of one's father or mother.

grape·fruit |grāp′ froot′| *n., pl.* **grapefruit** or **grapefruits** A large, round fruit that has yellow skin, is related to the orange, and has a somewhat sour taste.

graph |grăf| *n., pl.* **graphs** A drawing or diagram that shows the relationships between things: *This graph shows how prices have risen over the past ten years.*

grasp |grăsp| *v.* **grasped, grasping** To grab and hold firmly with or as if with the hand: *Grasp the railing so you won't fall.*

gray |grā| *n., pl.* **grays** A color made by mixing black and white.

great-grand·child |grāt′ grănd′ chīld′| *n., pl.* **great-grandchildren** A child of one's grandchild.

greet |grēt| *v.* **greeted, greeting** To welcome or speak to in a friendly or polite way: *We greeted our guests at the door.*

gro·cer·y |grō′ sə rē| *n., pl.* **groceries** A store selling food or household supplies.

group |grōōp| *n., pl.* **groups** A number of persons or things gathered or located together; a bunch: *A group of people are waiting for the bus.*

grouse |grous| *n., pl.* **grouse** *or* **grouses** A game bird, similar to turkey or a quail, that has a plump body and brownish or grayish feathers.

growth |grōth| *n., pl.* **growths** The process of becoming larger in size or becoming capable of doing well, especially in a particular climate or environment: *We saw the growth of some species of fish and the decline of others.*

guilt·y |gĭl′ tē| *adj.* **guiltier, guiltiest** Having committed a crime or bad deed: *The jury found them guilty of stealing.*

gym·na·si·um |jĭm nā′ zē əm| *n., pl.* **gymnasiums** A room or building with equipment for physical exercises and training and for indoor sports.

gym·nas·tics |jĭm năs′ tĭks| *pl. n. (used with a singular or plural verb)* Physical exercises done with the use of floor mats, stationary bars, and other equipment in a gymnasium.

hab·it |hăb′ ĭt| *n., pl.* **habits** An activity or action done so often that one does it without thinking: *I have the habit of getting up early every morning.*

ha·bit·u·al |hə bĭch′ ōō əl| *adj.* Done again and again: *Leah's pencil chewing became habitual.*

hai·ku |hī′ kōō| *n., pl.* **haiku** A Japanese lyric poem of a fixed seventeen-syllable form, usually on a subject that is drawn from nature.

half·heart·ed |hăf′ här′ tĭd| *adj.* Showing little eagerness or interest.

hall |hôl| *n., pl.* **halls** A passageway in a house or building; corridor.
◆ *These sound alike* **hall, haul.**

hand·some |hăn′ səm| *adj.* **handsomer, handsomest** Pleasing in appearance; good-looking.

hap·py |hăp′ ē| *adj.* **happier, happiest** Having, showing, or marked by a feeling of joy or pleasure: *This is the happiest day of my life.* *n.* **happiness** *Toby found happiness in her work.*

hard·ship |härd′ shĭp′| *n., pl.* **hardships** Something that causes suffering or difficulty: *The early pioneers suffered great hardships on the frontier.*

hare |hâr| *n., pl.* **hares** An animal that is related to and looks like a rabbit. A hare has longer ears and larger hind feet than a rabbit.
◆ *These sound alike* **hare, hair.**

har·mo·ny |här′ mə nē| *n., pl.* **harmonies** **1.** The sounding together of musical notes in a chord. **2.** A pleasing combination of the parts that make up a whole.

harsh |härsh| *adj.* **harsher, harshest** **1.** Unpleasant to hear or taste. **2.** Very severe or demanding; cruel.

har·vest |här′ vĭst| *n., pl.* **harvests** **1.** The act or process of gathering a crop: *The farmer hired extra workers for the harvest.* **2.** The crop that is gathered or is ready for gathering: *Everyone helped to bring in the corn harvest.*

haul |hôl| *v.* **hauled, hauling** To pull or carry with effort; drag: *We hauled the sled up the hill.*
◆ *These sound alike* **haul, hall.**

haunt |hônt| *v.* **haunted, haunting** **1.** To come to the mind of again and again: *A certain melody haunted Alex throughout the day.* **2.** To visit, live in, or appear to in the form of a ghost.

hawk |hôk| *n., pl.* **hawks** A large bird with a short, hooked bill, strong claws, and keen eyesight. Hawks catch small birds and other animals for food.

head·quar·ters |hĕd′ **kwôr**′ tərz| *pl. n.* A center of operations: *police headquarters.*

heal |hēl| *v.* **healed, healing** To make or become healthy again; mend: *The wound healed quickly.*
◆ *These sound alike* **heal, heel.**

health |hĕlth| *n.* **1.** The condition of the body or mind: *Bad eating habits can put you in poor health.* **2.** Freedom from disease or injury: *We wish you a speedy return to health.*

heel |hēl| *n., pl.* **heels** The rounded back part of the human foot.
◆ *These sound alike* **heel, heal.**

height |hīt| *n., pl.* **heights** **1.** The distance from bottom to top: *The height of the flagpole is twenty feet.* **2.** The distance from foot to head: *My height increased two inches this year.* **3.** The highest point; peak: *the height of the storm.*

heir |âr| *n., pl.* **heirs** A person who receives or has the right to receive the property of another person when the other person dies.

hel·i·port |hĕl′ ə pôrt′| *n., pl.* **heliports** A place for helicopters to take off and land.

herb |ûrb| or |hûrb| *n., pl.* **herbs** A plant whose leaves, roots, or other parts are used to flavor food or are used as medicine. Parsley and basil are herbs.

her·i·tage |hĕr′ ĭ tĭj| *n., pl.* **heritages** Something handed down to later generations from earlier generations: *Freedom of speech is part of our national heritage.*

hide |hīd| *v.* **hid** *or* **hidden, hiding** To keep or put out of sight: *The presents were hidden in the closet.*

hid·den |hĭd′ n| *v.* A past participle of **hide.** *adj.* Not visible; not exposed.

high-rise |hī′ rīz| *n., pl.* **high-rises** A tall building with many stories; skyscraper.

high-spir·it·ed |hī′ spĭr′ ĭ tĭd| *adj.* **1.** Having a proud or unbroken spirit; brave. **2.** Lively.

high·way |hī′ wā′| *n., pl.* **highways** A main public road.

his·tor·i·cal |hĭ stôr′ ĭ kəl| **1.** Of or relating to history. **2.** Based on or concerned with events in history.

his·to·ry |hĭs′ tə rē| *n., pl.* **histories** **1.** The continuing events of the past leading up to the present: *The invention of the printing press was one of the most important in history.* **2.** The study of past events as a special field of knowledge.

hit |hĭt| *v.* **hit, hitting** To propel by striking with a bat or racket.

hoard |hôrd| *n., pl.* **hoards** A supply that is stored away, often secretly. *v.* **hoarded, hoarding** To save and store away.
◆ *These sound alike* **hoard, horde.**

hol·i·day |hŏl′ ĭ dā′| *n., pl.* **holidays** A day or period of time set aside to honor someone or to celebrate a special event.

home·made |hōm′ mād′| *adj.* Made at home.

home·sick |hōm′ sĭk′| *adj.* Unhappy because one is away from one's home and family; longing for home.

hom·o·graph |hŏm′ ə grăf′| or |hō′ mə grăf′| *n., pl.* **homographs** A word that has the same spelling as another word but differs in meaning, origin, and sometimes in pronunciation. For example, **ring** (circle) and **ring** (sound).

hom·o·phone |hŏm′ ə fōn′| or |hō′ mə fōn′| *n., pl.* **homophones** A word that has the same sound as another word but differs in spelling, meaning, and origin. For example, **steel** and **steal.**

hon·est |ŏn′ ĭst| *adj.* Not lying, stealing, or cheating.

hon·or |ŏn′ ər| *n., pl.* **honors** **1.** Special respect or high regard: *We display the flag to show honor to the United States.* **2.** A special privilege or mark of excellence: *Election as class president is an honor.*

hon·or·a·ble |ŏn′ ər ə bəl| *adj.* Having or showing a strong sense of what is right or just: *an honorable person.*

horde |hôrd| *n., pl.* **hordes** A large crowd or swarm.
◆ *These sound alike* **horde, hoard.**

hor·ri·ble |hôr′ ə bəl| *adj.* **1.** Causing horror; dreadful. **2.** Very unpleasant.

horse |hôrs| *n., pl.* **horses** A large hoofed animal that has a long mane and tail.

hose |hōz| *n., pl.* **hose** *or* **hoses** **1.** A long flexible tube used for carrying fluid or air. **2.** Stockings or socks.

hos·pi·tal |hŏs′ pĭ təl| *n., pl.* **hospitals** A medical institution that treats sick and injured people.

house·hold |hous′ hōld′| *n., pl.* **households** A home and its activities.

how·ev·er |hou ĕv′ ər| *adv.* By whatever way or means: *However you get there, be there on time.* *conj.* In spite of that; nevertheless: *It was growing dark; however, we had a flashlight.*

howl |houl| *n., pl.* **howls** **1.** A long, wailing cry, such as the one made by a dog, wolf, or coyote. **2.** A loud cry, scream, or hoot.

hu·man |hyōō′ mən| *adj.* Of or characteristic of people: *the human body.* *n., pl.* **humans** A person.

hu·mor |hyōō′ mər| *n., pl.* **humors** The quality of being comical or funny: *I could find no humor in the dull jokes.*

hun·dred |hŭn′ drĭd| *n., pl.* **hundreds** The number, written 100, that is equal to the product of 10 X 10.

hun·gry |hŭng′ grē| *adj.* **hungrier, hungriest** Wanting food.

hurl |hûrl| *v.* **hurled, hurling** To throw with a great force; fling.

I

-ible A form of the suffix **-able.**

ice·berg |īs′ bûrg′| *n., pl.* **icebergs** A very large mass of ice floating in the ocean. Icebergs are pieces of a glacier that have broken off.

iceberg

i·de·a |ī dē′ ə| *n., pl.* **ideas** A thought or plan carefully formed in the mind: *I have some idea as to how I want to redecorate my bedroom.*

ill·ness |ĭl′ nĭs| *n., pl.* **illnesses** A sickness or disease: *Polio is a serious illness.*

im·age |ĭm′ ĭj| *n., pl.* **images** A picture in the mind: *Images of food came into the hungry child's head.*

i·mag·ine |ĭ măj′ ĭn| *v.* **imagined, imagining** **1.** To form a mental picture or idea of: *Can you imagine a blue horse with a yellow mane?* **2.** To use the imagination; pretend.

im·i·tate |ĭm′ ĭ tāt′| *v.* **imitated, imitating** To copy the actions, looks, or sounds of: *Little children imitate their parents.*

im·i·ta·tion |ĭm′ ĭ tā′ shən| *n., pl.* **imitations** **1.** The act or process of imitating or copying: *I learned the song through imitation.* **2.** Something made to look or seem just like something else; copy: *This vase is an imitation of one in the museum.*

im·por·tant |ĭm pôr′ tnt| *adj.* Strongly affecting the course of events or the nature of things; significant: *This is an important message.*

im·press |ĭm prĕs′| *v.* **impressed, impressing** To have a strong, often favorable effect on the mind or feelings of: *The size of the tall building impressed me.*

im·pres·sion |ĭm prĕsh′ ən| *n., pl.* **impressions** An effect, image, or feeling that stays in the mind: *My new friend made a good impression on my parents.*

im·pres·sion·a·ble |ĭm prĕsh′ ə nə bəl| *adj.* Easily influenced; suggestible.

Spelling Dictionary

im·pres·sion·ist |ĭm **prĕsh′** ə nĭst| *n., pl.* **impressionists** An artist who paints in a style that uses small brush strokes to give the impression of the natural light of a scene or an object.

im·pres·sion·is·tic |ĭm prĕsh′ ə **nĭs′** tĭk| *adj.* Of or relating to impressionism or impressionists.

im·pres·sive |ĭm **prĕs′** ĭv| *adj.* Making a strong, lasting impression: *A skyscraper is an impressive building.* —*adv.* **impressively** *She solved the problem impressively.*

im·prove |ĭm **prōōv′**| *v.* **improved, improving** To make or become better: *I improved my tennis serve by practicing.*

in-¹ A prefix that means "without, not": *inaccurate.*

in-² A prefix that means "in, within, or into": *inbound.*

in·com·plete |ĭn′ kəm **plēt′**| *adj.* Not complete: *This incomplete chess set is missing a pawn.* —*adv.* **incompletely** *The artist drew the scene incompletely.* —*n.* **incompleteness** *The incompleteness of this report bothers me.*

in·crease |ĭn **krēs′**| *v.* **increased, increasing** To make or become greater or larger: *I increased my spending money by taking a job after school. n.* |**ĭn′** krēs′|, *pl.* **increases** The act of increasing; growth: *When you get to high school, you will find an increase in homework.*

in·de·pend·ence |ĭn dĭ **pĕn′** dəns| *n.* The quality or condition of being independent or not governed by a foreign country: *The American Colonies won independence from Britain in the American Revolution.*

in·dus·try |**ĭn′** də strē| *n., pl.* **industries** A large-scale enterprise that provides a product or service: *Hollywood is the capital of the motion picture industry.*

in·flate |ĭn **flāt′**| *v.* **inflated, inflating** To fill with gas and expand: *Did you inflate the tires on the bicycle?*

in·form |ĭn **fôrm′**| *v.* **informed, informing** To tell about something; notify: *Please inform me as to the time of your arrival.*

in·her·it |ĭn **hĕr′** ĭt| *v.* **inherited, inheriting** To receive money or property after someone's death.

in·ject |ĭn **jĕkt′**| *v.* **injected, injecting** To force or drive a medicine into the body.

in·ning |**ĭn′** ĭng| *n., pl.* **innings** One of the divisions of a baseball game when each team comes to bat.

in·quir·y |ĭn **kwīr′** ē| or |**ĭn′** kwə rē| *n., pl.* **inquiries 1.** The act or process of asking in order to find out. **2.** A detailed examination of a matter; an investigation.

in·sist |ĭn **sĭst′**| *v.* **insisted, insisting** To demand; take a strong stand: *I insist on watching the ball game.*

in·spect |ĭn **spĕkt′**| *v.* **inspected, inspecting 1.** To look over carefully. **2.** To examine in an official or formal way.

in·spec·tion |ĭn **spĕk′** shən| *n., pl.* **inspections 1.** The act of inspecting. **2.** An official examination or review: *Elevators must undergo an annual safety inspection.*

in·spec·tor |ĭn **spĕk′** tər| *n., pl.* **inspectors** A person who examines or reviews things.

in·stall |ĭn **stôl′**| *v.* **installed, installing** To put in position for use or service: *They installed the telephone today.*

in·sult |ĭn **sŭlt′**| *v.* **insulted, insulting** To speak to or treat impolitely and disrespectfully: *Don't insult me by calling me dishonest.*

in·ter·na·tion·al |ĭn′ tər **năsh′** ə nəl| *adj.* Of, relating to, or carried on between two or more nations.

in·ter·pret |ĭn **tûr′** prĭt| *v.* **interpreted, interpreting** To tell the meaning or importance of; explain: *Can you interpret this graph?*

in·ter·sec·tion |ĭn tər **sĕk′** shən| *n., pl.* **intersections** The point where two or more things cross: *There is a traffic light at the intersection of the two streets.*

in·trude |ĭn **trōōd′**| *v.* **intruded, intruding** To break, come, or force in without being wanted or asked; trespass; invade: *Don't intrude on my privacy.*

in·vent |ĭn **vĕnt′**| *v.* **invented, inventing** To make or produce something that did not exist before: *Who invented the elevator?*

-ion A suffix that forms nouns and means "an act or process" or "the outcome of an act": *election.*

ir·ri·tate |ĭr′ ĭ tāt′| *v.* **irritated, irritating**
To make angry or impatient; annoy: *Your endless questions irritate me.*
ir·ri·ta·tion |ĭr ĭ tā′ shən| *n., pl.*
irritations 1. The act or process of irritating. **2.** The condition of being irritated. **3.** Something that irritates; an annoyance.
i·so·late |ī′ sə lāt′| *v.* **isolated, isolating**
To set or keep apart from others: *Isolate the mean puppy from the other dogs.*

J

jade |jād| *n., pl.* **jades** A hard, pale green or white stone. Jade is used for jewelry, ornaments, and statues.
jave·lin |jăv′ lĭn| *n., pl.* **javelins** A light spear that is thrown for distance in an athletic contest.

javelin

jew·el |jōō′ əl| *n., pl.* **jewels 1.** A precious stone; gem. **2.** A valuable ornament, as a ring or necklace, especially one made of precious metal and set with gems.
joint |joint| *n., pl.* **joints 1.** A place where two or more bones come together. **2.** A place where two or more things, such as pipes, come together.
jun·ior high school |jōōn′ yər hī′ skōōl′| *n., pl.* **junior high schools** A secondary school including the seventh, the eighth, and sometimes the ninth grades.

jus·tice |jŭs′ tĭs| *n., pl.* **justices 1.** The quality of being just or fair. **2.** The carrying out of the law or the way in which the law is carried out: *The courts make sure that justice is achieved.*

K

kay·ak |kī′ ăk′| *n., pl.* **kayaks** A canoe made of skins or canvas stretched over a light wooden frame. The top of a kayak is closed except for an opening in the middle in which the paddler sits.
keep |kēp| *v.* **kept, keeping** To hold in one's possession.
ker·nel |kûr′ nəl| *n., pl.* **kernels 1.** A grain or seed, especially of corn, wheat, or a similar cereal plant: *The kernels of corn were ground to make corn meal.* **2.** The part found inside the shell of a nut: *If you crack the walnut shell, you will find the kernel.*
kick·off |kĭk′ ôf′| *n., pl.* **kickoffs** A kick in football or soccer that begins play.
knap·sack |năp′ săk′| *n., pl.* **knapsacks** A canvas or leather bag that is designed to be carried on the back. A knapsack is used to hold supplies, as on a hike or march.
knowl·edge |nŏl′ ĭj| *n.* **1.** Facts and ideas; information: *Books are a great source of knowledge.* **2.** Understanding; awareness: *It may take a few years to gain solid knowledge of a new language.*

L

la·bel |lā′ bəl| *n., pl.* **labels** A tag or sticker that is attached to something to tell what it is or what it contains: *The label lists the contents of the can.*

lab·o·ra·to·ry |lăb′ rə tôr′ ē| *n., pl.* **laboratories** A room or building with special equipment for doing scientific tests and experiments.

La·bor Day |lā′ bər| *n.* A legal holiday in honor of workers that comes on the first Monday in September.

la·dy |lā′ dē| *n., pl.* **ladies** A woman: *A lady on the bus gave us directions.*

laid |lād| *v.* Past tense and past participle of **lay**: *He laid the books on his desk.*

lair |lâr| *n., pl.* **lairs** The den or home of a wild animal.

land |lănd| *v.* **landed, landing 1.** To come or bring to shore: *The boat landed at the dock.* **2.** To come down or bring to rest on a surface: *The pilot landed the plane.*

lan·guage |lăng′ gwĭj| *n., pl.* **languages 1.** Spoken or written human speech. People use language to communicate thoughts and feelings. **2.** A system of words and expressions shared by a people: *What is your native language?*

la·ser |lā′ zər| *n., pl.* **lasers** A device that sends out a very narrow and extremely powerful beam of light. Laser beams are used to cut through steel and perform delicate surgery.

laser

late·ly |lāt′ lē| *adv.* In the near past; recently; not long ago.

laugh·a·ble |lăf′ ə bəl| *adj.* Causing or likely to cause laughter or amusement.

laugh·ter |lăf′ tər| *n.* **1.** The act or sound of laughing. **2.** Happiness or amusement expressed by laughing.

launch[1] |lônch| *v.* **launched, launching 1.** To set afloat: *The new ship was launched today.* **2.** To begin or start: *We launched a new project.*

launch[2] |lônch| *n., pl.* **launches** A large motorboat.

lay·er |lā′ ər| *v.* **layered, layering** To put several thicknesses or sheets on top of each other.

leaf |lēf| *n., pl.* **leaves** A usually thin, flat, green plant part attached to a stem or stalk.

league |lēg| *n., pl.* **leagues** An association of sports teams that compete mainly among themselves: *Ten high schools formed a football league.*

learn |lûrn| *v.* **learned** or **learnt, learning 1.** To get knowledge of or skill in through study or instruction: *The third-graders are learning Spanish.* **2.** To find out: *I just learned about your accident.*

lease |lēs| *n., pl.* **leases** A written agreement by which an owner of property allows someone else to rent it for a certain period of time. *v.* **leased, leasing** To rent.

least |lēst| *adj.* Smallest in degree or size: *Making friends was Jacki's least worry.*

lec·ture |lĕk′ chər| *n., pl.* **lectures 1.** A speech providing information on a subject, given before a class. **2.** A serious scolding.

le·gal |lē′ gəl| *adj.* Based on or authorized by law; lawful: *Our parents are the legal owners of the house.*

le·gal·i·ty |lĭ găl′ ĭ tē| *n., pl.* **legalities** The fact of being legal; lawfulness.

leg·is·la·tion |lĕj′ ĭs lā′ shən| *n.* A law or group of laws that have been proposed or made: *The Senate passed legislation to raise the minimum wage.*

lei·sure |lē′ zhər| or |lĕzh′ ər| *n.* Free time in which to relax and do as one pleases.

-less A suffix that forms adjectives and means "not having" or "without": *harmless; shoeless.*

lev·el |lĕv′ əl| *n., pl.* **levels** A particular height: *I waded in until the water was at chest level.* *adj.* Having a flat, even surface; not tilted: *We found a level piece of ground for our picnic.*

lev·y |lĕv′ ē| *v.* **levied, levying** To order to be paid; to impose a tax or other fee: *The town levied a tax on new cars.*

Lew·is |lōō′ ĭs|, **Meriwether** 1774–1809. American Pacific Northwest explorer.

li·ar |lī′ ər| *n., pl.* **liars** A person who says things that are not true.

lib·er·ty |lĭb′ ər tē| *n., pl.* **liberties** Legal rights to do certain things without interference: *Freedom of speech is a basic liberty.*

li·brar·y |lī′ brĕr′ ē| *n., pl.* **libraries** A place where books, magazines, records, and reference materials are kept for reading or borrowing.

life·boat |līf′ bōt′| *n., pl.* **lifeboats** A strong boat used for saving lives at sea or from a shore: *Everyone got into lifeboats as the ship sank.*

light·house |līt′ hous′| *n., pl.* **lighthouses** A tower with a powerful light at the top that is used to guide ships.

light·ning bug |līt′ nĭng bŭg| *n., pl.* **lightning bugs** A firefly.

lil·y |lĭl′ ē| *n., pl.* **lilies** Any of several related plants that grow from bulbs and have tall, leafy stems and white or brightly colored flowers shaped like trumpets.

lime·light |līm′ līt′| *n.* The center of public attention: *The President is always in the limelight.*

lim·er·ick |lĭm′ ər ĭk| *n., pl.* **limericks** An amusing poem of five lines.

li·on |lī′ ən| *n., pl.* **lions** A very large light-brown wild cat of Africa and India.

lis·ten |lĭs′ ən| *v.* **listened, listening** **1.** To try to hear something: *If you listen, you can hear the ocean.* **2.** To pay attention.

lit·ter |lĭt′ ər| *n.* Pieces of paper, empty cans and bottles, and other waste material left lying around. *v.* **littered, littering** To make messy by leaving trash around: *Don't litter the picnic area.*

ă	pat	ō	go	th	thin
ā	pay	ô	paw, for	hw	which
â	care	oi	oil	zh	usual
ä	father	ŏŏ	book	ə	ago,
ĕ	pet	ōō	boot		item,
ē	be	yōō	cute		pencil,
ĭ	pit	ou	out		atom,
ī	ice	ŭ	cut		circus
î	near	û	fur	ər	butter
ŏ	pot	*th*	the		

live·ly |līv′ lē| *adj.* **livelier, liveliest** Full of life; energetic.

loaf |lōf| *n., pl.* **loaves** A mass of bread that is shaped and then baked in one piece: *We have part of a loaf of bread.*

loan |lōn| *v.* **loaned, loaning** To lend: *Please loan me your sleeping bag.*
♦ *These sound alike* **loan, lone.**

lob·by·ist |lŏb′ ē ĭst| *n., pl.* **lobbyists** A person who lobbies or tries to influence law makers: *Lobbyists discussed the issue with the Senator.*

lo·cal |lō′ kəl| *adj.* Of a certain limited area or place: *The town has its own local government.*

lo·cal·i·ty |lō kăl′ ĭ tē| *n., pl.* **localities** A particular place, region, or neighborhood.

lo·cate |lō′ kāt′| *v.* **located, locating** To find and show the position of.

lo·ca·tion |lō kā′ shən| *n., pl.* **locations** **1.** A position. **2.** A place away from a movie or television studio at which a scene is filmed.

lo·co·mo·tion |lō′ kə mō′ shən| *n., pl.* **locomotions** The act of moving or the ability to move from one place to another.

log·ic |lŏj′ ĭk| *n.* Rational thought; sound reasoning.

loi·ter |loi′ tər| *v.* **loitered, loitering** To stand around doing nothing; to linger; to not hurry.

lone |lōn| *adj.* **1.** Without others: *A lone sailor stood watch.* **2.** By itself: *A lone tree stood in the meadow.*
♦ *These sound alike* **lone, loan.**

lone·ly |lōn′ lē| *adj.* **lonelier, loneliest** Sad at being alone.

loop |lōōp| *n., pl.* **loops** A circular path or pattern.

loose |lo͞os| *adj.* **looser, loosest** **1.** Not fastened tightly: *Your shoelaces are loose.* **2.** Not confined or tied up; free: *Chickens were loose in the yard.* **3.** Not bound, bundled, or joined together: *Some loose pages fell out of the book.* —*adv.* **loosely** *She held the rope loosely.*

loo·sen |lo͞o′ sən| *v.* **loosened, loosening** To make or become loose or looser.

lord |lôrd| *n., pl.* **lords** A man of noble rank in Great Britain.

lose |lo͞oz| *v.* **lost, losing** **1.** To miss from one's possession; misplace; fail to find: *I lost my spelling book.* **2.** To be unable to keep: *I lost my balance and fell.* **3.** To give up in a natural process; shed: *Many trees lose their leaves in the fall.* **4.** To fail to win: *We lost both games.* —*n.* **loser** *Bill is a good loser.*

loy·al |loi′ əl| *adj.* Firm in supporting a person, country, or cause; faithful; true.

lug·gage |lŭg′ ĭj| *n.* Bags and suitcases that a person takes on a trip; baggage.

lu·nar |lo͞o′ nər| *adj.* Of, on, or having to do with the moon: *The spacecraft made a perfect lunar landing.*

lunch·eon |lŭn′ chən| *n., pl.* **luncheons** A midday meal; lunch.

lux·u·ry |lŭg′ zhə rē| or |lŭk′ shə rē| *n., pl.* **luxuries** Something that is not really needed but that gives great pleasure, enjoyment, or comfort: *A luxury is often expensive or hard to get.*

-ly A suffix that forms adverbs and means "in a certain way": *accidentally, happily.*

M

mag·a·zine |măg′ ə zēn′| or |măg′ ə zēn′| *n., pl.* **magazines** A publication that is issued regularly, as every week or month.

Ma·gel·lan |mə jĕl′ ən|, **Ferdinand** 1480?–1521. Portuguese navigator in the service of Spain; he died while commanding the first expedition that sailed around the world.

mag·ni·fy |măg′ nə fī′| *v.* **magnified, magnifying** To enlarge the appearance of: *A microscope magnifies bacteria.*

main |mān| *adj.* Most important; chief: *Look for the main idea in each paragraph.*
♦ *These sound alike* **main, mane.**

ma·jes·tic |mə jĕs′ tĭk| *adj.* Stately and dignified; regal: *The monarch gave a majestic wave.*

ma·jor |mā′ jər| *adj.* Larger, greater, or more important: *Students spend the major part of the day in school.*

ma·jor·i·ty |mə jôr′ ĭ tē| *n., pl.* **majorities** The greater number or part; more than half: *Girls make up the majority of the class.*

make-be·lieve |māk′ bĭ lēv′| *adj.* Pretended; imaginary.

male |māl| *n., pl.* **males** A man or boy.

mal·lard |măl′ ərd| *n., pl.* **mallards** A wild green-headed duck of North America, Europe, and northern Asia.

man·age |măn′ ĭj| *v.* **managed, managing** **1.** To have control over; direct: *Who will manage the business while your parents are away?* **2.** To succeed in doing something: *I managed to finish my work.*

mane |mān| *n., pl.* **manes** The long, heavy hair growing from the neck and head of an animal such as a horse or a male lion.
♦ *These sound alike* **mane, main.**

mane

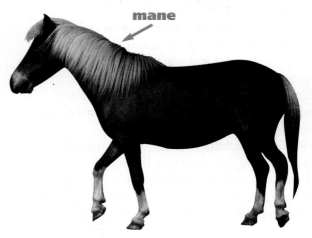

mar·a·thon |măr′ ə thŏn′| *n., pl.* **marathons** A race for runners over a distance of 26 miles, 385 yards.

mar·riage |măr′ ĭj| *n., pl.* **marriages** **1.** The condition of living together as husband and wife. **2.** Wedding: *The marriage will take place in September.*

Mar·tin Lu·ther King Day *n.* A holiday celebrating the birthday of Martin Luther King, Jr., a civil rights leader. This holiday falls on the third Monday in January.

mar·vel·ous |mär′ və ləs| *adj.*
1. Causing surprise, astonishment, or wonder: *You have a marvelous gift for science.* **2.** Of the highest or best kind or quality: *I just read a marvelous biography.*

mas·cot |măs′ kŏt′| *n., pl.* **mascots** Someone or something believed to bring good luck, often to a team: *The mascot of the football team is a donkey.*

mas·ter·piece |măs′ tər pēs′| *n., pl.* **masterpieces** An outstanding piece of work, especially an artist's or composer's greatest work.

mat·i·nee |măt′ n ā′| *n., pl.* **matinees** A theatrical performance or movie that is given or shown in the afternoon: *The matinee begins at 2 P.M.*

mat·ter |măt′ ər| *n., pl.* **matters** A subject of interest or concern: *I refuse to discuss the matter.* *v.* **mattered, mattering** To be important: *We tried to pretend that it didn't matter.*

May·flow·er |mā′ flou′ ər| *n.* The ship on which the Pilgrims sailed to America from England in 1620.

may·or |mā′ ər| *n., pl.* **mayors** The chief government official of a city or town.

meas·ure |mĕzh′ ər| *v.* **measured, measuring** To find the size, amount, capacity, or degree of: *We measured the room twice.*

meat |mēt| *n., pl.* **meats** The flesh of an animal eaten as food.
♦ *These sound alike* **meat, meet.**

me·chan·i·cal |mə kăn′ ĭ kəl| *adj.* Operated or performed by a machine: *The garage has a mechanical door that opens when you press a button.*

meet |mēt| *v.* **met, meeting** To come together; connect or touch: *The two rivers meet near the capital.* *n., pl.* **meets** A gathering for a sports competition: *The school held a track meet.*
♦ *These sound alike* **meet, meat.**

Me·mo·ri·al Day |mə môr′ ē əl| *n.* A holiday in honor of members of the United States armed forces who have died in wars. In most states Memorial Day is celebrated on the last Monday in May.

mem·o·ry |mĕm′ ə rē| *n., pl.* **memories**
1. The power or ability to remember. **2.** Something that is remembered: *My earliest memory is of my third birthday.*

-ment A suffix that forms nouns and means: **1.** Action or process: *government.* **2.** The result of an action or process: *measurement.* **3.** Condition: *amazement; retirement.*

mer·chant |mûr′ chənt| *n., pl.* **merchants** A person who buys and sells goods, especially a person who runs a store.

mes·sage |mĕs′ ĭj| *n., pl.* **messages**
1. Words that are sent from one person or group to another. **2.** A speech or other formal communication: *the President's message to Congress.*

met·al |mĕt′ l| *n., pl.* **metals** A substance, such as copper, iron, silver, or gold, that is usually shiny and hard, conducts heat and electricity, and can be hammered or cast into a desired shape.

mi·cro·scope |mī′ krə skōp′| *n., pl.* **microscopes** An instrument with a special lens for making a very small object appear larger, especially objects too small to be seen by the naked eye: *We examined the cell under the microscope.*

mid·dle |mĭd′ l| *n., pl.* **middles** A point or part that is the same distance from each side or end: *A deer stood in the middle of the road.*

mi·grate |mī′ grāt′| *v.* **migrated, migrating** **1.** To move from one country or region and settle in another. **2.** To move regularly from one region or climate to another: *Many birds migrate in the fall.*

mi·gra·tion |mī **grā′** shən| *n., pl.*
migrations **1.** The act or an example of
migrating. **2.** A group migrating together.

mild |mīld| *adj.* **milder, mildest** **1.** Gentle
in manner. **2.** Moderate in action or effect;
not stormy: *We had a mild winter.*

mil·len·ni·um |mə **lĕn′** ē əm| *n., pl.*
millenniums *or* **millennia** |mə **lĕn′** ē ə|
A period of one thousand years.

mil·lion |**mĭl′** yən| *n., pl.* **million** *or*
millions One thousand thousands; 1,000,000.

min·er |**mī′** nər| *n., pl.* **miners** A person
who works in a mine.
♦ *These sound alike* **miner, minor.**

min·er·al |**mĭn′** ər əl| *n., pl.* **minerals**
1. A natural substance, such as a diamond
or salt, that is not of plant or animal origin:
Many valuable gems are minerals. **2.** A natural
substance, such as ore, coal, or petroleum, that
is mined for human use: *He sold the rights to
the minerals on his land.*

mi·nor |**mī′** nər| *adj.* Smaller in amount,
size, extent, or importance.
♦ *These sound alike* **minor, miner.**

History

Miner may come from the Common
Celtic *meini*, meaning "ore." **Minor** comes
from the Latin word *minor*, meaning "less."

---

min·ute |**mĭn′** ĭt| *n., pl.* **minutes** A unit of
time equal to sixty seconds.

mir·ror |**mĭr′** ər| *n., pl.* **mirrors** A surface,
as of glass, that reflects the image of an object
placed in front of it.

mis·chief |**mĭs′** chĭf| *n.* **1.** Naughty or
bad behavior. **2.** Harm or damage caused by
someone or something.

mist |mĭst| *n., pl.* **mists** **1.** A mass of tiny
drops of water in the air. **2.** A mass of tiny drops
of any liquid, as perfume, sprayed into the air.

mis·take |mĭ **stāk′**| *n., pl.* **mistakes**
Something that is thought up, done, or figured
out in an incorrect way.

mix |mĭks| *v.* **mixed, mixing** To blend
or combine into a single mass or substance:

*Mix the flour, water, and eggs to form the bread
dough.*

mix·ture |**mĭks′** chər| *n., pl.* **mixtures**
Any combination of different ingredients,
things, or kinds; blend: *mixture of flour and
water.*

mod·el |**mŏd′** l| *n., pl.* **models** **1.** A small
copy: *I built a model of a sailboat.* **2.** A person
hired to display merchandise, such as clothing,
that is for sale. **3.** A person or thing that is a
good example: *The farm is a model of efficient
management.* *v.* **modeled, modeling** To
display by wearing. *adj.* Serving as a standard
of excellence: *Her handwriting is a model
example of neatness.*

mod·ule |**mŏj′** ool| *or* |**mŏd′** yool| *n.*
1. A standard or unit of measurement. **2.** Any
of the self-contained parts of a spacecraft, each
of which is used for a particular job or set of
jobs within the mission: *The captain operated
the spacecraft from the command module.*

moist |moist| *adj.* **moister, moistest**
Slightly wet; damp: *a moist towel.*

moist·en |**moi′** sən| *v.* **moistened,
moistening** To make moist; to dampen.

mois·ture |**mois′** chər| *n.* Liquid, as water,
that is present in the air or in the ground or
that forms tiny drops on a surface; dampness.

mo·ment |**mō′** mənt| *n., pl.* **moments**
A very short period of time; instant: *Wait a
moment while I wash my hands.*

mon·ster |**mŏn′** stər| *n., pl.* **monsters**
An imaginary creature that is huge and very
frightening.

mon·u·ment |**mŏn′** yə mənt| *n., pl.*
monuments **1.** Something, as a statue or
building, put up to help people continue
to remember a person, group, or thing.
2. A place, area, or region preserved by a
government for its beauty or significance.

mood |mood| *n., pl.* **moods** A person's state
of mind; a feeling: *Playing with my friends puts
me in a happy mood.*

more·o·ver |môr **ō′** vər| *adv.* Beyond
what has already been said; furthermore: *I'm
willing to paint my room, and moreover I'd
enjoy doing it.*

mor·tal |**môr′** tl| *adj.* **1.** Certain to die.
2. Causing death; fatal: *a mortal wound.*

mor·tal·i·ty |môr **tăl'** ĭ tē| *n., pl.*
mortalities **1.** The condition of being subject
to death: *The dying man thought about his
own mortality.* **2.** Death, especially of large
numbers of beings.

mo·sa·ic |mō **zā'** ĭk| *n., pl.* **mosaics**
A picture or design made on a surface by
fitting and cementing together small pieces
of colored tile, glass, or stone.

mos·qui·to |mə **skē'** tō| *n., pl.*
mosquitoes *or* **mosquitos** A small flying
insect. The female mosquito bites and sucks
blood from animals and human beings.

mo·tive |**mō'** tĭv| *n., pl.* **motives** A
reason that causes a person to act: *Curiosity
was Jamey's motive for reading books.*

mo·tor·cade |**mō'** tər kād'| *n., pl.*
motorcades A procession of motor vehicles.

motorcade

mound |mound| *n., pl.* **mounds** The
pitcher's area in the middle of a baseball
diamond raised about ten inches above the
ground.

moun·tain |**moun'** tən| *n., pl.* **mountains**
An area of land that rises to a great height.

moun·tain·ous |**moun'** tə nəs| *adj.*
Having many mountains.

move·ment |**mōōv'** mənt| *n., pl.*
movements The act or process of changing
position: *the slow movement of the hands on
the clock.*

mov·ie |**mōō'** vē| *n., pl.* **movies** A motion
picture.

mule |myōōl| *n., pl.* **mules** An animal that
is the offspring of a male donkey and a female
horse, generally thought of as being stubborn.

mus·cle |**mŭs'** əl| *n., pl.* **muscles** A type
of body tissue that can be contracted and
relaxed to cause movement or exert force.

mus·cu·lar |**mŭs'** kyə lər| *adj.* Having
strong muscles: *I have muscular legs from riding
my bicycle every single day.*

mu·sic |**myōō'** zĭk| *n.* **1.** The art of
combining tones or sounds in a pleasing or
meaningful way. **2.** Vocal or instrumental
sounds that have a tune and a beat.

mys·te·ry |**mĭs'** tə rē| *n., pl.* **mysteries**
1. Something that is not fully understood or
is kept secret: *That person's identity remains a
mystery.* **2.** A piece of fiction dealing with a
puzzling crime: *The mystery about the jewel
theft had a surprise ending.*

N

na·tion |**nā'** shən| *n., pl.* **nations** A group
of people who share the same territory and are
organized under a single government; country:
The United States is a nation.

na·tion·al |**nǎsh'** ə nəl| *adj.* Of, having to
do with, or belonging to a nation.

na·tion·al·i·ty |nǎsh' ə **nǎl'** ĭ tē| *n., pl.*
nationalities The condition of belonging to a
particular nation. Children born in the United
States are of American nationality.

na·tive |**nā'** tĭv| *adj.* Belonging to a person
because of the person's place of birth: *native
language.* *n., pl.* **natives** A person born in a
certain place or country: *I am a native of New
England.*

Spelling Dictionary

na·ture |**nā′** chər| *n., pl.* **natures** The world of living things and the outdoors; wildlife and natural scenery: *We slept outdoors to enjoy the beauties of nature.*

nee·dle |**nēd′** l| *n., pl.* **needles** A small, slender tool for sewing, usually made of polished steel. It has a sharp point at one end and an eye at the other end through which thread is passed.

ne·glect |nĭ **glĕkt′**| *v.* **neglected, neglecting** To fail to give proper care and attention to: *A good student doesn't neglect homework or class assignments.*

nerve |nûrv| *n., pl.* **nerves** **1.** Any of the bundles of fibers that carry messages between the brain or spinal cord and other parts of the body. **2.** Courage or daring: *It took all my nerve to jump that high fence.*

-ness A suffix that forms nouns and means "condition" or "quality." *Kindness* is the condition or quality of being kind.

net·work |**nĕt′** wûrk′| *n., pl.* **networks** A group of related radio or television stations that share programs.

neu·tral |**nōō′** trəl| or |**nyōō′** trəl| *adj.* **1.** Not taking sides in a war, quarrel, or contest: *The teacher was a neutral listener as the students debated the issue.* **2.** Having little color: *Gray is a neutral shade.*

nev·er·the·less |nĕv′ ər *th*ə **lĕs′**| *adv.* In spite of that; still; however: *The plan may fail, but we must try it nevertheless.*

news·cast |**nōōz′** kăst′| or |**nyōōz′** kăst′| *n., pl.* **newscasts** A broadcast of news on radio or television.

New Year's Day |**nōō′** yîrz| or |**nyōō′** yîrz| *n.* January 1, the first day of the year, a holiday in many parts of the world.

nick·el |**nĭk′** əl| *n., pl.* **nickels** A United States or Canadian coin worth five cents.

niece |nēs| *n., pl.* **nieces** The daughter of one's brother or sister.

nine·ty-nine |**nīn′** tē **nīn′**| *n.* The number written 99.

nom·i·nate |**nŏm′** ə nāt′| *v.* **nominated, nominating** To propose or select as a candidate for election, appointment to office, or an honor.

nor·mal |**nôr′** məl| *adj.* **1.** Of the usual or regular kind: *My weight is normal for my height.* **2.** Happening in a natural, healthy way: *The baby has a normal heartbeat.*

nor·mal·i·ty |nôr **măl′** ĭ tē| *n.* The condition of being normal: *After the flood the town quickly returned to normality.*

no·tice |**nō′** tĭs| *v.* **noticed, noticing** To take note of; pay attention to: *I sat in the last row and hoped nobody would notice me.*

nov·el¹ |**nŏv′** əl| *adj.* Very new, unusual, or different.

nov·el² |**nŏv′** əl| *n., pl.* **novels** A made-up story that is long enough to fill a book.

nui·sance |**nōō′** səns| or |**nyōō′** səns| *n., pl.* **nuisances** Someone or something that is annoying; a pest.

O

ob·ject¹ |**ŏb′** jĭkt| *n., pl.* **objects** Something that has shape and can be felt or seen: *There were several objects on the table.*

ob·ject² |əb **jĕkt′**| *v.* **objected, objecting** To express an opposing view or argument; to be against; disapprove of: *I object to long drives.*

ob·jec·tion |əb **jĕk′** shən| *n., pl.* **objections** The expression of an opposing point of view or argument: *You should have made an objection if you didn't like the idea.*

ob·vi·ous |**ŏb′** vē əs| *adj.* Easily seen or understood; clear: *The student made an obvious mistake in subtraction.*

o·cean |**ō′** shən| *n., pl.* **oceans** **1.** The great mass of salt water that covers about 72 percent of the earth's surface. **2.** One of the four main divisions of this mass of salt water: *The Arctic Ocean surrounds the North Pole.*

odd |ŏd| *adj.* **odder, oddest** Not ordinary or usual; peculiar: *The car is making an odd noise.*

of·fer |**ô′** fər| *v.* **offered, offering** **1.** To present for consideration; propose: *The editor offered some suggestions for improving the story.* **2.** To show readiness to do; volunteer. **3.** To put forward to be accepted or refused: *Julia offered me soup.*

of·fice |ô′ fĭs| *n., pl.* **offices** A place, as a room or series of rooms, in which the work of a business or profession is carried on.

of·fi·cer |ô′ fĭ sər| *n., pl.* **officers** A member of the police force.

of·fi·cial |ə fĭsh′ əl| *n., pl.* **officials** A person in a position of authority.

off-stage |ôf′ stāj′| *adv.* In or into the stage area not seen by the audience: *He walked off-stage.*

O·lym·pics |ō lĭm′ pĭks| *pl. n.* An international athletic competition held every four years in a different part of the world. The Olympics are divided into summer and winter games that alternate every two years. The modern Olympics are a revival of a festival of contests held in Olympia in ancient Greece.

on·ion |ŭn′ yən| *n., pl.* **onions** A plant with an edible round yellow bulb that is widely grown as a vegetable. The bulb has a strong smell and a sharp taste.

on·yx |ŏn′ ĭks| *n.* A type of quartz that occurs in bands of different colors, often black and white. Onyx may be dyed and carved.

o·pal |ō′ pəl| *n., pl.* **opals** A mineral having many rainbowlike colors, often used as a gem. It can be found in rock cavities.

op·er·ate |ŏp′ ə rāt′| *v.* **operated, operating** 1. To work or run: *This machine operates well.* 2. To perform surgery.

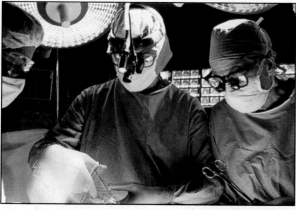
operate

op·po·nent |ə pō′ nənt| *n., pl.* **opponents** A person who is against another in a fight, contest, or debate; rival; not a friend.

op·pose |ə pōz′| *v.* **opposed, opposing** To be or fight against; resist: *Senator Huertas will oppose the plan for new taxes.*

op·tion |ŏp′ shən| *n., pl.* **options** The act of choosing; choice: *Luis has the option of going to summer camp or staying home.*

or·chard |ôr′ chərd| *n., pl.* **orchards** A piece of land where fruit trees are grown.

or·deal |ôr dēl′| *n., pl.* **ordeals** A very difficult or painful experience; hardship.

or·der |ôr′ dər| *v.* **ordered, ordering** 1. To give a command to: *The teacher ordered the class to open their books.* 2. To arrange things in a sequence one after another: *The books are ordered alphabetically.* 3. To place an order: *Please order a book from this catalog.*

or·der·less |ôr′ dər lĭs| *adj.* Without order: *The books on this shelf are orderless.*

or·der·ly |ôr′ dər lē| *adj.* Arranged in a neat and tidy way: *Let's all help to keep the kitchen orderly.* —*n.* **orderliness**

or·phan |ôr′ fən| *n., pl.* **orphans** A child whose parents are dead.

os·trich |ôs′ trĭch| *n., pl.* **ostriches** A large African bird that cannot fly but can run very fast. Ostriches have fluffy plumes.

ounce |ouns| *n., pl.* **ounces** A unit of weight and mass equal to 1/16 pound.

-ous A suffix that forms adjectives and means "full of" or "having the qualities of": *joyous.*

out·field |out′ fēld′| *n., pl.* **outfields** The playing area that extends outward from a baseball diamond and is divided into right, center, and left fields.

out·spo·ken |out spō′ kən| *adj.* Not speaking or spoken with reserve; frank and honest; bold: *You are too outspoken about your political views.*

o·va·tion |ō vā′ shən| *n., pl.* **ovations**
A loud and enthusiastic display of approval, usually in the form of shouting or hearty applause.

owe |ō| *v.* **owed, owing** **1.** To have to pay or repay: *We owe the store $20.* **2.** To be obliged for: *We owe the discovery of polio vaccine to a famous scientist.*

P

pack·age |păk′ ĭj| *n., pl.* **packages** A bundle of things packed together.

pale |pāl| *adj.* **paler, palest** Having skin that is lighter than usual, often because of illness; lacking color. —*n.* **paleness** *My paleness left when I recovered from the flu.*

par·ent |păr′ ənt| *n., pl.* **parents** A father or mother.

park·way |pärk′ wā′| *n., pl.* **parkways** A broad highway planted in certain areas with grass, bushes, and trees.

part·ner |pärt′ nər| *n., pl.* **partners** **1.** One of two or more persons associated in a business. **2.** Either of a pair of persons dancing together.

part of speech |pärt′ ŭv spēch′| or |pärt′ ŏv spēch′| *n., pl.* **parts of speech** A grammatical class, such as a noun, pronoun, verb, adjective, adverb, preposition, conjunction, or interjection, into which a word can be placed according to the way it is used in a phrase or sentence.

par·ty |pär′ tē| *n., pl.* **parties** A group of people who are organized for political activity: *Which party do your parents belong to?*

pas·sage |păs′ ĭj| *n., pl.* **passages** **1.** The act or process of passing: *The river is deep enough for safe passage.* **2.** A journey. **3.** A narrow path or channel. **4.** Approval of law by a legislative body. **5.** A part of a written work or piece of music.

pas·sen·ger |păs′ ən jər| *n., pl.* **passengers** A person riding in or on a vehicle or vessel: *There were twenty passengers on the bus.*

pass·port |păs′ pôrt| *n., pl.* **passports** A government document that gives a citizen permission to travel in foreign countries.

pas·ture |păs′ chər| *n., pl.* **pastures** Ground where animals graze.

pasture

pa·tri·ot |pā′ trē ət| *n., pl.* **patriots** A person who loves, supports, and defends his or her country.

pat·tern |păt′ ərn| *n., pl.* **patterns** An artistic design used for decoration: *The wallpaper has a pattern of flowers.*

pause |pôz| *n., pl.* **pauses** A brief stop. *v.* **paused, pausing** To stop briefly.

peace |pēs| *n.* **1.** The absence of war or fighting. **2.** Freedom from mental or emotional upset: *I need peace and quiet.*
♦ *These sound alike* peace, piece.

pea·nut |pē′ nŭt| *n., pl.* **peanuts** A vine similar to the pea that bears oily, edible, light-brown seeds that ripen underground; goober.

pearl |pûrl| *n., pl.* **pearls** A smooth, rounded, white or grayish growth formed inside the shells of oysters and used as a gem.

Pea·ry |pîr′ ē|, **Robert Edwin** 1856–1920. American naval officer and Arctic explorer; discovered North Pole in 1909.

ped·al |pĕd′ l| *n., pl.* **pedals** A lever, as on a piano, that is worked by the foot. *v.* **pedaled, pedaling** To ride a bicycle or tricycle: *It is hard to pedal up a steep hill.*

ped·es·tal |pĕd′ ĭ stəl| *n., pl.* **pedestals** A base or support, as for a column or a statue.

pe·des·tri·an |pə dĕs′ trē ən| *n., pl.* **pedestrians** A person traveling on foot: *The pedestrians crossed the street when the cars stopped for a red light.*

pe·dom·e·ter |pĭ **dŏm'** ĭ tər| *n., pl.*
pedometers An instrument that measures
the approximate distance a person takes
on foot by keeping track of the number of
steps taken.

peer |pîr| *v.* **peered, peering** To look
intently, closely, or with difficulty: *peer through
a microscope.*
◆ *These sound alike* **peer, pier.**

pen·al·ty |**pĕn'** əl tē| *n., pl.* **penalties**
Something that must be given up for breaking
a rule in a game or sport: *That foul cost our
football team a ten-yard penalty, and we lost
the game.*

pen·guin |**pĕn'** gwĭn| or |**pĕng'** gwĭn|
n., pl. **penguins** A sea bird that lives near the
South Pole, has webbed feet, and cannot fly.
A penguin has black and white feathers and
flipperlike wings.

per·cent·age |pər **sĕn'** tĭj| *n., pl.*
percentages A fraction with 100 as its
denominator: *What percentage of your time
do you spend asleep?*

per·fect |**pûr'** fĭkt| *adj.* Having no flaws,
mistakes, or defects.

per·haps |pər **hăps'**| *adv.* Maybe but not
definitely; possibly: *Perhaps you'll come with us.*

pe·ri·od |**pîr'** ē əd| *n., pl.* **periods** **1.** An
interval or portion of time: *A year is a period
of twelve months.* **2.** A punctuation mark (.)
used to indicate the end of a sentence or an
abbreviation. **3.** A time in history.

per·mit |pər **mĭt'**| *v.* **permitted,
permitting** To give permission to; allow:
*Standing is not permitted in the back of the
theater.* *n.* |**pûr'** mĭt'| or |pər **mĭt'**|, *pl.*
permits A written certificate of permission,
such as a license.

per·son |**pûr'** sən| *n., pl.* **persons** A
human; individual: *Any person who wants to
can come to the game.*

per·son·al |**pûr'** sə nəl| *adj.* Of, relating
to, or belonging to a person; private: *My clothes
are my personal property.*

pic·ture |**pĭk'** chər| *n., pl.* **pictures** A
painting, drawing, or photograph of a person
or thing.

piece |pēs| *n., pl.* **pieces** **1.** A portion of
something larger: *We bought a piece of land in

the country.* **2.** An object that is a member of
a group or class: *a piece of furniture.*
◆ *These sound alike* **piece, peace.**

pier |pîr| *n., pl.* **piers** A platform that
extends into water. A pier can be used to
protect a harbor or serve as a landing place
for ships and boats; a dock; wharf.
◆ *These sound alike* **pier, peer.**

pil·grim |**pĭl'** grĭm| *n., pl.* **pilgrims**
1. A person who travels to a sacred place.
2. **Pilgrim** One of the English settlers who
founded Plymouth Colony in New England
in 1620.

pil·lar |**pĭl'** ər| *n., pl.* **pillars** An upright
structure that serves as a support, as for a
bridge or a building, or stands alone as a
monument; column.

pin |pĭn| *n., pl.* **pins** A short, straight, stiff
piece of wire with a head at one end and a
sharp point at the other.
◇ *Idiom* **on pins and needles** In a state of
anxiety; nervous.

pitch·er |**pĭch'** ər| *n., pl.* **pitchers** The
baseball player who pitches the ball to the
batter.

pit·y |**pĭt'** ē| *n., pl.* **pities** A feeling of
sorrow or sympathy for the suffering of
another. *v.* **pitied, pitying** To feel sorry for.

plan |plăn| *v.* **planned, planning** To have
in mind; intend.

plat·form |**plăt'** fôrm'| *n., pl.* **platforms**
A formal statement of principles or policy,
as of a political party: *The party debated its
platform during the convention.*

play·wright |**plā'** rīt'| *n., pl.* **playwrights**
A person who writes plays.

Pronunciation Key

ă	pat	ō	go	th	thin
ā	pay	ô	paw, for	hw	which
â	care	oi	oil	zh	usual
ä	father	ŏŏ	book	ə	ago,
ĕ	pet	ōō	boot		item,
ē	be	yōō	cute		pencil,
ĭ	pit	ou	out		atom,
ī	ice	ŭ	cut		circus
î	near	û	fur	ər	butter
ŏ	pot	th	the		

Spelling Dictionary

pleas·ure |plĕzh′ ər| *n., pl.* **pleasures**
A feeling of happiness or enjoyment; delight:
She smiled with pleasure.

plight |plīt| *n., pl.* **plights** A serious
condition or a situation of difficulty or danger:
*The plight of the families living in the drought-
stricken area has not improved.*

Plym·outh |plĭm′ əth| *n.* A town in
Massachusetts where the Pilgrims landed in
1620. The colony was founded later that year.

po·em |pō′ əm| *n., pl.* **poems** A piece
of writing, often in rhyme, in which words
are chosen for their sound and beauty as well
as meaning.

po·et |pō′ ĭt| *n., pl.* **poets** One who writes
poems.

po·et·ic |pō ĕt′ ĭk| *adj.* Of, relating to, or
like poetry: *Poetic language is beautiful.*

poise |poiz| *v.* **poised, poising** To balance
or be balanced: *The horse poised for the jump.*
n. Sureness and confidence of manner: *The
child recited the poem with poise.*

poi·son i·vy |poi′ zən ī′ vē| *n.* A plant
with leaflets in groups of three that can cause
an itching skin rash if touched.

poison ivy

poi·son·ous |poi′ zə nəs| *adj.* Having
effects like that of poison: *The rattlesnake has
a poisonous bite.*

po·lar |pō′ lər| *adj.* Of, relating to, or near
the North Pole or the South Pole.

pole |pōl| *n., pl.* **poles** 1. A long slender
rod: *We used a branch as a fishing pole.* 2. An
upright post: *a telephone pole.*
 ◆ *These sound alike* **pole, poll.**

poll |pōl| *n., pl.* **polls** A survey made to find
out what people think.
 ◆ *These sound alike* **poll, pole.**

pol·lute |pə lōōt′| *v.* **polluted, polluting**
To make dirty or impure; contaminate:
Gasoline exhaust pollutes the air.

pol·lu·tion |pə lōō′ shən| *n.* The act of
polluting or condition of being polluted.

Po·lo |pō′ lō|, **Marco** 1254?–1324?
Venetian traveler and merchant who visited
China.

pop·u·lar |pŏp′ yə lər| *adj.* Enjoyed or
liked by many or most people: *Running is a
popular sport.*

pop·u·late |pŏp′ yə lāt′| *v.* **populated,
populating** 1. To supply with residents.
2. To live in; reside.

pop·u·la·tion |pŏp′ yə lā′ shən| *n., pl.*
populations The total number of people
living in a certain place.

pore[1] |pôr| *n., pl.* **pores** A tiny opening, as
in the skin or on the surface of a plant.
 ◆ *These sound alike* **pore, pour.**

pore[2] |pôr| *v.* **pored, poring** To examine
with great care and attention: *I pored over the
magazine.*
 ◆ *These sound alike* **pore, pour.**

port·a·ble |pôr′ tə bəl| *adj.* Capable of
being carried or moved: *We bought a portable
radio to take to the beach.*

por·ter |pôr′ tər| *n., pl.* **porters** A person
hired to carry baggage, as at a railroad station:
The porter helped us get the suitcases onto the train.

por·tray |pôr trā′| *v.* **portrayed,
portraying** To play the part of: *A young actor
is portraying a construction worker in the new
movie.*

pos·si·ble |pŏs′ ə bəl| *adj.* 1. Capable of
happening or being done: *It is possible to get to
the airport by bus.* 2. Capable of being used
for a certain purpose: *That field is a possible site
for the new school.*

post·age |pō′ stĭj| *n.* The charge for
mailing something.

post of·fice |pōst′ ô′ fĭs| *n., pl.* **post
offices** 1. A government department or
agency responsible for sending and delivering
mail. 2. A local office where mail is received,
sorted, and sent out.

po·ta·to |pə **tā′** tō| *n., pl.* **potatoes** A vegetable that has firm white flesh. Potatoes grow underground and are the thick, rounded stems of a leafy plant.

pour |pôr| *v.* **poured, pouring** To flow or cause to flow in a steady stream: *When you pour the milk, pour slowly.*

◆ *These sound alike* **pour, pore.**

pow·der |pou′ dər| *n., pl.* **powders 1.** A dry substance consisting of many very small particles. **2.** Something, such as a cosmetic, in the form of a powder.

pow·er·ful |pou′ ər fəl| *adj.* Having power, authority, or influence: *The United States of America is a powerful nation.*

prac·ti·cal |prăk′ tĭ′ kəl| *adj.* Having or serving a useful purpose: *It's not easy to turn an idea into a practical invention.*

prac·tice |prăk′ tĭs| *v.* **practiced, practicing 1.** To do or work over and over in order to acquire skill: *I practice playing the piano every day.* **2.** To make a habit of: *Learn to practice self-control.*

praise |prāz| *n., pl.* **praises** Approval or admiration: *Praise from Mom meant a lot to me.*

prank |prăngk| *n., pl.* **pranks** A playful trick or joke: *He liked to play funny pranks on his friends.*

pre- A prefix that means "earlier," "before," or "in advance": *preview.*

pre·am·ble |prē′ ăm′ bəl| *n., pl.* **preambles** An introduction to a formal document explaining its purpose or the reasons behind it.

pre·dict |prĭ dĭkt′| *v.* **predicted, predicting** To tell about in advance: *The weather report predicts showers.*

pre·fer |prĭ fûr′| *v.* **preferred, preferring** To like better: *I prefer books to television.*

pre·fix |prē′ fĭks| *n., pl.* **prefixes** A word part added to the beginning of a base word to change the meaning of the word. For example, the word parts *dis-* in *dislike*, *re-* in *repeat*, and *un-* in *unable* are prefixes.

pre·serve |prĭ zûrv′| *v.* **preserved, preserving 1.** To protect, as from injury or destruction: *We want to preserve our forests.* **2.** To protect food from spoiling, as by freezing, canning, or pickling.

Pronunciation Key

ă	pat	ō	go	th	thin
ā	pay	ô	paw, for	hw	which
â	care	oi	oil	zh	usual
ä	father	ŏŏ	book	ə	ago,
ĕ	pet	ōō	boot		item,
ē	be	yōō	cute		pencil,
ĭ	pit	ou	out		atom,
ī	ice	ŭ	cut		circus
î	near	û	fur	ər	butter
ŏ	pot	*th*	the		

pres·i·dent |prĕz′ ĭ dənt| *n., pl.* **presidents 1.** The chief executive of a republic, such as the United States. **2.** The chief officer of a company, organization, or institution.

pre·sume |prĭ zōōm′| *v.* **presumed, presuming** To suppose to be true; take for granted: *A good detective will not presume anything.*

pre·vent |prĭ vĕnt′| *v.* **prevented, preventing** To keep from happening.

pre·view |prē′ vyōō′| *n., pl.* **previews** A showing of something, as a movie, to an invited audience before presenting it to the public.

prim·i·tive |prĭm′ ĭ tĭv| *adj.* **1.** Of or in an early stage in the development of human culture: *Some of the primitive cave people were skillful artists.* **2.** Simple or crude: *The primitive table we built out of old wood collapsed.*

pro-¹ A prefix that means: **1.** Favor or support: *propose.* **2.** Acting as; substituting for: *pronoun.*

pro-² A prefix that means "before; in front of": *proceed.*

pro·ce·dure |prə sē′ jər| *n., pl.* **procedures** A way of doing something or getting something done, especially by a series of steps.

prof·it·a·ble |prŏf′ ĭ tə bəl| *adj.* Yielding a profit; money-making: *The computer industry is very profitable.*

pro·gram |prō′ grăm′| *n., pl.* **programs 1.** A list of information, as the order of events and the names of those taking part in a public performance or presentation. **2.** A performance, especially before an audience: *Which television programs do you like?*

Spelling Dictionary

proj·ect |**prŏj′** ĕkt′| *n., pl.* **projects**
1. A plan for doing something: *The major approved the building project.* **2.** A special study carried on by students: *a science project.*
v. **pro·ject** |prə **jĕkt′**| **projected, projecting**
1. To extend forward; to stick out: *The book projected beyond the shelf.* **2.** To cause an image to appear on a surface: *We projected the slides on the wall.*

pro·jec·tor |prə **jĕk′** tər| *n., pl.* **projectors**
A machine that projects an image onto a screen: *The teacher set up the movie projector and the class watched the film.*

projector

prom·i·nent |**prŏm′** ə nənt| *adj.* **1.** Very easy to see: *The new courthouse is quite prominent.* **2.** Widely known: *Our neighbor is a prominent scientist.*

pro·mote |prə **mōt′**| *v.* **promoted, promoting** **1.** To help the progress, development, or growth of; further: *Regular exercise promotes physical fitness.* **2.** To raise to a higher rank, position, or class: *She was promoted to the sixth grade.*

pro·mo·tion |prə **mō′** shən| *n., pl.* **promotions** **1.** The act of promoting; encouragement. **2.** Advancement in rank, position, or class: *a job promotion.*

pro·noun |**prō′** noun′| *n., pl.* **pronouns**
A word that can take the place of a noun. In the sentence *John takes the train when he travels*, the word *he* is a pronoun that takes the place of *John.*

proof |prŏof| *n., pl.* **proofs** Evidence of truth or accuracy: *We have no proof that the money was stolen.*

prop·er·ty |**prŏp′** ər tē| *n., pl.* **properties**
Something, as money or land, that is owned; possession.

pro·pose |prə **pōz′**| *v.* **proposed, proposing** To put forward for consideration; suggest: *I propose a trip to the museum.*

prop·o·si·tion |prŏp′ ə **zĭsh′** ən| *n., pl.* **propositions** Something proposed; offer.

pros·per |**prŏs′** pər| *v.* **prospered, prospering** To be fortunate or successful; thrive: *She works hard, and her business prospers.*

pro·tect |prə **tĕkt′**| *v.* **protected, protecting** To keep safe from harm, attack, or injury; guard: *Anti-pollution laws help protect our wildlife.*

pro·tec·tion |prə **tĕk′** shən| *n., pl.* **protections** **1.** The condition of being protected. **2.** The act of protecting. **3.** Someone or something that protects.

prov·erb |**prŏv′** ûrb′| *n., pl.* **proverbs**
A short, common saying that tells a truth. *"A rolling stone gathers no moss"* and *"Better late than never"* are proverbs.

pro·vide |prə **vīd′**| *v.* **provided, providing** To give something needed or useful; supply: *My father is providing me with help on my homework.*

pro·voke |prə **vōk′**| *v.* **provoked, provoking** To make angry; annoy: *The man's rudeness provoked me.*

prowl |proul| *v.* **prowled, prowling** To move about secretly and quietly as if looking for prey: *City cats prowl through alleys.*

pub·lish |**pŭb′** lĭsh| *v.* **published, publishing** To print and offer for public sale or distribution: *The newspaper published my letter.*

Pu·ri·tan |**pyŏor′** ĭ tn| *n., pl.* **Puritans** In the sixteenth and seventeenth centuries, a member of a religious group in England or the American Colonies that wanted simple forms of worship.

pur·suit |pər **sŏot′**| *n., pl.* **pursuits** The act of chasing in order to catch: *The detective went in pursuit of the criminals.*

puz·zle |**pŭz′** əl| *n., pl.* **puzzles**
1. Something that is hard to understand; mystery: *It's a puzzle to me how you can finish your work so fast.* **2.** A problem, toy, or game that makes one think and tests one's skill.

Q

quail |kwāl| *n., pl.* **quail** *or* **quails** A small, rather plump bird that has a short tail and brownish feathers.

quar·ter |kwôr′ tər| *n., pl.* **quarters**
1. Any of four equal parts into which something can be divided: *I cut the apple into quarters.* **2.** A coin used in the United States or Canada that is worth twenty-five cents. **3.** One of four time periods that make up a game. **4.** A district or section of a city. **5.** One fourth of the time it takes for the moon to revolve around the earth.

ques·tion |kwĕs′ chən| *n., pl.* **questions** Something that is asked: *I don't understand your question.* *v.* **questioned, questioning** To ask questions of: *My parents questioned me about my new job.*

ques·tion·naire |kwĕs′ chə nâr′| *n., pl.* **questionnaires** A printed form with a series of questions, often used to sample public opinion on a certain subject.

quick-wit·ted |kwĭk′ wĭt′ ĭd| *adj.* Mentally alert; clever.

qui·et |kwī′ ĭt| *adj.* **quieter, quietest** **1.** Marked by little or no noise; silent or nearly silent: *A library is a quiet place to study.* **2.** Free or nearly free from activity or motion; calm.

R

ra·di·o |rā′ dē ō| *n., pl.* **radios** **1.** A way of using energy waves to carry signals between points without using wires. **2.** The sending forth of programs of entertainment, news, and information in this way.

raise |rāz| *v.* **raised, raising** To move or lift to a higher position; boost: *I raised my arm and waved at my friend.* *n., pl.* **raises** An increase in amount, as in wages.

Pronunciation Key

ă	pat	ō	go	th	thin
ā	pay	ô	paw, for	hw	which
â	care	oi	oil	zh	usual
ä	father	ŏŏ	book	ə	ago,
ĕ	pet	ōō	boot		item,
ē	be	yōō	cute		pencil,
ĭ	pit	ou	out		atom,
ī	ice	ŭ	cut		circus
î	near	û	fur	ər	butter
ŏ	pot	th	the		

ran·dom |răn′ dəm| *adj.* Lacking a definite plan, pattern, or purpose: *I made a few random marks on the canvas.*
◇ *Idiom* **at random** Without a definite purpose or method; by chance.

rap·id |răp′ ĭd| *adj.* Marked by speed; fast.

rare |râr| *adj.* **rarer, rarest** **1.** Not often found, seen, or happening: *Our cat is a rare breed.* **2.** Unusually good; excellent: *a rare friendship.*

re- A prefix that means: **1.** Again: *refill.* **2.** Back; backward: *recalled.*

re·act |rē ăkt′| *v.* **reacted, reacting** To act in response, as to an experience or the behavior of another: *The audience reacted with pleasure to the play.*

re·ac·tion |rē ăk′ shən| *n., pl.* **reactions** A response to something: *I developed a rash as a reaction to the medicine.*

rear |rîr| *n., pl.* **rears** The area or direction closest to or at the back.

rea·son·a·ble |rē′ zə nə bəl| *adj.* Showing good judgment; sensible or logical: *We came up with a reasonable solution.*

re·bel |rĭ bĕl′| *v.* **rebelled, rebelling** To resist or fight against a government or an authority.

re·build |rē bĭld′| *v.* **rebuilt, rebuilding** To build again; reconstruct: *rebuild a house.*

rec·ord |rĕk′ ərd| *n., pl.* **records** A disk that can be played on a phonograph.

re·cord |rĭ kôrd′| *v.* **recorded, recording** To set down in writing: *Record the time you spent on each test question.*

re·cy·cle |rē sī′ kəl| *v.* **recycled, recycling** To treat materials that have been thrown away in order to use them again: *The city recycles glass, cans, and paper.*

Spelling Dictionary

re·duce |rĭ dōōs′| *v.* **reduced, reducing**
To make or become smaller.

reel |rēl| *n., pl.* **reels** A spoollike device that
is used for winding something flexible, such as
fishing line or film: *Put the first reel of film in
the projector.*

ref·e·ree |rĕf′ ə rē′| *n., pl.* **referees** An
official who enforces the rules in a sports
contest: *The referee called a foul on one of the
basketball players.*

referee

ref·uge |rĕf′ yōōj| *n., pl.* **refuges**
Protection or shelter from danger or trouble.

re·gard |rĭ gärd′| *v.* **regarded, regarding**
To hold in affection or esteem; think highly
of. *n., pl.* **regards** Consideration: *Have you
no regard for Tammy's feelings?*

re·gion |rē′ jən| *n., pl.* **regions** An area
without distinct boundaries: *In this region of
the country there are few tall trees.*

reg·is·ter |rĕj′ ĭ stər| *v.* **registered,
registering** To record or have one's name
recorded on an official written list: *You must
register to be able to vote.*

reg·u·lar |rĕg′ yə lər| *adj.* **1.** Usual or
normal; standard: *Those shirts are $5.00 below
the regular price.* **2.** Appearing again and
again: *a regular customer.*

reg·u·lar·i·ty |rĕg′ yə lăr′ ĭ tē| *n., pl.*
regularities 1. Something that is usual or
standard. **2.** Something that happens again
and again.

reg·u·late |rĕg′ yə lāt′| *v.* **regulated,
regulating** To control or direct according to
rules: *The government regulates the printing
of money.*

reg·u·la·tion |rĕg′ yə lā′ shən| *n., pl.*
regulations 1. The act of regulating. **2.** A
rule of law: *a traffic regulation.*

re·hearse |rĭ hûrs′| *v.* **rehearsed,
rehearsing** To practice in preparation for a
public performance: *rehearsing our lines.*

re·ject |rĭ jĕkt′| *v.* **rejected, rejecting**
To refuse to accept or consider.

rel·a·tive |rĕl′ ə tĭv| *n., pl.* **relatives**
A person related to another by family: *None
of Katie's relatives live near her.*

re·lax |rĭ lăks′| *v.* **relaxed, relaxing** To
make or become less tight or tense: *Try to relax
your muscles.*

re·mark·a·ble |rĭ mär′ kə bəl| *adj.*
That which is worthy of notice; extraordinary:
*The landing on the moon was a remarkable
achievement.*

re·mem·ber |rĭ mĕm′ bər| *v.*
remembered, remembering 1. To bring
back to the mind; think of again: *I could not
remember how to stop the machine.* **2.** To keep
carefully in one's memory: *Remember that we
have to leave early tonight.*

re·mind |rĭ mīnd′| *v.* **reminded,
reminding** To cause someone to remember or
think of something.

re·mote con·trol |rĭ mōt′ kən trōl′| *n.,
pl.* **remote controls** The control of an activity,
process, or machine from a distance, especially
by a radio or electricity: *You can operate this
robot by remote control.*

re·or·der |rē ôr′ dər | *v.* **reordered,
reordering 1.** To straighten out or put in
order again. **2.** To place an order again.

re·pair |rĭ pâr′| *v.* **repaired, repairing**
To put back into proper or useful condition;
fix; mend.

re·peat |rĭ pēt′| *v.* **repeated, repeating**
To say, do, or go through again.

re·ply |rĭ plī′| *v.* **replied, replying** To say
or give an answer: *I replied that I would go.*
n., pl. **replies** An answer or response: *I didn't
hear your reply to my question.*

re·port |rĭ pôrt′| *n., pl.* **reports 1.** A
spoken or written description: *weather report.*
2. A formal account of the activities of a group.
v. **reported, reporting 1.** To provide an
account for publication. **2.** To present oneself.

rep·re·sent |rĕp′ rĭ **zĕnt′**| v. **represented,
representing** To act for: *Two Senators are
elected to represent each state in Congress.*

re·proach |rĭ **prōch′**| v. **reproached,
reproaching** To criticize severely, blame.
n., pl. **reproaches** Blame; disapproval.

Re·pub·li·can |rĭ **pŭb′** lĭ kən| n., pl.
Republicans A member of the Republican Party:
The Republicans introduced a bill into Congress.

re·side |rĭ **zīd′**| v. **resided, residing** To
make one's home; live: *The Smiths resided in
Los Angeles for a year.*

res·i·dent |rĕz′ ĭ dənt| n., pl. **residents**
A person who lives in a particular place.

re·sist |rĭ **zist′**| v. **resisted, resisting** To
work against; oppose: *The lock resisted our
efforts to open it.*

re·spond |rĭ **spŏnd′**| v. **responded,
responding** To make a reply; answer: *I'll
respond to your question in a minute.*

re·spon·si·ble |rĭ **spŏn′** sə bəl| adj.
1. Having a certain duty or obligation: *We
are responsible for cleaning our rooms.* **2.** Being
the cause or source of something: *Viruses are
responsible for many diseases.*

re·sult |rĭ **zŭlt′**| n., pl. **results** Something
that happens because of something else. v.
resulted, resulting 1. To come about as a
result of something: *Floods resulted from the
hurricane.* **2.** To lead to a certain result: *Hard
work results in success.*

re·tire |rĭ **tīr′**| v. **retired, retiring** To give
up one's work, business, or career, usually
because of advancing age: *He will retire from
baseball.* —n. **retirement** *Nancy's father took
an early retirement.*

re·venge |rĭ **vĕnj′**| v. **revenged, revenging**
To injure or harm in return for an earlier
injury or harm; to get even.

rev·er·ence |rĕv′ ər əns| n. A feeling
of awe and deep respect mixed with love;
adoration: *Janet looked at the beautiful painting
with reverence.*

re·vers·i·ble |rĭ **vûr′** sə bəl| adj. Capable
of being worn or used with either side out,
often having a different color, pattern, or fabric
on the opposite side.

re·view |rĭ **vyoō′**| n., pl. **reviews** The act
or process of studying again.

Pronunciation Key

ă	pat	ō	go	th	thin
ā	pay	ô	paw, for	hw	which
â	care	oi	oil	zh	usual
ä	father	ŏŏ	book	ə	ago,
ĕ	pet	ōō	boot		item,
ē	be	yōō	cute		pencil,
ĭ	pit	ou	out		atom,
ī	ice	ŭ	cut		circus
î	near	û	fur	ər	butter
ŏ	pot	th	the		

rev·o·lu·tion |rĕv′ ə **lōō′** shən| n., pl.
revolutions A complete change in government
or rule: *In the American Revolution British rule
was overthrown.*

rhyme |rīm| v. **rhymed, rhyming**
To correspond in sound: *"Hour" rhymes
with "sour."*

rhythm |**rĭth′** əm| n., pl. **rhythms** A
sound pattern with a series of regularly
accented beats: *We clapped our hands to the
rhythm of the song.*

right of way |rīt′ əv **wā′**| n., pl. **rights
of way** or **right of ways** The right of one
person, vessel, or vehicle to pass in front of
another: *Police and emergency vehicles always
have the right of way.*

ri·ot |**rī′** ət| n., pl. **riots** Disturbance
created by a large number of people.

rise |rīz| v. **rose, risen, rising 1.** To go
up; ascend: *The kite is rising in the air.* **2.** To
improve in rank or condition: *Education will
help you rise in the world.*

ri·val·ry |**rī′** vəl rē| n., pl. **rivalries** The
effort of striving to equal or outdo another;
competition.

ro·bot |**rō′** bət| or |**rō′** bŏt′| n., pl. **robots**
A machine that can perform human tasks
or imitate human actions. A robot has a
computer that processes information, such
as commands.

History

Robot comes from the Czech word *robota*,
meaning "forced labor; hard, boring work."

Spelling Dictionary

ro·de·o |rō′ dē ō′| or |rō **dā′** ō|
n., pl. **rodeos** A show in which cowhands
display their skill in riding horses and steers
and compete in events such as roping cattle.

role |rōl| *n., pl.* **roles** A part played by an
actor: *I tried out for the role of the hero in the
class play.*

ro·man·tic |rō **măn′** tĭk| *adj.* Of, relating
to, or marked by love or romance: *I read a
romantic novel.*

rook·ie |rŏŏk′ ē| *n., pl.* **rookies** A person
who lacks training: *The rookies on the police
force were carefully supervised.*

rough |rŭf| *adj.* **rougher, roughest**
1. Bumpy or uneven; not smooth: *Hickory
trees have rough bark.* **2.** Not calm.

route |rŏŏt| or |rout| *n., pl.* **routes**
A road, path, or lane of travel between two
places.

roy·al |roi′ əl| *adj.* Of or having to do
with a queen or king: *The royal family led
the procession.*

rub |rŭb| *v.* **rubbed, rubbing** To press
something against a surface and move it
back and forth: *We rubbed the table with a
clean cloth.*

ru·by |rŏŏ′ bē| *n., pl.* **rubies** A deep-red
precious stone found in riverbeds.

rude |rŏŏd| *adj.* **ruder, rudest** Not
considerate of others; impolite: *It was rude of
Josh to take a third piece of pie when others had
not eaten any yet.*

rug·ged |rŭg′ ĭd| *adj.* Having a
rough surface or jagged outline: *rugged
mountains.*

ru·in |rŏŏ′ ĭn| *v.* **ruined, ruining** To
damage beyond repair; wreck: *Water from the
overflowing bathtub ruined the new carpeting in
the hallway.*

rule |rŏŏl| *n., pl.* **rules** A statement
or principle that controls behavior or
action: *a rule against running in the school
halls.* *v.* **ruled, ruling** To have power or
authority over; to govern: *The king and
queen ruled the land for many years.*

rus·tic |rŭs′ tĭk| *adj.* Of or typical of the
country; rural: *Smithtown is a rustic community
in the mountains.*

S

sac·ri·fice |săk′ rə fīs′| *n., pl.* **sacrifices**
An offering: *a sacrifice of grain and meat.* *v.*
sacrificed, sacrificing To give up something
valuable for the sake of someone or something
else.

safe |sāf| *adj.* **safer, safest** Free from
danger, risk, or threat of harm. —*adv.* **safely**
We got home safely before the storm began.

sales·per·son |sālz′ pûr′ sən| *n., pl.*
salespersons A person who sells goods or
services.

sa·lute |sə lŏŏt′| *v.* **saluted, saluting**
1. To show respect by raising the right hand
stiffly to the forehead or by firing guns. **2.** To
greet with a polite gesture. *n., pl.* **salutes** An
act of saluting.

sam·ple |săm′ pəl| *n., pl.* **samples** A part
of a larger group, used for estimating what the
larger group is like: *A sample of 500 people were
questioned for a survey.*

sand·wich |sănd′ wĭch| *n., pl.*
sandwiches Two or more slices of bread with
a filling between them.

sap·phire |săf′ īr′| *n., pl.* **sapphires** A
hard, deep-blue precious stone that is valued as
a gem.

scal·lop |skŏl′ əp| or |skăl′ əp| *v.*
scalloped, scalloping To bake in a casserole
with a sauce and often with bread crumbs.

scar |skär| *n., pl.* **scars** A mark left on the
skin by a healed wound. *v.* **scarred, scarring**
To mark with or form a scar: *The deep wound
scarred Nina's knee.*

scare |skâr| *v.* **scared, scaring** To frighten
or become frightened.

scar·y |skâr′ ē| *adj.* **scarier, scariest**
Frightening; terrifying.

scene |sēn| *n., pl.* **scenes** **1.** The place
where an action or event takes place: *The tow
truck finally arrived at the scene of the wreck.*
2. A short section of a play or movie.
♦ *These sound alike* **scene, seen.**

sce·nic |sē′ nĭk| *adj.* Of attractive natural
scenery: *We drove along a scenic route in the
mountains.*

sched·ule |skĕj′ o͞ol| or |skĕj′ əl| *n., pl.*
schedules A list of the times for departures
and arrivals: *According to the schedule, the plane
will take off at four o'clock.*

schol·ar |skŏl′ ər| *n., pl.* **scholars** A
person who has a great deal of knowledge.

schwa |shwä| *n.* A weak vowel sound
found in unstressed syllables in words. The
symbol for the schwa sound is |ə|. Different
vowel letters can spell the *schwa* sound.

sci·ence |sī′ əns| *n., pl.* **sciences** **1.** The
study and explanation of things that happen
in nature and the universe. **2.** An area of
knowledge in which observation, experiments,
and study are used.

scoop |sko͞op| *n., pl.* **scoops** **1.** A utensil
that is like a small shovel, used to take up
or dish out foods. **2.** The amount a scoop
holds: *Add another scoop of flour to the dough.*
v. **scooped, scooping** To lift out with or as
if with a scoop; to dish out.

scowl |skoul| *v.* **scowled, scowling** To
lower the eyebrows in anger or disapproval;
frown.

screen·play |skrēn′ plā′| *n., pl.*
screenplays The script for a motion picture.

script |skrĭpt| *n., pl.* **scripts** The written text
of a play or movie or of a radio or television
show, often divided into acts and scenes.

seal |sēl| *n., pl.* **seals** A design used as an
official mark of authority. *v.* **sealed, sealing**
To close or fasten tightly.

seat belt |sēt′ bĕlt′| *n., pl.* **seat belts** A
safety strap or harness that is designed to hold a
person securely in a seat, as in a car or airplane.

seat belt

seek |sēk| *v.* **sought, seeking** To try to
find or get: *We are seeking a new place to live.*

seen |sēn| Past participle of **see**: *I have seen
that movie.*
♦ *These sound alike* **seen, scene.**

self-as·sured |sĕlf′ ə sho͝ ord′| *adj.*
Having or showing confidence in oneself.

Sen·ate |sĕn′ ĭt| *n., pl.* **senates** The upper
house of the United States Congress. Its
members are elected every six years.

sen·si·tive |sĕn′ sĭ tĭv| *adj.* **1.** Sore:
My bruise is still sensitive. **2.** Easily affected,
influenced, or hurt: *Don't be so sensitive to
criticism.*

sen·sor |sĕn′ sər| or |sĕn′ sôr′| *n., pl.*
sensors A device, such as a thermostat, that
reacts in a predictable way to a particular type of
change, such as a change in light or temperature.

se·ries |sîr′ ēz| *n., pl.* **series** A television
or radio show that is presented at regular
intervals: *a comedy series.*

se·ri·ous |sîr′ ē əs| *adj.* **1.** Grave; not
humorous: *Mike wondered what was wrong
when he saw the serious look on his father's face.*
2. Important: *Getting married is a serious step.*
—*n.* **seriousness** *Alex did not understand the
seriousness of the problem.*

serv·ant |sûr′ vənt| *n., pl.* **servants**
1. A person who works for wages in someone
else's household. **2.** A person who is hired to
perform services for another: *Police officers are
public servants.*

serv·ice |sûr′ vĭs| *n., pl.* **services** **1.** The
act or work of helping others; aid: *They spend
their lives in service to the poor.* **2.** The act or
manner of satisfying customers' requests: *The
service at that restaurant is very slow.*

Spelling Dictionary

ses·sion |sĕsh′ ən| *n., pl.* **sessions**
A meeting or series of meetings of a court or legislature.

set |sĕt| *n., pl.* **sets** The scenery, furniture, and other objects on the stage of a play or movie.

set·tle·ment |sĕt′ l mənt| *n., pl.*
settlements A small community; village:
a fishing settlement.

shad·ow |shăd′ ō| *n., pl.* **shadows**
1. A shaded area made when light is blocked.
2. Partial darkness.

sharp |shärp| *adj.* **sharper, sharpest** Not rounded or blunt; pointed.

shel·ter |shĕl′ tər| *v.* **sheltered, sheltering**
To provide protection or cover for: *We sheltered the injured animal until it got well.*

Shen·an·do·ah Na·tion·al Park
|shĕn′ ən dō′ ə| A scenic area of north Virginia on the crest of the Blue Ridge Mountains.

ship |shĭp| *n., pl.* **ships** A large vessel that can travel in deep water. A ship can be powered by a motor or sails. *v.* **shipped, shipping 1.** To transport or send: *We ship our fresh vegetables to market by truck.* **2.** To put on board a ship.

ship·yard |shĭp′ yärd′| *n., pl.* **shipyards**
A place where ships are built, repaired, and equipped.

shipyard

shoot |shoōt| *v.* **shot, shooting** To hit, wound, or kill with a bullet, an arrow, or another projectile fired from a weapon.

short·age |shôr′ tĭj| *n., pl.* **shortages**
An amount of something that is not enough; lack; scarcity.

short·stop |shôrt′ stŏp′| *n., pl.* **shortstops**
The position between second and third bases in baseball.

shoul·der |shōl′ dər| *n., pl.* **shoulders**
The part of the human body between the neck and the upper arm.

shov·el |shŭv′ əl| *n., pl.* **shovels** A tool with a long handle and a flattened scoop:
I dug out the ditch with a shovel. *v.* **shoveled, shoveling** To pick up or move with a shovel:
Shovel the snow.

shown |shōn| *v.* A past participle of **show:**
The librarian has shown us where to find books about birds.

shred |shrĕd| *v.* **shredded** *or* **shred, shredding** To cut or tear into small strips.

side·kick |sīd′ kĭk| *n., pl.* **sidekicks**
Slang. A close friend; pal.

sigh |sī| *v.* **sighed, sighing** To let out a long, deep breath because of fatigue, sorrow, or relief.

sight·see·ing |sīt′ sē′ ĭng| *n.* The act or pastime of touring places of interest. —*n.*
sightseer *Anne led a tour through the museum for the sightseers.*

sign |sīn| *n., pl.* **signs** Something, such as a poster, that conveys information. *v.* **signed, signing** To write one's name on, as a form.

sig·nal |sĭg′ nəl| *n., pl.* **signals** A sign, gesture, or device that gives a command, a warning, or other information.

si·lent |sī′ lənt| *adj.* Making or having no sound; quiet.

sim·i·lar |sĭm′ ə lər| *adj.* Alike but not exactly the same.

sim·ple |sĭm′ pəl| *adj.* **simpler, simplest**
Not complicated; easy: *The directions are simple.*

sim·plic·i·ty |sĭm plĭs′ ĭ tē| *n.* The condition or quality of being uncomplicated or easy.

sim·pli·fy |sĭm′ plə fī′| *v.* **simplified, simplifying** To make or become less complicated or easier.

sim·ply |sĭm′ plē| *adv.* **1.** In an uncomplicated or easy way; plainly. **2.** Merely; just: *I was simply standing there.*

sin·cere |sĭn sîr′| *adj.* **sincerer, sincerest** Not lying or pretending; honest; genuine: *a sincere apology.*

sin·gle |sĭng′ gəl| *adj.* **1.** Not with another or others; one: *There is a single biscuit left on the plate.* **2.** Not married. **3.** A hit in baseball that allows the batter to reach first base.

site |sīt| *n., pl.* **sites** A position or location.

skill |skĭl| *n., pl.* **skills** The ability to do something well.

skim |skĭm| *v.* **skimmed, skimming 1.** To remove (floating matter) from a liquid: *Skim cream off the top of the milk.* **2.** To read quickly, skipping over parts.

slam |slăm| *v.* **slammed, slamming** To shut forcefully and noisily.

slept |slĕpt| *v.* Past tense and past participle of **sleep:** *The baby slept late today.*

slide |slīd| *n., pl.* **slides** A small glass plate on which objects are placed for examination by microscope: *Look at the slide with the flower pollen on it.*

slight |slīt| *adj.* **slighter, slightest 1.** Small in amount or degree. **2.** Small in size; slender.

slip·per·y |slĭp′ ə rē| *adj.* **slipperier, slipperiest** Tending to slip; tending to cause one to lose one's balance or grasp; slick.

slope |slōp| *v.* **sloped, sloping** To slant upward or downward.

slug·gish |slŭg′ ĭsh| *adj.* Moving or acting in a slow way; not lively.

smear |smîr| *v.* **smeared, smearing** To cover or spread with a sticky or greasy substance. *n., pl.* **smears 1.** A stain or blotch. **2.** A substance or preparation placed on a slide for microscopic study.

smog |smôg| *n.* Fog mixed with smoke.

snap |snăp| *v.* **snapped, snapping 1.** To make or cause to make a sharp cracking sound. **2.** To break or cause to break suddenly with a sharp sound.

snare |snâr| *n., pl.* **snares** A device, such as a noose, that is used for trapping birds and small animals; a trap.

ă	pat	ō	go	th	thin
ā	pay	ô	paw, for	hw	which
â	care	oi	oil	zh	usual
ä	father	ŏŏ	book	ə	ago,
ĕ	pet	ōō	boot		item,
ē	be	yōō	cute		pencil,
ĭ	pit	ou	out		atom,
ī	ice	ŭ	cut		circus
î	near	û	fur	ər	butter
ŏ	pot	th	the		

snow·ball |snō′ bôl′| *n., pl.* **snowballs** A ball of pressed snow.

soar |sôr| *v.* **soared, soaring** To rise, fly, or glide high in the air.
♦ *These sound alike* **soar, sore.**

soft |sôft| *adj.* **softer, softest 1.** Not hard or firm: *She squeezed the soft melon.* **2.** Smooth, fine, or pleasing to the touch: *She petted a soft, gray kitten.* —*n.* **softness** *Lamb's wool is known for its softness.*

sole¹ |sōl| *n., pl.* **soles** The bottom of a shoe, boot, or slipper.
♦ *These sound alike* **sole, soul.**

sole² |sōl| *adj.* Being the only one; single.
♦ *These sound alike* **sole, soul.**

sol·id |sŏl′ ĭd| *adj.* **1.** Not hollow: *The chef carved a swan out of a solid block of ice.* **2.** Strong and firm: *The house has a solid foundation.*

sol·i·tar·y |sŏl′ ĭ tĕr′ ē| *adj.* Being or living alone: *I saw a solitary runner at the side of the road.*

sol·i·tude |sŏl′ ĭ tūd′| or |sŏl′ ĭ tyōōd′| *n.* Time alone away from others: *Mother likes to spend one hour a day in solitude.*

so·lo |sō′ lō| *n., pl.* **solos** A performance by a single person.

solve |sŏlv| or |sôlv| *v.* **solved, solving** To find an answer or solution to: *She finally solved the mystery.*

som·ber |sŏm′ bər| *adj.* **1.** Dark and dull; gloomy: *The somber sky was the first sign of the approaching storm.* **2.** Serious: *The bad news put us in a somber mood.*

som·er·sault |sŭm′ ər sôlt′| *n., pl.* **somersaults** The act of rolling the body in a complete circle, heels over head.

sore |sôr| *adj.* **sorer, sorest** Suffering pain, hurting: *I am sore from running.*
◆ *These sound alike* **sore, soar.**
◇ *Idiom* **stick out like a sore thumb** To be obvious or visible: *That purple car sticks out like a sore thumb.*

sor·row |sŏr′ ō| *n., pl.* **sorrows** Grief or sadness caused by loss or injury.

soul |sōl| *n., pl.* **souls** The part of a person considered to include the capabilities to think, feel, and act.
◆ *These sound alike* **soul, sole.**

sound·track |sound′ trăk′| *n., pl.* **soundtracks** A narrow strip at the edge of a motion-picture film that carries a recording of the sound.

south |south| *n.* The direction to the left side of a person who faces the sunset.

space |spās| *n., pl.* **spaces** The distance or open area between or within objects or between points.

spa·cious |spā′ shəs| *adj.* Having much space; roomy.

spar·kle |spär′ kəl| *v.* **sparkled, sparkling** To give off sparks of light; glitter: *Diamonds sparkle.* *n., pl.* **sparkles** A spark of light.

spe·cial |spĕsh′ əl| *adj.* Different from what is common or usual: *Birthdays are special occasions.* *n., pl.* **specials** Something arranged for a particular occasion: *lunch special.*

spec·ta·cle |spĕk′ tə kəl| *n., pl.* **spectacles** An unusual or impressive public show, as of fireworks.

spec·ta·tor |spĕk′ tā′ tər| *n., pl.* **spectators** A person who watches an event but does not take part in it; viewer.

spec·trum |spĕk′ trəm| *n., pl.* **spectrums** The bands of color that are seen when light, especially light from the sun, is broken up, as by a prism. You can see the colors of the spectrum in a rainbow.

speech |spēch| *n., pl.* **speeches** A public talk or address: *The President's speech was broadcast at nine o'clock P.M.*

speech·less |spēch′ lĭs| *adj.* Not able to speak for a short time because of shock, fear, or joy.

speed·om·e·ter |spĭ dŏm′ ĭ tər| *n., pl.* **speedometers** A device that measures and indicates speed, as of an automobile or bicycle.

speedometer

spic·y |spī′ sē| *adj.* **spicier, spiciest** Seasoned with or containing spice; a plant substance such as nutmeg or pepper that has a pleasant or strong smell.

spin·ach |spĭn′ ĭch| *n.* A plant grown for its dark green leaves. Spinach is eaten as a vegetable.

split |splĭt| *v.* **split, splitting 1.** To divide or become divided into parts, especially lengthwise: *We split logs for the campfire.* **2.** To break, burst, or rip apart with force: *Pressure caused the container to split.*

spon·sor |spŏn′ sər| *n., pl.* **sponsors** A person or organization that pays the costs of a radio or television program in order to advertise a product or service.

sports·cast |spôrts′ kăst′| *n., pl.* **sportscasts** A radio or television broadcast of a sports event.

spot |spŏt| *n. pl.* **spots 1.** A small mark or stain. **2.** An area that is different, as in color, from the area around it: *My dog has brown fur with white spots.* **3.** A place or location *v.* **spotted, spotting 1.** To mark or cause to be marked with spots. **2.** To find or locate: *It was hard to spot you in the crowd.*

spy |spī| *v.* **spied, spying 1.** To watch secretly and for unfriendly reasons: *Soldiers were spying on the enemy camp.* **2.** to catch sight of: *I spied a blue jay on a branch.*

squad |skwŏd| *n., pl.* **squads** An organized team or group, as of police officers.

square |skwâr| *n., pl.* **squares** A rectangle having four equal sides.

squeeze |skwēz| *v.* **squeezed, squeezing** To press together with force: *The baby squeezed the rubber toy.*

squirm |skwûrm| *v.* **squirmed, squirming** To twist about; wiggle.

squirt |skwûrt| *v.* **squirted, squirting** To send out or be sent out in a thin, fast stream.

sta·di·um |stā′ dē əm| *n., pl.* **stadiums** A large structure in which athletic events are held; arena.

staff |stăf| *n., pl.* **staffs** *or* **staves** **1.** A long stick carried to help in walking. **2.** A pole on which a flag flies. **3.** An organized group of employees: *the staff of camp counselors.* **4.** The set of five horizontal lines and the spaces between them on which musical notes are written.

stage·hand |stāj′ hănd′| *n., pl.* **stagehands** A person who works backstage in a theater.

stain |stān| *n., pl.* **stains** A discolored mark or spot.

stair |stâr| *n., pl.* **stairs** **1.** **stairs** A series or flight of steps; staircase. **2.** One of a flight of steps.

stalk¹ |stôk| *n., pl.* **stalks** **1.** The stem of a plant. **2.** A part that is attached to or supports a leaf or flower.

stalk² |stôk| *v.* **stalked, stalking** To move in a sly way as if tracking prey: *The tiger stalked through the jungle.*

stan·za |stăn′ zə| *n., pl.* **stanzas** A group of lines that makes up a division of a poem.

star·ry-eyed |stär′ ē īd′| *adj.* Full of youthful hope and enthusiasm.

sta·tion·ar·y |stā′ shə něr′ ē| *adj.* **1.** Not changing: *The price remained stationary.* **2.** Not capable of being moved; fixed in place: *The towers of a suspension bridge are stationary.*
♦ *These sound alike* **stationary, stationery.**

sta·tion·er·y |stā′ shə něr′ ē| *n.* Materials, such as paper, notebooks, pens, and envelopes, that are used in writing.
♦ *These sound alike* **stationery, stationary.**

stat·ute |stăch′ ōōt| *n., pl.* **statutes** A law.

Pronunciation Key

ă	pat	ō	go	th	thin
ā	pay	ô	paw, for	hw	which
â	care	oi	oil	zh	usual
ä	father	ŏŏ	book	ə	ago,
ĕ	pet	ōō	boot		item,
ē	be	yōō	cute		pencil,
ĭ	pit	ou	out		atom,
ī	ice	ŭ	cut		circus
î	near	û	fur	ər	butter
ŏ	pot	*th*	*the*		

steal |stēl| *v.* **stole, stolen, stealing** **1.** To take without right or permission. **2.** In baseball, to gain (another base) without the ball being batted, by running to the base during the delivery of the pitch.

steer |stîr| *v.* **steered, steering** To direct the course of or guide: *The pilot steered the ship to the dock.*

stern |stûrn| *n., pl.* **sterns** The rear part of a ship or boat.

stim·u·late |stĭm′ yə lāt′| *v.* **stimulated, stimulating** To make active or more active; excite; arouse: *The book stimulates my imagination.*

stir |stûr| *v.* **stirred, stirring** To mix by using repeated circular motions: *I stirred the vegetables into the soup.*

stole |stōl| *v.* Past tense of **steal:** *When the pitcher threw the ball, Luis stole second base.*

strat·e·gy |străt′ ə jē| *n., pl.* **strategies** A clever system or plan of action: *Our strategy is to give a surprise party for them.*

stray |strā| *n., pl.* **strays** A person or animal that has wandered away from home. *adj.* Wandering or having wandered away from home; lost.

stress |strĕs| *n.* The emphasis placed upon the syllable spoken most strongly in a word.

stride |strīd| *v.* **strode, stridden, striding** To walk with long steps. *n., pl.* **strides** A long step.

strike |strīk| *v.* **struck, striking** To hit with or as if with the hand: *I struck the ball with the bat.*

strip |strĭp| *v.* **stripped, stripping** To remove the covering from: *I stripped the peel from the banana.*

Spelling Dictionary

stroke |strōk| *n., pl.* **strokes** The time indicated by the striking of a bell or a gong: *She had to be home at the stroke of eight o'clock.* *v.* **stroked, stroking** To move the hand over gently.

stroll |strōl| *v.* **strolled, strolling** To walk or wander around in a slow, relaxed way. *n., pl.* **strolls** A slow, relaxed walk.

stub·born |stŭb′ ərn| *adj.* Not willing to change a purpose or opinion in spite of urging or requests from others: *The stubborn child refused to wear boots.*

stuck |stŭk| *v.* Past tense and past participle of **stick:** *The car got stuck in the mud.*

stu·dent |stood′ nt| or |styood′ nt| *n., pl.* **students** A person who studies, as in a school; pupil.

stud·y |stŭd′ ē| *n., pl.* **studies** The act or process of learning; an effort to learn: *Much study went into the new program.* *v.* **studied, studying** To examine closely and carefully: *Study the questions before you try to answer them.*

stun |stŭn| *v.* **stunned, stunning 1.** To daze or make senseless by or as if by a blow. **2.** To shock or confuse.

stunt |stŭnt| *n., pl.* **stunts** An act showing unusual skill or daring: *The action-packed movie was full of dangerous stunts performed by specially trained actors.*

sub·due |səb doo′| or |səb dyoo′| *v.* **subdued, subduing** To quiet or bring under control: *I managed to subdue my fear and speak up.*

sub·ject |sŭb′ jĭkt| *n., pl.* **subjects 1.** Something thought about or discussed; topic. **2.** The word or group of words in a sentence that tells what the sentence is about. |səb jĕkt′| *v.* **subjected, subjecting** To cause to undergo: *My doctor subjected me to some tests.*

sub·mit |səb mĭt′| *v.* **submitted, submitting** To yield to someone else's commands; give in.

suc·ceed |sək sēd′| *v.* **succeeded, succeeding** To carry out something desired or attempted: *We succeeded in our repairs.*

suf·fer |sŭf′ ər| *v.* **suffered, suffering** To feel pain, hurt, or distress: *suffering from illness.*

suf·fix |sŭf′ ĭks| *n., pl.* **suffixes** A word part added to the end of a base word to form a new word. The word part *-less* in *careless* is a suffix.

suit·a·ble |soo′ tə bəl| *adj.* Right for a purpose or occasion; appropriate; proper.

sum·mit |sŭm′ ĭt| *n., pl.* **summits** The highest point or part; peak; not the base: *the summit of the mountain.*

summit

su·per·hu·man |soo′ pər hyoo′ mən| *adj.* Being or seeming to be beyond ordinary or normal human ability: *It would take superhuman strength to move that boulder.*

su·per·la·tive |soo pûr′ lə tĭv| *adj.* Being the very best: *The singer gave a superlative performance.*

su·per·mar·ket |soo′ pər mär′ kĭt| *n., pl.* **supermarkets** A large store that sells food and household goods.

sup·port |sə pôrt′| *v.* **supported, supporting 1.** To keep from falling; hold in position: *Two steel towers supported the bridge.* **2.** To act in a lesser role to a leading actor: *John supported Lara, who had the starring role.*

sur·geon |sûr′ jən| *n., pl.* **surgeons** A doctor who specializes in treating injury and disease by cutting into and removing or repairing parts of the body.

sur·vey |sûr′ vā| *n., pl.* **surveys** A big investigation, as a sampling of opinions: *A survey of the voters showed that people want honest government.*

sur·vi·vor |sər vī′ vər| *n., pl.* **survivors** Someone or something that has stayed alive: *There were many survivors of the plane crash.*

sus·pect |sŭs′ pĕkt′| *n., pl.* **suspects** A person who is thought to be guilty of something without proof.

sus·pense |sə **spĕns′**| *n.* **1.** The condition or quality of being undecided. **2.** Anxious uncertainty about what will happen. —*adj.* **suspenseful** *This mystery novel is very suspenseful and quite entertaining.*

sus·pi·cious |sə **spĭsh′** əs| *adj.* Distrustful; doubtful. —*adv.* **suspiciously** *The police officer looked at me suspiciously.*

sway |swā| *v.* **swayed, swaying** To swing or cause to swing back and forth or from side to side: *The willow trees were swaying in the wind.*

sweep |swēp| *v.* **swept, sweeping** **1.** To clean with a broom or brush. **2.** To move or flow with steady force: *A strong wind sweeps across the lake all winter.*

sweet |swēt| *adj.* Having a pleasant taste like that of sugar.

sweet·heart |swēt′ härt′| *n., pl.* **sweethearts** **1.** A person whom one loves. **2.** A lovable person.

swept |swĕpt| *v.* Past tense and past participle of **sweep:** *He swept the floor with a broom.*

swift |swĭft| *adj.* **swifter, swiftest** Moving or able to move very fast; quick; speedy.

swim |swĭm| *v.* **swam, swum, swimming** To move through water by moving the arms, legs, or fins.

syl·la·ble |sĭl′ ə bəl| *n., pl.* **syllables** A word or a word part that has one vowel sound.

syn·o·nym |sĭn′ ə nĭm| *n., pl.* **synonyms** A word having the same or similar meaning as that of another word.

T

tai·lor |tā′ lər| *n., pl.* **tailors** A person who makes, repairs, or alters clothing.

tax·a·tion |tăk sā′ shən| *n.* The act of imposing taxes, or requiring that people or businesses pay money in order to support a government.

tel·e·cast |tĕl′ ĭ kăst′| *v.* **telecasted, telecasting** To broadcast by television. *n., pl.* **telecasts** *A television broadcast.*

Pronunciation Key

ă	pat	ō	go	th	**thin**
ā	pay	ô	paw, for	hw	**which**
â	care	oi	**oil**	zh	usual
ä	father	ŏŏ	book	ə	ago,
ĕ	pet	ōō	boot		item,
ē	be	yōō	cute		pencil,
ĭ	pit	ou	**out**		atom,
ī	ice	ŭ	cut		circus
î	near	û	fur	ər	butter
ŏ	pot	*th*	*the*		

tel·e·gram |tĕl′ ĭ grăm′| *n., pl.* **telegrams** A message sent by wire or radio to a receiving station.

tel·e·phone |tĕl′ ə fōn′| *n., pl.* **telephones** An instrument that reproduces and receives sound, especially speech.

tel·e·scope |tĕl′ ĭ skōp′| *n., pl.* **telescopes** A device that uses an arrangement of lenses or mirrors in a long tube to make distant objects appear closer.

tel·e·thon |tĕl′ ə thŏn′| *n. pl.* **telethons** A lengthy television program to raise funds for a charity.

tel·e·vise |tĕl′ ə vīz′| *v.* **televised, televising** To broadcast by television.

tel·e·vi·sion |tĕl′ ə vĭzh′ ən| *n., pl.* **televisions** **1.** A system for sending and receiving visual images of objects and actions with the sounds that go with them. **2.** A device that receives and reproduces the images and sounds sent by a television broadcast system.

tense |tĕns| *adj.* **tenser, tensest** Anxious or nervous.

ten·sion |tĕn′ shən| *n., pl.* **tensions** **1.** The act of stretching or the condition of being stretched. **2.** Stress that affects nerves, emotions, or relationships with other people; strain: *Meeting the deadline caused tension in the office.*

term |tûrm| *n., pl.* **terms** **1.** A word that has a certain meaning, usually in a special vocabulary: *"Shutout" is a sports term.* **2.** A period of time, especially one with definite limits: *a term of office.*

ter·ri·ble |tĕr′ ə bəl| *adj.* **1.** Causing great fear; dreadful. **2.** Very great or extreme; severe: *a terrible storm.* **3.** Very bad: *That was a terrible movie.*

Spelling Dictionary

test tube |tĕst′ to͞ob′| or |tĕst′ tyo͞ob′| *n., pl.* **test tubes** A tube of glass that is usually open at one end and rounded at the other, used in the laboratory for experiments.

tex·ture |tĕks′ chər| *n., pl.* **textures** The look or feel of a surface: *Velvet has a soft, smooth texture.*

Thanks·giv·ing Day |thăngks gĭv′ ĭng| *n.* A holiday for giving thanks. Thanksgiving Day is the fourth Thursday of November in the United States. It is the second Monday of October in Canada.

the·a·ter |thē′ ə tər| *n., pl.* **theaters** **1.** A building where plays or movies are presented. **2.** The work of writing, producing, or acting in plays.

there·fore |*th*âr′ fôr′| *adv.* For that reason; as a result: *I overslept and was therefore late getting to school.*

thief |thēf| *n., pl.* **thieves** A person who steals; a robber.

thigh |thī| *n., pl.* **thighs** The part of the human leg that extends from the hip to the knee.

thirst |thûrst| *n., pl.* **thirsts** **1.** A dry feeling in the mouth related to the need to drink. **2.** A desire to drink liquids.

thou·sand |thou′ zənd| *n., pl.* **thousands** The number, written 1000, that is equal to the product of 10 X 100.

through·out |thro͞o out′| *prep.* In, to, through, or during every part of: *Elections were held throughout the country. adv.* In or through every part: *I found this book interesting throughout.*

throw |thrō| *v.* **threw, thrown, throwing** To send through the air with a fast motion of the arm; fling: *We threw the ball back and forth.*

thrown |thrōn| *v.* Past participle of **throw**: *Jeff has thrown the ball under the fence.*

thun·der |thŭn′ dər| *n.* The deep, rumbling noise that goes with or comes after a flash of lightning.

thus |thŭs| *adv.* As a result: *Balsa wood is softer and thus it is easier to carve.*

ti·ny |tī′ nē| *adj.* **tinier, tiniest** Extremely small.

ti·tle |tīt′ l| *n., pl.* **titles** An identifying name given to a book, painting, song, or other work.

to·geth·er |tə ge*th*′ ər| *adv.* In or into a single group or place; with each other: *Many people were crowded together. We went to school together.*

to·mor·row |tə môr′ ō| *n.* **1.** The day after today **2.** The near future. *adv.* On or for the day after today: *I will return your book tomorrow.*

to·paz |tō′ păz′| *n., pl.* **topazes** A mineral, usually yellow, that is used as a gem.

torch |tôrch| *n., pl.* **torches** A device that shoots out a hot flame, as for welding or cutting metals.

tore |tôr| *v.* Past tense of **tear**: *He tore his shirt on a nail.*

◇ *Idiom* **tore his [her] hair out** Suffered greatly; became very anxious.

to·tal |tōt′ l| *n., pl.* **totals** **1.** A number gotten by adding; sum. **2.** An entire amount. *adj.* Absolute; complete: *Our play was a total success.*

touch·down |tŭch′ doun′| *n., pl.* **touchdowns** A score of six points in football, usually made by running with the ball, or catching a teammate's pass, across the opposing team's goal line.

tough |tŭf| *adj.* **tougher, toughest** Strong and not likely to break or tear with use or wear.

tow·er |tou′ ər| *n., pl.* **towers** A very tall building or a tall structure that is part of a larger building.

tox·ic |tŏk′ sĭk| *adj.* Of, relating to, or caused by a poison: *The child was allergic to bee stings and had a toxic reaction.*

trace |trās| *v.* **traced, tracing** **1.** To follow the track, course, or trail of: *The post office tried to trace the lost letter.* **2.** To copy, as a drawing, by following lines seen through a sheet of transparent paper.

track |trăk| *n., pl.* **tracks** **1.** A path, course, or trail made for racing, running, or hiking. **2.** A rail or set of rails for vehicles such as trains to run on.

trac·tor |trăk′ tər| *n., pl.* **tractors** A vehicle that is driven by an engine and is equipped with large tires that have deep treads. A tractor is used especially for pulling farm machinery, such as a plow or thresher.

tractor

traf·fic |trăf′ ĭk| *n.* The movement of vehicles and people along roads and streets, of ships on the seas, or of aircraft in the sky.

trans·mit |trăns mĭt′| *v.* **transmitted, transmitting 1.** To send from one person, place, or thing to another. **2.** To send out an electric or electronic signal by wire or radio.

trans·port |trăns pôrt′| *v.* **transported, transporting** To carry from one place to another.

trans·pose |trăns pōz′| *v.* **transposed, transposing** To put in a new order.

treas·ure |trĕzh′ ər| *n., pl.* **treasures 1.** Wealth, such as jewels or money, that has been collected or hidden. **2.** A very precious or valuable person or thing.

trea·ty |trē′ tē| *n., pl.* **treaties** An official agreement between two or more countries, national governments, or rulers: *The war ended and a peace treaty was signed.*

trek |trĕk| *n., pl.* **treks** A long and difficult journey.

trem·or |trĕm′ ər| *n., pl.* **tremors** A shaking or vibrating movement, especially of the earth.

tres·pass |trĕs′ pəs| *v.* **trespassed, trespassing** To go onto someone's property without permission; intrude.

tri·al |trī′ əl| *n., pl.* **trials** The studying and deciding of a case in a court of law.

Pronunciation Key

ă	pat	ō	go	th	**th**in
ā	pay	ô	paw, for	hw	**wh**ich
â	care	oi	oil	zh	u**s**ual
ä	father	ŏŏ	book	ə	**a**go,
ĕ	pet	ōō	boot		item,
ē	be	yōō	cute		pencil,
ĭ	pit	ou	out		atom,
ī	ice	ŭ	cut		circus
î	near	û	fur	ər	butter
ŏ	pot	*th*	**th**e		

trip·le |trĭp′ əl| *n., pl.* **triples** In baseball, a hit that allows a batter to reach third base safely.

troop |trōōp| *n., pl.* **troops 1.** A group of persons, animals, or things: *police troop.* **2.** A group of soldiers mounted on horses or riding in motor vehicles.

tro·phy |trō′ fē| *n., pl.* **trophies** A prize given or received as a symbol of victory or achievement: *The basketball team won the play-off game and received a trophy.*

true |trōō| *adj.* **truer, truest** Being in agreement with fact or reality; accurate: *Is it true that you are moving this summer?*

trunk |trŭngk| *n., pl.* **trunks 1.** A sturdy box in which clothes or belongings can be packed for travel or storage. **2.** The covered compartment of an automobile, used for storage.

tu·lip |tōō′ lĭp| or |tyōō′ lĭp| *n., pl.* **tulips** A garden plant that grows from a bulb and has colored cup-shaped flowers. Tulips are planted in the fall and bloom in the spring and early summer.

tun·nel |tŭn′ əl| *n., pl.* **tunnels** An underground or underwater passage.

turn·pike |tûrn′ pīk′| *n., pl.* **turnpikes** A wide highway that drivers pay a toll to use.

twice |twīs| *adv.* Two times: *He saw the movie twice.*

twirl |twûrl| *v.* **twirled, twirling** To spin.

typ·i·cal |tĭp′ ĭ kəl| *adj.* Showing the special traits or characteristics of a group, kind, or class; usual; ordinary: *A typical summer day in Arizona is hot and dry.*

Spelling Dictionary

U

um·pire |ŭm′ pīr′| *n., pl.* **umpires**
A person who rules on plays in sports, such as baseball: *The umpire called a strike, and the batter was out.*

un- A prefix that means: **1.** Not: *unable, unhappy.* **2.** Lack of: *unemployment.*

un·a·ble |ŭn′ ā′ bəl| *adj.* Not able; lacking the power to do something: *I was unable to catch the school bus.*

un·a·ware |ŭn′ ə wâr′| *adj.* Not aware or conscious: *My brother and sister were unaware of my presence.*

un·e·ven |ŭn ē′ vən| *adj.* **unevener, unevenest** **1.** Not level, smooth, or straight: *The surface of the bumpy road is uneven.* **2.** Not balanced; unequal.

un·for·tu·nate |ŭn fôr′ chə nĭt| *adj.* Not fortunate; not lucky.

uni- A prefix that means "one, single": *unicycle.*

u·ni·corn |yoo′ nĭ kôrn′| *n., pl.* **unicorns** An imaginary animal similar to a horse but with a single long horn in the middle of the forehead.

u·ni·form |yoo′ nə fôrm′| *n., pl.* **uniforms** Clothing that identifies those who wear it as members of a certain group, such as a police force.

u·ni·fy |yoo′ nə fī′| *v.* **unified, unifying** To make or form into a whole; unite; join: *Patriotism unified the community.*

un·in·ter·est·ed |ŭn ĭn′ trĭ stĭd| or |ŭn ĭn′ tə rĕs tĭd| *adj.* Having no interest; indifferent.

un·known |ŭn nōn′| *adj.* **1.** Not known or familiar; strange: *We bought a drawing by an unknown artist.* **2.** Not identified: *The cause of the fire was unknown.*

un·nec·es·sar·y |ŭn nĕs′ ĭ sĕr′ ē| *adj.* Not necessary or required; needless.

un·sink·a·ble |ŭn sĭngk′ ə bəl| *adj.* Not able to go under the surface or to be sunk.

un·skilled |ŭn skĭld′| *adj.* Lacking skill or special training.

un·sure |ŭn shoor′| *adj.* Not sure; uncertain: *I am unsure about this homework assignment.*

up-to-date |ŭp′ tə dāt′| *adj.* Showing or using the latest improvements, facts, or style: *We bought a new, up-to-date home computer.*

use |yooz| *v.* **used, using** To bring or put into service for a purpose: *Use the soap when you wash.*

u·su·al |yoo′ zhoo əl| *adj.* Happening at regular intervals or all the time; customary; common.

V

va·can·cy |vā′ kən sē| *n., pl.* **vacancies** **1.** The condition of being vacant. **2.** An unoccupied job, position, or place, such as a motel room.

va·cant |vā′ kənt| *adj.* Not occupied or rented.

va·cate |vā′ kāt′| *v.* **vacated, vacating** To go away from and no longer occupy: *We vacated our apartment when we bought a house.*

va·ca·tion |vā kā′ shən| *n., pl.* **vacations** A time of rest from work, school, or other regular activities: *This summer my family is going on a camping vacation.*

vac·u·um |văk′ yoo əm| or |văk′ yoom| *n., pl.* **vacuums** **1.** A space that does not have any air in it. A perfect vacuum probably does not exist. **2.** A vacuum cleaner.

Val·en·tine's Day |văl′ ən tīnz| *n.* February 14, a day when people send valentines to their friends, relatives, and sweethearts.

val·u·a·ble |văl′ yoo ə bəl| *adj.* Worth a lot of money; precious: *This is a valuable necklace.* *n., pl.* **valuables** A valuable personal possession, as jewelry: *We have a safe to put our valuables in.*

val·ue |văl′ yoo| *n., pl.* **values** **1.** What something is worth in exchange for something else: *These shoes will give you good value for your money.* **2.** The quality that makes something worth having; importance: *You should recognize the value of a good education.*

van·ish |văn′ ĭsh| *v.* **vanished, vanishing** To disappear or become invisible: *My smile vanished when Martha told me the bad news.*

va·ri·e·ty |və **rī'** ĭ tē| *n., pl.* **varieties**
1. Difference or change; lack of sameness: *We enjoy variety in our meals.* **2.** A number of different kinds within the same group or category: *Our library has a wide variety of books.*

vault |vôlt| *v.* **vaulted, vaulting** To jump or leap over, especially with the help of one's hands or a pole.

ve·hi·cle |**vē'** ĭ kəl| *n., pl.* **vehicles** Something used for carrying people or goods from one place to another, especially one that moves on wheels or runners. Cars, bicycles, and airplanes are vehicles.

vel·vet |**věl'** vĭt| *n., pl.* **velvets** A soft fabric with a short, thick pile. Velvet is made of silk, cotton, rayon, or other materials.

ve·ran·da |və **răn'** də| *n., pl.* **verandas** A long porch or balcony, usually with a roof, that runs along one or more sides of a building.

veranda

Vet·er·ans Day |**vět'** ər ənz| *n.* November 11, a holiday in memory of the peace treaty ending World War I in 1918 and in honor of veterans of the armed services.

ve·to |**vē'** tō| *n., pl.* **vetoes** The right or power of a president, governor, or mayor to reject a bill that has been passed by a legislature and to keep it from becoming a law. *v.* **vetoed, vetoing** To prevent from becoming law by using the power of veto: *The President vetoed the tax bill.*

vic·to·ry |**vĭk'** tə rē| *n., pl.* **victories** The defeat of an opponent or enemy; success.

vid·e·o |**vĭd'** ē ō'| *n., pl.* **videos** A recording on special tape of a television program or movie for later playback and viewing.

view |vyōō| *n., pl.* **views** Range of field of sight: *The airplane disappeared from view.* *v.* **viewed, viewing** To look at: *We viewed the stars through a telescope.*

vil·lage |**vĭl'** ĭj| *n., pl.* **villages** **1.** A group of houses that make up a community smaller than a town. **2.** The people who live in a village.

vil·lain |**vĭl'** ən| *n., pl.* **villains** **1.** A wicked person; not a hero. **2.** A main character who harms or threatens the good or heroic characters in a story or play.

vin·e·gar |**vĭn'** ĭ gər| *n., pl.* **vinegars** A sour liquid that is made by fermenting wine, cider, or other liquids. Vinegar is used in flavoring and preserving food and in salad dressing.

vi·o·let |**vī'** ə lĭt| *n., pl.* **violets** **1.** A low-growing plant having small flowers that are usually bluish purple but can be yellow or white. **2.** A reddish blue color.

vis·it |**vĭz'** ĭt| *v.* **visited, visiting** **1.** To go or come to see: *Visit your doctor once a year.* **2.** To stay with as a guest: *I am visiting an old friend in California.*

vi·tal |**vīt'** l| *adj.* **1.** Necessary to life: *The heart and lungs are vital organs.* **2.** Very important; essential; necessary: *A good education is vital to a successful career.*

vot·er |**vō'** tər| *n., pl.* **voters** A person who casts a ballot or otherwise votes in an election.

voy·age |**voi'** ĭj| *n., pl.* **voyages** A long journey to a distant place, made on a ship, aircraft, or spacecraft.

Spelling Dictionary

W

waist |wāst| *n., pl.* **waists** The part of the human body between the ribs and the hips.
♦ *These sound alike* **waist, waste.**

wait |wāt| *v.* **waited, waiting** To do nothing or stay in a place until something expected happens: *Wait for me here.*
♦ *These sound alike* **wait, weight.**

wan·der |wŏn′ dər| *v.* **wandered, wandering** To move from place to place without a special purpose or destination; roam: *We wandered around town.*

ware·house |wâr′ hous′| *n., pl.* **warehouses** A large building where goods are stored.

warn |wôrn| *v.* **warned, warning** To make aware of danger; alert: *The news report warned us that the roads were icy.*
♦ *These sound alike* **warn, worn.**

war·rant |wôr′ ənt| *n., pl.* **warrants** An official paper that gives the police authority, as for making a search or an arrest.

waste |wāst| *n., pl.* **wastes** Worthless or useless material, such as garbage. *adj.* Worthless or useless: *Throw out that waste paper.*
♦ *These sound alike* **waste, waist.**

waste·bas·ket |wāst′ băs′ kĭt| *n., pl.* **wastebaskets** An open container that is used to hold things to be thrown away.

watch·ful |wŏch′ fəl| *adj.* On the lookout; alert.

wa·ter·mel·on |wô′ tər měl′ ən| *n., pl.* **watermelons** A very large melon with a hard, thick, green rind and sweet, watery pink or reddish flesh.

way·side |wā′ sīd| *n., pl.* **waysides** The side or edge of a road: *He stopped the car by the wayside.*

weap·on |wěp′ ən| *n., pl.* **weapons** Something, such as a gun or claw, that is used in defense or attack.

week·end |wēk′ ěnd′| *n., pl.* **weekends** The period of time from Friday evening through Sunday evening.

weep |wēp| *v.* **wept, weeping** To cry.

weight |wāt| *n., pl.* **weights** The measure of how heavy something is: *The weight of the box is 100 pounds.*
♦ *These sound alike* **weight, wait.**

wel·fare |wěl′ fâr′| *n.* Health, happiness, or prosperity; well-being.

wheel·chair |hwēl′ châr′| *n., pl.* **wheelchairs** A chair on wheels in which a sick or disabled person can move about.

where·a·bouts |hwâr′ ə bouts′| *n.* (used with a singular or plural verb) The place where someone or something is: *My friend's whereabouts is (or are) unknown.*

wheth·er |hwěth′ ər| *conj.* **1.** Used to show a choice between things: *Whether we win or lose, we will be glad we tried.* **2.** If.

whip |hwĭp| *v.* **whipped, whipping** To beat something, such as cream, into a foam.

whir |hwûr| *v.* **whirred, whirring** To move quickly with a buzzing or humming sound.

whis·tle |hwĭs′ əl| *n., pl.* **whistles 1.** A device that makes a high, clear sound when air is blown through it. **2.** A sound made by or as if by whistling.

who·ev·er |hoo ěv′ ər| *pron.* Anyone that: *Whoever wants my sandwich can have it.*

wild |wīld| *adj.* **wilder, wildest** Not grown, cared for, or controlled by people: *The polar bear is a wild animal.*

wil·der·ness |wĭl′ dər nĭs| *n., pl.* **wildernesses** A region in a wild, natural state in which there are few or no people.

wild·life |wīld′ līf′| *n.* Wild plants and animals, especially wild animals living in their natural surroundings.

win |wĭn| *v.* **won, winning 1.** To gain victory in a game, contest, or battle: *Which team won?* **2.** To achieve success in an effort or venture.

win·ner |wĭn′ ər| *n., pl.* **winners** A person or group that wins.

wis·dom |wĭz′ dəm| *n.* Intelligence and good judgment in knowing what to do and being able to tell the difference between good and bad and right and wrong; not foolishness or ignorance.

wise |wīz| *adj.* **wiser, wisest** Having or showing intelligence and good judgment: *A wise student studies for tests.*

wit·ness |wĭt' nĭs| *n., pl.* **witnesses**
1. Someone who has seen or heard something; observer: *I was a witness to the traffic accident.*
2. A person who is called to testify before a court of law and promises to tell the truth.

word root |wôrd rōŏt| or |wôrd rŏŏt|
n., pl. **word roots** A word part from which other words are formed. It adds meaning to the word. For example, *pedal* includes the word root *ped,* meaning "foot."

world |wûrld| *n., pl.* **worlds** The earth: *The world is round.*

worse |wûrs| *adj.* Comparative of **bad.** Less well.

wor·ship |wûr' shĭp| *n.* Religious ceremonies and prayers. *v.* **worshiped, worshiping** *or* **worshipped, worshipping** To honor and love.

worth |wûrth| *n.* The quality that makes someone or something expensive, valuable, useful, or important: *Your education will prove its worth. adj.* Equal in value to: *This rare baseball card is worth $27.50.*

worth·less |wûrth' lĭs| *adj.* Without worth; useless.

worth·while |wûrth' hwīl'| *adj.* Worth the time, effort, or cost involved; valuable; important.

wor·thy |wûr' thē| *adj.* **worthier, worthiest** Having worth, merit, or value; useful or valuable: *Raising money for the homeless is a worthy cause.* —*n.* **worthiness** *Sasha was confident of her worthiness as a pitcher.*

wrote |rōt| *v.* Past tense of **write**: *She wrote an excellent book report.*

year |yîr| *n., pl.* **years** **1.** A period of twelve months. **2.** A period of time, usually less than twelve months, devoted to a special activity: *The school year begins in September and ends in June.*

yearn |yûrn| *v.* **yearned, yearning** To have a deep desire; long; want very much: *I yearn to see my old friends again.*

Yel·low·stone Na·tion·al Park
|yĕl' ō stōn'| Oldest and largest of United States national parks, mostly in northwest Wyoming, where the geyser Old Faithful is located.

Yellowstone National Park

yes·ter·day |yĕs' tər dē| or |yĕs' tər dā| *n.* The day before today: *Yesterday was windy. adv.* On the day before today.

yield |yēld| *v.* **yielded, yielding** To allow to another: *At a stop sign, yield to the car on your right.*

Yo·sem·i·te Na·tion·al Park
|yō sĕm' ĭ tē| An area of east central California that has high waterfalls and mountain scenery.

youth |yōōth| *n., pl.* **youths** **1.** The time of life between being a child and being an adult: *They had worked hard since their youth.* **2.** A young person, especially a boy or young man.

Content Index

Numbers in **boldface** indicate pages on which a skill is introduced as well as references to the Capitalization and Punctuation Guide.

Dictionary Skills

accent marks, **62**, **182**
definitions, **26**, 76, 122, 160
dictionary, using a, 20, 38, 50, 128, 140, 212, **278**
entry words, **20**, **278**
    as base words, **128**, 140, 212, **278**
guide words, **20**, **278**
homographs, **122**, **278**
homophones, **68**
parts of an entry, 20, 26, 68, 128, **278**
parts of speech, **92**, 98, 200
prefixes, **212**
pronunciation key, **50**
pronunciations, 38, 50, 98, 200
sample sentences and phrases, **26**
spelling table, **38**, 276–277
stressed syllables, **62**, 98, **182**
suffixes, **140**
word histories, **170**

Language Arts Skills

abbreviations, **247–248**
    initials, **248**
    state names, **247**
    titles of people, **159**, **247**
    words in addresses, **247**
    words in business, **247**
apostrophes
    in contractions, **219**, **250**
    in possessive nouns, **57**, **250**
capitalization, **249–250**
    of days, months, and holidays, **249**
    of first word in a sentence, **249**
    in letters, **250**, 252–253
    in outlines, **250**
    of the pronoun *I*, **249**
    of proper nouns and adjectives, **87**, **249**
    in quotations, **147**, **248**
    of titles, **159**, **165**, 194, **248–249**
colons, **177**, **251**, 253
commas
    between adjectives, **251**
    in compound sentences, **33**, **251**
    in dates, **195**, 252–253
    after greeting and closing in letters, **177**, **251**, 252–253
    after introductory words, **111**, **251**
    between names of city and state, **195**, **251**, 252–253
    with nouns in direct address, **135**, **251**
    in quotations, **248**
    in a series, **105**, **251**
comparing with *good* and *bad*, **75**
contractions, **219**
end marks, **15**, **250**
parts of a letter, **177**, **190**, **195**, 252–253
possessive nouns, **57**, 250
quotations
    capitalizing, **147**, **248**
    punctuating, **147**, **248**
titles
    capitalizing, **159**, **165**, 194, **248**, **249**
    with quotation marks, **165**, **248**
    underlining, **165**, **248**
using *I* and *me*, **207**

Literature

46, 82, 118, 154, 190, 226

Phonics

13, 19, 25, 31, 37, 42, 43, 44, 45, 49, 55, 67, 73, 78, 80, 81, 91, 97, 103, 109, 114, 117, 121, 139, 145, 152, 153, 157, 175, 181, 186, 199, 211, 229, 230, 231, 232, 234, 235, 240, 241, 276–277

Proofreading

for abbreviations, **159**
for capitalization
    in abbreviations, **159**
    in direct quotations, **147**
    of proper nouns and adjectives, **87**, 119
    of titles, **159**, **165**
for colons, **177**
for commas
    between city and state, **195**
    in compound sentences, **33**
    in dates, **195**
    with introductory words, **111**
    in letters, **177**, **195**
    with nouns in direct address, **135**
    in a series, **105**
for contractions, **219**
for end marks, **15**, 47, 155
for forms of *good* and *bad*, **75**

for *I* and *me*, **207**
for parts of a letter, **177**
for possessive nouns, **57,** 83
for quotation marks, **147**
for spelling, 15, 21, 27, 33, 39, 47, 51, 57, 63, 69, 75, 83, 87, 93, 99, 105, 111, 119, 123, 129, 135, 141, 147, 155, 159, 165, 171, 177, 183, 191, 195, 201, 207, 213, 219, 227
for titles
  of people, **159,** 191
  of written works, **165**

Spelling

See Table of Contents.
alphabetical order, 20, 26, 68, 92, 110, 128, 158, 170, 194
self-assessment, 14, 20, 26, 32, 38, 50, 56, 62, 68, 74, 86, 92, 98, 104, 110, 122, 128, 134, 140, 146, 158, 164, 170, 176, 182, 194, 200, 206, 212, 218
spelling strategies, 13, 19, 25, 31, 37, 42–45, 55, 61, 67, 73, 78–81, 85, 91, 97, 103, 109, 114–117, 121, 127, 133, 139, 145, 150–153, 157, 163, 169, 175, 181, 186–189, 193, 199, 205, 211, 217, 222–225, 229–246
See also Vocabulary.

Spelling Across the Curriculum

business, 209
careers, 35

health, 197
home economics, 137
language arts, 53, 113, 143
math, 71
performing arts, 77, 131, 185
physical education, 29
recreation, 17, 65, 221
science, 41, 59, 95, 125
social studies, 23, 89, 101, 107, 149, 161, 167, 173, 179, 203, 215

Spelling and Meaning

consonant changes, 25, 37, 45, 97, 145, 153, 157, 181, 270–271
vowel changes, 13, 19, 67, 73, 81, 91, 109, 117, 175, 199, 205, 211, 217, 271–273
word forms, 31, 49, 55, 61, 85, 103, 121, 133, 139, 163
word parts
  Greek word parts, 184, 189, 275
  Latin word roots, 40, 70, 94, 100, 127, 148, 169, 193, 202, 208, 225, 274–275

Thinking Skills

analogies, **37,** 44, 55, 80, 116, 145, 151, 163, 187, 211, 224, 232, 237, 239, 240, 246
analyzing. *See* first two pages of each Basic Unit. *See also* 14, 23, 26, 32, 42, 45, 50, 56, 62, 65, 74, 79–81, 86, 89, 92, 95,

98, 104, 110, 114–115, 117, 122, 128, 134, 141, 150, 152–153, 164, 173, 176, 182, 187–189, 194, 200, 203, 206, 218, 222–223, 230–239, 241–242, 244–246
classifying. *See* first page of each Basic Unit. *See also* 31, 38, 42, 78, 80, 91, 115, 121, 155, 186, 188, 217, 222, 229, 231, 234–235, 241, 243, 245
comparing, 95
contrasting, 95, 104
creative thinking, 15, 16, 21, 22, 27, 33, 39, 41, 45, 51, 57, 63, 75, 77, 81, 87, 89, 93, 94, 95, 99, 105, 106, 111, 113, 123, 129, 135, 137, 141, 147, 159, 161, 165, 171, 177, 185, 195, 196, 207, 208, 213, 219
critical thinking, 17, 23, 29, 35, 53, 59, 65, 71, 76, 101, 107, 125, 131, 143, 149, 161, 167, 173, 179, 197, 203, 209, 215, 221
distinguishing between facts and opinions, 190–191, 226–227
making generalizations. *See* first page of each Basic Unit.
making inferences, 13, 14, 17, 19, 20, 23, 25–26, 29, 31, 32, 37, 41, 42–44, 46, 50, 53, 55, 56, 59, 61, 65, 67, 68, 71, 73, 74, 77, 78–80, 85, 89, 91, 92, 95, 98, 101, 103, 107, 109, 110, 113, 114–116, 118,

Content Index

121, 122, 125, 127, 128, 131, 134, 137, 139, 143, 145, 149, 151–152, 154, 157, 158, 161, 164, 167, 169–170, 173, 175–176, 179, 181–182, 185, 186–187, 194, 197, 203, 205–206, 209, 212, 215, 217, 218, 221, 222–224, 226, 229–246

persuasion, 105, 177, 190–191

predicting outcomes, 118

sequencing, 69, 82–83, 171, 183

summarizing, 75, 129

using graphic organizers, 16, 28, 34, 70, 88, 94, 100, 112, 119, 148, 149, 166, 172, 184, 196, 208, 214, 220

Vocabulary

See also Spelling and Meaning.

antonyms, 20, 43–44, 55, 73, 80, 104, 109, 115–116, 127, **139**, 145, 151–152, **166**, 217, 235, 243

base words, **126**–128, 132–133, 138–140, 157, 168–169, 172, 174, 180, 187–188, 192, 198–199, 212, 222, 239, 242

blended words, **58**

building word families, 112, 196

cloze activities, 14, 17, 19, 23, 29, 31, 34–35, 41–43, 53, 56, 59, 65, 67, 68, 70–71, 77–79, 91–92, 95, 101, 104, 107, 113–114,

116, 125, 127, 131, 134, 137, 143, 149, 157, 161, 167, 169, 173, 179, 181, 184–187, 194, 197, 203, 208–209, 215, 220–221, 223, 231–233, 235, 237–240, 242, 245–246

compound words, **60**–63, 64, 79, 84–87, 114, 233, 235

content area vocabulary, 17, 23, 29, 35, 41, 53, 59, 65, 71, 77, 89, 95, 101, 107, 113, 125, 131, 137, 143, 149, 161, 167, 173, 179, 185, 197, 203, 209, 215, 221

definitions, 13, 19, 20, 25–26, 32, 35, 37, 42–44, 49, 55, 61, 67, 73–74, 78–80, 85, 91, 97, 103, 106, 109, 114–116, 121–122, 127–128, 133, 139, 145–146, 148–152, 157–158, 163–164, 169–170, 175–176, 181, 186–188, 193, 199, 205, 211, 217, 218, 222–224, 229–231, 233–234, 236–238, 240–241, 243–244

easily confused words, 34

exact words, 28, 130, 178

homographs, **122**

homophones, 49, 55, **66**–69, 79–80, 233

idioms, **52**

multiple-meaning words, 76, 136, 160

prefixes, 100, **168**–169, 172, 181, 198–200, 202, 212, 217, 222, 242, 244

regional differences, **142**

rhyming words, 14, 16, 19, 37, 42, 56, 73, 150, 164, 176, 199, 222, 244

suffixes, **138**–141, 174, 180–181, 187, 192–193, 196, 204–206, 211, 220, 222, 239, 242

synonyms, **22**, 25, 78, 97, 103, 109, 116, 121, 127, 133, 150, 152, 164, 199, 214, 224, 233–234, 236, 242–245

thesaurus, using a, **22**, 28, 130, 178, 254–255

transition words, **88**

word histories, 122, 124, 170

word parts

Greek word parts, 184, 189, 275

Latin word roots, 40, **70**, 94, 100, 127, 148, 168, 169, 193, 198, 202, 208, 225, 242, 274–275

words from names, **106**

Writing

types of writing

ad, 123

book jacket blurb, 141

book titles, 165

bulletin board notice, 77

captions, 22, 76, 148, 160, 178

character sketch, 219

conversation, 135

creative writing, 16, 22, 27, 33, 39, 41, 51, 57, 93, 95, 111, 123, 137, 141, 147, 159, 185, 207,

208

description, 27, 155

discussion, 203

headlines, 208

instructions, 83

interview, 33

invitation, 87

journal entry, 15

letter, 105, 177, 191, 195,
   252–253

list, 63, 165, 201

news report, 171

newspaper headline, 208

opinion, 89, 113

personal story, 47, 213

persuasive letter, 105,
   191

poem, 41

post card, 159

quotations, 147

report, 227

review, 75, 129

rhyming couplets, 137

riddles, 39

sentences, 16, 20, 38, 58,
   62, 64, 86, 100, 106,
   112, 130, 134, 136, 160,
   164, 166, 172, 196, 206,
   214, 218

similes, 95

song, 207

speech, 21

story, 51, 57, 93, 119

survey, 69

television plan, 185

television schedule, 183

traffic report, 99

writing process

   description, 155

   instructions, 83

   personal narrative, 47

   persuasive letter, 191

   research report, 227

   story, 119

Credits

Handwriting Models

a b c d e f g h i
j k l m n o p q r
s t u v w x y z

A B C D E F G H I
J K L M N O P Q R
S T U V W X Y Z

Words Often Misspelled

You probably use many of the words on this list when you write. If you cannot think of the spelling of a word, you can always check this list. The words are in alphabetical order.

A
again
all right
a lot
also
always
another
anyone
anything
anyway

B
beautiful
because
before
believe
brought
buy

C
cannot
can't
caught
clothes
coming
cousin

D
didn't
different
don't

E
enough
every
everybody

everyone
everything

F
family
field
finally
friend

G
getting
going
guess

H
happened
happily
haven't
heard
here

I
I'd
I'll
instead
its
it's

K
knew
know

M
might
millimeter

morning
mother's

O
o'clock
once

P
people
pretty
probably

R
really
right

S
Saturday
school
someone
sometimes
stopped
suppose
swimming

T
that's
their
there
there's
they
they're
thought
through
to
tonight

too
tried
two

U
until
usually

W
weird
we're
whole
would
wouldn't
write
writing

Y
your
you're